« Strategy »
for Tomorrow

A 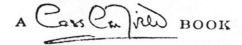 BOOK

# «« Strategy »»
# for Tomorrow

## HANSON W. BALDWIN

Written under the auspices of
**The Center for Strategic and International Studies,**
Georgetown University, Washington, D.C.

HARPER & ROW, PUBLISHERS
NEW YORK AND EVANSTON

Maps by Jean Paul Tremblay

LIBRARY OF CONGRESS CATALOG CARD NUMBER: 71-108937

# Contents

# Maps

# «« 1 »»
# Man and Power

OF ARMS and the Man I sing at a time when Americans are sick of war and the world talks of disarmament and détente.

But there is reason.

Man does not live without hopes and dreams; his reach must always exceed his grasp.

Yet war in some form—organized, armed conflict—has been, throughout history, the most persistent and repetitive manifestation of Man's propensity to utilize physical power as the ultimate argument. War is a human institution which is certain to remain a global social phenomenon.

This book is concerned with strategy—particularly military strategy—and is based upon the self-evident conclusion that power in all its forms—political, economic, military, psychological, physical, moral and spiritual—is, and will remain, a dominant factor in the affairs of nations and of men.

To stress the facts of power, the certainty of conflict and the inevitability of future war is no cause for despair. There is no cynicism in the acceptance of things as they are. The hard-thinking pragmatist is more likely to achieve a brave new world than the emotional idealist; the politician who promises the impossible is far more likely to be a Pied Piper to disaster than the realist.

To be against war is not enough; there have been periodic revolts against violence since the days of Lysistrata, yet war has persisted. The Dr. Spocks, the pacifists of this generation, are nothing new to history; who now remembers the Oxford students of pre–World War II who swore never to bear arms for King and Country? Indeed, the war-weariness of the American people—in half a century, World War I, World War II, Korea, Vietnam and many lesser sanguinary incidents—has often been, ironically, expressed in an invocation of organized violence. The "little wars"—student rebellions, racial troubles—reflect man's innate disposition toward violence.

Thus the study of war and the recognition that war is a recurrent phenomenon, are not, per se, despite the beliefs of so many sincere but mistaken persons, an incitement to war. Rather, the hope of tomorrow lies, not in wishful thinking, not in "dreaming of things as they never were," but in a careful awareness of things as they are, a formulation of what is worth fighting for and what is not worth fighting for and a study of how to decrease the frequency of wars and limit their extent.

Once again today, for the nth time in living memory, the vision of a brave new warless world is being conjured up for the American people.

Many people—frustrated, exasperated, weary of war—foresee the dawn of a peaceful new era. War, they say (illogically, with the dead of Korea and Vietnam and countless other conflicts irrefutable evidence to the contrary), has become impossible in the nuclear age. Political pluralism will breed global internationalism. Supersonic aircraft, modern communications and the miracles of the technological revolution can be exploited to bring about the Brotherhood of Man; the world can truly become One World, and man can stop killing his fellow man.

Less hopeful—or more realistic—observers anticipate no such sweeping improvement in the world of man, but believe that a tremendous psychological breakthrough in the logjam of problems inherited from World War II may clear the way for a global political settlement. Even so hardheaded an idealist as Walt Rostow, former head of the State Department Policy Planning Council,

2

recently forecast an era of greater stability. The "aggressive, romantic revolutionaries" seem to be passing from the world scene, he said, and "the struggle in Vietnam might be the last great confrontation of the postwar era."

Such misplaced optimism, much of it due to the sense of psychological frustration Vietnam bred in some sections of the American public, could well lead to political and psychological euphoria—a kind of national complacency—or to withdrawal from the world around us. It has, indeed, already led to a kind of neo-isolationism and to an antimilitary and anti-Establishment ground swell. As a people we have long been wishful thinkers eager to turn dream into reality, ready to think well of any nation, people or men, lacking the hardheadedness that comes only with a long view of history. As a people we have too long been prone to fight a war and forget it, to put the bloodshed and the misery and the muck behind us, to tear down the structure of security so painfully built up during war and to hail a new future instead of seeing the postwar world as the same old world with patches on it. Twice now we have fought, in World Wars I and II, "wars to end war"; there are voices in the land today suggesting that the end of the war in Vietnam will lead to a stable, even a warless, world, that if the U.S. limits arms, the U.S.S.R. will follow suit.

This, put in a nutshell, is poppycock.

A content of idealism, a hope for tomorrow, a reach exceeding our grasp are essential ingredients of United States foreign policy and, in fact, of man's life, but they should never obscure the dirty facts of history, or disguise the aggressive traits of man. There is no easy cure for the illness of war; we cannot now anticipate a golden age.

Both the study of history and the study of man provide the basic facts to refute the wishful thinkers.

Viewed against the centuries, Vietnam and the other wars of the twentieth century have been merely additional episodes of violence in the long history of man's inhumanity to man. Historically war in some form has been a recurrent—almost a continuous—phenomenon since man started keeping records. To Americans, Vietnam has been the *only* war of recent years, but while it raged there

3

were at least ten other contemporary conflicts in other parts of the world—some of them not comparable in size or scope to Vietnam, but conflicts in which the dead were just as dead, the wounded in as much agony as were the casualties of Vietnam. Wars of a sort —expressed in the violence of arms tribal, national, regional, civil, revolutionary, religious, guerrilla—raged in Yemen, in South Arabia, along the Arab-Israeli borders, in the land of the Kurds, in Nagaland in India, incipiently along the Chinese-Indian frontier, perhaps in Tibet and even in China, in the Hukbalahap area in the Philippines, in Colombia and Venezuela, in Nigeria and the Sudan, intermittently in the Congo and the Portuguese African colonies, and some would even say in the streets of America.

Even if one indulges in semantics and dismisses all these manifestations of man's addiction to armed violence as "disorders" or "insurrections" rather than "wars," one can find no comfort from history's record.

In 1940 the Carnegie Endowment for International Peace in a memorandum, "Wars of the World," reviewed the history of mankind and, quoting from Ivan S. Bloch's famous treatise, *The Future of War*, noted that "An analysis . . . shows that from the years 1496 B.C. to the year 1861—a cycle of 3,357 years, [there] were but 227 years of peace and 3,130 years of war; in other words, there were thirteen years of war for every year of peace."

It is, of course, true that world wars—really large wars—have recurred with far less frequency. Exactly a quarter of a century elapsed between the beginnings of World Wars I and II. Between the Napoleonic Wars, a convulsion that shook Europe, and World War I lay a century widely regarded as an era of peace and stability —the Victorian age, the "golden age" of prosperity. It *was* such an era—but not for those who died or were maimed in the world's battlefields. Between Napoleon's conquests and the Battle of the Marne, the United States fought Britain in the War of 1812, Mexico in 1846-48, tore itself apart in a great Civil War, dispossessed the Indians in a score of small but bloody conflicts and defeated Spain. These "golden years" saw, too, the conquest of India by Britain, the rise of Germany in Europe with all the wars that resulted, the Crimean War, the Franco-Prussian War, the Chino-Japanese War,

4

the Russo-Japanese War, the Boer War and a host of other conflicts, some of them years in duration. The "piping times of peace" of the nineteenth century is a contradiction in terms.

In the modern era, war defined as armed conflict between organized groups has *not* become less frequent but more so. True, since the start of the nuclear age man has demonstrated some restraint in the exercise of his awesome new technological power; no world war, no nuclear war, no unlimited war, has occurred since World War II.

But this is sparse comfort. Of the forty to more than sixty sizable wars—the exact number depends on the incidents of organized and armed violence that one includes—that have occurred since World War II, many have been major in terms of men involved, in costs, in casualties and in results. And one calculation indicates that the annual global incidence of violence increased from thirty-four in 1958 to fifty-eight in 1965.[1]

The United States has fought two major wars since 1945. In thirty-seven months in Korea, both sides—the UN Command and the Chinese and North Korean Communists—sustained a total of more than 2.5 million casualties (dead, wounded and missing); in Vietnam since 1961 (through 1969) by incomplete estimates both sides have suffered a total of about 765,000 dead. The Nigerian civil war cost an estimated 1 million dead, mostly civilians. Even the brief India-Pakistan war was major in terms of economic and political consequences to both countries.

Thus the term "limited war" can cover a spectrum of conflict from a squad of armed men to a nation; its results in military, political or economic terms can be almost as far-reaching, in some instances, as those of a so-called world or major war, and to the battlefield dead, death is catholic in its impartiality whether inflicted by the fireball of an A-bomb or the iron shards of a booby trap.

Thus history provides some pretty convincing statistics—if the past is any guide to the future—that peace is not just around the corner.

But there are other guides. Quincy Wright (in *A Study of War*) and many others have made brave attempts to analyze war

5

and to determine its causes. The deeper students, including Wright, have emphasized what the economic determinists, the political determinists, the idealists and the chauvinists, the most extreme One-Worlders and the narrowest parochial patriots dislike to admit —that, in Wright's phrase, "There is no single cause of war. Peace is an equilibrium among many forces."[2]

Some contemporary optimists have concluded that man's political groups and economic development foster this equilibrium and that the very power of his weapons have made war less likely. But Wright felt that "war tends to increase both in frequency and in severity in times of rapid technological and cultural change because adjustment, which always involves habituation, is a function of time."[3]

Those who accept this statement can take small comfort from it, for there has probably never in history been a period of such major technological and cultural change as that of the twentieth century. From coal to nuclear power, from the horse-and-buggy to the internal combustion engine, from word of mouth to radio, from horseback to supersonic jets in one lifetime is technological change with a vengeance, and the cultural changes that have accompanied the technological revolution have crossed all national frontiers. Indeed, one of the great crises of our civilization has been aptly described as the crisis of values; the old beliefs are largely dead or dying; man gropes in a wilderness of change—technological, cultural and spiritual.

If one accepts the truth of Wright's thesis, the recurrence and frequency of war through the ages would seem to indicate that man since his beginnings has been, somewhere in the world, in a perpetual state of "rapid technological and cultural change."

Despite the pedantic and sometimes esoteric search for war's causes, the only common denominator is man himself. As Plato phrased it, "Wars, battles, and revolutions come from the body and the lusts of the body." Man is a fighting animal, though men do not like to admit it.

Robert Ardrey in his beautiful speculative book, *African Genesis*, traces some of the findings of modern anthropology to postulate that in the slow process of evolution man was born of "risen apes,

6

not fallen angels, and the apes were armed killers besides." He sees man as "dominated by ineradicable animal instincts . . . the most sophisticated predator the world has ever known," and war as "the most natural mode of human expression since the beginnings of recorded history."[4]

Instinctual urges or "behavioral patterns, some as ancient as recorded life," inherited through the aeons from our animal ancestors and from the burly-browed cave men of our beginnings, are still buried deep within us, Mr. Ardrey suggests in *African Genesis* and in his later sequel, *The Territorial Imperative.*[5] It is the nature of man, not the economic or political systems he has created, that causes war.

It is true that many scientists pooh-pooh Mr. Ardrey as an amateur and that to anthropologists in particular this playwright-turned-scientist is a controversial figure. But one cannot easily dismiss *On Aggression* by Konrad Lorenz, a book which deals with the "fighting instinct in beast and man which is directed against members of the same species."

As in Cro-Magnon man, the aggressive instinct remains a kind of "primeval drive"; it "impels an Alexander or a Napoleon to sacrifice millions of lives in his attempt to unite the world under his scepter." The riddle of why "human beings behave so unreasonably" can be answered only if one assumes that "human behavior . . . far from being determined by reason and cultural tradition alone, is still subject to all the laws prevailing in all phylogenetically adapted instinctive behavior."[6]

These two expositions—so challenging to the old traditional beliefs in man's sharp differentiation from the animal and in man's inborn "goodness"—gain strength from the fact that both authors are optimists; Lorenz sees "humor and knowledge" and the sublimation of the aggressive instinct (though never its elimination) as the hope of tomorrow; Ardrey believes the utilization and sublimation of man's territorial instinct may develop into a possible curb to his self-destructiveness.

But that man is his own worst enemy and that in him lie the seeds of war, these and many other realistic students agree. Their studies of animal behavior and their exposition of the past with their lessons for the present are far more convincing than their predictions for the future. For tomorrow they substitute hopes for science, and assume that man will use the rational processes which throughout history he has invariably ignored.

Judged by the past and by any study of man, war, it is clear, is a human institution which is so much a part of our traditions, our history, our mores, our habit patterns and our instincts that it seems probable that some form of organized, armed conflict between groups of human beings is here to stay for an indefinite future—perhaps for as long as man.

" . . . war is so much the consequence of human attitudes and instincts that it does not seem likely to disappear until something wonderfully new happens to mankind. And that . . . as Thomas More said of the advent of Utopia, will not be for some time."[7]

Certainly the elimination of war is not just a matter of ending current conflicts; it will be—at the very best—a long, slow, tragic effort, perhaps doomed to failure in the future as it has been in the past.

But could not man hope for a lesser achievement with the end of the Vietnam war—the beginning of a period of greater stabilization, the solution of some of the vexing problems that have disturbed the world for the last quarter-century?

Even the brief survey of the world's problems presented in the following chapters shows that the answer is bound to be mixed.

Vietnam has been only one incident in the convulsive age in which we live. Tremendous and pressing global problems promise an enduring complexity.

Man, in uncontrolled proliferation, is crowding himself off an earth he has despoiled and polluted.

The limitation of arms has not really started.

The problems left over from World War II are far from settled today, three decades later.

The old bonds—NATO, CENTO, SEATO, the Warsaw Pact—are weakening. But they are being replaced not by One World bonds but by small-power groupings, by nationalism, by violent struggle within nations, by pluralism.

Divided Germany, divided Korea, the two-China situation in the Far East; the Israeli-Arab conflict; the Soviet push for power in the Middle East; the Pakistan-India confrontation; Nigeria; Africa—these are only a few of the major political problems to which the ending of the Vietnam war, when it comes, will provide no answer. Above all, there is the troubled awakening of sleeping China, and the new confrontation that appears to be shaping up in the heart of Central Asia and along the Manchurian frontier.

The United States of the twentieth century has had power thrust upon it. Often, not by choice, not even by plan, certainly not by inclination, it has filled, as in Southeast Asia, the vacuums of power left by the collapse of ancient empires.

We are of the world—part of it—a much smaller world in geopolitical terms than in the days of our forefathers, and inevitably, inexorably, immutably, we share its many problems.

No man is an island unto himself.

We cannot escape frustrations by ignoring them; we cannot turn back the technological clock and find safety in isolation.

"Nuclear pacifism," Dr. William R. Kintner has written, "offers no escape from our dilemma. The balance must be struck between the defense of values and the defense of life. Pure physical survival cannot be raised to the Number One value of humanity, for we must be concerned, not only for life itself, but also for the quality of life."[8]

So the end of the Vietnam war will not bring a new world overnight. The "Time of Troubles" in which we live will last long after the echo of the guns of Vietnam has died into history.

Conflict between man and man, tribes and races and nations—and with it, war in some form—will persist tomorrow. Therefore the marshaling of resources, the utilization of power to achieve national goals, the formulation of strategic concepts will continue to preoccupy the planners of tomorrow.

But a strategy for tomorrow must build upon the lessons of yesterday.

# «« 2 »»
# Of Recent History

UNLESS ONE LEARNS from history, one is condemned to repeat it. Too often, this simple lesson is forgotten; Americans are not great students of the past, and tragically and needlessly each succeeding generation relearns the bitter lessons of yesterday. In blood and misery, in war after war, the truisms taught in political science courses and in the war colleges must be experienced the hard way.

Yet the political, strategic and military plans and policies of the United States must be based upon the experience of the past and must derive their substance from the soil of yesterday and today. The United States should study the lessons of history.

The fundamental lesson of warfare is that no major war is worth fighting unless it leads to a greater degree of stability, at least temporarily, and at least in the geographic area of conflict. Wars are the ultimate means of settling problems; unless they settle the problem under dispute without substituting an equally serious problem for the one resolved, they have been fought in vain. World War II led, for the United States, to precisely this result; in one sense, indeed, Vietnam was a by-product of World War II. For the menace of a totalitarian and expansionist Germany was substituted the menace of a totalitarian and expansionist Russian (and Chinese) Communism. We won the war but lost the peace. The political aims of any war must be paramount; they must be clearly elucidated, and the strategy and the manner of fighting the war must contribute to the achievement of the results desired. It is not enough to postulate victory as the end.

A second great lesson of warfare, emphasized by the experience of Vietnam, is that the costs of achieving the end results desired must be carefully weighed *before* involvement to determine, as far as possible, whether the game is worth the candle. Do the vital interests of the United States require the nation's involvement in a shooting war?

In the modern world of foreshortened distances and shrunken dimensions U.S. interests are, of course, global. But not all of them by any means are *vital.* The defense of American interests must be tailored to their importance; some might require diplomacy, some economic or political or psychological measures, a very few war itself. A clear definition of interests—of the stakes involved—and a balancing of the risks and losses anticipated against the gains to be achieved should be part of a continuing assessment of the world situation. An essential part of such an assessment must be the matching of national resources against estimated costs; the available resources are the final determinant of a pragmatic policy.

These truisms deserve re-emphasis for it is clear no such hardheaded appraisal was made before the event in Vietnam.

Realistic appraisals of world problems cannot be made without the closest sort of liaison between responsible government departments and agencies and the frankest sort of expression by the participants. The National Security Council and its various corollary agencies were established for just this purpose. But the Council —or any other body—is no more effective than the use that is made of it. President Johnson and, particularly, President Kennedy made most of their decisions outside its channels; the Council was illutilized, or totally ignored.

During the tenure of Secretary of Defense Robert S. McNamara in the Pentagon, military expertise and military experience were downgraded; political and management appraisals of military needs overrode military judgments. Military appraisals sometimes failed to reach the echelon of the Commander in Chief. The Secretary of Defense should be, of course—regardless of the walk of life from

11

which he is drawn—primarily a political figure, and he is expected to make political and management judgments. And often the Secretary may well be right, his uniformed advisers wrong. The military had no monopoly of perspicacity in Vietnam, or in Korea, or in World Wars I and II. But the training, the professional experience, they represent is a national resource; their point of view is a major factor which must be considered in Presidential decision-making. It must be an input to be weighed, not just manipulated. The mechanism of government fails unless the military viewpoint—even if it is in disagreement among the services—is reflected comprehensively and honestly and in detail to the Commander in Chief, the President.

This fundamental requirement was not fulfilled in the case of Vietnam. The working habits of both President Kennedy and President Johnson; the personality of Mr. McNamara and his distaste for disagreement; the ascendancy of the computer-minded, cost-effectiveness operational analyst and management specialist; and the subordination of the Joint Chiefs of Staff all contributed to what was a fundamental failure—the failure to elucidate at the top level of government the military costs and requirements of victory in Vietnam.

Sound estimates of the costs and requirements were available *before* the first U.S. combat troops were committed in March, 1965. Both the Army Chief of Staff and the Marine Commandant are on record, in the early months of 1965 before our massive build-up in Vietnam, as estimating that victory there would require 500,000 to 800,000 men and would take years of effort. It is hard to believe that the President received these estimates or, if he received them, that he fully understood their meaning; if he had, it seems unlikely that U.S. interests—the stakes involved—would have seemed worth the costs.

But this mistake was almost immediately compounded, in the summer of 1965 when the President announced a major build-up of U.S. combat forces in Vietnam, by the nation's failure to mobilize its reserve forces. The failure meant strain and drawdown on all the regular armed forces and established a policy of gradualism, of very slow build-up, which could be matched, relatively, by the enemy.

The military had anticipated and prepared for mobilization; again it is difficult to believe that the President fully understood the inevitable consequences of his failure to utilize rapidly and decisively the nation's might. Somewhere between the responsible heads of the armed services in the Pentagon and the Commander in Chief communications broke down or meanings were obscured.

The Joint Chiefs of Staff during the crucial period of U.S. intervention in Vietnam were composed primarily of men little known to the public—men with no real public image. They were not "yes-men," but they were selected by the President and Mr. McNamara because it was felt "they would not kick over the traces." They were not men who would "pound the table." They were not strong Chiefs of Staff in the tradition of "Ernie" King or George Marshall. They were torn between their primary military obligation—to obey their President's orders and their sense of loyalty to their Secretary and their Commander in Chief and his policies—and their corollary responsibility to Congress and the people. Their oath of office—to support and defend the Constitution of the United States—dramatizes this difficult but essential dichotomy. The Joint Chiefs, in fact the uniformed officers of all services, owe loyalty and obedience to the Commander in Chief, but they also have an obligation to Congress, as well as to the President, to provide frank appraisals of all military matters. Their fundamental fidelity is to the nation, not to any single administration, and the founding fathers undoubtedly intended to emphasize the dual loyalties involved.

This conflict—inherent in the constitutional responsibility of Congress for the maintenance of a sound defense—was not new to history, but during the Vietnam war the excessive centralization of power in the executive branch of government—particularly in the person of Mr. McNamara—and, until 1968, the diminished role of Congress combined, with other factors, to minimize the importance of military advice.

The personalities of the Joint Chiefs of Staff were, however, less important than the President's propensity to utilize McNamara as the funnel through which most military information was channeled. Presidential work habits, methods and character and personality often change the course of history, and no organizational chart—

13

no matter how meticulous—can include these imponderable factors. President Johnson had relatively few military associations as Senator or Vice President. As President, he had a mistrust of the military. Like President Kennedy, he was neither used to nor inclined to use a staff system. Both Presidents consulted widely by telephone or in person; both sought discrepant advice. But it was essentially *political* advice. There was no such closeness of contact between the Commander in Chief and his responsible advisers in uniform as existed between President Roosevelt, President Truman or President Eisenhower and their Chiefs of Staff.

The law provides that the Secretary of Defense and the Joint Chiefs of Staff collectively shall be the "principal military advisors to the President." But to make sure that the President receives an unvarnished military judgment there must be constant communication between the men in uniform and the Commander in Chief.

Yet, the Chairman of the Joint Chiefs of Staff, who has considerable military prestige and some authority but little direct responsibility, was the only member of the Joint Chiefs who saw the President with any regularity in the crucial years 1965–68. In the period from mid-1965 to June, 1966, when our basic Vietnam policies were being formulated and implemented, the Chairman saw the President once or twice a week. Compare this with the daily contacts between Admiral William D. Leahy and President Roosevelt during World War II, and the frequent telephone conversations and personal meetings between F.D.R. and General Marshall and Admiral King.

The Chairman rarely saw the President alone; only about once in every eight or nine White House visits. He was almost always accompanied either by the Secretary of Defense or his deputy, who never hesitated to "second-guess" the Chairman and to dilute and contradict his statements. The individual members of the Joint Chiefs—the responsible heads of the fighting services: the Army, Navy, Air Force, Marines—seldom saw the President privately. In the crucial twelve months from June, 1965, to June, 1966, when large numbers of U.S. ground troops were committed to Vietnam and the bombing of the North was started, the Air Chief of Staff

14

had about four private individual meetings with the President, the Commandant of the Marine Corps about the same number of meetings; the Chief of Staff of the Army saw the President privately twice. It was in this period that the Joint Chiefs reached what one of them described later as a "plateau of frustration"; their advice to the Commander in Chief was either "not getting through" or was so downgraded in the process that it was of minimal value in decision-making.

The legal requirement of the National Security Act that the President must receive *military* advice from men in uniform was largely frustrated during the formative years of Vietnam. In the Kennedy and, particularly, in the Johnson administrations, the civilians in the Pentagon, with little or no military experience but with tremendous authority, though little legal and less actual responsibility, had usurped the military role. The Secretary of Defense, aided by his civilian assistants, had become virtually the sole military adviser to the President.

The dangers that may stem from this situation are, as Vietnam showed, twofold. The first is that the purely *military* advice which the Pentagon is supposed to provide to the White House may be too much watered down by nonmilitary factors. The second is that all-powerful civilians, in the role of management analysts, rather than the much-feared military "men on horseback," may develop a military party line, which could be just as dangerous to the country in its ultimate consequences as a political party line.

As Lyman B. Kirkpatrick, Jr. has written, ". . . where civilian authorities dominate the decision-making process in matters exclusively military . . . then national catastrophe may result."[1]

Every war the United States has fought has shown that military factors must be considered by the President himself—not merely by his subordinates—as part of the top-level decision-making process. These factors may be overweighed in the decision-making process by political or economic or other considerations. But the President himself must make these judgments, for the stakes, during wartime, are lives—the lives of the younger generation of Americans.

Similarly, the development of an inflexible military policy or military strategy, from which no dissent is possible, is a sure road

15

to defeat and disaster. Hitler demonstrated this truism in World War II.

Our conspicuous failures in Vietnam were failures in command and control at the top levels in Washington, a product not only of personalities but also of the closely centralized organization that has evolved in the Pentagon since the passage of the unification act after World War II.

Checks and balances are a fundamental part of the American system of government, and if democracy and freedom are to be preserved, checks and balances are required within the executive branch as well as in the Congress–Supreme Court–federal–state system. Military checks and balances are almost as important as political ones, for political as well as military reasons.

The founding fathers understood this and created a state militia (now a National Guard) which was originally a creature of the individual states. More and more the Federal Government has extended its control over the Guard; its military effectiveness has certainly been increased, but at a price in political-military balance. The individual voices of the services, of the Guard and of the Reserve, and the now abolished chiefs of arms and services in the Army and the powerful bureau system in the Navy Department— all supported by or coupled with Congressional authority—once insured that no single "man on horseback," in or out of uniform, could establish a Pentagon hegemony and develop a military "party line," much less a personal political satrapy.

The centralization of power in the Pentagon in the office of the Secretary of Defense, the elimination of the service secretaries from the Cabinet and the subordination of the service departments and the creation of a Chairman of the Joint Chiefs of Staff, with great prestige and considerable power, all contributed to the development and creation of a tremendously powerful executive department, with military influence subordinated to all-powerful computer-management experts in and out of uniform.

The elimination, to a large degree, of the military checks and balances that once characterized our security organization, and the decline of Congressional authority under the "strong President"

16

concept of the Kennedy and Johnson administrations, postulate a future danger.

Vietnam has shown that management efficiency and a single military "line," or theory, are not necessarily synonymous with either combat effectiveness or the successful accomplishment of a policy objective.

The tendency toward centralization in the Pentagon had its counterpart in Vietnam in the operational field. Probably never in American experience has a theater commander had as much responsibility and as little real authority as General William C. Westmoreland. The President, the Secretary of Defense, the Chairman of the Joint Chiefs of Staff, and even Assistant Secretaries of Defense and staff assistants outside the chain of command exercised some degree of operational control or intervened at many different levels in the command structure. The Washington command post almost became the CP of a battalion commander. In the early stages of the war flight operations were so strictly controlled from Washington or Hawaii that target selection, flight profiles, numbers of sorties, armament loads and other details were stipulated from thousands of miles away. In the Tonkin Gulf incident the commander of one of the destroyers under torpedo boat attack was dunned and harried by messages from Washington while he was trying to interpret radar blips and fight his ship.

Until very late in the war, the failures of command, organization and control were as conspicuous in Saigon as in Washington. Gradually, we assumed responsibility in Saigon, but without authority. The lack of a combined unified command (with the South Vietnamese) handicapped the war effort, and our guilt complex about the overthrow of the Diem government and the murder of Diem made us overtender about the reactions of subsequent Vietnamese governments. We did not control events within South Vietnam—where the political, economic, social and military battles had ultimately to be won—in proportion to the immense effort that we exerted.

In part this hands-off attitude was due to two shibboleths that have become ingrained in American minds and that have handicapped the reasonable application of American power overseas.

17

Both are products of the U.S. propensity for moralizing and our tendency to generalize guideline principles into immutable laws. The self-determination of peoples and nonintervention in the internal affairs of other nations have, misapplied, caused us needless loss and anguish. The former, carried to extremes, can only lead to anarchy, as we have seen in the tribal conflicts in Africa and the strife in U.S. city streets; the latter, followed rigorously in wartime in a country like Vietnam, represents a well-nigh complete abdication of power, or rather its application without adequate guidance. We are constantly seeking, too, to walk down the path of power only with those governments groomed in our own image—the so-called democracies. The futility of attempting to establish Western-style democratic regimes in many of the undeveloped, illiterate nations of the world should be self-evident.

Though many of the mistakes in command, organization and control were in part the product of American attitudes, the primary failure was in coupling authority to responsibility. As Sir Robert Thompson, the British authority on counterinsurgency operations, has written: ". . . the Ambassador must be a pro-consul with absolute authority locally over all policy and agencies."[2]

Sir Robert and others have also correctly stressed what was one of the primary failures of the early years in Vietnam—our concentration upon defeating the enemy's military forces with essentially a foreign and alien army (our own), while neglecting, or minimizing, the basic governmental and political reforms necessary to make South Vietnam a viable entity. Priority should have been placed on strengthening the government and the civil service; the build-up of a national police; and, finally, upon the Vietnamization—the strengthening of the combat capabilities of the South Vietnamese armed forces—which is only now being adequately emphasized.

The new breed of American management experts, the self-perpetuating empires of government bureaus in Washington, and the fascination of the bureaucrats with statistics and computers had, during the Kennedy-Johnson-McNamara regime, a tendency to make a complex war still more complex and far more costly in terms of both dollars and personnel. In Vietnam countless studies —many of them of little pertinence—confused rather than clarified.

18

It may be fascinating to discover that the dreams of the Popular Forces are only .05 per cent sexual, but it is not likely to win the war [wrote Sir Robert Thompson]. It merely suggests to me that they are underpaid and underfed and everyone knows that anyway. The cabinets of United States Departments are stuffed with research reports which few have read and upon which no action is going to be taken. A minor facet of this unproductive activity is that these people tie up, while they are in the country, a fair proportion of the better trained and educated Vietnamese who could be much more usefully employed.[3]

The speed and effectiveness of modern communications, plus centralization in Washington, and the unwillingness, or inability, of the President and the Secretary of Defense to delegate authority, to tell their subordinates what to do but not how to do it, unquestionably reduced effectiveness and increased casualties. The top policy-makers lost sight of the woods because of the individual trees; there was a preoccupation with minutiae, while basic policy decisions too often were made without adequate advice or sufficient examination. The result: unnecessary casualties; there is no doubt, for instance, that American pilots paid with their lives for mistaken attempts to control all details from Washington or from Hawaii.

Overcontrol of military forces and the dictation of tactical and technical procedures by men thousands of miles from the battlefield thus contributed to the end they were intended to prevent: increased bloodshed.

In Vietnam, from the original commitment of U.S. ground combat units and the start of the bombing of the North in 1965, the United States followed what President Johnson called a "policy of gradualism"—a policy of slowly increasing the military pressure, of upping the ante, against the enemy. In modern military parlance, this could be called escalation—raising the stakes by increasing the forces committed and strengthening the actions taken.

Escalation always favors the stronger side—if it is done rapidly, with decision and with a power that the weaker enemy cannot quickly match relatively. But if it is done slowly, hesitatingly and with uncertainty—as it was done in Vietnam—the enemy, particularly if he is helped from outside his country—as was true in Viet-

19

nam—can match, relatively, each slow increase in strength. A hesitant policy telegraphs a national weakness of will, an uncertainty or indecisiveness which a determined enemy will always exploit. Evidence of determination and a few thousand men early in a war may well be worth far sterner and stronger measures later.

In Vietnam what was possible with minimum risks in 1964 and 1965—blockade of the North Vietnamese coast and a strong air interdiction campaign—was not possible without undue risks and losses in 1968: the U.S.S.R. had become too much involved; the enemy defenses had been too greatly strengthened. In nearly every instance the policy of "gradualism"—of delay—led to frustration. We bombed the oil storage and fuel complex of North Vietnam, but not until after the North Vietnamese had dispersed their supplies; we bombed the North Vietnamese airfields, but not until after they had dispersed their planes. U.S. air power was hobbled by political restrictions while the North Vietnamese steadily built up the most formidable air-defense system in the world and exacted higher and higher losses. The policy of gradualism which governed the whole course of the war in Vietnam was precisely the wrong way to fight any kind of war; it inevitably led to frustration and it lengthened and made far more costly what was certain to be—no matter how military pressure was applied—a long war.

This policy of gradualism, and the failure of the administration to explain adequately the nature of the war in Vietnam and our war aims, contributed to the natural impatience of the American people. In any guerrilla war public opinion is probably the most important single battlefield. The French clearly won the military battles in Algeria, but they lost the war when they lost the support of public opinion at home and abroad. By its very nature guerrilla war—or a "war of national liberation," as Premier Khrushchev described it—is a war of attrition, bound to be long-drawn-out and, at best, frustrating.

This is particularly true when the guerrillas are supplied from neighboring countries immune to attack. The British required twelve years to eliminate a far smaller and simpler guerrilla insurgence in Malaya; in the Philippines, after two decades, the Hukbalahaps still exist, at least in kernel form. In Cyprus, in Palestine and in many other countries, the difficulties of stamping out terrorism and hit-and-run guerrillas have been illustrated by history. Guerrilla wars, in any area where the guerrillas have become well established and can be supplied from outside the area of operations, are certain to be long and wearing wars of attrition.

A clear understanding of this and of the nature of the war and a continually candid appraisal of the progress of the war by the government are essential to public support. Honesty and frankness are a basic tool of war particularly in the age of electronic communication—when the television screen has brought the blood and horrors of the battlefield into the living room. The capsuled comments of the "TV generals" and the exhausted remarks of some battle-scarred "grunt," or weary corporal, had a lot to do, during the Vietnam war, with the shaping of public opinion.

The government bore a major share of the blame for the nation's war-weariness; its overoptimism lulled and deceived the American people; its lack of honesty and consistency confused them; the "credibility gap"—particularly in Washington and also in the early years in Saigon—was real and understandable. The Secretary of Defense and the President were not believed because they too often manipulated the truth.

Yet the public media share the blame. Oversimplification of the news and emotional editorialization marked the coverage of the Vietnamese conflict. Young men with little competence to do so squeezed sweeping judgments of the past and prophecies for the future into a half-column of space or a few seconds on the TV screen. And the breach between the government and the public media was not wholly of the government's making. As in every war, there was some excellent reportage and some highly irresponsible coverage; what distinguished Vietnam during the formative years (until 1968) was the almost consistently antiadministration outlook of a large segment of the press, and the irrelevant, emotional, over-simplified or erroneous judgments of many of the reporters.

For the first time in American experience since the Civil War intense antiwar and antimilitary sentiment developed in the United States before the war was over. The public media reflected this and, in part, caused it in a chicken-and-egg relationship that is inextrica-

21

bly mixed. There were many frustrating factors: the way we became involved without a declaration of war; the scale of the commitment; the nature of the conflict, with no great battles won or territory conquered; the essentially negative objectives—not to conquer but to prevent conquest; the endless nature of the guerrilla fighting; what was to most Americans an alien culture and an unattractive environment; and the failure of the public to discern clear signs of progress—all contributed to war-weariness and disillusionment.

Thus the public media were not by any means the only factors in the gradual development of a climate of futility that became pronounced after the enemy's militarily abortive, but psychologically successful, Tet offensive. Nevertheless, with some marked and shining exceptions, the Vietnam war was *not* journalism's finest hour. Some reporters and commentators, most of them trained in the old school of objectivity and fairness and experienced in foreign and military correspondence, maintained a high standard, and some contributed reportage in magnificent depth and detail. But not most.

Vietnam was the kind of war—a complex crazy quilt of political, economic and psychological factors—in which almost anything you said about it was true. But many representatives of television broadcasting companies, press associations and individual newspapers—reflecting perhaps the division back home, the bias of their editors or publishers or their own emotions—selected essentially the negative factors. Uncle Sam, or the administration, or the services, or (in particular) the much-abused South Vietnamese Government and armed forces became the whipping boy for public frustration. Many of the new young reporters, particularly in the television medium, wanted to be their own Lincoln Steffens; they ignored a basic guideline—that it is much easier to be a muckraker than to provide a balanced report.

Some confused the "passion to inform" with the "passion to perform," as General Maxwell D. Taylor phrased it, in an address to the Association of the U.S. Army on October 30, 1968: ". . . in Vietnam some reporters and commentators have felt that their task is not to describe the events but to shape them, not to report on foreign policy but to make it."

22

Instant journalism encouraged the development of thirty-second pundits, and the reporting, selecting and editing of the news—on both TV screens and in newspapers—forswore much of the objectivity of the past and tended to emphasize the dramatic, the exciting, the sensational at the cost of perspective and fairness. Many editorial writers and columnists—particularly in the *New York Times* and the Washington *Post,* the bellwethers of American journalism—abandoned balance and fairness, lost perspective and accentuated the negative.

The new style in journalism—in some ways a throwback to the last century's subjective journalism—is a far cry from the principles of thirty or forty years ago when the adverb "only" would be removed from a reporter's copy by the editors because it was deemed to convey an editorial judgment.

Today the emphasis is first on reader interest instead of accuracy, and on somewhat freewheeling interpretation rather than objectivity. This subjectivity was, in part, responsible for a distorted view of the Vietnam war. But there were other factors and attitudes which shaped the American outlook.

Many Americans, shocked by their vicarious exposure, via TV, to war's brutality, assumed a sense of guilt. They bought whole the "big bully" fiction of the enemy's propaganda, as did much of the world. This was, in fact, an image which was never wholly erased, particularly in the minds of our Western European allies. Our own actions occasionally fortified the false impression. In Vietnam our one-year rotation policy meant that we fielded a "turnover" army —in some ways the most inexperienced in recent history. The top- and middle-grade leadership was in general excellent, but at platoon and company level lieutenants and captains and noncoms, fresh from the corner drugstore, succeeded each other with lightning rapidity. Professional expertise and discipline declined, and occasionally restraint suffered. The alleged Songmy massacre of civilians, for instance, greatly hurt the United States in the eyes of the world, even though the slayings were regarded by the Army itself as "criminal," and even though the U.S. Army is the only one in modern history which has publicly preferred charges of such gravity against its own men in the midst of war.

23

Thus a just moral cause—the defense of a people against terrorism and force—was transformed in the hearts and minds of many into an unjust one; the United States, with its immense power, was pictured as trying to destroy the tiny country of North Vietnam. The facts were conveniently forgotten: the almost unlimited manpower of the North Vietnamese, backed by China, and the industrial and arms support of the two giants of world Communism, Russia and China.

The cruelty of war led, too, to revulsion—a commendable human reaction, but one which if translated into the extreme political and psychological reactions which characterized Vietnam might well lead to a nation's decline and fall. This factor was coupled with a naïve, almost a sophomoric, "thing" about democracy. The South Vietnamese Government was condemned, almost *in toto*, not only because it was inefficient and corrupt but because it did not live up to our image of the one-man-one-vote principle. To the American people, who have been leading participants in global history since 1917, the relatively primitive political methods of a small, illiterate Asiatic country, beset by enemies in the midst of war, should have come as no surprise.

There was another vast difference between Vietnam and World War II, or even Korea. The enemy made clear-cut physical attacks in organized military force upon the United States, or upon friends of the United States, in World War II and Korea. In World War II the opposition of the left-wing intellectuals in the United States, who play such a large role in molding public opinion, was transformed to support for the war when Hitler invaded Russia. And Hitler's persecution of the Jews unified the important and influential Jewish community in America—important alike in the publishing and other communications media, in economics and finance and in politics—against him.

These factors were lacking in Vietnam. There was subtle, often covert aggression; we were fighting against the Communists, not with them; there was no overt Jewish persecution: Jewish emotions in the United States were focused, not on Vietnam but on the plight of Israel in the Middle East. There had been, moreover, a revolution in values in the United States and in the world which under-

24

mined the old concepts and the old loyalties.

The left-wing elements in American life, strengthened by the racial troubles at home and by the revolts of the students, were a fertile field for Communist propaganda. The narrow parochialism of many so-called liberal views, and their ignorance of or distortion of the facts, added to the morally sincere but pragmatically feckless recommendations of so many of the do-gooders—often an unwitting force for evil in American life—greatly oversimplified a complex conflict and deeply influenced large segments of the American public.

The demand for simplistic solutions—"Withdraw now"—solutions which even a high school junior in political science should have rejected, became powerful political factors in 1968 and even more so in 1969. Thus President Johnson lost the one battle essential to victory in a guerrilla war—the struggle for the hearts and minds of his own people. Vietnam clearly demonstrated that at the Washington command-post level in particular, and at the "country team" level in general, the nation has not yet achieved the proper melding and smooth direction of all forms of power to achieve a complex political end.

As George Fielding Eliot and Cornelius D. Sullivan put it, in a Vietnam study prepared for the Center for Strategic and International Studies at Georgetown University, "In the total picture, the executive decision making apparatus seems to have operated very badly in the higher direction of the war."

Robert Hotz, editor of *Aviation Week and Space Technology*, capsuled the basic error in an editorial: ". . . the real failure has not been in our arms but in our policy."[4] Or, as others have put it, the divorcement of politics and power.

Another lesson of Vietnam—and a prime one—is the necessity of conserving and marshaling the economic strength of the nation, as well as its psychological strength. During the Vietnam war the government tried to fight a major war with business as usual; it was determined to have guns and butter, and to maintain important commitments around the world while sending seven thousand miles overseas the largest expeditionary forces since World War II. The immense resources of America made this possible during the

25

first eighteen months, but inevitable economic retribution caught up. There were no price and wage controls, or for that matter any real material controls. There was a steady inflation, and the President, having cut taxes in the early stages, found Congress reluctant to raise them again without major cuts in the federal budget. The dollar gap threatened gold, and the United States, as a result of high-level mismanagement, found itself in 1967, 1968 and 1969 in a financial crisis. Early economic foresight and, above all, political courage to adopt unpalatable and restrictive economic controls are essential in a major war; the longer the administration waits, the more difficult the problem of control. For both economic and psychological reasons a "business-as-usual," "guns-*and*-butter" policy can be disastrous to the accomplishment of war aims, and, indeed, to the national vitality.[5]

Korea and, particularly, Vietnam—and the atomic trauma which has too often inhibited American foreign policy—have obscured what should be a self-evident truism in the nuclear age: that the United States can fight a limited war, a counterinsurgency war, a conventional war, only under the umbrella of an annihilating strategic nuclear-delivery capability. An annihilating strategic nuclear-delivery capability means—or should mean—what it implies: the capability of annihilating the military, political and economic power of the U.S.S.R. and Communist China regardless of what they do first. In regions where the interests of the great superstates conflict the risk of committing any kind of conventional force appreciably increases if we fail to maintain our nuclear capabilities. If the U.S.S.R. and her Communist allies should achieve nuclear superiority, Moscow would be able to choose the time and place and manner of conquest and we would be powerless to prevent it.

We appear to have forgotten this fundamental principle, for in the past few years Russia has gone a long way indeed in reducing our once overwhelming nuclear superiority. As long as atomic weapons remain part of the arsenal of man, the United States must retain the capability of destroying Soviet Russia no matter what she does first. Any nonproliferation treaty, any treaty for the control of nuclear armaments, must be judged against this yardstick: what does it mean to the future security of America? As long as nuclear armaments exist without foolproof controls, we must be prepared to fight World War III; only thus can we deter it.

This does *not* mean indiscriminate, massive escalation, or preemptive nuclear assault. This does *not* mean that if we become involved again in war, we must, *ipso facto*, lay about blindly, smashing cities and destroying peoples. In the atomic age a *delenda est Carthago* policy—never morally justifiable—would be a two-edged sword and would mean mutual destruction. The objectives of any war worth fighting must always be a more stable peace.

Yet we must learn to *fight limited wars without limiting our power so greatly that we exhaust ourselves and defeat our objective.* Power must have restraints, but once military power is invoked it must be used rapidly, heavily, decisively, to achieve our objective, no matter how defined, or it becomes aimless violence.

We have allowed the term "limited war" to become a shibboleth; we have forgotten that it takes two to fight limited wars. Strategy is the science of alternatives; we have, by our own actions or lack of actions, reduced too greatly the options available to us. During much of the 1950's we emphasized too greatly nuclear strategy and tactics; during much of the 1960's we have emphasized too greatly conventional strategy and tactics—and particularly limited war.

Limited war should mean, first and primarily, the definition of aims and objectives and the limited political end to be achieved. But in practice—in two limited wars, Korea and Vietnam—we have used American manpower and spent American blood unstintingly,[6] while limiting weapons and hobbling strategy and tactics. We have practiced manpower escalation, while limiting technological escalation, and the result has been military and political frustration. The problem of the future is not simply *how* to limit wars but how to limit them without condemning ourselves to long wearing wars of attrition, how to limit them *without* frustrating our political ojectives.

Vietnam suggests that the first and fundamental requirement for fighting limited wars successfully is to lead from strength, not from weakness. While overstated and oversimplified, the "Never Again" school that became so important in U.S. strategic discussions after Korea has some historical validity. Historically, the utilization of mass armies has usually led to mass slaughter. The decline of the British Empire can almost certainly be traced to the awful casualties of Ypres and the Somme and the trench stalemate of World War I. Whole generations of the best and finest of British youth, the heritage of the future, were wiped out in the holocaust of fire and steel; thousands of others, who were the potential leaders of Britain, were scarred and crippled, physically, emotionally or mentally. Winston Churchill's preoccupation in World War II with a strategy which would minimize British loss of life was well founded.

Thus the "Never Again" school in American military policy has some validity, particularly to the area of earth to which it was applied—the Asiatic continent. For the United States, compared with Communist China and Asia as a whole, is weak in manpower, strong in technology; Asia, with its limitless millions and its casual regard for human life, is bound to have an advantage in any conflict in which manpower is the principal factor. To lead from strength, then, one must fashion a strategy which maximizes the natural advantages and the inherent skills of one's own nation and minimizes the strengths of the enemy.

Vietnam emphasized, too, the high importance of selectivity in strategy; intervention anywhere and everywhere is a sure invitation to disaster. The geographic areas to be defended must be important; the conditions for success present, even if obscured.

In Vietnam, T. E. Lawrence's classic formula that "irregular war or rebellion could be proved to be an exact science and an inevitable success, granted certain factors and if pursued along certain lines," was supported by nature, geography and our own policy failures. "Rebellion," Lawrence wrote, in his famous *Encyclopaedia Britannica* article, "must have an unassailable base. . . . It must have a sophisticated alien enemy, in the form of a disciplined army of occupation . . . too few to adjust number to space. . . . It must have a friendly population, not actively friendly, but sympathetic to the point of not betraying rebel movements to the enemy."[7]

Colonel Amos A. Jordan, Jr., drawing upon the experience of Vietnam, concludes, too sweepingly, that "as modern technology has ruled out general war as a rational policy instrument, so modern participatory politics have made limited war as an instrument of

28

policy impracticable, except when a state is in extremis, or its truly vital interests are at stake—or conceivably when such a conflict is under a multilateral banner."[8]

A multilateral intervention, particularly if "sanctified" by the United Nations, is far more likely to win some degree of international support. President Eisenhower's decision against intervening at Dienbienphu was based, in large part, upon the refusal of Britain and other powers to join us, and his instinct was correct. In Vietnam, anomalously, the total forces of our allies (excluding the South Vietnamese)—South Koreans, Australians, New Zealanders, Thais and Filipinos—outnumbered the total of non-American, non-Korean forces during the Korean War. But they did not fight in Vietnam under the UN banner, a symbol which appeals so greatly to the intellectual liberals and opinion-makers of the world.

Vietnam has not—in summary—demonstrated either the end of insurrectionary wars or their inevitable success. Insurrectionary wars of some sort are here to stay regardless of the outcome in Vietnam, and whether or not the United States fights them. But

> If the Americans are forced, whether for military or for political reasons, to pull out of Vietnam, their defeat, however disguised, will be hailed by revolutionaries everywhere as the final vindication of the theory of People's Revolutionary War—a demonstration that even a super-power can be defeated by a peasant army. In that event, the efforts now being made to launch such insurrections, or sustain them, in Africa and Latin-America, would be redoubled.[9]

Inevitably, whether or not the United States returns to isolation (and such a return can be only temporary), there will be more but different Vietnams with many and differing results.

Vietnam has, above all, emphasized that military intervention cannot substitute for political intervention. Politics is the name of the game in insurrectionary situations; the political factors are dominant, or, as Robert Shaplen has put it, "We seemed unwilling [in Vietnam] to confront the harsh and unpalatable fact that in today's world . . . subtle but firm political involvement in the affairs of other countries with whom we are engaged in a common enterprise is often the only way to get results and avoid military as well as political disasters."[10]

Vietnam re-emphasized many military truisms—particularly the characteristics, the limitations and the capabilities of air power, sea power and ground power, which each new generation of policymakers seems to have to learn anew.

The capabilities and the limitations of air power, in particular, were misunderstood in Vietnam, especially by the public, but also to some degree by the government and even by Air Force leaders. In part, we were victims of our own propaganda. Air power is a dramatic military instrument, and the leaders of a young Air Force who have had to fight to achieve co-equal status with the other services have never been given to understatement. Most of them have been drawn from the "big bomber" ranks, or have been selected for high positions for political as well as military reasons. The same charge that Major General Claire Chennault made when a young officer at the Air Force Tactical School prior to World War II, that tactical air power and fighter aircraft had been too much subordinated to "big bomber" doctrine, had equal validity just prior to Vietnam.

The Air Force is a service with charisma; it appeals to the public, who like to believe in the promise of quick and easy victories, relatively bloodless for our side, won in the wild blue yonder. But victory in the air requires the most advanced technology, the most intense training and the most careful and precise targeting achievable. The military principles of mass and momentum apply to air war as well as to surface operations, and weight of metal is still a key factor—a lesson learned in World War II, overlooked prior to Vietnam.

Dr. John S. Foster, Jr., the Defense Department's Director of Research and Engineering, in testimony to a Senate committee on July 10, 1968, noted that the nation's "conventional tactical warfare capability . . . was not adequate for continued, limited non-nuclear warfare." He said there had been too "much dependence on nuclear weapons in the 1953–1961 period," but he failed to emphasize that the "bomber generals" had controlled Air Force destinies ever since the beginning of World War II.

He also conveniently omitted mentioning one of the basic flaws in the Kennedy-Johnson-McNamara air power policies. Kennedy and McNamara switched Air Force emphasis from a heavy reliance on nuclear bombs to conventional bombing. But, faced with the huge expenditures essential to full preparation for a conventional air war, they failed to grasp the nettle. It was these prospective expenditures which had persuaded the Eisenhower administration to place principal (and initially far too much) reliance upon the nuclear deterrent. To take out an airfield with nuclear weapons may require one or two sorties; with conventional bombs, the operation —as Vietnam has again shown—must be constantly repeated and hundreds of missions are required. A conventional air war, *ipso facto*, requires thousands of planes and a production line for planes, pilots and spare parts to maintain a high level of effort despite losses. The numbers of planes and pilots, and the spare parts— greatly reduced by McNamara's penny-pinching policies—were inadequate even to the needs of the very limited and strictly controlled air war in Vietnam. And, as Dr. Foster noted:

> . . . we encountered some awkwardness in trying to apply our sophisticated systems, particularly air power, to the insurgency-limited war environment.
>
> We have been plagued with our inability to find an elusive, unsophisticated enemy and decisively hit him. We did not have a good, all-weather or night attack capability.
>
> We were unable to pinpoint SAM [Surface to Air Missiles], or AAA [Antiaircraft Artillery] control radars. These were the same shortcomings (with the exception of the SAM problem) we had in Korea.

The fiction that air power won World War II was perpetuated, for a time, in Korea, when Operation Strangle (which failed to strangle) was proclaimed as a war-winning gambit.

But in Vietnam air power—in large part through no fault of its own—has suffered in the public mind too much de-emphasis; it has been wrongly blamed for failures that were not its doing, and has not won recognition for its real accomplishments.

When the bombing of North Vietnam started, at least a segment of the administration was persuaded that a limited and selective

31

bombardment of the North could quickly persuade the Communist leadership either (a) to negotiate or (b) to halt or reduce their support of the Vietcong in the South. Later it was believed that the air bombardment would reduce the morale of the North Vietnamese people and erode their will to resist.

Neither appreciation was sound; neither was grounded in experience. Even the all-out, no-holds-barred aerial bombing campaigns of World War II, culminating with the frightful fire-bomb raids on Tokyo and the nuclear annihilation of Hiroshima and Nagasaki, did not crush the will of the enemy. Indeed, it is doubtful that the will of a people can have much effect—except over a very long period —upon a dictatorial or authoritarian government. The effort to persuade by power must be applied directly to the government; yet a Communist government, or a fanatic authoritarian one, is notoriously difficult to persuade. (In Hitler's case, of course, where unconditional surrender was the Allied objective, he had everything to gain and nothing to lose by continued resistance even though it was hopeless.) Even in limited war the punishment inflicted by air power must be so great that the alternative offered would be attractive.

But in Vietnam air power was so limited, hobbled and restricted by the administration that its political, psychological and morale effects—rarely definitive in any case except with the use of nuclear weapons—were minimized. The bombing of North Vietnam probably resulted in more lift for the morale of South Vietnam, and particularly for the stability of the South Vietnamese Government, than it accomplished in depressing the morale of the North, or shaking Ho Chi Minh's government.

In the air war the administration's policy of gradualism was followed with disastrous effects. In 1965 the Joint Chiefs of Staff recommended that some ninety-four key targets in North Vietnam be destroyed within a space of some two to three weeks in an overwhelming blitz. North Vietnam's air defenses were then weak and the cumulative effect of destroying all of these targets rapidly might, indeed, have shaken the North Vietnamese hierarchy, and certainly would have greatly impeded their aid to the Vietcong.

Yet the basic military principles of mass and momentum and

32

shock effect were completely ignored; not all of the ninety-four targets had been struck when bombing was halted in 1968, and instead of three weeks, the power of the United States Air Force and Navy was applied in driblets over three years. The natural result was that the North Vietnamese air defenses increased tremendously (with Soviet and Chinese help) in power, extent and sophistication; our own air losses increased seriously, and the results achieved were neutralized by the enemy's dispersion, concealment and protection of his important sources of strength—fuel supplies, electric generators, etc.

Any air campaign, like a naval blockade, is a campaign of attrition; the enemy must be worn down by air destruction faster than his economy and his logistics can repair the havoc. As we discovered in World War II and Korea, it requires major effort and a vast amount of conventional bomb tonnage to degrade the capabilities and deplete the energies of a resolute foe faster than the enemy can recoup them, whether the environment be a sophisticated industrial one or a primitive economy.

The interdiction campaign against North Vietnam was similarly hobbled by restrictions incredibly naïve in a military sense and politically stupid. The main source of the enemy's supplies from 1965 on were outside North and South Vietnam; Russia and China produced the arms, the fuel, the food and the manufactured products without which the war could not have been continued. Most of these were funneled into the country through Haiphong and two other, much smaller North Vietnamese ports, by railroad and, to a lesser extent, by road from China and increasingly in the later stages through Cambodia by sea, by river and by land. The bottlenecks were the North Vietnamese and, later, the Cambodian ports, including the docks and unloading facilities and anchorages. When President Johnson finally, in the summer of 1967, permitted close-in bombing around Haiphong and Hanoi, more was accomplished in three months to block the flow of supplies to the South than had been accomplished in the prior two years. But the effort was short-lived; bad weather, and then political restrictions, which transformed the air above the 19th parallel into a sanctuary, made first the heartland of North Vietnam, and later, when the bombing

33

was completely halted, the entire country, immune to punishment. In a few months—between March of 1968 and the fall—much that had been so painfully destroyed at the cost of so many American lives was rebuilt, and North Vietnam in a military sense was about as strong as ever.

"We made the classic blunder in Vietnam," a high-ranking officer has noted. "We committed our infantry before we isolated the objective."

Despite severe restrictions, the interdiction campaign unquestionably reduced and hampered the flow of men and supplies to South Vietnam—by how much it is impossible to say. No inderdiction campaign ever waged has ever stopped such a flow completely, even when all the odds favored air power (as in Italy in World War II and in Korea). And any air interdiction campaign has been effective in hurting definitively the over-all combat capabilities of the enemy only when coupled with heavy ground fighting; the air is the hammer, the ground the anvil against which the foe's strength must be crushed. If the enemy is not forced by our own ground actions to use up and expend his supplies at a more rapid rate than he can resupply himself over damaged and blown bridges and cratered roads and railroads, then air interdiction will be futile.

Even without the political restrictions imposed upon it air power could never, therefore, have been spectacularly successful in Vietnam in inhibiting enemy ground activity in the South. No plane, no number of planes, can stop individuals from filtering undetected down jungle trails. In South Vietnam the enemy had built up large stockpiles of supplies, weapons and equipment; he grew, or purchased, most of his food locally, or in nearby Cambodia; he even manufactured some of his weapons in jungle hideouts. The Vietcong was in many ways a primitive enemy, and his wants were few. Most important, with the sanctuaries of the jungles and Cambodia and Laos near at hand he could normally choose or reject ground combat as he willed. Since there was no continuous ground front and only intermittent engagement, there was no continuous expenditure of ammunition and equipment and the enemy's supply lines had ample time to replenish his stocks. Given these facts, the limitations of the environment, the existence of sanctuaries and the political restrictions imposed, it is remarkable that air power accomplished what it did. That it eased the combat operations of U.S. and South Vietnamese ground forces and saved Allied lives, even at the cost of pilot casualties, is clear; without the air interdiction campaign, restricted even though it was, the fighting in South Vietnam would have been far more bloody.

Where air power operated under ideal military circumstances— as in the Battle of Khesanh—it demonstrated its capabilities. At Khesanh, air was the hammer, the Marine garrison the anvil between which the enemy was bloodily crushed. B-52 bombers and tactical fighter-bombers, plus heavy artillery bombardments, destroyed the enemy and his supply lines faster than they could be replaced; a full-fledged attack upon Khesanh was never mounted.

Elsewhere in South Vietnam the versatility and flexibility of air power provided the margin of superiority which often turned defeat into victory. The helicopter gave the ground troops undreamed-of mobility and made vertical envelopment of the enemy a viable tactic. Transport and supply aircraft provided logistic lifelines which the Victcong could not cut. Tactical fighter-bombers, armed helicopters and a whole stable of Commando-type aircraft provided an around-the-clock air support for Allied ground forces that on the whole was superb in its efficiency and often decisive in its effect. Reconnaissance aircraft with infrared "people sniffers," side-looking radar, cameras and other exotic detection and sensing devices emphasized to a greater degree than ever before the intelligence capability of air power.

Thus the history of Vietnam demonstrates that air superiority is an absolutely indispensable instrument of military power to the United States, and indeed to any sophisticated nation. Without it one may hope to prevent defeat, but he cannot expect victory. With it anything is possible; above all, your own loss in blood and sweat and tears is minimized.

Yet it is dangerous to generalize too much from the experience of Vietnam. We faced an enemy in the South with no planes of his own and little antiaircraft support; in the North the enemy's defenses represented the most sophisticated air-defense system the United States had ever faced, yet it was notably short of aircraft,

35

and was, undoubtedly, a "piece of cake" compared with the air defenses of Moscow. And no nuclear weapons were used. We found that the "blitz" effects of air power—its tremendous morale effects —have even less consequence in a jungle environment and against a simple economy than in the closely packed industrialized regions of Western Europe, where they were never decisive.

The characteristics and limitations of air power are thus conspicuous:

It is an essential part of the military team, but in nearly all circumstances it is not capable of an "independent" victory; i.e., it requires the cooperative efforts of ground and sea power to provide a war-winning strategy. If one can speak of victory in an *all-out nuclear war*, air power, operating alone or independently (in the form primarily of missiles, with piloted planes useful for transport and logistic backup and in reconnaissance roles), could destroy both an enemy's capability and an enemy's will to resist. In a *limited nuclear* war it is conceivable that air power alone might, under certain circumstances—such as the defense of an island base (with antiaircraft nuclear-headed missiles and fighters)—be the decisive arm. But in *conventional wars* of any sort, in nearly all *limited wars*, it is part of the team—an indispensable partner, but still only a partner.

Air power can devastate, punish and destroy, but it cannot dominate, hold and control ground or surface areas. It can delay and harass and hamper surface communications, but acting alone it cannot completely cut them. It can reduce, perhaps—in some circumstances, decisively—an enemy's capability, if not his will, to resist. But it cannot put the seal on victory.

It can overfly the oceans and can lift heavy weapons and masses of troops quickly to any point on the earth's surface. Yet it is dependent on surface transportation for backup and support, for the fuel for its giant transport planes, for spare parts, for the steel matting for runways, for bulk cargoes, etc. It can transport men but not all the things a man needs to make him a soldier.

Above all, the speed of reaction of land-based air power is dependent primarily upon the availability of adequate and secure airfields close to the center of crisis.

36

Missile power, which is included, generically, in the Air Force's definition of "aerospace power," has demonstrated its distinct limitations and yet specialized capabilities in limited war. Surface-to-surface bombardment missiles with ranges varying from a few thousand yards to thousands of miles have unquestionably largely (but not wholly) replaced the piloted bomber in nuclear war of any type. Yet in Vietnam no bombardment missile that was cost-competitive with the fighter-bomber and that at the same time had sufficient accuracy to destroy targets with conventional warheads was available. However, new tactical missiles with very small CEP's (circular error, probable), and far cheaper than Pershing or Polaris, are certain to supplement piloted aircraft in the delivery of explosives against tactical as well as strategic targets. Antiaircraft missiles were less effective, in the environment of counterinsurgency war, than antiaircraft guns, but both, employed with modern radar and interceptors, greatly strengthened air defenses. Air-to-surface missiles, after disappointing beginnings, increased their power and accuracy, and air-to-air missiles proved to be essential to the modern fighter, but at the same time were no substitute for aircraft cannon.

The advent of missile warfare, in other words, has greatly complicated the entire spectrum of war, particularly because counterelectronic warfare—the jamming, spoofing or evasion of the enemy's radar or guidance systems—has now become so essential a part of all war. But missiles, though indispensable, are not definitive or conclusive. The lesson in war is driven home again and again: a man with a gun in the woods is still as important as he was in the French and Indian Wars; new weapons and new tactics have supplemented but not replaced the old. There is no ultimate weapon; there is no easy, simplistic answer to war technically or tactically.

Sea power, like air power, has the tremendous advantage of mobility. The speed of a ship, of course, is a fraction of that of the plane, but it possesses a bulk-cargo-carrying capacity and an economy—in terms of costs per ton-mile—which no plane can match. Some 98 percent of the tonnage required to prosecute the war in Vietnam was transported there by ships; indeed, most of the troop units (as distinct from replacements) were ferried to Vietnam by sea.

U.S. control of the seas was a fundamental requirement for the projection of U.S. power to Southeast Asia; without it the war could not have been fought. The aircraft carrier provided the mobile landing field which enabled air operations long before land airfields were available. Another important advantage of the aircraft carrier, at least under the peculiar conditions prevailing in Vietnam, was its immunity to attack. Thousands of U.S. aircraft of all types were destroyed or damaged by enemy mortar, rocket or sabotage attacks on U.S. land airfields. Sea-based air power was invulnerable to such attacks. On the other hand, operational accidents—and particularly carrier fires—destroyed many naval planes.

Two naval weaknesses at the start of U.S. operations in Vietnam —a lack of shallow-water, river and coastal patrol craft and inadequate naval gunfire (both of them painfully developed in World War II)—were gradually remedied, but not until late in 1968, when the 16-inch guns of the battleship *New Jersey* became available, did the Navy provide even a fraction of its potential gunfire-support capability. Nevertheless, water patrols, surveillance and inspection aided materially in reducing the flow of enemy men and supplies into South Vietnam, and naval gunfire support helped many operations ashore. Similarly, amphibious operations—particularly in the northern I Corps area, where the U.S. Marines worked closely with the Seventh Fleet—permitted envelopment tactics which frequently resulted in disproportionate casualties to the enemy.

Perhaps most important was the logistic support and security that control of the sea permitted. In effect, our coastal enclaves were secure bases, with their backs to the sea, with ships as their depots, and the United States, seven thousand miles away, as their warehouse.

Yet, as in the case of air power, the naval lessons of Vietnam must be accepted with reserve. Like air power, sea power was hobbled by political restrictions. One of sea power's strongest weapons—the blockade—was never invoked, and mine-laying in enemy coastal waters (as distinct from enemy rivers) was never permitted. Blockade, like air bombardment, is a strategy of attrition, but Vietnam became—like every guerrilla war—a war of attrition, and Washington forswore the use of its strongest cards. Moreover, our command of the sea was never seriously challenged—save on the rivers, where the Navy's patrol boats engaged in constant duels with the land. The North Vietnamese Navy was inconsequential in strength, and neither the Russians nor the Chinese chose to challenge the United States with their formidable submarine fleets. Nor did enemy air power attack our ships; coastal-defense batteries were the major threat the Seventh Fleet faced.

Once again, sea power proved its absolute indispensability to the life of a great nation. The protection of the seaborne lines of supply to our friends and allies and of the vital arteries through which flow the strategic lifeblood of industry, and the projection of U.S. military power to any overseas area, cannot be accomplished without the whole panoply of sea power—oceangoing surface ships of many types; coastal patrol and river craft; planes and submarines. Today it can project its power, by planes and missiles, far inland and convey its amphibious forces, by helicopters and landing craft, to more shallow beachheads. But like air power, the Navy's guns and missiles and planes and ships can smash and destroy and partially interdict, but they cannot, except in narrow areas and for limited times, provide absolute control over sea and contiguous land areas. Control of the sea is an evanescent factor, to be fought for and won again and again—against submarines, planes, blockade runners, camouflaged barges, high-speed patrol craft, night operations—as long as the enemy persists.

Like air power, sea power is an indispensable part of the team, but, like air power, sea power alone cannot insure victory in any sizable conventional war. In specialized cases, where all an enemy's supply lines are by sea, sea power could be the decisive factor, but an insurrection of the hill tribes in Burma is not likely to be overawed by the Seventh Fleet, cruising up and down in the Indian Ocean.

Vietnam demonstrated, as never before, that the "grunt" (the GI) with rifle and bayonet is vital—to the domination, control, interdiction and pacification of land areas. Only the soldier with his feet in the mud can ultimately confirm the conquest of land areas. The fire power, the destructiveness, the mobility of the other services cannot substitute for the sentinel at his post, day and night, in all weathers.

Yet the soldier's traditional task—control of land areas—was threatened as never before in Vietnam. The tactics of terrorism by an enemy who melts into the civilian population, the hit-and-run attacks of guerrillas and the Communist mixture of political, psychological, social, economic and military measures have postulated in Vietnam a greater challenge to the ground soldier's traditional role than at any time in our history. In an insurgency environment the task of providing security to the people is an immense one; yet it is fundamentally security that is the key to counterinsurgency. Vietnam was a test—some think a calculated test—of Communism's recipe for world conquest, of what Khrushchev called "wars of national liberation," of what Mao tse-tung sees as a worldwide peasant or agrarian revolution.

The United States picked up the gauntlet, but it has not found the full answer—save at undue cost in blood, sweat and tears—to the challenge of tomorrow, the challenge of unconventional warfare.

Finally, there was the basic lesson—fundamental to every war—which many of our leaders have never learned. During Vietnam, for the first time in United States history, the administration followed, even until the end, a policy of "just-enough-but-not-too-much." There were, according to McNamara, to be none of the great and wasteful surpluses of military equipment that had followed every other war in which the nation participated. The result was a slowness in starting or restarting production lines and in placing orders, an overcareful calculation of anticipated expenditures, a parsimony of material and dollars which resulted in intermittent shortages or scarcities of many items in Vietnam (ammunition, generators, spare parts, etc.) and, above all, caused a major "drawdown" on aircraft, inventories and the combat effectiveness of U.S. forces around the world.

The disgraceful *Pueblo* incident off Korea in early 1968 illustrated graphically the weakness in ready military strength of the United States in areas other than in Vietnam. Yet, parenthetically, it should be obvious that during any period in which the nation is

40

fighting a war of any kind in one area, it should be more ready than ever before to fight another war elsewhere. Despite careful caution and precise calculations, unwanted conflicts occur; the Middle Eastern crisis of 1967 demonstrated this.

The penny-pinching war in Vietnam—an incredible performance for the wealthiest nation in the world—was, in major part, a product of the President's political failure to grasp the nettle of a war economy, to impose economic controls and to mobilize. Yet Secretary McNamara not only abetted and encouraged this policy, but his own actions in the Pentagon—exemplified by endless studies and analyses and rigid control—did much to extend lead times required to produce new weapons systems, and to hamper technological development. The contention by some mistaken scientists that a technological plateau had been reached influenced decision-makers in the Washington of 1961–68, and the contention of others that a deliberate acceptance of parity with Russia in strategic weapons would smooth the way to a peaceful world influenced many others, Mr. McNamara among them. Yet in these crucial years there was no sign of Soviet abstention in weapons development; U.S. inaction bred Soviet action. The technological revolution, it became clear, was far from over—one single development, the laser (a concentrated beam of light), could, potentially, upset the present balance of power.

It is clear that stinting research and development funds today can lead to supreme danger tomorrow; if the United States lags in weapons development today, it will become a second-class military (and political) power tomorrow.

The late Mark S. Watson of the Baltimore *Sun* put all this succinctly and dramatically in a volume he authored in the U.S. Army World War II official history series:

> ... the facts of war are often in total opposition to the facts of peace. An industrialist trained in economy will employ for a given job just enough means to perform the job. He will avoid all excessive use of manpower and material alike. Nothing could be more rational than this instinctive economy of force. But war is irrational and war is waste, fundamentally. ... Unlike the industrialist just mentioned, the efficient commander does not seek to use just enough means, but an

41

excess of means. A military force that is just strong enough to take a position will suffer heavy casualties in doing so; a force vastly superior to the enemy's will do the job without serious loss of men and (often more important still) with no loss of the all-important commodity, time; it can thereafter plunge straight ahead to the next task, catching the enemy unaware and thus gaining victory after victory and driving a bewildered enemy into panic.

To the untrained observer all of this is clear enough after the fact, but rarely is it acceptable in advance, when the mere suggestion of getting more men, more goods, more speed than are demonstrably needed is interpreted as a statement of bald intention to "waste." The military planner in peacetime must make the civilian mind accept the principle of "wastefulness" in this sense as an ideal to be sought. . . . The nation that winds up a war with a surplus of equipment is likely to be the nation that wins the conflict. The lessons of war are painfully learned, yet with war over are quickly forgotten until it is time to begin learning them again by the same painful process as before.[11]

Thus any viable strategy must be based upon the experience and the lessons of the past, but it must be shaped and molded to the world of tomorrow.

<<< 3 >>>

# The World of Tomorrow

THE WORLD of tomorrow, as in all past eras of man, will be a world of struggle and uncertainty, of dreams realized and hopes confounded. But particularly for the United States, a nation with so brief and brilliant a past, the decade of the 1970's represents a Great Divide. The country's actions and reactions to the world around us, to external and internal challenge, will shape the course of our tomorrows and will determine whether the nation will continue a great power or will start upon the downward slope of history which all great powers have followed in the past.

After less than two hundred years of national identity and half a century as a truly global power, the United States faces political, economic, social, technological and military problems of unprecedented complexity. It is beset, internally, by dissidence and disorder; externally by the modern barbarians. The 1970's will determine whether or not the pessimistic predictions of Thomas B. Macaulay in 1857, and the philosopher George Santayana in 1921, will be refuted or confirmed:

> Either [wrote Macaulay] some Caesar or Napoleon will seize the reins of government with a strong hand; or your republic will be as fearfully plundered and laid waste by barbarians in the twentieth century as the Roman Empire was in the fifth—with this difference

... that your Huns and Vandals will have been engendered within your own country by your own institutions.[1]

Democracy [Santayana said] is often mentioned in the same breath with liberty, as if they meant the same thing. . . . The disinherited many, led by the disinherited few . . . would abolish those private interests which are the factors in any cooperation, and would reduce everybody to forced membership and forced services in one universal flock, without property, family, country or religion.[2]

It is easy to dismiss these gloomy observations and Oswald Spengler's equally depressing predictions in his *Decline of the West* as the dated products of another era. Yet their pertinence to the problems of tomorrow is undeniable.

The contemporary phrases so often used to describe today's predicaments—"the generation gap"; the "revolution of rising expectations"; the "crisis in values"; "the dollar gap"; the "technological revolution"; the "population explosion"; the "peasant revolution"; the "revolt against the Establishment"; "the drug culture"—represent semantic clothing for the bare facts of crisis. The problem of tomorrow is not only how to adjust to change—for change is always with us—but how to make the really gigantic adjustments necessary without the debilitation of the American system or the destruction of civilization.

Despite the unpredictable variables that will shape tomorrow's world, there are some historical constants that can serve as guidelines to the new dimensions of strategy.

Geography has not changed, even though distances, rivers, swamps and jungles, mountains and terrain contours, and even oceans have less importance as natural obstacles and barriers than in the past. The time-space factor has been revolutionized by supersonic speeds, and weapon ranges have become global. The vertical outflanking of surface barriers is a vital factor in a nuclear war of annihilation, but is not necessarily decisive—as Vietnam has shown —in a limited war. Jungles, rivers, mountains still dictate to ground armies; the seas—the skies above and the depths below—still control the operations of navies.

The Mackinder-Spykman[3] geopolitical concept of the world as divided into a vast continental "heartland" of Eurasia, surrounded by Eurasian "rimland," or maritime, countries, bordering the seas, with North America as a kind of continental island, will still be essentially valid in the years to come. But foreshortened geography has pulled the continents much closer together; increased weapon ranges and unprecedented power have increased the vulnerability and reduced the security of every nation on earth; air and missile power can now overfly the rimlands, and political and economic factors, as well as the technological revolution, have focused new attention on South America and Africa.

The technological revolution, which has compressed distances, has also emphasized two new media—aerospace and the depths of the seas. These new dimensions have complicated strategic problems but have not altered the basic principles of strategy—mass, momentum, speed ("to git thar fust with the most"), surprise, concentration, mobility and so on. The commander of tomorrow will possess more fully than ever before in history the capability of implementing many of the principles of war enumerated by strategic thinkers since the days of Sun Tzu. Yet all plans and policies and strategies will be overshadowed by the atomic cloud. Never before has the strategist had the capability of destroying great nation-states, or of returning world civilization to the Dark Ages; this awesome responsibility will limit and confine and guide all the strategic plans of the future.

What Arnold Toynbee has described as "The Time of Troubles" in which we live will continue throughout the twentieth century. World Wars I and II destroyed nations and empires; we will be picking up the pieces for decades to come. But the enormous dislocations of these global conflicts were tremendously complicated by revolutions or developments that are still continuing—and will long continue:

*The technological revolution,* still unfinished. No "plateau" has been reached—or is ever reached—in science; man will continue to discover, and to develop, regardless of the restrictions he may place upon himself. Any arms-control agreements can only slow, not halt, this process; the problem of control is enormously complicated by the close relationship between military and industrial development.

*The population explosion.* The immense and continuing growth in numbers of the world's peoples threatens the environment—the world itself. Agronomists, with careful figures, argue that if man uses scientific agriculture and employs available resources adequately, he can feed himself and his increase indefinitely. The theory is sound, the practice feeble. The nations with maximum population problems, such as India, are the very ones that have found it impossible—given their religious taboos, their backward processes, their inadequate administrative structure—to feed themselves. C. P. Snow, the British scientist-philosopher, in a pessimistic lecture delivered at Westminster College in November, 1968, foresaw the danger—perhaps beginning in the 1975–80 period—of "local famines," spreading "into a sea of hunger."[4] Famines, or food insufficiencies, are periodic in the world of today and will continue in the world of tomorrow, and the pressure of increasing population will make for instability.

*Industrialization.* The industrialization of areas of the world that were once purely agrarian economies, with consequent social, political and economic dislocation, will continue.

*Racial problems.* Racial antagonisms and frictions will persist, as they have throughout history, in the United States, Africa, Britain and elsewhere, and in some instances—notably in the United States, Rhodesia, South Africa, Portuguese Africa—will have a major politico-economic influence upon domestic and foreign policies. In the United States in particular the homogeneity of the past —normally an important factor in military power—has gone forever. The once roughly similar national and racial origin of the vast majority of the *voting* population has been succeeded by a divided nation—Negroes, Mexican Americans, Puerto Ricans and others—with widely differing values and outlooks. No synthesis of these variant views is likely in the foreseeable future. The Negro minority is far too large—larger than the populations of most of the Negro nations of the world—to be assimilated except over the centuries.

*Resources and environment.* The man-made problem of diminishing natural resources and pollution of the natural environment (air, water, land) will not be solved quickly. However, a start has

46

been made on both problems, and time will not soon run out. But the scramble for resources is certain to continue and to intensify. *Regional and local problems.* Many of these—Berlin, divided Germany, divided Korea, the two-China situation, Vietnam itself— are a heritage of World War II, with no solution in sight. All of them are dangerous friction points, certain to exacerbate great-power and medium-power relationships.

*Conflicting ideologies.* Differing and antagonistic political and religious beliefs are as old as man and will persist as long as man. Communism is here to stay. Its extremism has been somewhat modified by time, and its missionary zeal for Communizing the world may be further eroded as the Russian and Chinese revolutions age and are able to satisfy to a greater degree the economic and social hopes of their peoples. Nevertheless the doctrines of Communism—and particularly the methods employed (the ends justify *any* means)—will continue to present global challenges to a Western world bred in the doctrines of the Magna Carta and Jefferson. To those who feel that Communism is no longer a malevolent force, history has its own best refutation. The brutal and bloody suppression of the Hungarian bid for freedom in 1956, and—with a different cast but the same ruthlessness—the invasion of Czechoslovakia in 1968 and the liquidation of millions of Chinese "oppositionists" by Mao Tse-tung and of hundreds of thousands of "revisionists" by Ho Chi Minh, should be a sufficient indication that any real détente with present or prospective Communist rulers, unless it is on their terms, is impossible. Communist power made these crimes possible, but Communist ideology required them. Similarly, religious antagonisms—Moslem versus Hindu in the Indian subcontinent; Arab versus Jew in the Middle East; tribe versus tribe in Africa—will persist as facts of life. Indeed, conflicts of ideologies may dominate tomorrow; they stir human beings to greater emotion than any other cause of conflict. In the Middle East the liquidation of Israel has become to many Arabs as much an ideological—a religious—tenet as a political one. These antagonisms will wax and wane, but they will not end; they are part and parcel of man.

Thus the United States will face in the remainder of the twentieth

47

century precisely the same topical problems that confront it today; the focus, the emphasis, will differ, but the problems will remain.

Nevertheless the world of tomorrow is certain to differ greatly— politically, socially, economically—from the world of today.

The increasing speed of communications will knit the world together physically if not spiritually. It will be physically possible for every man to be his brother's keeper; this morning's injustices in the Congo will be emblazoned on tonight's TV screen. Yet there is an irritating factor in such a community of emotion; most men do not wish to be their brothers' keepers, or to be guarded and guided by others. Proximity does not necessarily breed respect; often it exacerbates differences. The idea that cultural exchanges, student visits or mutual airline privileges will overweigh political and other differences and create "One World" is a mirage. Man will retain his sturdy individualism and his major national and ethnic differences and friction points.

The very speed of modern communications is, in part, responsible for what might be called the political fractionalization of the world, and the development—now well advanced—of a multipolar system. Ideas know no boundaries; a desire for freedom, for better living, for more learning, spreads beyond frontiers regardless of walls and "Iron Curtains" and radio jamming. But this does not necessarily promote political stabilization; social revolution can produce chaos for all as well as a better life for many. It makes for ferment, and can—as in Hungary, Czechoslovakia, South Korea, Vietnam—lead to repression and to dangerous political crises. For it is clear that, despite our vaunted twentieth-century civilization, the Communist governments and many other world rulers view freedom of expression as a threat to their rule. They live, as George Ball told the United Nations, in darkness; they cannot stand the light of truth or freedom; they fear that heresy will undermine their regimes and destroy their system. Dictatorships have never resolved the problem of the succession of power, nor have they ever learned how to meet dissidence except by force. In the long-term view, the invocation of bald and brutal force—as in Hungary and Czechoslovakia—can only weaken Communist rule, but in the foreseeable future the neo-Stalinists and hard-liners in the Kremlin are almost certain to repress, or attempt to repress, flagrant deviations from the Moscow line.

The Communists have found, too, that the mass education of their peoples, which was absolutely essential to their continued progress in technology, bred its own problems; a little knowledge is a dangerous thing, learning a heady wine. Men started to think for themselves, and thus an irreconcilable conflict between government and governed was joined. The process continues, the end is not yet; the yeast of change contributes to the rising expectations of the captive peoples, with ultimate consequences no man can foretell. Yet this trend is certain to create continued tensions in the Communist states; the xenophobic suspicions of the Russian and Chinese minds, stoked by the fears of the Communist rulers, are certain to meet the struggle for freedom head-on in violent and unpredictable collision. This force for change is thus a factor that makes for continued instability in the history of tomorrow, not only in the Communist and autocratic countries but also—as we have seen in our slums—in our own nation.

Politically, the world of tomorrow, far from being "One World," is certain to be many worlds. The bipolar world that emerged from World War II has gone, possibly never to return. The United States and Soviet Russia, the two superstates that dominated the first decade after World War II, are still superstates superior in power to any other nation on earth. Yet the groupings that coalesced around them, the division of the world into tidy "Communist" and "non-Communist" compartments or spheres of influence, have disappeared. The coalitions and alliances of both sides have sloughed away; new political and economic power centers have developed; a third force of "gray," neutral or nonaligned nations has become a major factor, and throughout the world there are many undeveloped new states, with little political, economic, military or psychological viability, that are "up for grabs."

The Communist global grouping is by no means politically monolithic, as it once appeared to be. Soviet Russia has had increasing difficulty since the advent of Tito's "revisionism" in Yugoslavia in asserting her ideological, political and power primacy. Tiny Albania sloughed away to follow the hard line of Mao Tse-tung, and twice Moscow has had to invoke military power against her helpless satellites in Eastern Europe. Even so, Rumania has followed a para-independent line in developing its concepts of Communism; the Communist rulers of Poland have been forced to come to terms with the power of the Catholic Church; and the ferment of greater freedom still stirs in all of Eastern Europe.

There are conflicting and potentially dangerous forces in Eastern Europe: the dislike for and fear of Germany and of German irredentism about its lost territories; the general mistrust felt by the Poles, Germans and Hungarians for the Czechoslovaks; the Yugoslav "heresy" of independent Communism; the age-old rivalry of Teuton and Slav. Nationalism and the ancient frictions are still powerful forces in Eastern and Central Europe, and, despite the common obeisance paid to Lenin and to Marx, there are almost as many forms of Communism as there are nations.

Two common factors unite Russia and her Eastern European satellites—geography and Soviet military and economic power. Eastern Europe is still viewed in Moscow's eyes as a buffer zone against the West, a protection—in time and space—against land invasion. The satellites are enforced allies, not too reliable in deep adversity, but allies nevertheless. Yet the deep crisis of values, dramatized by Hungary and Czechoslovakia, remains.

But the schism between Soviet Russia and Communist China is a great and probably a lasting one—political and territorial and demographic, as well as ideological. It is one which is likely to persist in the world of tomorrow, even after Mao Tse-tung and some of the old-line Bolshevists in Peking die or are replaced. The death of Mao Tse-tung will release unpredictable forces within China and in China's relationship to Moscow. Mao's successors may indeed see their own—and their country's—future in terms of cooperation with the U.S.S.R. This development could vastly increase the difficulties and the perplexities of the United States and of the West—particularly in Asia. But it is essentially a short-term danger—a danger of the next one to three decades.

For in the long-term view, as China increases in strength and prestige, the power differences between Peking and Moscow are certain to loom large. The border frictions and territorial rivalries in Central Asia, near Afghanistan and along the Siberian frontier will remain potential trouble areas. But the fundamental cause for continued dichotomy between the two great Communist powers is the development of Communist China, a nation with by far the greatest population on earth, into a nuclear and industrialized power. The prospect of a modern powerful state, bursting with the energy of 700 million people, next to the underpopulated wealth of Siberia can be of little comfort to Moscow, regardless of common ideologies.

Even so, the Sino-Soviet friction will not result in transforming either one or the other country into an "ally" of the United States. The roseate dream of many Americans that has translated an occasional commonality of interest between Moscow and Washington into, first, détente and, then, an "alliance" mutually directed against the "Yellow Peril" has little basis in reality. Either China or Russia or both would have to change their ideological stripes to make such a restructured world possible.

The grouping of the so-called Western, or "free," nations has similarly been fractionalized in the past decade, and there is no prospect that it will resume its old pattern. Britain, without an empire, with backward industrial practices and a social security system beyond her means, has faced continuing economic crises. The consequent enforced reduction of her military power, and her deliberate politico-military withdrawal from east of Suez, weakened the ready military strength of the West.

France, under De Gaulle, experienced an economic and psychological renaissance and has become a nuclear power and a modern wealthy industrialized state. But her gains have been checked by the demand of the many for more, and except on paper she has sloughed away from the NATO alliance to follow a para-independent course. For much of the postwar era De Gaulle towered above his contemporaries, but the changes and reforms he effected have not permanently eliminated the centrifugal nature of French politics. His successors face an era of factionalism, and the foreign offices of the world must reckon with French domestic turbulence, political and economic, as a factor in French foreign policy.

West Germany, with a booming economy and renewed strength,

51

has become—as would be expected—less pliable to the wishes of Washington and London and Paris; as the leading economic power of Western Europe it is exerting an increasingly magnetic effect upon Eastern Europe and its neighbors in the West. But its military strength has not matched its remarkable economic growth; in part, economic growth was possible because Germany's allies provided military security.

Germany, under NATO, has had the best of both worlds. But one cannot expect Bonn to assume a greater share of the burden of her own—and Western Europe's—defense if she is not treated as a full and equal partner. Yet the nuclear nonproliferation treaty, which excludes Germany and all other non-nuclear powers in perpetuity from nuclear weapons, is still regarded by some in Germany as unfair discrimination—and is viewed as a dangerous precedent, despite Bonn's decision to sign the treaty. The bogy of German politics is that the United States and the U.S.S.R. will come to some sort of terms over Bonn's head and will perpetuate Germany's division and her insecurity.

But a countervailing concern—it amounts to a deep-seated fear in Moscow, shared to a lesser degree by the United States and her allies—is that somehow a renascent Germany might come to occupy a balance of power in Europe and play off East against West. It is quite clear that the U.S.S.R.'s painfully constructed puppet empire and its Warsaw Pact military alliance would fall apart if a reunited Germany were allied with the West, or were to play an independent (neutralist) role. Clearly, therefore, the U.S.S.R. is unlikely—as long as it has the power—to permit the reunification of Germany, *except on its terms.* Yet the magnetic attraction of the two parts of Germany, a nation artificially divided, is certain to continue, and the motive of *revanche,* of irredentism—both encouraged by significant rightist extremists in Germany—will continue to obscure the future of Europe. And, just as a divided Germany holds one of the major keys to the history of tomorrow, so a divided Berlin may determine the history of Germany. Berlin is perhaps the single most explosive issue in the global politics of the decades to come. It is an exposed and vulnerable salient in the heart of Communist hegemony; yet as Berlin goes, so may go Germany.

52

Too often, we think of the division of Europe into Western and Soviet "spheres of influence" as a permanent phenomenon. The "Iron Curtain" is defined as fixed and constant; neither side dares to tear it down. Yet nothing is immutable in politics; the long-term future of Europe is far from stable.

In the Mediterranean area the political and military weakening of the bonds of the NATO alliance and the creation of new and more independent power centers have continued. England and Spain are still at odds about Gibraltar, and Spain is excluded from NATO. Portugal's colonial policies have alienated NATO partners. Italy, with a Communist or Communist-allied left-wing electorate averaging a consistent 25 to 33 percent, has moved somewhat more to the left; her economic interests have dictated oil and pipeline agreements with the Communists, and a somewhat more independent stance. But she is shaky, politically and economically, and moving toward extremes of right and left. The new-found freedom of North Africa has resulted in a plethora of small but fiery states, with Algeria deeply committed, by extensive Soviet military and economic aid, to a political stance sympathetic to Russia.

The right flank of NATO—always an unnatural alliance—has all but disintegrated. Turkey and Greece are still at odds over Cyprus, with no solution in sight, and Turkey, irked by strong U.S. political pressure for a settlement of the Cyprus problem, has cooled off toward both the United States and NATO and is once again mending her fences with Russia. Greece has been weakened by a military coup, and the entire Allied flank has been turned by a large Soviet political-military presence in Egypt and Syria.

The Suez Canal, with the advent of huge supertankers and the construction of oil pipelines from Middle Eastern fields to the Mediterranean, is no longer vital strategically or commercially to Western Europe. The shorter sea passage to India and the Far East that it offers is nevertheless of economic and military importance to all powers, particularly Russia. It is significant that the Suez–Red Sea area has been, like other maritime nodal points throughout the world (Panama and Singapore), a focal point of Communist expansion.

There is no doubt that the entire complexion of NATO has

changed and that one of the major unknowns in the years ahead will be the type of organization that may replace or supplement it. The age-old dream of a politically effective United States of Europe appears to be more remote than ever.

Yet Western Europe in the decade to come—if not in the long-term future—will remain the most important geographic entity, politically and economically, in the world, outranked only by U.S. power. Collectively, its well-developed industry and technology, its highly literate and skilled peoples, its commonality of political and cultural heritage, its modern closely knit communications, and its strategic importance as a peninsula of the Eurasian continent guarding the great sea approaches to the heartland of Eurasia make it of primary importance. In time, it will be eclipsed by new power centers in Asia, but for the foreseeable future Western Europe (including the British Isles) will continue to be of unique economic-industrial importance.

And, despite the decline of NATO and the fissions of nationalism in the Soviet puppet empire, it is clear that Europe is divided into "spheres of influence." The line between Communism and the Free World is well marked in Europe, blurred only in Berlin. Eastern Europe, as U.S. failure to act in Hungary in 1956 and in Czechoslovakia in 1968 has shown, is, from a power and political point of view, a recognized Russian fief; whereas the "rimlands" of Western Europe are clearly linked to the United States.

It is in the Eastern Mediterranean—Middle Eastern area that a most marked deterioration of the Western position has occurred since the brief Arab-Israeli war of 1967. The end of the British and French empires completed a process started in World War I—the fractionalization of the area into many small political entities, each endowed with memories of ancient greatness, but none with the physical assets to regain the glories of the past. The vacuum of power left by the withdrawal of the British Raj has been partially filled by increasing Soviet influence in Egypt, Syria, Iraq, Algeria and other Arab states; U.S. and Soviet naval power in the Mediterranean; and the development of Israel. The United States and Western Europe have major oil interests in the area, and strong emotional ties bind the powerful Jewish community in the United

54

States to Israel. A very unstable balance, and the irreconcilable conflict between Israel and the Arabs, will make the Middle East an arena of conflict for years to come.

Similarly, the diminution of British power in that vast maritime area of the world from the Cape of Good Hope to Australia and from Aden to Singapore has left the Indian Ocean area a politico-military vacuum. India, with its immense problems—social stratification, lack of homogeneity, religious and ethnic taboos, shibboleths and frictions, overpopulation, linguistic differences, famine, backwardness and lethargy—cannot be expected to fill this vacuum. Like Pakistan, New Delhi will long be preoccupied with its own immense internal problems and its chauvinistic rivalries. Neither India nor Pakistan will develop major economic or military potential in this century.

In Southeast Asia the smudged line between Communism and non-Communism has never been clearly drawn; here are potentially rich lands—Burma, Thailand, Vietnam, Indonesia—with teeming populations, much ignorance and disease and undeveloped economies, vulnerable to Communist penetration. The problems of Southeast Asia will be a constant political factor in the rest of the twentieth century; the British withdrawal from Singapore emphasizes once again the vacuum of power that exists in the area—a vacuum that both Russia, with its naval and economic might, and China, with its land power and the advantage of propinquity, are trying to fill.

The development of a more or less monolithic China, under centralized control, with industrial development and nuclear-missile power emphasized by its rulers, is a dominant fact of the twentieth century in Asia. It is bound to be, in the long run, a destabilizing factor—particularly if the fiery, hard-line ideology of Mao Tse-tung is continued by his successors—but unsettling, no matter who rules. The Sino-Soviet rivalry and the struggle of China for dominance and spheres of influence in its frontier areas are certain to keep vast areas in intermittent ferment—the Taiwan Straits, including Taiwan and the Nationalist-held offshore islands; Southeast Asia; Tibet and the Indian frontier; Afghanistan and Sinkiang; Central Asia; Mongolia and Manchuria and Korea.

The future of Asia will be complicated and profoundly influenced by the rise of another great power center—Japan. From complete defeat in World War II to the world's third greatest industrial power in two decades, from a nation unable to feed itself before World War II to a rice-exporting country today, is the amazing record of the most energetic, literate and developed industrialized economy in the East.

Like Germany, part of Japan's renaissance from the ashes of defeat has been due to her dependence upon the United States for her security, to the huge sums of U.S. money expended in Japan and to the preferential treatment accorded her by her American conquerors. In fact, the Japanese have never had it so good. Hiroshima, the revulsion caused by defeat and the constitution fathered by the American proconsul of the occupation era, General Douglas MacArthur, have made a major impression upon the present generation of Japanese. They would like to be of the world commercially and economically, but withdrawn from it politically.

Yet the basic Japanese character has not changed, and Japan is not immune to the same tides that have swept the rest of the world. The struggle between left and right is certain to become more acute in the years ahead. The Communists and extreme left-wing groups in Japan are well organized; the extreme right is quiescent, yet the rise of the Soka Gakkai, the militant parareligious Buddhist sect, has been phenomenal, and deep in the Japanese subconscious the samurai values still live. Japan's internal political development will depend in large measure upon how she faces the world and its problems, and in turn upon how the world—and the United States in particular—reacts to Japan. A whole host of issues—trade with China; relations with Soviet Russia and the United States; Okinawa; Southeast Asia; Japanese defense forces—will complicate the immediate future. Like Germany in Europe, Japan will be the political pivot point of the Western Pacific–Eastern Asia area. Many years from now its power may be eclipsed by a developed China, but in the immediate years, as Japan goes, so may go much of Asia.

In the world of tomorrow Africa, Latin America, Australia–New Zealand and the Pacific islands will remain politically peripheral.

This does not mean these vast and wealthy areas of the world will be unimportant to its future history. They are certain to influence that history—far more so in the rest of the twentieth century than they did in its first seventy years—but they will not dictate it. For major power resides elsewhere, and Africa and Latin America are divided into small states, many of them only marginal nations, some of them clearly lacking the homogeneity, the material power or the trained leadership to remain nations.

Africa is the question-mark continent. Its immediate potentialities for trouble are far greater than its capabilities for stability. It is potentially wealthy, inherently powerless—a collection of tribal groupings, most of its people illiterate and backward, united (after a fashion and intermittently) only by the magic catchword of "freedom," by racial and tribal antagonisms and by definite, though primitive, economic aspirations. Because its population is primarily black, because of its colonial past and because of the rapidity of modern communications and the major racial cleavage in the United States, the racial problem in Africa has become a global political one, with consequences which have involved—but probably will not engulf—the great powers.

Most of the black nations of Africa—former colonies of the great powers—have been so immersed in tribal rivalries, economic and political difficulties and their inexpert attempts at self-government that they have retrogressed, rather than advanced, in their new-found freedom. Regionalism, separatism, tribalism are a part of African life. Coups and tribal wars and civil war—as in the Congo and Nigeria—are the heritage of history in most of Free Africa; the peoples have paid a heavy price for the façade of liberty. There have been exceptions. But there is no end in sight to Africa's convulsions; they will continue as part of the inescapable price of freedom and political maturity.

It is ironic that the most developed and most stable parts of Africa are those ruled by a white minority—South Africa and Rhodesia. It is also ironic that South Africa, in particular, by virtue of geographic position, dominating the Cape of Good Hope, is of more strategic importance to the United States and the Western world than any other part of Africa south of the Sahara, and it also

57

has greater economic importance.

Portugal is a NATO ally, and its geographic position near the entrance to the Mediterranean and its strategically placed Atlantic islands also have considerable military significance.

The United States and much of the Western world, along with the U.S.S.R. and the Communist world, have joined in condemnation of the South African, Rhodesian and Portuguese racial political policies. This condemnation has been supported by a multination economic embargo against Rhodesia. The embargo has been largely ineffective economically and completely ineffective politically, as embargoes have been in the past; it has merely resulted in heightened tensions and bitter feelings. Thus Africa is torn by tensions, and the United States is in the anomalous position of sponsoring political policies which conflict with its strategic interests. We are in a position in Africa of "damned-if-we-do-and-damned-if-we-don't." This unhappy continent is certain to be in a continuing state of turmoil. Its danger for the world is that rivalries for raw materials, Africa's own internal frictions and its racial conflicts may involve the great powers, a danger already foreshadowed in Nigeria and the Congo.

The future of Latin America, an immense area with great potential wealth—much of it unexploited—but little ready strength, is likely to be more of the same. Latin America is a land marked by extremes—where the wealthy few rule the impoverished many; where public office is often synonymous with personal gain; where the Roman Catholic Church, in its most conservative form, commands the allegiance of many of the peoples and has, until recently, represented (except for some few but violent Catholic revolutionaries) a reactionary force; where democracy is in most cases merely a word. Most of the countries in Latin America have at best a small middle class, and thus the natural buffer against violent revolution is lacking. Communism has staked out strong beachheads in virtually every country of the area; the indigenous conditions for plots and counterplots, coups and countercoups, violence and revolution, dictators and "men on horseback," will not soon change.[5] The mixture, in most countries, of Indians, Negroes, Spanish and Portuguese; the excitable temperament of the peoples, weak govern-

58

ments and insecure political and economic conditions mean continued instability. One can expect coups and revolutions, bloodshed and trouble in Latin America.

But the likelihood of major exported trouble from this area is not, at the moment, high. Castro seeks to export revolution, but his capabilities for doing so—particularly after the defeat and death of his lieutenant, Che Guevara, in Bolivia—are not major, so long as Soviet Russia maintains its past emphasis on a policy of trade with, and peaceful penetration of, Latin America rather than sponsoring violent revolution. The great neighbor to the north, the United States, could be the focus of major hostility by Latin America, which always lies under the shadow of Uncle Sam. But today the menace to their own rule of Communism is of almost as much concern to many Latin-American governments as is Uncle Sam, who can also be Uncle Sugar. The prospects for tomorrow, therefore, while in no sense offering the hope of stability and great progress, contain less explosive ingredients than Asia. There will be guerrilla movements, underground plots, assassinations and terrorism (as in Guatemala), gun-running, the sequestration and confiscation of American-owned firms, Catholic radicalism, strikes and coups, and the contagion of Commmunism may spread beyond Cuba, but there is little likelihood that an ideological or political forest fire will engulf the continent and threaten the United States.

Australia–New Zealand and most of Pacific Micronesia lie in relatively tranquil backwaters of world conflicts. Australia's chief strategic concern is necessarily linked to New Guinea and the great Indonesian Archipelago to her north, and to Southeast Asia. A white country, she is potentially threatened with inundation by the overcrowded masses of Asia, but, short of her conquest, her immigration policies will prevent this. Both Australia and New Zealand now depend more upon the United States than upon Britain for security, and Australia is an important link between the Pacific and Indian oceans. These powers and the islands of the Pacific will not be immune to the winds of change, but there are few prospects of major internal troubles, and they are not likely to cause the winds to shift.

The world of tomorrow thus will continue to be a world of great-power rivalries, of multipolar ambitions and frictions, of conflicting ideologies, of economic and technological development.

In many ways, the age-old struggle of the "haves" and the "have-nots" will dominate; the "revolution of rising expectations"—the hopes of many of the world's peoples for a better life—will test and challenge alike the resources and ingenuity of capitalism and Communism. In the world, as in the United States, the yearning for stability and order will clash again and again with the thrust for freedom and the need for change.

Many political economists see the future in terms of capital needs, with the undeveloped nations of Asia, Africa and Latin America as the focus of change and the requirements of development far exceeding the capabilities of world capital. Viewed in global rather than in narrow economic terms, this is perhaps an oversimplistic concept, yet the human dynamics of the many wanting more is part of the problem of tomorrow. The wants, if interpreted literally, are so many that there is no possibility of their total fulfillment; economic as well as political and military priorities will be essential, and frustration rather than satisfaction the end result.

Leonard A. Lecht estimated in 1966 that U.S. "contributions to the international non-financial organizations, military aid, and the 'Food for Peace' program" would require an "estimated level of spending of $3.1 billion a year for minimum programs in the 1970's."[6] These figures, now somewhat dated, are supplemented by other estimates which are far higher and, if all forms of foreign aid are included, reach politically impossible sums.

The clear-cut trend, as the 1970's start—a reflection of political priorities, social exigencies and the Vietnam reaction—is downward in foreign aid. Aid will not be stopped, but foreign aid is almost certain to be far more carefully vetted and restricted in the years ahead than it often was in the past.

Thus the rest of the twentieth century must be viewed in terms of conflict and compromise, action and reaction, between the nations and the peoples, the resources and the needs, the ideas and the facts of life in the very small world of tomorrow.

The history of the next thirty years will turn, to a great degree, upon three factors: the capability and the willingness of the United States to relieve, or at least stabilize, some of its most acute internal problems, while simultaneously maintaining its great-power role in the world; the determination of Soviet Russia to escape the land-locked prison of its heartland to penetrate or outflank the rimlands and to debouch, with its maritime power, upon the high seas of the world; and the attempt of Communist China to become a unified nation and a major industrial and nuclear-missile power. In Europe the roles of Germany and France, in Asia of Japan, will in turn tremendously influence these factors, and the whole world situation will be affected by the explosive volatility of the small and un-developed nations of the Middle East, Asia, Africa and Latin America. In this kind of world, regional organizations and alliances may well play important roles in economic development and politi-cal and military security. The United Nations—with or without Chinese Communist membership—will continue to act as a global forum, where in the forensics of debate the heat of passion can be dissipated in angry words rather than in angry actions. The UN has a particular meaning to the little powers and the backward ones; for them—if the great powers agree—it can act as shield and buffer. It flatters their egos; in its halls the weak can confront the powerful with the similitude of equal footing. It is a meeting place for ideas and a lever for the application of moral suasion. It, and its various instruments, can also have some economic importance, particularly to the undeveloped nations, and it can help to promote the limita-tion of arms.

But the UN is not, and will never be in our lifetimes, the answer to the ills of the world. It has no inherent power; it does not equal the sum of its parts. Its impotency has never been better illustrated than in the events surrounding the Israeli-Arab war of 1967. Its police force is *ad hoc* and nominal, and there is little likelihood, except in special situations, that it can become an effective military instrument. It has politico-military usefulness, particularly in the settlement of small disputes, in dampening frictions, in patrolling and policing agreements. But it cannot be expected to substitute for a great power; it is not one and it cannot act as one. Division between the superstates or between any of the larger powers leaves it helpless; the UN, in such a case, can only wring its hands and pray. Thus neither the United States nor any other major power can depend upon the United Nations for either military or political security; if our powder is to be kept dry, we must do it.

Make no mistake about it; the rest of the twentieth century will be far more dangerous to the American dream and to the world than its first seventy years. Americans are tired of involvement in wars and troubles; neo-isolationism has become, even to the Walter Lippmanns of today, a respectable philosophy, and security expenditures and foreign aid will compete unfavorably with domestic needs. There will be the same propensity to cut military budgets and to reduce ready military strength that has followed every other war in which the United States has been involved.

Politically, there has been, ever since 1960, a continuing trend in the United States toward instability, a surge away from the old two-party system toward extremes of the right and the left. This trend, stoked by racial tensions and past frustrations, will probably continue. In foreign policy it will make itself felt in what Samuel P. Huntington has described as "a fundamental change in American attitudes . . . toward American involvement in international affairs."[7] Mr. Huntington noted the recurrent tendency of American public opinion toward "introversion," and predicted that "no more Vietnams" would be a "likely guideline of American policy for the foreseeable future."[8] "The current retreat from world involvement," Mr. Huntington agreed, has now started, is likely to continue throughout the 1970's and may well inhibit overseas involvements.

However, he noted that the United States will face, in its foreign relations, many crises, which will somehow have to be met: authoritarian breakdowns, communal wars, peasant revolutions and anti-American assaults. And, at home, the retreat from the world around us will conflict with the moral content of U.S. foreign policy —what former Ambassador Edwin Reischauer has called the moral imperative to help those who need help.

This internal conflict between what Ithiel de Sola Pool has described as an "isolationist impulse to avoid involvement in other people's problems and an internationalist impulse to promote our own values in the world" will be sharpened and perhaps decided, as de Sola Pool has pointed out, by nuclear proliferation. "Treaty or no treaty, there are many . . . who will live to see several undeveloped countries with the means to launch nuclear war."[9]

These domestic conflicts and changes in American attitudes come at a time of major political and economic instability, of maximum danger, when Soviet ambitions are looking toward far horizons, when the Soviet merchant fleet is expanding rapidly into the world's largest, and when U.S. political and military options have been sharply circumscribed by the major increase in strength (particularly nuclear-missile power) of the Communist powers. The technological revolution has opened its most dangerous phase, one in which the future can be won or lost in the laboratories.

Today, as the United States tries to shape its security policies for tomorrow, the realities of Communist power are not comforting.

By 1970 the Russians had achieved numerical superiority over the United States in numbers of land-based intercontinental ballistic missiles, and the "throw-weight," or payload, of these missiles considerably exceeded ours. Moscow deploys about 600 to 1,000 medium-range, land-based missiles, some of them mobile, capable of reaching any targets in Europe or North Africa; the United States and her allies have none. The U.S.S.R. is well ahead of the United States in missile defense. Her extensive series of nuclear tests in 1961–62, which broke the test moratorium, provided her with detailed knowledge of the high-altitude effects of large-scale nuclear explosions. A ballistic-missile area-defense system has been deployed around Moscow, which probably soon will be amplified and supplemented by a new system to defend much of the rest of the country. Our ABM is still under development; the Russians are far ahead.

In both numbers and quality of sea-based missiles the United States is still clearly superior to Soviet Russia, but the lead is diminishing; the U.S.S.R. is making extensive efforts to catch up. In bombers and strategic bombing techniques, particularly at intercontinental ranges, the United States has an advantage in quality, though none in quantity. But the Soviet antiaircraft defense system, fortified by new radars, modified low-altitude missiles and a stable of new high-speed fighter-interceptors, is of increasing strength. By 1975 some few of the Soviet ICBM's—nearly all of which are now in heavily hardened underground silos—may be mobile, and many of them will probably be fitted with MIRV's (Multiple Independently Targetable Re-entry Vehicles)—several warheads for each missile, each capable of guidance to a separate target. Similarly, before 1975 the U.S. quantitative lead in numbers of sea-based missiles, which was between 4 and 6 to 1 in our favor in 1968, may be reduced—unless Washington moves rapidly—to between 1 and 1.5 to 1.[10]

The prospect of Soviet superiority, or even of parity, in nuclear weapons is not a comforting one. It is, as Zbigniew Brzezinski argues, "a major shift" in the world's power equation, which

> will . . . contribute to an increasingly complex posture, defiant of clear-cut calculations and inimical to psychological self-assurance.
> Whether this condition will lead to greater mutual restraint or, on the contrary, prompts more maneuver and bluffing cannot be answered with certainty, but there may be some reason for entertaining a dose of pessimism. . . .
> . . . deterrence may just not work as well in the future.[11]

Nor are the U.S.-Soviet discussions on the limitation of strategic weapons, which are just beginning, likely to alter this equation of power, in some ways disadvantageous to us, in our favor. Even if an agreement is negotiated, there can be no certainty it "will lead to greater mutual restraint."

The strategic challenge from Red China is yet undeveloped. The virtual civil war that raged in China in 1965–68—part of the political-ideological conflict which Communism always breeds—has slowed nuclear and missile development. Nevertheless Red China already has short-range tactical missiles and a nuclear-bomb capability within light-bomber radius (700 to 1,000 miles) of her frontiers. By 1975 Peking may have a small but respectable armory of nuclear and thermonuclear weapons, several score—perhaps several hundred—medium-range missiles (up to about 2,000 miles), and perhaps some ICBM's, as well as some submarine-launched missiles.

Thus the nuclear monopoly and the once great superiority in strategic nuclear-delivery capability the United States enjoyed for a period after World War II has now been largely neutralized. Yet the technological revolution is still unfinished, and breakthroughs —or major developments in offensive or defensive weapons—could alter the power equation in the years to come.

Other elements of Soviet military strength have made similar progress in the past decade. The Soviet Navy, once a shallow-water coastal-defensive force, which guarded the flank of the Red Army, is now the world's second naval power, with the largest submarine fleet and with a growing modern force of surface ships. At least two helicopter carriers, a considerable number of a new type of double-ended LST's, a small but highly trained Marine amphibious force, and cruisers and destroyers armed with long-range surface-to-air and surface-to-surface missiles provide new capabilities to Moscow.

In time Moscow will extend her land-based air power to sea bases, either by the construction of attack aircraft carriers or by the development of vertical take-off and landing planes, capable of rising from the small decks of many types of ships. A permanent Soviet naval force is now established in the Mediterranean; squadrons flying the hammer and sickle cruise in the Persian Gulf–Indian Ocean area; and Soviet submarines, intelligence trawlers and surface ships are frequently sighted in all the seas of the world. Supported by a merchant fleet growing faster than that of any other nation, and by the most modern fishing fleet in the world, Russia obviously is attempting to break out of her past landlocked isolation to global horizons.

The Soviet Army, though reduced in numbers since the advent of the strategic missile forces, is still one of the largest and most powerful armies in the world, with a peacetime structure of almost 150 divisions, capable of rapid fleshing out and expansion. It is equipped with modern arms of every type and is particularly strong in armor and artillery. It is heavily supported by Soviet tactical air power, numbering at least 3,200—perhaps 4,000—aircraft.

Peking's greatest military strength is—and will remain, for some years to come—her ground army. It is an army which has been somewhat weakened in recent years, torn by the dissidence which has been a product of Mao Tse-tung's "cultural revolution." But it is hardy, resolute, large—and with an almost limitless source of replacements. It is well equipped with infantry weapons, supported by many mortars and light to medium artillery; it is weak in armor and in supporting tactical air power. It is the largest army, numerically, in the world—somewhere between 2,250,000 and 2,750,000 men, organized in about 118 divisions, including some small paratroop units.

China's air power and naval strength are weak; her technological efforts have been largely concentrated on nuclear weapons and strategic missiles. But Peking has shown a surprising capability— not yet across the board as in Russia, but selectively—in certain elements of modern military strength. China can now manufacture a limited number of Mig-type jet aircraft, and her radar has proven to be of high quality. The most important elements of her naval power are Soviet-type submarines, two of them, at least, equipped with tubes for launching ballistic missiles, and *Komar*-type motor torpedo boats, armed with the Styx antishipping winged missiles of the same type used by the Egyptians against the Israeli destroyer *Elath*.

The Red Army, backed by the People's Militia, and by the largest population on earth, is a formidable defensive force, and—within marching distance of its frontiers—a formidable offensive one. Its sheer mass power overshadows all the contiguous areas of Asia.

But, except for a limited nuclear threat, Red China has little offensive capability beyond the immediate range of its land frontiers. It is an undeveloped giant; its development could shake the world.

U.S. military power, as contrasted to that of the U.S.S.R. and China, has a much stronger technological-industrial base, and—on the whole—an advantage in quality in nuclear-delivery systems and strategic missiles. Our Army, modernized by Vietnam, is nevertheless small in numbers though great in fire power and mobility as compared with the larger armies of the Communist powers. Our chief advantage is at sea; our naval strength—despite marked Russian progress—is still superior to that of Soviet Russia. Over all, the collective U.S. Air Force–U.S. Navy–U.S. Army air capability is probably superior, tactically and technically, to that of the Communists.

Compared with these military giants, the armed forces of the rest of the nations of the world are small in size and inferior in technology. But they possess very considerable importance both regionally and locally, and under certain circumstances they could represent a kind of balance of power. Both England and France belong to the "nuclear club," a political-diplomatic and, in some circumstances, military asset which distinguishes them from other nations. It has been popular in the West to denigrate the French atomic capabilities; this is a mistake. For these capabilities will represent by 1975 not only a political card but also a military one. If French missile submarines have the capability of destroying Moscow (or Peking)—regardless of what Moscow might do first—a very great element of doubt and danger must enter any equation for Communist aggression.

In ground power and ground-support air power, West Germany in Europe and South Korea in Asia are of major importance in their areas, with Japan probably assuming a greater and greater military role. The Soviet satellite countries of Eastern Europe add a formidable number of ground divisions, with some supporting air power, to the Soviet forces, even though the satellite armies would be of doubtful dependability in case of acute crisis.

What, then, does the future hold? It will be, like the world of the past, a world of danger, but of more danger to the many than ever before in history. For the age of the two "scorpions in a bottle" is still with us; a plentiful stockpile of atomic weapons is now held by five nations, and the technological revolution continues. Some reduction in the tempo of the strategic-weapons race may be achieved by the U.S.-U.S.S.R. discussions on arms limitations and by strenuous international efforts; much will depend upon the attitude of China, and whether or not the United States leads from strength rather than weakness. But no complete arms-control agreement is foreseeable; indeed, from the point of view of the United States "general and complete disarmament" (a principle to which all the major powers have hypocritically lent lip service) would be a disaster. For if populations were reduced to sticks and stones, the greatest numbers would invariably triumph. In any case, no arms-control agreement fashioned by man can be immune to violations envisaged by man. In the twentieth century the arms race may be checked, but it will not be halted.

In one sense, indeed, the period of maximum danger is upon us, for the once great superiority of the United States in nuclear armaments has to a large extent been neutralized, and at the same time political and, to a lesser extent, economic power have been dispersed to new and, in some cases, less responsible entities. Yet a countervailing force fends off catastrophe: governments and peoples have been awed by the overwhelming power of modern arms and, so far in the atomic age, have demonstrated, even in crisis, a sane and cautious restraint.

But nuclear war is possible; it is too easily and too often dismissed as "unthinkable." As Herman Kahn has pointed out, one must think about the unthinkable; if we blandly accept the "impossibility" of nuclear war without doing anything about it, we shall be "Red or Dead" or both. Thus, in maximum terms, the danger of tomorrow is nuclear war, or, alternatively, political slavery.

But the *probable* as distinct from the *maximum possible* dangers are both more insidious and less obvious. Russia, at least, has demonstrated a desire, in her own self-interest, for mutual coexistence —though, in the words of William R. Kintner and Harriet Fast Scott, she "is unswervingly committed to a nuclear strategy."[12] But she has not foresworn the "wars of national liberation," the so-called "just" wars, of which Vietnam was one example. There has been in the Communist bloc (with the exception, so far, of China) the moderating tendency to be expected in any revolution. Lenin's goal of world conquest has not been abandoned, but there is no deadline, and the ideological thrust of Soviet Communism has been opportunistic, following normally what it considered the course of least resistance. Russia is still, and long will be, governed by ruthless men, and the last part of the twentieth century will be more dangerous than the first because of the development of Russian power and because of the continuing struggle in Russia for power. The U.S.S.R. now has the means—the power that was once lacking

—to export Communism by force; it is a power still inadequate for world conquest, but one still growing and now obviously dedicated to a global geopolitical goal.

In short, as Gerald L. Steibel has put it in a pamphlet, *Détente: Dilemma or Disaster?*, prepared for the National Strategy Information Center, "the Soviet Union's policies, allocation of resources, weapons inventories and, above all, its deeds, are those of a nation geared for major struggle and perhaps major war."

In the words of Admiral Arleigh Burke, chairman of the Center for Strategic and International Studies at Georgetown University, (summarizing a recent panel report of the Center on key trends in Kremlin policies) "the Soviets are likely to confront us with increased Soviet chauvinism, ideological hardening throughout the bloc, greater military strength and instabilities within Kremlin leadership.

"These factors [the panelists concluded] could lead to a Soviet policy of more competitive intervention in international political and military affairs."[13]

This "competitive intervention" has already taken the form of rate-cutting, vigorous commercial trading and barter deals. Diplomatically, it may employ, as it has already done with Turkey and Iran, fence-mending tactics with China, with West Germany and with the United States. Moscow will utilize the SALT (Strategic Arms Limitation Talks) negotiations, agreements with Bonn, and Warsaw Pact and NATO talks to encourage the relaxation that has already occurred in the West and foster the re-emergence of national rivalries and the disunity and fractionalization of Western alliances. NATO appears to be most threatened by this process.

Yet this is not a course without risks for Moscow itself. For the process of relaxation can scarcely be localized; it could "infect" the Communist countries and lead (particularly Moscow's fence-mending with West Germany) to disarray in the bloc.

No matter how viewed, Russia's obvious intent to achieve and to exercise global power will be a destabilizing factor; it must lead to uncertain tomorrows.

The most important single indication of Soviet ambitions is the now resumed push of Russia toward warm-water seas and open

69

oceans, the thrust outward from the heartland past the rimlands of Eurasia toward blue water. Russia's maritime expansion goes far beyond the needs of the heartland's security. Upon the continuation, tempo and extent of this expansion much of the history of the future depends.

The second major factor in the world of tomorrow will be the development of China and the course it takes. During its first years under a Communist dictatorship China has been loud in virulent words, cautious—except in Korea—in actions. But, like Russia of the past, China has not possessed the power for far-flung adventures or risky gambles. But that her rulers and some of her peoples aspire to a kind of Asiatic hegemony there is little doubt; and she will attempt to achieve industrial-technological strength.

> The nature of the world in which the Americans, the Chinese and the Russians live suggests that relations among these states and their peoples will remain delicate and hazardous. We shall no doubt remain locked in a shrinking world, suspicious of and hostile towards each other, unable on one hand to conquer or overthrow the other but equally unable to disengage and flee into some kind of armed security. . . . In such a position, we in the United States should maintain our economic, political, and spiritual vitality and our military strength, cooperate with other peoples who share our general goals and who are committed to peaceful progress, and continue to demonstrate that we are as resolute as in 1776 or in 1942 to defend our interests.[14]

It would be astigmatic, however, to look upon the world of tomorrow in the polarized terms of the past; the problem of the rest of the twentieth century is not merely the conflict between Communism and anti-Communism, between expanding Russian and Chinese power and other nations. It is far more insidious, far more complex; the pluralistic world of the future carries within it many seeds of conflict, and the problems that challenge men are immense and unpredictable.

The vast world movements of today represent a kind of convulsive spasm of history. They will be greatly complicated by the struggles of the many to achieve more, by the inadequate attempts of the world's developed areas to fill the vacuum of hope in the undeveloped regions, by conflict and strife and passion.

Throughout the rest of the twentieth century there will be crisis points throughout the world, breeding grounds for trouble and for war. The unsolved problem areas can be easily identified: Berlin and divided Germany; the Taiwan Strait and the two-China situation; divided Korea; divided South Vietnam; Southeast Asia; Africa; Latin America; Cyprus; the Arabian Peninsula–Persian Gulf area; and particularly the explosive, volatile Middle East. Other "hot spots," now unforeseen, will develop in the years to come—some only of passing local importance, others more dangerous and more durable.

All of this need not mean major war—perhaps not even another Vietnam or Korea—but it certainly postulates a world of recurrent crisis and unending trouble.

The challenge to the United States is, at its maximum, a challenge to our past role as a modern, civilized world power; at a minimum, a challenge to our patience, our political institutions, our economy.

How to meet the challenge of security in the years ahead without becoming a garrison state or a bankrupt state is the major task of U.S. foreign policy, U.S. security policy, U.S. grand strategy. No matter what route we attempt to follow—the path of optimum international cooperation through the United Nations and other agencies; neo-isolationism and a Fortress America neutralism; or attempts to police the world—the United States will require ready military strength to defend our vital interests, backed up and supported by a modern industrial-technological base. The challenge to the strategy for tomorrow is to match the cloth to the suit—to compress expanding commitments into shrinking resources.

71

«« 4 »»

# Colossus under Strain

THE ADMONITION OF Thomas Fuller in 1731—"Let not thy Will roar, an thy Power can but whisper"—is as sound today as it was two centuries ago.

The United States, with the strongest economic and technological power base in the world, can roar globally, but its power is neither constant nor infinite. National power waxes and wanes; it is a product not only of its physical components but of the intangibles of will and skills and national character.

The American dream has been built upon an economy of plenty, an economy of surpluses, an economy of waste. We have become a machine civilization—an economy constructed upon nuclear power, thermal power, electrical power, water power. We have become an automated and urbanized society, which, with fewer and fewer farmers, produces more and more food surpluses. Mass production and the technocratic age were born in America. For three decades power and the United States have come to be synonymous.

Yet in the years to come there will be infinite demands upon finite resources. More and more the United States must adjust to the realization that its frontiers have been tamed, its continent conquered, its wildernesses filled up, its resources reduced. More and more in the years to come, an economy of selectivity must replace an economy of waste. More and more in the years to come, the United States will move from the ranks of the "have" nations, rich in strategic materials and resources, into the ranks of the "have -not" nations, dependent upon raw materials produced beyond their own frontiers. More and more as the years pass, the future of the nation will depend upon the proper matching of *commitments* (or *requirements* or *interests*) to *resources* (or *capabilities*).

The equation of national power is implacable. Its absolute imperative is simple in statement, difficult in observance: the nation's commitments must never exceed the nation's resources.

What are those resources now and what will they be tomorrow?

In terms of geographic size, the United States is less than half as large as the U.S.S.R., slightly smaller than China, a factor of increased strategic significance in the age of nuclear weapons and radioactive fallout. In terms of geographic position and climate, the United States has a pronounced advantage. Far more of its territory lies within the Temperate Zone; unlike landlocked Russia, it has three great seacoasts and its farmlands are rich and bountiful. It can feed its people and much of the world besides; it has not had to fear, as have Russia and China, periodic crop failures and famines. As a continental island, it lies far from the source of most of the world's major problems—the Eurasian land mass.

U.S. and Russian population and population growth are approximately equal; China's population—by far the largest in the world —is almost four times that of the United States.

The United States is a highly developed economy—essentially an industrial urbanized nation. Its steel production (in 1967) of 127 million tons is the world's largest (the U.S.S.R., 110 million tons; Japan, 53 million tons). It produces more coal, more copper, more titanium, than any other nation; its petroleum production of more than 3 billion barrels annually (from domestic sources alone) exceeds Russia's by more than a billion barrels a year.*

Its gross national product—the sum of goods plus services— totaled $866 billion in 1967, and will probably approximate $1.2 trillion in 1975; Russia's GNP is estimated at approximately half ours. Rate of real growth (minus inflation) is estimated at 4 to 4.5

*Detailed comparison will be found in the Appendices.

73

percent annually for the United States, 4 to 7 percent annually for Russia.†[1]

The continental United States is also rich in raw materials, some of them untapped. The new finds in Alaska add tremendously to petroleum reserves and mineral deposits. Other great deposits—iron ore in Labrador; natural gas and oil in northwestern Canada—are close to U.S. frontiers, easily available to U.S. industry. But there are major deficiencies in so-called strategic raw materials—minerals or other products essential to the functioning of modern industry and to the development of military power. We are, as compared with Russia, a developed nation, with respect to geological exploration and exploitation of the earth's riches; the U.S.S.R. is constantly discovering new sources of supply. It is true that the United States still has a vast reserve of untapped treasure, both on land and beneath the adjoining sea floors, and Canada and Alaska are troves of riches. But Russia has vast, untapped and, indeed, unknown mineral wealth, and within her own frontiers she can find most—though not all—of the products modern technology demands.

From the point of view of mineral and raw-material self-sufficiency, the United States passed the great divide from the "have" to the "have-not" nations more than a decade ago when our imports of such materials first exceeded our exports.

There are twenty-three so-called strategic materials, some of which are not found at all in the United States or are in scarce supply, yet essential to our economy.* Some of them are supplied by Canada, Mexico or other countries in the Western Hemisphere, but every continent on earth and many of the islands provide the United States with materials vital to her strength and prosperity. At least one of these essential items is purchased from Russia.

On the whole, the facts of national power are comforting. Yet they require interpretation and amplification.

National power is no greater than the national will and resolution, and that in turn is a product of many factors—the environment; the political and governmental system; the nature, the

†See Appendix II.
*See Appendix III.

character and the skills of the people.

Russia is still essentially an agrarian economy, though it is fast becoming industrialized. China's teeming peasants provided the backbone of her Communist revolution and are the sinews of her strength. The United States is no longer the land of wide-open spaces; it is an urban and industrialized society with most of its peoples far from the soil. Like Russia and China, the United States has many ethnic minorities, and one group—the Negro—is not assimilable in less than generations.

The United States enjoys the advantages of any highly developed technological culture. Its peoples on the whole are better educated, more technically inclined, with more skills than those of Russia and China. We are used to the machine, and we use it and depend upon it far more than any other people in the world. We are clustered in cities—great urban sprawls that have become in many areas almost a continuous megalopolis—at once the glory and the blight of our civilization.

These concentrations of human beings are not adequately reflected in the so-called population-density figures—the average number of persons per square mile of territory. In the United States the population density (1960 census) was 21 per square kilometer; in European Russia (1959 figures) it was 32 per square kilometer; in Siberia or Asiatic Russia 3 persons per square kilometer, with an over-all density for all of Russia of 10 per square kilometer.

But the United States (1960, 1965 figures) includes 147 of what United Nations demographers call "urban agglomerations," cities and adjoining densely populated suburbs, each totaling more than 100,000 people. Of these 147, 28 had populations of more than 1,000,000, with the New York metropolitan area—11,348,000 people—topping the list. The U.S.S.R., in comparison, had, in 1966, only three "urban agglomerations" of more than 100,000 people. All three exceeded 1,000,000 population each, with the largest, Moscow, numbering 6,463,000 people.

These comparative statistics have acquired a new and awful meaning in the nuclear age; great concentrations of people and machines increase a nation's vulnerability to sudden destruction, and complicate civilian defense to a point of no return. More land area and less concentration of population on the other hand, provide the advantage of dispersion. Nevertheless the destructive effects—and particularly the radioactive fallout—of large nuclear explosions extend over such vast distances that Moscow can take scant comfort; vulnerability is a relative term.

An industrial-technological society, built upon machines and cybernetics, must pay the price for its own brilliance; subtly the machine changes the character of a people. Americans have not yet lost all of the ancient virtues: resolution, improvisation, energy. But we are losing many of them; we are not exempt from the crisis of values which has shaken the Western world. Many observers have noted a growing softness about our society, a sloth and ease and comfort which are not conducive to reaction to challenge. The work-less-and-make-more syndrome has affected the national psychology. In fact, the politico-social climate of the times has produced leader after leader, government after government, which promises more ease, more leisure, less work, less challenge. John F. Kennedy posed the problem: "Ask not what your country can do for you; ask what you can do for your country."

But the answer was not affirmative.

It is important to note these trends, for the national character and the national will are the country's principal resource for the future —more important, by far, than its green acres and its smoking factories. These are trends; they are not a fixed and irreversible character mutation, and there are still millions of Americans who retain the characteristics that made the nation great—indeed, the new generations, revolting against the standards of the old, have shed many of the false values and hypocrisies of yesterday.

Nevertheless, as Hal Borland has written in his beautifully poetic *Countryman:*

> With almost cyclic inevitability, cultures that were based on individual freedom from work became decadent, cynical, and weak rather than vital and happy and strong. The work-is-a-curse myth led to war and ultimate disaster . . . every civilization has been at its strongest, in human terms at least, when it was in some stage of the pioneering phase; when man was out there building a civilized society at the near edge of a wilderness, dreaming not of a sweatless

76

utopia but of accomplishment with his own thew and muscle. . . .
Both civilization and culture must be rooted somewhere, and all
roots grow best in the soil itself.[2]

There is no doubt that America is no longer a pioneer society,
no longer an agrarian country, and that the impatience, the tensions, the ills and evils of a cluttered, industrialized, urbanized
nation are now part of the national character.

There are advantages and disadvantages, too, in the form of
government developed in the United States. We are no longer a
republic, as conceived by the founding fathers, but a democracy
which at times and places has assumed many of the characteristics
of mobocracy. Sometimes it seems that we are trying to apply the
old democratic principles of a tiny Greek city-state, or a New
England town meeting of the last century, to the government of a
nation of 200 million diverse people. The U.S. Government has
become administratively tightly centralized and hence more rigid,
less adaptable to local conditions, more bureaucratic and hence less
efficient, and it has become paternalistic though not yet self-delud-
ing like the Communist hierarchy. Our system is more flexible than
the systems of the Communist or authoritarian powers, but less
resolute, less quick to act in moments of crisis. It promises more to
the people and demands less of them, hence reducing the self-
reliance which has been the past hallmark of the American character. On the other hand, in its attempts to meet its promises the tax
burden has risen astronomically—to such an extent that tax evasion, once practiced by only the few, or a marked reduction of
incentive, once a characteristic of the many, seems certain. On the
other hand, our system, unlike any authoritarian system, has until
now shown itself capable of tolerating major dissent and able to
innovate, and it periodically transfers power without the deadly and
crucial struggles that continue to beset the Communist leadership.

In sum, the strengths and the weaknesses of America—the resources of political and economic system, of national character and
technocratic society, of heart and mind and brain and brawn, and,
above all, of machine—make the United States by far the richest
nation in the world and the most powerful—a colossus of history.

But it is a colossus under strain.

77

We are today a nation built upon promissory notes, drawn upon the next generation; in some sense we have mortgaged the future to pay for the past. Our national indebtedness is by far the greatest in history, and we have become a welfare state. An unending spiral of inflation has weakened the dollar. The real and urgent requirement for human needs, for modernization of our cities and transportation systems, adds to the demands of the domestic sector of our economy.

The needs of national security—what can be spent for defense, space, foreign affairs—will thus be far more strictly limited and must be more closely defined than in the past. The dollar gap alone has shown that U.S. foreign expenditures must be curtailed; a sound economic base is the foundation of any national security program.

Yet, as we noted, the gross national product is increasing at a healthy rate—about 4 to 4.5 percent a year.

In an economic sense, we can afford nearly any level of defense spending provided it is properly balanced by adequate taxation and limited domestic budgets. In recent years we have been spending about 8 to 10 percent of our GNP annually for defense (excluding foreign aid and space). By 1975 this level of spending could provide a defense budget of between $96 and $120 billions annually. But this is the absolute upper level, a "ceiling" which almost certainly will not be reached, barring a major war or crisis. For political realities, rather than economic stringency alone, indicate a far lower level (after Vietnam) of defense spending, something on the order of $72 to $80 billions, about 6 to 7 percent of the GNP. The demands for domestic spending and the rising resentment of high taxes indicate that it would be unrealistic to anticipate a defense budget much larger than this in the early 1970's. In fact, a spending level of $70 to $75 billion has been established as a goal for the next five years.

Domestic political factors and the needs of the domestic economy, plus the prevalent "antimilitary" attitude of a large, vocal section of the people, will act as powerful restraints upon the U.S. defense budget in the early 1970's. Russia, with a less powerful economy but a rigid political system, will experience fewer restraints. At the expense of fewer consumer goods, she can and will devote a considerably larger proportion of her over-all budget and GNP to defense and defense-allied projects such as space and the merchant marine than the United States will do. In terms of weapons procurement, her armed forces will be nurtured by an "economy of plenty," whereas ours will be experiencing, at least for the immediate future, an era of retrenchment, cutback and scarcity. Thus the President may face the dilemma postulated before the last election: he must spend billions more on defense to compensate for years of past neglect, for age and obsolescence, for drawdown of stockpiles during the Vietnam war, or he may have to reconcile himself and the nation to acceptance of Soviet superiority in some major elements of military power. And the other side of the coin is equally stark: if the nation's immense problems on the home front are not eased, there is little point in drawing up blueprints for defense against foreign foes.

The basic problem confronting the nation is an economy that is commencing to be one of scarcity. There are, as Leonard A. Lecht has put it, "a complex of competing claims on resources. . . . The costs of the entire complex are estimated to exceed the resources we are capable of generating without severe strains on our social and economic institutions."[3]

But the nub of the problem is commitments: what do we defend? We can insure a reasonable security only if we tailor the suit to fit the cloth; we cannot stretch a finite economy to infinite demands without disaster.

Those who argue that we have been stretched thin, that we are overextended, that we cannot be the world's policeman, can point, with considerable persuasiveness, to the long list of multilateral and bilateral treaties and agreements which commit, or appear to commit, the United States to some form of *defense* support to a minimum of forty nations, perhaps to more than a hundred.*[4] In addition to these explicit agreements, there appear to be many implicit ones, which do not appear to have the force of a treaty, but which may, nevertheless, involve us even more powerfully than legal terminology. The bond of a common tongue which ties us to England, the cultural and historical links to Western Europe, the

*See Appendix IV.

sympathy of many Americans—particularly of the politically powerful Jewish community—for Israel and the ethnic ties of various U.S. groups to other countries represent at least emotional commitments, which may become political commitments in time of crisis.

But *commitments*—despite the most precise legal terminology—are not necessarily binding unless cemented by mutual *interests*. Commitments, and even interests, can and do change, and commitments promising the ultimate sanction—the use of military force—are based upon quicksand unless important or vital interests of the nations concerned are involved. Even a vital interest can become a less important one. At one time, for instance, the uranium ore of the Congo was of major importance to the development of a U.S. nuclear capability. The exploitation of other sources of fissionable material has reduced materially our *interest* in this source, and we certainly have no *commitment* to defend the Congo.

Stephen Maxwell comments, for instance, that "any commitment the Americans have to keep India from being overrun by the Chinese is not a commitment *to* the Indians or their government, but a consequence of the existence of an American interest in restraining China, and giving confidence to other governments in Asia."[5]

A commitment is *political;* an interest implies as its ultimate defense a *military* reaction. A *vital* interest is one which involves the fundamental welfare or security of a nation, one of such tremendous importance that it justifies, if absolutely essential, invocation of the "ultimate weapon"—the A-bomb—even though its use might destroy the user as well as his opponent. This "rationality of the irrational"—a determination to use a weapon under certain circumstances which would mean self-destruction as well as enemy destruction—can be a powerful deterrent to infringement of a nation's *vital* interests, provided those interests are clearly defined and the penalty for infringement is both credible and unambiguous.

But the problem of defining what is vital and of "posting" it—of putting up a political fence marked in large letters, "No Trespassing"—is at once difficult and subtle. It is not always desirable to be specific in diplomacy. Ambiguity can provide a political advantage;

80

a clear-cut statement that certain countries or regions were not considered of major importance to U.S. interests could weaken deterrence and help to invite aggression, as former Secretary of State Dean Acheson discovered in the Korean aggression.

And, as Vietnam has shown, what may simply start as a secondary *interest* (and a commitment) can become, when military sanctions are invoked, an important, even a vital, interest, because of escalation and involvement. Interests involve intangible, as well as tangible, factors: prestige, honor, pride and even attitudes; what may be vital to defend today may not be vital tomorrow.

A continuing review of U.S. commitments, and particularly of U.S. interests, is therefore an important task in any analysis of national security policies.

Selectivity and a list of priorities are essential not only in our own national interests but for the sake of world stability.

To determine priorities, one must determine interests. "First, we must . . . ask ourselves whether the nation or region in question is of any direct relevance to our national security. To put it another way, would 'hostile' control of that nation or region pose any real threat to our national security . . . ?"[6]

The first and fundamental priority in any listing of U.S. security interests in the United States—the nation itself, the sound base on which our armed forces must depend, from which they draw their support, from which they must deploy. A secure home base is the first requirement for military security.

In the preatomic age the security of the home base could be assured; today in the age of missiles and nuclear weapons no absolute security is possible. Nevertheless a reasonable degree of relative security is achievable, and is, indeed, vital, if the nation is to survive.

The United States, in geopolitical terms, is part of a continental "island," which forms, with South America, a hemispheric island. Our own "insular" security would be breached if Canada, Mexico or the Latin-American nations were to come under the aegis not alone of a foreign ideology, as in Cuba, but of a major foreign power, as at the time of the Cuban missile crisis. The Monroe Doctrine,

81

conceived in a different age, is still geopolitically sound in the twentiety century; we cannot afford to permit the domination* of any part of the Western Hemisphere—particularly north of the Equator—by a foreign power.

The Western Hemisphere's geographic, economic, psychological and political interests are almost matched in importance by Western Europe's economic, political and cultural significance. This is a region of the world which, in the short-term future, at least, is indispensable to our freedom. If all Western Europe should be merged into a Communist empire, or conquered by Russian troops, Moscow would control the greatest economic conglomerate in the world, and the United States would ultimately be outmatched.

North America, including the Caribbean area, can, in other words, be classified as part of a "categorical" imperative (this we must defend if we are to exist as a nation); Western Europe as "vital."[7]

The United States also has interests which may be classified as vital in the preservation of a free and independent Japan friendly to the West, and of an independent South Korea, and in the freedom and security of the offshore islands and land masses fringing Asia, extending from the Aleutians to Australia and New Zealand. A retreat by the United States from these island positions would imply a geopolitical defeat of tremendous magnitude; the U.S. security frontier would be pushed back to the mid-Pacific.

The Middle East is a region of incalculable consequence, which, if not vital, is certainly of high importance. The economic stakes, particularly in the form of petroleum production, are very high (though of less significance than they were two decades ago). The area is a land bridge between three continents, birthplace of three great religions, and the natural focus of world shipping and airline routes, and now a center of Arab-Israeli passions and Soviet ambitions.

Southeast Asia has also become, largely because of our commit-

*But "domination" may have many gradations. We have found it possible, though unpleasant and dangerous, to live with a Communist Cuba, greatly influenced by Soviet Russia. "Domination" in a strategic sense would mean the establishment of bases or military facilities by a foreign power; i.e., the U.S.S.R. or Communist China. This could not be safely tolerated.

82

ments during the Vietnam war, a region of importance to the American future; whether we like it or not, our interests are involved—importantly involved—in Vietnam, Thailand and the other states of the area. Outright defeat in Vietnam or a precipitate American withdrawal would have disastrous global consequences.

It is to our interests to avoid the domination of India and Pakistan by Chinese or Russian Communism, but this interest is more negative than positive, and has a lower order of priority than the others listed.

The rest of the world—and particularly most of Africa south of the Sahara—is of fringe importance to the United States today; if it were unified under one great conqueror tomorrow, it could become of major importance. It is to our interests to prevent this.

To the United States the world around us has shades and gradations of meaning, which are never constant. Save for a few categorical imperatives, involving the self-preservation of the nation, national interests are forever changing. A new advance in technology may demand exotic minerals found only in a remote region of the earth; denial, to us, of the source of supply might halt or handicap economic, military or social progress. Nor are all interests to be viewed solely in physical terms; emotional ties and intangible bonds—the moral imperatives that often drive men to war—are sometimes no less strong than the vital requirements of geography, of land and space and economics.

And the world today, though far from the "One World" of Wendell Willkie's phrase, is a far more compact and interdependent whole than in the days of our forefathers. If Khrushchev had dropped a shoe in Madagascar, the echo would have been heard in Rome or Washington. Thus small events may blossom into major headlines and minor interests become major ones.

There can be no fixed and immutable prescription for national security; there can be no constant definition of an American grand strategy; change demands adjustment. But strategy—the determination of what to defend and how to do it—has one overriding and enduring imperative: the security of the home base, the viability of its political, social, cultural and economic institutions, the defense of the nation.

83

«« 5 »»

# This We Must Defend

*"This fortress built by Nature for herself
Against infection and the hand of war . . ."*

IN GEOPOLITICAL TERMS, the United States of the twentieth century represents the "fortress" England of which Shakespeare wrote.

The continental island of North America is separated from the great powers of Europe and Asia by the Atlantic and the Pacific, the Arctic and the Antarctic. In the missile-jet age, with supersonic speeds and foreshortened geography, the broad oceans of yesterday have shrunk to the dimensions of a moat—the English Channel of the eighteenth and nineteenth centuries. Nevertheless blue water and blue skies provide the United States with a rampart against *ground* attack as impregnable today as the English Channel proved to be in history's yesterdays.

Unlike the nations of Europe and Asia, which have been exposed for centuries to predatory attacks across vulnerable ground frontiers, the United States—with a friendly and interdependent Canada to the north and small and weak nations to the south—has no fear of serious ground invasion.

This simplifies U.S. strategy and eases the problem of hemispheric defense. Unless a major and potentially hostile power dominates large land areas in the Western Hemisphere and exploits and develops them as strong, offensive bases, the threat of enemy ground power to the United States is an inconsequential risk. And the development of any such foreign base could be accomplished only by breaching the ramparts of sea and sky which surround the Americas. Thus a maritime strategy for the United States is a natural geopolitical derivative—an imperative of our security.

This favorable geographic position is unequaled by that of any other major power. The fear of ground invasion which has dominated so much of Eurasia's strategic thinking for generations, and which still colors Soviet and Chinese and German political policies, has no counterpart in the United States.

Nevertheless the "fortress built by Nature" is no stronger than its defenders. Geography confers advantages; man must exploit them.

And in the nuclear-missile age the problem of any defense is far more acute and imperative than in any era of the past. The technological revolution has meant that, for the first time in history, any nation on earth—no matter how remote—is potentially exposed to devastation, possibly to annihilation. Time and space have been telescoped; wholesale death can arrive on the wings of the dawn. Powerful deterrents, instant readiness and swift reactions are the essential factors in defense in the atomic age.

There are two interrelated problems in hemispheric strategy: defense against nuclear attack and defense against lesser types of aggression.

The immense importance of the nation's nuclear forces as the basic foundation of any global security system has been somewhat obscured publicly by the past decade's emphasis on limited wars and guerrilla conflicts, by the tendency of many to view atomic war as "unthinkable," and by the sheer obscurantism or emotional bias of many of the political and atomic scientists who have dealt with the subject.

The nation's strategic forces—our nuclear arsenal and offensive and defensive long-range delivery vehicles and weapons systems—are the first and final line of defense, the only military hope of preserving a free nation. Conventional forces require, if they are to operate successfully, the shield against enemy nuclear annihilation

85

that only our own nuclear forces can provide. Not only in the Western Hemisphere, but throughout the world, United States armed forces fight successfully only within the shadow, beneath the umbrella, of a nuclear superiority.

The most difficult, the most expensive, the most vital and the greatest task of American strategy today is nuclear defense. Without it there is no defense, there can be no national security. With it there can be no perfect defense, no absolute security.

But this is not new to history; no fortress, no Maginot Line, no defensive system ever built has long remained impregnable; there is no absolute security—and there never will be—in the life of man.

The implications of an enemy nuclear attack to the life of the nation are so staggering that nuclear defense must have absolute priority in any U.S. grand strategy. The defense of the continental United States is a categorical imperative.

Former Secretary of Defense Robert S. McNamara, in his 1969 Posture Statement to Congress, estimated that both the United States and the Soviet Union would suffer up to 120 million fatalities in the event of an all-out nuclear exchange in the mid-1970's.[1]

His coldly computerized rationale, which tended to downgrade the importance of an antiballistic missile defense, can and has been faulted by many critics, but the thrust of his statement—the horrible cost of a nuclear war computed in megadeaths—can have no effective refutation. The prime requirement of any continental defense, of any grand strategy, is therefore to arm ourselves in such a manner as to deter nuclear war, to inhibit any enemy from utilizing nuclear weapons, and to limit damage to the United States, and, as far as possible, to our allies, if such a war should occur.

Put in the official terminology of the nation's basic national security objective, this means:

"... to preserve the United States as a free and independent nation, safeguarding its fundamental values and to preserve its freedom to pursue its national objectives as the leading world power." From this, we produce our basic military objective, to deter aggression at any level and, should deterrence fail, to terminate hostilities, in concert with our allies, under conditions of relative advantage while limiting damage to the United States and minimizing damage to the United States' and allied interests.[2]

THIS WE MUST DEFEND

After World War I offensive weapons increased their advantage over defensive systems. With the development of the hydrogen bomb and intercontinental missiles the offense appeared to have won a final and definitive victory in its age-old struggle with the defense. There was "no place to hide," and the "absolute weapon" —the nuclear bomb—had given the offense such predominance that the only defense appeared to be offense—the threat of retaliation in kind.

But the technological revolution has by no means ended, and the judgments of those who draw immutable conclusions from existing capabilities and present data are certain to be swept into the dustbin of history.

It is still true today—and is likely to be true throughout the next two decades—that the best defense is a stout offense, that a U.S. capability of devastating any enemy regardless of what the enemy does first is the best deterrent to attack. It is still true that this so-called "assured destruction" capability—the capability of destroying an enemy's political and industrial, social and military system even if the enemy attacks first—is the cornerstone of continental defense.

"Assured destruction" is the absolute and irreducible minimum requirement. But what does this jargon mean?

It must mean the capability of inflicting upon any enemy unacceptable damage regardless of how the nuclear interchange starts. But damage that might be unacceptable to the United States might be considered acceptable by tougher governments and peoples. What unacceptable damage means is thus a matter of subjective judgment, and, as such, may be grossly in error. Former Secretary of Defense McNamara once defined it, illustratively, as a capability of inflicting upon the U.S.S.R. the destruction of 50 percent of her industry and 20 to 25 percent of her people.[3] To rational rulers any such losses would be unacceptable and the deterrent would be real.

But there would probably be no war if all men were rational; the risk of irrationality will be forever with us.

The problem of nuclear defense is further complicated by other factors. Irrationality and the errors of subjective judgment introduce dangerous unknowns into the equation; so, too, does the factor of credibility.

Will the enemy believe us? Does he put the same evaluation, first, upon our power and, second, upon our will to use it that we do?

Because of the many unknowns in the equation of deterrence there is room for a wide margin of error. Yet the penalty of miscalculation of an enemy's intentions or capabilities could be the life of the nation. Thus a generous—a very generous—allowance for such error must be made in calculating our nuclear-deterrence requirements.

But an assured destruction capability alone is not enough; it would not assure the termination of hostilities "under conditions of relative advantage while limiting damage to the United States."

To speak of "winning" a nuclear war is a contradiction in terms; after a large nuclear interchange between major powers both of them—and probably many of their allies—would be devastated. Nevertheless one side or the other would emerge with *less* damage, *more* strength than the other; one side would end with a "relative advantage."

General Douglas MacArthur's "There is no substitute for victory" applies to a nuclear war—*and particularly to its deterrence*—as much as it does to a conventional war—though one must, of course, define "victory" in new and ominous terms. What this really means is that "assured destruction" is not enough; one must develop a "damage-limiting" capability. This can be sought by a combination of offensive and defensive weapons systems: ICBM's targeted against enemy missile silos, airfields and enemy second-strike capabilities; antisubmarine and air-defense systems, and antiballistic missile systems.

Given the present state of the art, none of these measures offers immediate hope of limiting damage to the United Sates to what we would define as "acceptable" levels. The speed and power of the modern offensive make sudden surprise attack by strategic weapons almost impossible to anticipate or to forestall. And there is, for the United Sates, another constraint: our political policies preclude a first strike. Our strategy and our technology must therefore be built upon the assumption of a second strike, after the enemy has attacked us. This means we must have weapons systems capable of surviving the immense blast, fire and radioactive effects of widespread nuclear detonations. The second-strike requirement terrifically complicates the problem of limiting damage and of maintaining sufficient offensive strength to assure unacceptable destruction to any enemy.

Our antimissile defensive system, for instance, must be built around a microsecond accuracy. Its radar and electronics must survive the huge discharges of energy that accompany every nuclear explosion, and the radar must be able to distinguish and sort out decoys from actual nuclear warheads. But above all the defensive missiles must be "tied in" to our offensive ones with such precision that the blast of our defensive intercepting missiles does not destroy or throw off course our outgoing offensive missiles. The scenario of such an attack must anticipate launchings of defensive and offensive missiles at microsecond intervals on precalculated trajectories which will "clear" each other. The computer that can control all this has not yet been built.

Thus damage limitation—given the state of the art today—is far more difficult to achieve for a nation committed to withholding its punch until an enemy punches us. And it is clear that strengthening our offensive capabilities and increasing their invulnerability offer greater hope today of deterring nuclear war, and thus of limiting damage to ourselves, than the strengthening of our defensive systems.

The defense is definitely at a disadvantage today.

But the race between defense and offense never stands still; technology never turns back. Tomorrow a missile defense system may be developed which will intercept ballistic missiles during midcourse, or soon after launching, rather than in their terminal phase. Laser technology, solar mirrors to focus the rays of the sun, pellet barrages, manned space interceptors with electronic countermeasure capabilities—these and "more things in heaven and earth . . . than are dreamt of"—may completely alter the future relations between offense and defense.

In the past decade, as a number of scientists have shown, the defense has increased its effectiveness vis-à-vis the offense, from both a technological and a cost viewpoint. The exaggerations of the opposition about the cost of a missile defensive system have been well publicized. Yet the ABM Safeguard system is, as Albert Wohlstetter has pointed out, "a modest program":

> The average annual cost of the completed program, on a five year basis, is less than one fifth of what we were spending for active defense against manned bombers at the end of the 1950's. Nor is it at all likely to start a quantitative arms spiral. Indeed . . . there has been no quantitative arms race in the strategic offense and defense budget, no "ever-accelerating increase," nor, in fact, any long-term increase at all. The budget for strategic offense and defense forces in fiscal 1962 was $11.3 billion. This proposed fiscal 1970 budget . . . comes to about $8.3 billion. Adjusted for price changes, the 1962 figure was well over 50 per cent higher than that for 1970.[4]

Even given the limitations of today's defensive technology, the consequences of nuclear war are so catastrophic that nearly any damage-limitation measures would appear to be justifiable. In one of his arguments against an ABM system, former Secretary of Defense McNamara, using computer studies, calculated that even an extensive system might, under certain conditions, save only a few million lives. Indeed, in one coldly horrible table in his last Posture Statement to Congress, which summarized the numbers of fatalities on both sides in an all-out nuclear interchange in the mid-1970's, a footnote conceded that "at fatality levels of approximately 100 million or more, differences of 10 to 20 million in the calculated results are less than the margin of error in the estimates."[5]

Given the calculated megadeaths of nuclear war, a few million lives saved may not appear to be cost-effective. But in moral, human and political and economic terms, any strategy that does not attempt to minimize to the optimum limits of technology the death and destruction caused by a nuclear strike is not a national security strategy; it has lost sight of the first objective of armed forces: the security of the nation against external attack.

The necessity for a damage-limiting as well as an assured destruction strategy rests on even stronger foundations. It has been popular among part of the scientific and intellectual community to resist either qualitative or quantitative strengthening of the nation's nuclear capabilities. New developments, like an ABM system, or

90

MIRV's (Multiple Independently Targetable Re-entry Vehicles), would, it was said, speed up an arms race and would ultimately reduce—not increase—U.S. security. On the other hand, approximate nuclear parity with the U.S.S.R. would be "stabilizing"; if we did not develop new weapons systems, Russia would not do so.

This is probably the most perniciously mistaken doctrine that has yet been advanced under the guise of strategy. It is a doctrine that if followed to its bitter end is almost certain to lead to harrowing alternatives. History is against it; technology is opposed to it; and recent experience has indicated overwhelmingly that no matter what the United States does, the U.S.S.R. and Communist China will develop their weapons technology to the limit of their capabilities. (The size of their forces may well be affected by the size of our own armed services and their evaluation of our intentions and capabilities. But they do not believe in a "technological plateau"; they will develop their qualitative capabilities to the full.)

The strategy of parity is not, and never can be unless it is accompanied by an absolutely foolproof, on-the-site inspection system, a stabilizing strategy. Rather, it represents a dangerously uneasy balance of terror, which could be upset overnight by a Soviet technological breakthrough or even by a secret and massive building program.

The mere adoption of such a strategy would have—indeed, has had—immediate destabilizing effects. The deliberate relinquishment of nuclear superiority by the United States reduces the credibility of the deterrent; Moscow may come to believe that she has the capability not only to deter a U.S. nuclear attack but to emerge from a nuclear interchange as the stronger power. Her impression of the will and resolution of the United States—already weakened by the mild reaction of the United States to the seizure of the naval ship *Pueblo* on the high seas, the shooting down of a naval reconnaissance plane off Korea and the rape of Czechoslovakia and our suppliant attitude about peace in Vietnam and arms limitations—will certainly be reduced. And if we found Soviet political actions truculent and difficult in the period when we had an overwhelming nuclear advantage, how can anyone expect a more stable world in a period when the U.S.S.R. has achieved parity or superiority? The inhibitions to strong U.S. action anywhere in the world would be overwhelming, and the tremendous political disadvantages of parity or inferiority would inevitably become apparent—when it was too late.

The dangers of Soviet nuclear superiority are subtle and manifold; indeed, the catastrophe might not even be detected by the public until we had passed the point of no return. The ultimate threat is not so much the specter of sudden and devastating atomic annihilation of the nation, for, in any scenario one can envisage, the United States probably would retain—even if it accepted an acknowledged inferiority—some capability to inflict terrible damage on the Soviet Union. But nuclear superiority would greatly strengthen Moscow's pre-emptive diplomacy all over the world; we would hesitate, indeed, to offer any defense of peripheral interests in the face of Soviet nuclear superiority. Would we risk, for instance, a naval confrontation in the Gulf of Aden if we knew Russia possessed nuclear superiority? Nuclear blackmail in subtle form could cost us the world. This is not an insensate nightmare but a dangerous possibility. One can never forget Moscow's missile and atomic threats at the time of the Suez crisis, and her audacious emplacement in 1962 of missiles in Cuba.

One would expect that the Kremlin would, at first, utilize nuclear superiority coolly. Moscow might be expected to both proclaim and demonstrate its strength, and Moscow propagandists would emphasize to the American people and to our government the superiority of their position. Their demands would be low-key and seemingly reasonable, but progressive and more and more far-reaching. The road of atomic appeasement can be one of no turning; it could force or persuade us to accept solutions to world problems that would be favorable to the U.S.S.R., disadvantageous to the United States.

There are more ways than one to lose the world to Communism. Put in an oversimplified and extreme form, the strategy of nuclear parity or nuclear inferiority or of unilateral arms limitation is a strategy of defeat, not a strategy of national security.

Thus any strategy for defense of the continental island and the Western Hemisphere—indeed, any world strategy—must start with a definite and clear-cut nuclear superiority to any potential enemy or combination of enemies—a superiority that is clearly discernible by the enemy. It must be both an assured destruction and a damage-limitation strategy that is built upon continuing technological developments.

No administration can settle for less than this unless there is a global and policed arms-limitation agreement, subject to adequate verification and control.

But nuclear superiority today means not only—and not so much —a bigger bang, a more powerful warhead (although this is important), but superior delivery vehicles or weapons systems. To our continental island, attack can come only through space, in the atmosphere or on or under the sea; similarly, our nuclear deterrent can be projected against any enemy only through the same media. The cornerstone of any U.S. grand strategy must therefore be command of the aerospace above us and of the sea around us. A modern maritime strategy must be keyed to the oceans of air and space as well as the oceans of water. Similarly, the successful application of lesser forms of military power in defense of the United States and the Western Hemisphere requires predominant sea-air power. A successful sea-air strategy means the capability to utilize the sea and the atmosphere, as well as space above it, for our own purposes, while denying, insofar as technologically possible, similar use to an enemy.

The defense of the United States starts in the "empyrean blue" —in space. It has been said that he who controls space absolutely controls the world absolutely. This is today a catchy phrase without too much substantive meaning; for the technological capability to control space "absolutely"—i.e., to use it as we wish while denying any enemy use of space—is not in sight.

However, the military uses of space are so diverse and, today, so little developed that caution dictates restraint in predicting possibilities of tomorrow.

Ballistic missiles launched from anywhere on the earth's surface follow a parabolic course through space to target. The Fractional Orbital Bombardment System developed by the Russians is, as its

Dr. Strangelove designation implies, a missile with nuclear warhead which follows a low orbital course around the earth, and on command can be brought down on its target after a partial circumnavigation. It is, so far, less accurate than a conventional ballistic missile, but it shortens the defender's warning time to about three to five minutes. Nuclear weapons in complete orbit or stationed in outer space are future technological possibilities, even though the great powers have agreed that space should be used for peaceful purposes.

Today by far the most important military utilization of space is intelligence-collection and monitoring. Satellites equipped with high-resolution cameras, electronic, radiological, infrared and other sensors provide information about both enemy capabilities and, in some cases, intentions. They can collect data about the numbers and locations of missile silos and provide early warning of missile launchings and nuclear explosions.

A system of such satellites, tied in by telemetering equipment to ground computers, will be able tomorrow to provide track charts of nearly all surface ships on all the oceans of the world and to pick up major mechanized troop movements. The fullest possible development of reconnaissance, intelligence-collection and monitoring satellites is an exploitation of defensive technology which is essential to any strategy of security—with or without arms control.[6]

Weather, navigation, communication and mapping satellites, already operational, will be subject to major refinement and will obviously have important military, as well as nonmilitary, uses.

For the United States the major weakness in our space armory is the lack of a manned satellite interceptor. Close-up monitoring and visual inspection may be essential tomorrow to determine whether or not a "bogy," or unknown satellite, is a weapon of war or a peaceful explorer. A manned orbiting laboratory—now apparently the goal of Soviet space programs—is also important to basic space research. The development of these technologies and of new generations of ballistic missiles will permit the United States to build up rapidly an offensive space capability if prohibitions against the stationing of weapons in space should be disregarded by potential enemies.

94

For the United States the 70 percent of the earth's surface that is water and that part of the space above the earth (the atmosphere) that is used by piloted aircraft and air-breathing missiles are even more basic to our security. As launching bases for strategic missiles, the sea and the air offer the tremendous advantages of dispersion —vast areas where no man lives—and they permit a mobility impossible on land. The subsurfaces of the sea provide another advantage—concealment.

The sea-based missile—and particularly the submarine-launched missile—has, indeed, so many strategic advantages that it is clear it must become in the next two decades the principal component of our strategic nuclear forces. In the past, Polaris submarines have been ancillary to our land-based missile silos. The range of their missiles was initially limited, their accuracy was slightly less, the power of their warheads smaller, and there were maintenance, navigation and communication problems. And in cost-effectiveness terms the submarine-based missile suffered in comparison to the Minuteman silos.

But technology has altered the equation drastically in favor of the sea-based missile, whereas so far, the chief virtue of the submarine as a launching platform—its capability to conceal itself and thus to insure protection against any enemy surprise attack—has not been breached. It is true, of course, that putting all one's eggs in one basket, or placing complete reliance on a single weapons system, is never a sound solution of a security problem. A single enemy technological breakthrough might make such a system obsolete overnight. There is no immediate prospect that the submarine will soon be stripped of its concealment; the sea is a murky medium, and sound ranging and detection, with all its inaccuracies and its unpredictable factors, is still an inadequate defense. But multiple weapons systems tremendously complicate the enemy's defensive problem from a technological, a military and strategic and an economic point of view; multiple systems, wisely mixed, are cost-effective.

No sensible strategist would urge, therefore, complete reliance upon a sea-based missile system, but technology and costs have already suggested, and indeed demanded, that our basic and major

95

nuclear deterrent must go to sea.

The production of missiles and warheads of tremendous power, and of MIRV's, has made the development of a stronger and more extensive sea-based deterrent imperative to a strategy of assured destruction. MIRV—the mating of many individually guided warheads or dummies or decoys to a single missile—increases the probability of the destruction of fixed land-based missile sites and enormously complicates the problem of the defense.

To meet this threat, the defense can: (1) strengthen existing missile silos by increased "hardening" (more concrete, steel and earth, and better shielding against the tremendous surges of power released by nuclear explosions); (2) disperse our retaliatory forces by building more land-based missile launchers and bomber bases; (3) provide antiballistic missile defensive systems; (4) build mobile land-based systems which cannot be "zeroed in" ahead of time by any enemy; (5) keep long-range bombers equipped with standoff, air-launched missiles constantly in the air; (6) put more missiles at sea.

The land-based sites have none of the problems inevitably associated with mobile systems; they excel as far as simplicity and ease of maintenance are concerned. But in nearly every other respect, including costs, and particularly in the basic capability of survivability, the sea-based missile now has a *pronounced* advantage. The submarine-launched missile, in particular, provides the "assured destruction" capability which is the cornerstone of deterrence.

It has both mobility and concealment; it is not a prepositioned target; its whereabouts are not known to the enemy. It has range enough to reach any target on earth, power enough to destroy any city, accuracy enough to destroy nearly any hard target. It can be kept instantly ready for firing upon orders from Washington, yet—since it is not subject to destruction by an enemy surprise attack—the dangerous compulsion of quick reaction to early warnings is not a factor. There is time for evaluation and Presidential decision. Moreover, the submarine-launched missile inherently contributes to a damage-limiting strategy. For it is emplaced at sea; dispersion is achieved in the wide stretches of the uninhabited oceans, not in

96

the congested areas of the populated land. It invites the lightning of enemy nuclear strikes toward the open sea, not toward the vulnerable land. And—most important of all—it increases the credibility of the deterrent, for there is now no known, or prospective, means of destroying all submarine-based missiles in a surprise attack. It gives pause even to the rash aggressor, for no enemy can rationally anticipate a successful first strike.

Ballistic missiles mounted on surface ships do not have the same degree of invulnerability as submarine-launched ballistic missiles. But, except for concealment, they have the other advantages enjoyed by a submarine-launched ballistic missile system, and they are much less costly than any other mobile launching system or than fixed, hardened sites. Sooner or later most major naval vessels will probably carry ballistic or air-breathing dual-purpose missiles, for use against other ships or land targets, with ranges of 100 to 1,000 or more miles. Some merchant-type hulls may also be specially fitted as missile launchers.

Our offensive missiles are the principal reliance, now and in the foreseeable future, of the deterrent to nuclear war, but defensive missiles can also contribute to deterrence. Defensive missiles can contribute—at present fractionally, in the future perhaps to a more major degree—to a damage-limiting strategy. The degree to which they can reduce casualties and limit damage will depend, ultimately, upon technology; today there appears to be little hope of shielding any nation from a saturation missile attack.

Nevertheless a United States without defensive missiles confronting a Russia with defensive missiles immediately accepts political, psychological and military disadvantages. More important, the failure to deploy at least a minimal ABM system would handicap our technological development of an improved system, for only by actual deployment and field operation can any such system achieve sound growth improvements. The U.S. Sentinel-Safeguard system, based upon an exoatmospheric rocket with large nuclear warhead, intended to intercept incoming missiles outside the atmosphere, supplemented by a shorter-range high-speed Sprint missile for last-ditch, in-the-atmosphere defense, offers defensive promise for tomorrow.

It can be both an area and a spot defensive system, and as such can be developed into a defensive system for urban areas and for the entire nation, as well as a tighter local defense for ICBM missile silos and military sites.

It should be deployed first on a small scale, and later—if and when its technological growth offers greater defensive returns—it should be extended.

A damage-limiting strategy should also include some civil defense measures. The protection of any great numbers of persons—particularly those living in urban complexes—against the blast and heat of large-scale nuclear detonations appears to be impractical, but some degree of protection against fallout is feasible. The present program of utilizing, adapting, strengthening or modifying existing facilities—deep subways, concrete and steel buildings, abandoned mines and caves, basement shelters—is a sensible one, and economically entirely feasible. It does not really meet the needs—but nothing, at present, does. A nationwide, government-supported system of deep shelters, involving huge costs, does not now appear to be worth the effort. For no one has resolved the problem of how to resume national life—how, indeed, to sustain individual life—after the bombs have burst, the fighting stopped and the survivors have emerged from the shelters to a ravaged and poisoned land. Civil defense is thus a part of any damage-limiting strategy, but its technology must be, for the time being at least, adaptive, experimental and developmental; it should not consume a major share of the defense budget; the money can be better spent for active, rather than passive, defensive measures.

The missile has become the major strategic weapon for both offense and defense. But it has not replaced the piloted aircraft.

The bomber—particularly the bomber mated to the missile—has an important technological future. Bombers, equipped with standoff missiles and capable of low-altitude flight profiles, already have a formidable offensive capability against present air defenses. The ranges and accuracies of air-to-ground missiles will increase, and, in time, an air-launched ballistic missile—a descendant of the ill-fated Skybolt—with 1,000-mile range will be in service. The bomber, as a missile-launching platform, will then come fully of

THIS WE MUST DEFEND

age, and will add a formidable and well-nigh invulnerable component to our deterrent capability. The air-launched missile will not
enjoy invisibility like the submarine, for modern radar will in time
extend its range through the air to tremendous distances. But the
bomber's speed and great mobility will enable it to "swim" nearly
anywhere in an ocean of air and to threaten enemy defenses from
any quarter. Its disadvantages will be the limited power of the
missile warhead, relative inaccuracy, very high costs and the necessity for frequent returns to vulnerable fixed bases for refueling,
maintenance and crew rotation. A nuclear-powered bomber, with
an indefinite airborne endurance, would reduce these disadvan
tages, but even so combat effectiveness would indicate a limited
commitment only.

But in addition to their important roles as missile platforms,
long-range bombers have other missions in future war. Under favorable conditions, because they can overfly the target, they can
deliver explosive loads more accurately than any other weapons
system. They are essential for poststrike reconnaissance. And, as
Vietnam has shown, the bomber is important in limited war. With
its huge load-carrying capacity, and its ability to bomb undetected
from great altitudes, the heavy bomber added tremendous power to
U.S. capabilities—power which must be retained tomorrow.

The categorical imperative of continental defense requires air
superiority—a defensive system against attack by piloted planes
which is strong enough to exact a very high toll—perhaps 60 to 90
percent—of any attacking force. Effective air defense today means
a long-range-warning capability against aircraft and air-breathing
missiles flying at any altitudes and a capability of destroying those
aircraft before they launch standoff missiles. A future air-defense
complex requires an integrated system of rapid communications,
ground-based long-range and control radar, antiaircraft missiles
and guns, AWACS (Airborne Warning and Control System) and
long-range interceptors with a "look-down-shoot-down" capability, i.e., airborne radar which can distinguish and track low-flying
aircraft and airborne weapons which can destroy such planes.

There is a final essential element of continental defense which,
properly developed, can add materially to the capability and credi-

99

bility of a damage-limiting strategy, and hence to the deterrent. It is a sea-based defensive system—first against enemy submarines and submarine- or ship-launched missiles, second against enemy land-based missiles. The factor of redundancy—the capability of a defensive system designed for one purpose to be applied to an additional purpose—aids this defense; for instance, both antiaircraft and antiballistic missile systems can be utilized against sea-launched missiles. But the basic requirement is early warning, and the opaque character of the sea and the dependence of the defense primarily upon sound to penetrate the sea's depths make adequate early warning difficult.

Fortunately, we are aided by geography: all Soviet submarines, in transit to open waters—except those based on Petropavlovsk in Kamchatka—must pass through relatively narrow sea passages, where the detection problem is eased. Antisubmarine barriers—fixed sound and electronic installations, submarines, surface ships, and land-based and sea-based aircraft—can provide reasonably accurate surveillance. Sensitive hydrophones in fixed positions in deep water, beneath the ocean's thermal layers, can literally "hear" the sound of a submarine's propellers thousands of miles away. Arrays of these listening devices in deep water off the continental shelf, off the British Isles and at other points around the world transmit the sounds they pick up—and the directions from which the sounds came—by cables to recorders and computers ashore. Comparison of the signals can provide rough fixes of the source of the sound and also indicate its nature—Soviet nuclear submarine, tramp steamer, U.S. submarine or what not. Passive sonar arrays of this type have been in use for some time, and although their findings are not precise, they have proved themselves an indispensable part of the complex defense required against modern submarines.

But probably the best defense against an enemy missile submarine is another submarine, faster, more maneuverable, quieter. An effective defense against enemy missile submarines—given the present state of the art—appears to mean a U.S. submarine "tailing" each of the enemy missile subs. (This also appears to be the Soviet "answer" to our missile submarines.)

SABMIS (Ship-based Antiballistic Missile System) promises another technological exploitation of the medium of the sea to strengthen any U.S. damage-limiting strategy. SABMIS simply envisages a seagoing version of an antiballistic missile system. The Army's Sprint or Spartan, or both, modified for shipboard launching, and the huge radars and computers that control them, would be built into one or more surface ships. These ships would then patrol in forward positions—far from U.S. shores—beneath the ballistic trajectories that any land-based missiles fired against the United States or our allies would have to follow. The concept has tremendous importance. It would provide antiballistic missile defense in depth—a forward intercept zone provided by the SABMIS; two land-based terminal intercept zones provided by Spartan and Sprint. The ship-based system, moreover, might make possible the interception of enemy missiles in mid-course—even, in some cases, in launch phases of the trajectory before multiple warheads separated to start their individually guided courses toward different targets. If such a concept should prove technologically feasible, a strong defense against ballistic missiles might be possible. But the technological problems are major and costs will be high.

It is thus clear that the adequate application of a modern maritime strategy to control of the aerospace-sea environment around us will not be cheap or easy. Indeed, no formula for the defense of the United States can yield more than a relative security. But today the nuclear threat posits such a menace to the very life of the nation that constant vigilance, the highest possible degree of military readiness and maximum sustained strength are vital. For the first time in American history since the days of the Indian Wars we face "open" frontiers. For the first time since the early settlers built watchtowers and wooden walls around their towns, the United States has had to build "stockades" around its coasts. For the first time since the pioneers plowed their fields with their guns under their arms, we go about our business with "hot-gunned" fighters roaring over our heads and missiles pointed ever skyward.

We have achieved by these efforts only a relative security; so far, any potential enemy has reckoned that the game is not worth the candle; the cost of aggression would be too great. But deterrents do not remain static, and any strategic concept is no better than the

101

"hardware"—in terms of weapons systems and the will to use them —that backs it.

Today the United States faces a period of unprecedented peril. Russia had in operation or in construction in early 1970 launching sites for about 1,500 intercontinental ballistic missiles (450 more than the U.S.), more than 300 of them sites for the giant SS-9 missile which can carry a 9-to-25-megaton warhead (the Minuteman carries a 1-megaton warhead). Contruction and expansion in numbers is continuing at high speed. Dr. John S. Foster, Jr., the Defense Department's Director of Research and Engineering, has estimated that some 420 SS-9's, each carrying three 4-to-5-megaton MIRV's, each with a quarter-mile accuracy (well within the Soviet state of the art), could destroy about 95 percent of our 1,000 land-based Minutemen. Russia can achieve this capability in three years or less. At the same time she is constructing at unprecedented rates large numbers of high-speed nuclear-powered attack submarines in efforts to produce a fleet of submersibles that could "saturate" our sea-based missile system by shadowing our missile submarines in the depths of the sea.

Professor Albert Wohlstetter of the University of Chicago, in statements to a Senate subcommittee, stressed the technological challenge of tomorrow:

> The stereotype repeated throughout the 1960's that our security has declined while our strategic force grew at an accelerating rate is grossly wrong on both counts.
>
> In the past some key programs increased the protected second-strike capacity of the force, while cutting at the same time billions of dollars from the spending projected, and our security is much greater in the 1960's, since we have protected and made more responsive our strategic force.
>
> In the 1970's, unless we continue to make appropriate decisions to meet technological change, once again the viability of a large part of our second-strike force will be put in question. Several related innovations, but in particular the development of a rocket booster carrying many re-entry vehicles (MIRV's), raise once again the possibility of attack ratios favoring the attacker.[7]

102

To retain a relative security, to convince any enemy of the credibility of our deterrent, will require constant change. Obsolescence will doom some elements of any defensive system; excessive costs for marginal gains will kill others aborning.

But there is one constant in any formula for defense. The United States is doomed unless its military technology—its basic scientific and technical know-how, and its applied development—is second to none, and unless this technology is persistently and imaginatively applied to the fundamental mission of retaining superiority at sea and in the air.

The Union of Soviet Socialist Republics has clearly understood this priority and has translated it into the greatest challenge the United States has ever faced. Moscow already has adopted a maritime-aerospace strategy, and in the past decade she has achieved not only a global high-seas posture of strength but a nuclear capability in many ways superior to our own. The hour is later than most Americans realize.

The "heartland" of the United States defense—the inner ramparts that must be strongly held in the Western Hemisphere—include Alaska and the Aleutians, the Canadian Arctic islands, particularly Baffin Island, Greenland, all of continental North America and the sea-land-air space of the Caribbean, Mexico and Central America through Venezuela and northern Colombia. The outer ramparts include the rest of the South American continent and its outlying islands. The hump of Brazil, a dominant feature in South Atlantic strategy, represents a major bastion in these outer ramparts, important to control of South Atlantic maritime routes —the shipping lanes around the Cape of Good Hope and the Horn.

The Falkland Islands, southern Argentina and Chile have assumed a new importance in the missile age as potential sites for radar and early-warning stations against the threat of "wrong-way" over-the-South-Pole missiles and the FOBS (Fractional Orbital Bombardment System).

The Arctic Ocean and its bordering land masses represent to the United States a new strategic frontier. The Arctic's frozen surfaces no longer bar navigation; nuclear-powered missile submarines can

103

now cruise beneath the ice, surface in a *polynya*—a "lake" or rift or hole in the ice—and launch their missiles. Long-range bombers can leap above the Pole. The most direct air-missile routes to the United States approach the nation across the North Atlantic, Arctic, Alaska and Greenland.

Long before the era of the missile, General "Billy" Mitchell foresaw—and somewhat exaggerated—the strategic importance of Alaska as an offensive and defensive air complex, and as a dominant flanking position to the Pacific great-circle shipping routes. Today, in our smaller world of modern technology, Alaska represents only a part, though a major part, of our northern ramparts. Its vast land mass (about one-fifth the size of the continental United States); sparse population (about 241,000 people); oil and mineral wealth; proximity to Soviet Siberia and to the shortest great-circle air and shipping routes to Japan; and its buffer geographic position relative to U.S. centers of population and industry give Alaska a strategic importance to the United States unmatched by any other Arctic land area. This importance is enhanced by the fact that it is one of the fifty states of the Union; it is the only Arctic territory under the U.S. flag, and hence military installations on its soil are not subject to the political, psychological and economic disadvantages of U.S. bases on foreign soil.

Alaska's present fundamental importance—as a key link in our early-warning system—may somewhat, but not greatly, diminish with development of over-the-horizon, long-range radar, airborne early-warning systems and other monitors. But the BMEWS (Ballistic Missile Early Warning System) station at Clear, Alaska, which complements similar stations at Thule, Greenland, and Flyingdale Moors, England, will probably remain an essential backstop to any other system. The so-called DEW (Distant Early Warning) Line of radar stations for detection of enemy bombers, extending from the Aleutians, around Alaska, across Canada and down through Greenland to Newfoundland, is being superseded by new technology and is being modified or thinned out. But the early-warning coverage which Alaska offers to the Pacific Northwest, Canada and much of the Northern and Western United States is still essential to the overlapping pattern of monitoring now provided by the three great BMEWS stations.

Alaska's great airfields also provide forward bases for reconnaissance and intelligence missions of high importance to the nation's over-all security. The state's geographic location close to Siberia, dominating the Pacific exit of the Soviet Arctic Sea route, and athwart the prevailing winds from west to east, make it an ideal intelligence platform for electronic monitoring, observation of the Soviet Kamchatka missile range, sampling of radioactivity vented in Soviet underground atomic tests, and in ice patrol and antishipping patrols.

Alaska, with its long appendage of the Aleutian Islands, is a forward observation post and first line of defense against Soviet bases at Vladivostok, Nikolayevsk and in Kamchatka.

In addition to its sentinel role, Alaska is important as an offensive-defensive area which, properly exploited, could checkmate and neutralize Soviet missile installations across the Bering Strait and in much of Siberia. Much of Alaska is still a wilderness. The bulk of its population is clustered around two cities, Anchorage and Fairbanks. Its mountains and forests offer, from the purely geographic military point of view, ideal sites for medium- and long-range missile emplacements, far from great industries and densely populated areas, yet close to potential enemy installations. But the military advantages of remoteness and sparsity of population, unequalled by any other land area under the American flag, are reduced by the high construction and maintenance costs these very factors —and the rigorous climate of Alaska—impose. The cost factor militates against turning Alaska into any vast missile base, nor are extensive installations there necessary or desirable.

But its unique military advantages do warrant the construction of a limited number of missile sites in the interior, despite the extra costs involved. Air bases already provide dispersion capabilities for our bombers; in the missile age a region like Alaska with few people and great open spaces is a strategic "dream." These missiles would provide some clear-cut advantages: dispersion of our deterrent force; a defensive discouragement to any Soviet build-up in the Alaskan area; a counter to Soviet missiles in Siberia.

The defense of Alaska against non-nuclear attack has been, and will almost certainly continue to be, based upon control of the seas and the maintenance of a so-called insular theory of defense. The important populated areas of Fairbanks and Anchorage, surrounded by air bases and military installations, are viewed as islands in a sea of snow and muskeg to be defended by planes and airborne troops. The perimeter of the state is considered an outpost or warning line.

Because of the narrow width of the Bering Strait and the proximity of the Soviet Chukchi Peninsula and the military complex of Kamchatka, the Fairbanks-Anchorage "islands" must be defended by highly ready mobile ground forces, by well-disposed antiaircraft missiles and guns, and by fighter-interceptors, operating in some cases from advanced bases. The present garrison of two small brigades of ground troops, one disposed near each of the "island" cities, is adequate as a permanent force, provided: (1) there is an instant backup available by air transport from the strategic reserve in the continental United States; (2) the two brigades are excellently equipped and trained and acclimated to operations in wild terrain and severe climate; and (3) helicopters and transport aircraft are available within Alaska, capable of moving the troops quickly to any point within the state. There can be no real fear of serious ground invasion of the "Lower Forty-eight," or of Canada, by way of Alaska, though the Russians conceivably might well mount a ground diversion there (as the Japanese did in the Aleutians in World War II). The ground communications are too sparse, the terrain too rugged, the climate too difficult; any army that landed in Alaska with its objective Seattle might ultimately reach Seattle, but not as an army—merely as half-frozen, ragged, defeated prisoners of war.

The conventional threat, in other words, is not massive invasion —despite the short distance across the Bering Strait. In Alaska the United States has the tremendous advantage of the "interior" military position, operating on shorter supply lines; the Russians must move around the arc of a circle over far greater distances from their main supply bases. The threat, therefore, is quiet, perhaps covert, infiltration by small groups of individuals; sabotage of key installations such as BMEWS; or a deliberate diversion. The perimeter

106

early-warning monitoring systems the United States now mans, supplemented by long-range ground and air patrols and reconnaissance and by Eskimo and Indian National Guard scouts, all backed by the fighter squadrons and brigades at Fairbanks and Anchorage, provide an adequate defense.

In the age of BMEWS, over-the-horizon radar and satellite early-warning systems, the Canadian Arctic has less importance to continental defense than it did when the Distant Early Warning Line of conventional radar was erected in the 1950's. A few forward airstrips, capable of handling fighters and troop transports, are useful in meeting the threat of air or airborne attack. The base at Frobisher Bay, Baffin Island, commands the Hudson Strait, entrance to Hudson Bay, and the Davis Strait, and, with bases in Labrador and Newfoundland, is important for ice patrol and maritime patrol. Thule, in Greenland, site of a great BMEWS station, is also potentially important as a dispersal base for long-range bombers.

Continental defense, in the age of missiles, must start well beyond our frontiers. The Denmark Strait, between Greenland and Iceland, the Iceland-Faeroes "gap," and the sea passages between the Faeroes and the United Kingdom are sortie routes for Soviet submarines, transiting from their bases to missile patrol, or anti-shipping stations. Iceland is a key flanking approach to the North American continent, highly important as an early-warning position and as a base for antisubmarine and shipping patrols. The sea passages it commands require now—in this age of "two scorpions in a bottle"—surveillance above, on and under the sea.

With modern underwater hydrophone arrays, monitoring cables, radar and antisubmarine "barriers" (planes, surface ships, submarines), surveillance of these narrow sea passages can be highly effective—but no more effective than the utilization we make of the natural geographic advantages we enjoy. These straits are, indeed, the key to the North Atlantic; unless we monitor them in peacetime, we could be surprised in time of crisis; unless we dominate them in war, our lines of supply to Europe could be severed, or, at worst, we might be defeated and devastated.

In the broad reaches of the North Atlantic, the Portuguese

Azores and British Bermuda represent island outpost lines for continental defense, of value in antisubmarine and antishipping patrols, as early-warning stations and as emergency staging bases for transport aircraft.

To the United States, the Caribbean Sea–Gulf of Mexico–Panama Canal area, with its great wind-swept waters, its exotic island archipelagoes, its agricultural and mineral wealth, is of major importance to continental defense. It is the nexus of the shipping lanes of the world; the oil of Venezuela, the bauxite of Jamaica, the manganese of Brazil, the copper of Chile, tin, iron ore, fibers, coffee, bananas and sugar move through its waters to the United States. It dominates not only north-south trade with Latin America, but east-west trade from Western Europe and the Eastern coastal ports of the United States to Western ports and the Pacific.

The obsolescent Panama Canal cannot today handle many of the modern Navy's great ships or the larger tankers or ore ships. Nevertheless the nuclear submarine, the smaller carriers and all smaller ships can transit it, and in time a more adequate canal—at sea level or with tidal locks—will replace it somewhere in Central America. Effective physical (or military) control of that canal is a basic requirement of an adequate continental defense position. The United States must be able to deny the canal to the ships of any potential enemy in times of war and crisis, and it must be able to utilize the canal to shuttle men-of-war quickly between the oceans, but above all for logistic and supply purposes. During the Vietnam war approximately 98 percent of the tonnage shipped to Vietnam was carried in ships' bottoms. Of this amount about 33 percent was loaded in East and Gulf coast ports and was shipped to Vietnam via the Panama Canal.

The Caribbean Sea and its fringing islands command the Atlantic approaches to any Central American canal, to the Gulf of Mexico and to the Southeastern coast of the United States. If any of its islands or surrounding land masses should come under the domination of a major hostile power, the continental ramparts would be breached and, under certain conditions—as the Cuban missile crisis of 1962 demonstrated—a deadly, indeed a vital, danger to the

108

security of the United States might develop. Alternatively, a Communist-dominated Caribbean nation posits the threat of creeping conquest; it could be a focal infection spot used for the export of Communism to Latin America.

Because of the proximity of the area to the continental United States and our developed strength, an overt military challenge to the Monroe Doctrine by Russia or any other potential power—in the form of *military conquest or the deliberate construction of a foreign air-sea missile base*—is unlikely, though not impossible. It occurred once, it could occur again. In any case, Communist domination of any of the countries of the area poses a major political problem to the United States, causes a diversion of a portion of our military strength, requires constant watchfulness and, as the technological revolution continues, poses some worrisome security problems.

Castro's Communist Government in Cuba—supported by, and supporting, Moscow—illustrates the problem graphically.

Strength, size and position give Cuba a strategic potential as the most important single island in the Caribbean area. It commands the "strategic chokepoint" of the Windward Passage—main entrance to the Caribbean for Atlantic shipping—and it lies athwart the Florida Straits. From the perspective of the United States, it has military operational utility.

The United States Naval Base at Guantánamo Bay, known to generations of Americans as "Gitmo," is a 45-square-mile, $76 million investment. It has two airstrips, including an 8,000-foot strip for jets, one of the best naval anchorages in the Carribean and 1,400 buildings. Normally about 4,000 to 6,000 Americans are stationed there, and another 4,000 to 5,000 are aboard ships of the fleet operating from Gitmo, while almost 1,600 civil service employees work in the shops.

Since the Spanish-American War, the base at Guantánamo has been developed into perhaps the most important naval facility outside our shores in the Western Hemisphere. The base has liabilities. The army of civil workers who operate its facilities and the 24 miles of fence line and 10 miles of seacoast make the base's internal-security problem a complex one. Sabotage and terrorism would be

109

difficult though not impossible to meet. The base has no fresh-water supply of its own. Water used to be piped from a pumping station on the Yateras River, four miles outside the reservation, to tanks on the base. In early 1964 this supply was cut off by Castro. Washington reacted by cutting the Yateras River pipeline permanently, importing water by tankers, and ordering the base to make itself self-sufficient in water supply by construction of a desalinization plant, well-digging and other means. The base is now fully capable of getting along without the Yateras River supply. Finally, high Cuban hills outside the reservation dominate parts of the base. If Soviet-type antiship missiles or long-range artillery were emplaced on these hills, it might well make the airstrips unusable and the anchorage in the bay untenable for ships.

Again, this theoretical advantage to Castro is more than compensated for by the liabilities that would be incurred if this gambit were actually used. Denial of the use of the base to our ships and planes could be no more than temporary and would mean open hostilities, which would immediately expose Cuba to massive (conventional) assault. As a matter of fact, the Marine garrison at Guantánamo has long had plans to seize the dominating hill masses close by if Castro should press the button.

So much for the military limitations of Gitmo. Its military assets are of three types.

It is an important training base used by all ships in the Atlantic at one time or another for shakedown and refresher training. A Fleet Training Group, Atlantic, under the Commander in Chief, Atlantic, is based at Guantánamo to aid ship training. As a training base it is complemented by the newer base at Roosevelt Roads, Puerto Rico (and nearby Vieques). Modern missile ships use the longer-firing ranges available outside Roosevelt Roads. Guantánamo is, of course, replaceable as a training base, but it has many facilities that Roosevelt Roads presently lacks, and these could be duplicated in Puerto Rico only at high cost.

In addition to its training and fleet-support role, Guantánamo Bay has logistical or supply importance. It has naval and air supply and repair facilities unavailable at any other Caribbean base, and it offers a staging base for fighter aircraft, or troop-carrying or cargo

110

aircraft, en route from the United States to Latin America. Guantánamo's strategic location makes it an extremely useful (though not indispensable) base in any limited war or for the basing of reserve power in any crisis or quasi-war situation (similar to the crises of 1963 in the Dominican Republic and Haiti). Its usefulness would vary, of course, depending upon the area of crisis. In World War II it was a convoy port, where Atlantic and Caribbean convoys made up and sortied. Antisubmarine and shipping surveillance patrol planes of the Navy still base intermittently at Gitmo. Guantánamo Bay is one of the links in a chain of bases including Florida, Roosevelt Roads (Puerto Rico), and Chaguaramos (Trinidad). In a time of limited war this chain would permit the United States to control the Caribbean–Gulf of Mexico area, maintain surveillance of all shipping in the area and protect the Atlantic approaches to the Panama Canal.

In nuclear war Guantánamo Bay would have little utility except as a dispersal port for U.S. naval power. Like the Panama Canal, for which it acts as a link in the Atlantic defenses, the base would play virtually no role in an all-out nuclear interchange. (The canal itself, for that matter, could be blocked or hopelessly wrecked by one well-placed nuclear warhead.) Potentially Gitmo could be useful as a ballistic-missile early-warning station if the need should arise to establish such stations to cover the southern approaches to the United States. However, other more favorable locations might be found for the giant radars required. The base could also be used to provide early warning of enemy aircraft and as a link in the undersea sound-detection system, to provide early warning of the approach to our coasts of enemy missile submarines.

Guantánamo's usefulness as a base is thus of optimum importance in limited-war situations or in cold war crises, particularly in situations involving conflict, or the risk of conflict, in any of the Caribbean countries. Since the political stability of these countries is at best dubious, and since Washington has repeatedly felt compelled to undertake armed intervention in the Caribbean, this consideration is of obvious importance.

Finally, Guantánamo Bay has a political importance to the United States that transcends its military usefulness. The treaty

111

(last reaffirmed in 1934) that governs our use of the base is remarkably similar to the treaty that underlies our rights in the Canal Zone. We enjoy in the area of the base "complete jurisdiction and control"—or the *de facto* exercise of sovereign rights—over almost 29,000 acres of land and water. "Ultimate sovereignty" (not defined in the treaty) is Cuban, but our "complete jurisdiction and control" continue indefinitely unless the United States "abandons" the base or formally agrees with Cuba to revision of the treaty terms. The treaty cannot be revised or abrogated by Cuba alone; it requires mutual consent.

Revision of the treaty terms for Guantánamo will inevitably lead to revisionism elsewhere—in Panama, in Trinidad, globally. What happens to Guantánamo will profoundly influence what happens to the Canal Zone, to our base in Trinidad and, indeed, to our bases all over the world, and particularly to our position in Latin America. United States power and prestige are involved in Gitmo, whether we like it or not.

But Cuba, to the United States, is more than a naval base at Guantánamo Bay. The "presence" and cooperation of a friendly Cuban government on the island have major military implications in Latin America. Some Latin-American leaders are openly ambivalent; they publicly decry the Castro leadership but privately admire the man who has successfully defied the majesty and power of the United States. Cuba can be an example, a bellwether. The political importance of Cuba is obvious, but the military implications of a friendly government there are too often overlooked. A friendly government would mean the denial to any potential enemy of the military and political advantages (many of them potential, some actual) that now accrue to such an enemy through the Fidel Castro regime. The cooperation of a friendly government in Cuba would mean elimination of a base for a hostile power. What are the possibile military uses to the U.S.S.R. of a Communist Cuba? There are six primary uses:

*1. Missile base.* First and most important, in the global equation of power, is the potential utility of Cuba as a missile and/or aircraft base. It would be a mistake to overestimate this importance, but it would also be a mistake to underestimate it.

Soviet missiles in Cuba in 1962 accomplished a number of purposes:

They were emplaced on our southern periphery, where radar and missile early warning were weak or completely lacking.

These emplacements brought within enemy firing range most of SAC's bomber bases, many of our air-defense installations and many of our land-based missile sites. Their presence, even though they were never fired, tended to alter, though not to overturn, the balance of strategic power by neutralizing some of these sites.

The nation's great cities were brought within easy missile range by the Cuban sites. Some of these cities were already threatened by Russian-based ICBM's. Our cities thus became double hostages to Moscow, even though Moscow itself would have been doomed by the long-range power of the United States.

Cuban-based missiles and, to a lesser extent, long-range aircraft with atomic bombs made our defensive task more difficult. Above all, they brought a sharp new awareness of terror and threat to the American mainland—an awareness of nuclear danger that had not existed in the public mind to anything like the same degree before the Cuban missile crisis.

What of the future?

Most intelligence agencies and military men believe (though they cannot provide 100 percent proof) that the Soviet nuclear-tipped MRBM's (Medium Range Ballistic Missiles) and IRBM's (Intermediate Range Ballistic Missiles) that produced the 1962 missile crisis were actually removed from Cuba.

But caves on the island are known to be packed with military equipment of various sorts, and if missiles are not included in these below-ground inventories today, it is perfectly possible that they may be tomorrow. All the missiles that played their brief role in the limelight of world crisis in 1962 were liquid-fueled missiles. Liquid-fueled missiles require a relatively long countdown and must be supported by fairly complex fueling trucks and facilities. The 2,200-mile missile requires permanent installations and lengthy construction. But the Soviet 1,000-mile mobile ballistic missile was described by Secretary of Defense Robert S. McNamara as capable of being moved from one site to another and re-emplaced within six days. Other sources have since estimated that these mobile Russian missiles—like the German V-2, which could be launched from any hard, flat and level area—might be emplaced in sixteen to eighteen hours.

Even if these estimates represent an exaggeration, it is certain that future generations of Soviet mobile missiles will, like our own, be fueled by solid propellants or stable, storable liquids. Solid fuel reduces the time for countdown and also eliminates a complex of fueling trucks, volatile liquids and pumping systems. It makes the missile more mobile, easier to conceal and far easier to move about and to emplace. If such missiles, with their simplified supporting equipment, were transported to Cuba and carefully hidden, it is quite conceivable that they could be removed from concealment under cover of darkness and erected ready for firing in predetermined positions by the following dawn or soon after. This rather dreadful potentiality, it should be emphasized, is not an actuality today, but it is well within the capabilities of Soviet military science in future years.

Cuban missile sites would provide other benefits from the Russian point of view. They would increase geographic dispersion of Communist missile bases and oblige the United States to allocate some of its nuclear-deterrent forces to neutralize them. They would be so close to U.S. shores that some of the fallout from our own counterattacking weapons might be disseminated in the United States. And since accuracy is, to a degree, a factor of range, the closeness of Cuban missile sites to their targets would ensure more hits.

All these advantages might be nullified, in a strictly military sense, in some future time, by technological developments. When Russia has acquired a large fleet of nuclear-propelled, missile-firing submarines and has constructed many heavily protected easily concealed launching sites for solid-fueled ICBM's on her own soil, the cost-effectiveness equation (particularly the difficulties of logistics) might dictate the permanent abandonment of Cuba as a potential Soviet missile site. But this time is not yet at hand. And even then a Cuban base for Soviet missile submarines would ease Russian logistic problems and would enable Moscow to maintain a larger number of submarines on patrol off our coast.

Soviet bombers based in Cuba would offer less of a threat, though a tangible one. Bombers are harder to conceal than missiles. Even if underground hangars were available (at great cost), long adjacent airstrips would be necessary for take-off. Surprise by air attack based on Cuba is entirely possible, as recent undetected penetrations of the Florida air space by Cuban planes have shown. But our defense against piloted aircraft is well developed, and speed and altitude limitations of the plane would make this threat a far less dangerous one than that of the missile.

A mobile strike force of conventional ground forces, with their paraphernalia of equipment—tanks, artillery, rockets and perhaps tactical nuclear weapons—would have very little chance of achieving surprise, or even of moving far beyond Cuba's shores. The necessary concentration of troop-carrying aircraft or of amphibious and naval shipping required to transport the troops beyond Cuban waters would signal any attack far in advance.

Thus Cuba, as a potential missile base, still offers to Russia some important military advantages—particularly now that Russian nuclear-delivery capability approaches parity with the United States. The actual utilization of this potential by Moscow would probably be considered by the Communists to involve unacceptable political and military risks, unless there was virtual certainty in Moscow that the missiles could be secretly transported to, and concealed in, Cuba pending the time when they might serve a political or psychological or even a military purpose on the chessboard of world conflict.

Thus, in sum, utilization of Cuba as a missile base by the U.S.S.R. would clearly be within the future military and technical competence of the Russians, but missiles in Cuba would imply a willingness on Moscow's part to accept the risks of global nuclear war.

2. *Naval base.* The second, and probably far more likely, potential utilization of a Communist Cuba by Russia is as a naval and submarine base or refueling and replenishment station. Announcement has already been made, though without many details, that

Soviet Russia would aid Cuba in the development of a port and facilities for fishing fleets. Russian trawlers, as well as Cuban fishing vessels, are using Cuban ports. About a dozen Soviet trawlers are intermittently based on the island. During the missile crisis of 1962 there was a considerable concentration of Soviet submarines off Cuba, and there have been persistent but unconfirmed reports since then that one or more Soviet destroyers or submarines were to be transferred to the Cuban Navy. Soviet naval vessels have made an unprecedented visit to Cuban waters.

A fueling facility for submarines, trawlers and small craft, and machine shops capable of making minor repairs (the shops in the U.S. Naval Base at Guantánamo Bay are the best on the island), are an entirely feasible development and could be mutually beneficial, both economically and militarily, to the U.S.S.R. and Cuba. Such a "base" would permit Soviet vessels, and particularly Soviet missile submarines, to remain on station in Western Hemisphere waters for far longer cycles than if those vessels were limited to Soviet mainland bases or to refueling tankers at sea.

The U.S.S.R. has transferred a sizable number of *Komar-* and *Osa*-type missile torpedo boats to Cuba. These high-speed craft have a deadly sting (as the sinking of the Israeli destroyer *Elath* showed). Their limited range and sea-keeping capability are, however, sufficient to permit patrol of the Cuban coast and the contiguous narrow passages into the Caribbean; they could force the rerouting of shipping in time of crisis, and they certainly add to the pre-emptive value of Castro's and Moscow's diplomacy.

*3. Intelligence center.* The third potential importance of a Communist Cuba to Russia is as an intelligence base, or center, for the open and secret collection of information of all sorts about the United States and the Caribbean. Cuba is ideally situated for such a purpose. Vital shipping lanes skirt its shores, and visual reconnaissance from Cuba can easily check the types, nationalities and sizes of ships that pass. Nearby are Cape Kennedy and the U.S. Atlantic Missile Range, used for both military and civilian earth satellite and space shots and for missile testing of Polaris, Minuteman and other military missiles. Electronic monitoring of the extensive radio and radar transmissions needed for such a range has undoubtedly been

116

conducted from Cuban-based "listening" stations for some time. Indeed, the Russians could, if they wished, erect a large radar in Cuba that would provide them with much the same type of information about missile launchings, trajectories and ranges that is provided the United States by giant radars in Turkey and the Aleutians.

Soviet trawlers with electronic equipment have long been prowling the Florida coast and, indeed, the entire Atlantic coast. These are equipped with recording devices that transcribe all military electronic transmissions from United States radar or radio stations and detect the "pulse rate," frequency and location of such stations. Some of these trawlers are based in Cuba. Aircraft based in Cuba are capable of overflying parts of the American Southeast and of photographic reconnaissance. (Soviet commercial flights to Cuba already skirt our coasts.)

Finally, Cuba offers an ideal base for the infiltration of intelligence agents or "spies" of various kinds (mixed, for instance, among legitimate refugees) to the United States mainland, to Puerto Rico, to other Caribbean islands or to Central and South America. Cuba is being used actively as a Russian intelligence outpost today; unquestionably, its most important intelligence function is the monitoring of U.S. missile-range transmissions and of U.S. military radio and radar stations.

*4. Tracking station.* Another possible use of the Cuban island position by Russia is as a site for instrumentation, control and communications equipment for Soviet space shots. Heretofore Russian monitoring and control stations have either been entirely within the boundaries of the Soviet Union or based aboard ship. Today Russia is reportedly building a space-tracking station in Cuba.

*5. Base for subversion.* As a Communist base in the heart of the Western Hemisphere, Cuba is useful to Russian Communism as a base for the export of subversion, propaganda, sabotage and guerrillas. The island has already been used as such a base in a small degree; the troubles in Venezuela and, to some extent, in Bolivia, Chile and Panama can be traced in part to influences emanating from Cuba. As such a base, Cuba represents a threat to the unstable

117

regimes and poverty-stricken volatile masses of the Caribbean islands (including U.S. Puerto Rico) and Central America in particular, and to all of Latin America in general. With its inadequate sea power and its proximity to the overpowering sea and air power of the United States, Cuba poses little danger of a formal large-scale or organized invasion of another country. But a tramp steamer or a submarine or a fishing vessel or a plane can easily carry a platoon of men. There is no possible way, short of complete blockade and "search-and-seizure," to prevent the infiltration of other Latin-American countries by small groups of hard-core Communists, highly trained in the specialties of sabotage and subversion, of propaganda and guerrilla war, and of inciting revolution and overthrowing governments. Nor is there any way to stop gun-running from Cuba, as a base, to other countries of the hemisphere. Today Cuba is serving this Russian purpose well. It is a training base for many Latin-American specialists in revolution and ferment—a staging base, to be used, when needed, for the expansion of Communism in the Western Hemisphere.

*6. Military diversion.* There is, finally, for Russia the military diversionary value of Cuba. This would be of most importance were Cuba to become a well-developed missile base, for in such a case it would be absolutely essential for the United States to earmark a sizable part of its strategic power to eliminate the Cuban missile sites before their missiles could be launched. In limited war, or in times of mobilization for crisis elsewhere, Cuba could divert a sizable portion of our ready strength long enough to "foul up" time schedules and influence other operations. Even with no imminent crisis in sight, and all missiles supposedly removed, Cuba today diverts fractional but important elements of our military strength in many different forms.

Surveillance by maritime patrol aircraft of shipping bound to and from Cuba requires the more or less constant use of at least one (sometimes several) U.S. naval patrol planes. It also necessitates a careful global reporting system that tabulates, when known, the cargoes and ports of call of all Soviet bloc ships that call at the island.

Photoreconnaissance—in the absence of on-the-spot inspection, which neither Fidel Castro nor the Russians have ever granted—is obviously of vital importance, as the missile crisis of 1962 showed. Photorecon flights have, however, certain limitations and liabilities. Comparative chronological photographs of the same area can reveal unusual activity, or new installations on the surface, sometimes even if camouflaged, but they cannot reveal what is stored underground, or carefully hidden in warehouses, buildings or dense forests. In view of the rapidity with which modern missiles can be erected, frequent flights would be required if Washington was to guard itself fully against another nasty surprise similar to that of September and October, 1962. For no one flight, even at high altitude, can possibly cover the entire island of Cuba adequately. Repeated and relatively frequent flights are necessary for full coverage. Thus Cuba as a Russian base diverts the efforts of the Strategic Air Command's photoreconnaissance aircraft, which make what the Pentagon euphemistically calls "periodic" flights near, and over, the island. To provide the low-level photos that are essential to accurate interpretation of any telltale signs the high-level mosaics may yield, several Navy, Marine, and Air Force high-speed jet photorecon planes must always be available. These planes have not, however, been used over Cuba for months, a fact that reduces our intelligence capability and increases our risks.

There is a political liability and increased risk in the use of low-level flights: Our aircraft would fly within easy range of Russian and Cuban antiaircraft guns, and would be so obvious to Castro's armed forces that he would probably charge aggression. Despite these political and psychological liabilities, low-level and night reconnaissance may, at some future time, be necessary if intelligence estimates indicate that Russia has developed very mobile, quickly emplaced solid-fueled or storable-liquid-fueled missiles.

Because of the political and psychological liabilities of too thorough photoreconnaissance, the United States must supplement in Cuba its "seeing-eye" aircraft with one of the most intensive intelligence efforts mounted by this country against any single objective. This must take many forms: electronic intelligence; monitoring of all radio and radar transmissions from Cuba; raids by refugees or agents; operation of spies or agents within Cuba; and infiltration by small parties of armed men, with intelligence, sabotage or guerrilla missions, into Cuba. The Central Intelligence Agency and the armed services must participate in these activities —the former on what may be a substantial scale, with its own "fishing vessels," speedboats and aircraft.

Since Fidel Castro came to power in Cuba, and particularly since Russia began to utilize Cuba for military purposes, the United States has constantly maintained a naval amphibious squadron with a reinforced Marine battalion landing team (about 1,700 men) in the Caribbean or close to it. The Marines are either aboard ship cruising within a few hours of Cuba or at Vieques, an island near Puerto Rico. This force can be useful, of course, as contemporary history has shown, in any trouble spot in the Caribbean, but its focus is Cuba. The garrison of Guantánamo has also been somewhat strengthened. Behind these first-line units, the Army, the Navy and the Marines maintain alert forces ready for quick transportation by sea or by air to the Caribbean area. And along the Florida coast, particularly from Key West to north of Miami, radar stations and air-defense facilities have had to be strengthened, and some of the nation's best fighter-interceptors have been assigned to the area.

What the collective manpower total and dollar cost of all these precautions amount to is the Pentagon's secret. But even measured against the gargantuan yardstick of the defense budget, it is not insignificant. Cuba as a Russian-equipped base costs us many millions annually, and it demands a diversion of a sizable fraction of our most specialized and skilled forces to what is essentially a static, defensive task on our own doorstep.

The most discouraging and ominous part of this military equation from the American point of view is that Russia, with very little additional effort (perhaps even feigned effort), can force the United States to raise the ante considerably. A sudden increase in the number of Soviet ships sent to Cuba, unusual engineering work in Cuba's mountains, overt displays of strengthened military power, the threat of new missiles, and the eruption of trouble fostered by infiltrators trained in Cuba, in other Caribbean islands or in Central America would necessitate the immediate allocation of additional United States military power to the Caribbean area. In this game

THIS WE MUST DEFEND

Russia holds the cards. Moscow can play it hard or soft and force our effort to ebb or flow with her actions. We cannot—and must not —forget that in the fall of 1962 some forty-odd missiles and perhaps (at a maximum) 40,000 Russians forced the mobilization and concentration by the United States of more than half a million soldiers, sailors, Marines and airmen. All this suggests that the island of Cuba, by virtue of geography (and recently by virtue of the Russian transfusions of military power), is of long-term and continuing importance in Caribbean, hemispheric and global strategy.

The Cuban situation alone, even if exploited as fully as possible by Moscow, could not alter the global balance of power. The superior power position of the United States does not depend upon what happens in Cuba. But a Cuba developed as a Soviet base could be one important element in the world equation of power. A strong Soviet military position in Cuba could divert sizable segments of U.S. military strength, could neutralize some of our nuclear retaliatory capability and could thus become an important political pawn in, for instance, another Berlin crisis.

Cuba is not vital to us as a base. But unless future U.S. security is to suffer a continuous and unpredictable series of alarms and retreats, it should be denied as a base to any potential enemy. Under certain circumstances—the discovery of Soviet long-range missiles on the island, for instance—immediate military invasion by the United States might be necessary. Other circumstances, such as a major increase in the export of arms, saboteurs and terrorists to Latin America, might require less stringent, but definite, action, such as a partial blockade. In any case, as long as Soviet Russia uses Cuba for its purposes, statesmen and military planners in the United States will have nightmares.

Thus a Communist-dominated Cuba, or for that matter any Communist country in the Caribbean area aided by Russia (or Red China), represents a breach in the ramparts of continental defense, and must be regarded with the utmost seriousness.[8]

The Panama Canal represents a special problem to U.S. grand strategy. In the days of a one-ocean navy, it was vital for the quick transfer of naval vessels from ocean to ocean. (The battleship

*Oregon*'s dash around Cape Horn in the Spanish-American War dramatized the importance of an isthmian canal.) Today, with a multiocean fleet and bases on both coasts, the canal is no longer vital to U.S. security. But it retains major importance—particularly as a logistic and supply route. In the Cuban missile crisis, during the Vietnam war and in other emergencies large numbers of troops and great quantities of military supplies have been moved in ships via the Panama Canal to the areas of crisis. It represents the cheapest means of transport—particularly for bulk tonnage.

The canal, of course, has military weaknesses; it could be eliminated quickly—and would, in any case, have little importance—in a nuclear war. It is difficult to defend against determined saboteurs in a conventional war. But its political and economic, as much as its continued military, importance make it worth defending—indeed, essential to defend. As a nodal waterway and bottleneck of world shipping, it represents a focus of Communist ambitions; it is not by chance that Moscow has concentrated considerable effort on such important maritime passageways as the Malacca Strait, Suez and Panama.

The canal's political importance is clear; it symbolizes U.S. power, authority and fairness. Like Guantánamo in Cuba, it is of more negative than positive importance—Russian or Communist control or domination of the canal would represent a far greater disadvantage to us than the advantages offered by U.S. control. The Communist gambit in Panama, as in Egypt, is clear: to promote control of international waterways by Communist puppets, or to collectivize such control, under the guise of "internationalization." Internationalization has a beguiling ring, and, indeed, under certain ironclad conditions, might offer some advantages. But any real collectivized control, unless insured by U.S. power, might well result in Communist control. And cession by the United States of a dominant military interest in any isthmian canal would certainly lead to grave political and diplomatic problems elsewhere in Latin America; it would be taken as a precedent of weakness. The nations south of the border often damn the "gringo" and rant about Yankee "imperialism," but they respect firmness and strength.

The canal's economic importance to hemispheric and intercontinental shipping is also clear. Without it freight and charter rates would be certain to increase, and prices of the essential commodities imported from the far corners of the world would rise. The volume of traffic that flows through it is constantly increasing.

The canal "base," whether in Panama or elsewhere, has an ancillary military importance, which transcends the defense of the canal. The Army's Southern Command is situated there, and counterinsurgency and other schools, including jungle warfare training, for U.S. and Latin-American military personnel operate in a tropical environment. It is the supervisory nexus of the U.S. military aid and advisory effort throughout the Southern Hemisphere. Normally, the United States maintains one brigade and a Special Forces group in Panama, capable of quick transportation by air anywhere within the hemisphere. The somewhat bleak outlook for the Latin America of tomorrow—an area certain to be roiled by trouble—would indicate the advisability of a slightly strengthened force.

The present lock canal has many technical limitations and faces traffic saturation. Alternatives under consideration include a sea-level canal at the same site or elsewhere in Panama or Colombia. Economically, a new or modernized canal is badly needed. Politically, a new canal, particularly if the site is to be a new one, offers the United States an opportunity for resolving some of the problems that have troubled U.S.-Panamanian relations.

Panama is, in reality, an artificial country, created by the United States and supported, directly or indirectly, by the United States. The politicians and the wealthy "Fifty Families" of Panama have long used a kind of political blackmail—a demagogic appeal to the masses—to try to force more and more concessions from the United States. Communist agitation and our own mistakes and weaknesses have contributed to instability.

But the road of concession after concession has no turning. Weakness breeds contempt, and nothing we can offer will induce permanent stability in Panama, where there is—as in so many other areas of Latin America—a frightening irresponsibility on the part of the government toward the governed.

A new canal outside Panama could doom Panama and its principal cities, Colón and Panama City, clustered at either end of the present canal, to economic stagnation, perhaps—without U.S. help —to disaster. This is a powerful bargaining card, yet the emotional tinder of public opinion and the irresponsible character of most Panamanian leadership require the most subtle and careful gamesmanship.

A new canal inside or outside Panama, or the old canal modernized, should be managed and administered by a board of trustees or managers representing those American countries who are major users of the canal, with the United States and the host country (Panama or Colombia) in the majority. If the present Canal Zone is maintained, no further concessions to Panamanian sovereignty should be made; if a new canal is developed, sovereignty of the required area could well remain with the host country, provided adequate provision were made for actual physical and military control and defense of the canal by U.S. forces. Any new treaty *must* provide for such *de facto* control, no matter how its provisions may be sugar-coated or disguised, and therefore the treaty must contain provisions regarding military-base rights, training areas, airfields and so on.

In return for these rights the United States might well agree to the regulation of tolls, and the distribution of profits from tolls (if any) by the nations represented on the governing board. The bulk of the funds needed to modernize the present canal or to build a new one and the engineering know-how would be provided by the United States. Thus, in effect, the United States would pay, in dollar terms, for what is essentially an investment in U.S. and Latin-American security. Basically, what the United States requires for any isthmian canal is the right for its ships—and the ships of all nations—to transit it efficiently and quickly in time of peace, and the capability to use it in war and to deny its use to any enemy.

Isthmian bases are important not only to the defense of the canal but as deployment and staging bases between North and South America. Any Latin-American defense force would find them useful to its operations.

The Caribbean screen of islands provides the outlying defenses for the Atlantic approaches to the canal. In the Pacific the Cocos and the Galápagos Islands and the Mexican ports could provide early-warning sites and *ad hoc,* or temporary, bases in time of war. In South America the strategic points are the Recife-Natal area on the bulge of Brazil; the Brazilian island of Fernando de Noronha, off its coast (already used as an instrument site in the Atlantic Missile Range); and, further south, the Falkland Islands or continental sites, dominating the sea approaches around Cape Horn and guarding the missile trajectories across Antarctica.

The vast, wealthy and undeveloped South American continent has tremendous economic potential and indirect strategic consequence. But it is of more negative than positive military importance today. We cannot tolerate its monopolistic utilization, its political domination or military conquest by any unfriendly power, but we do not, in time of peace, require its territory for our strategic defense. What is essential is that the political contagion of Communism or any other world-devouring ideology must not spread from Europe or Africa to its shores; what is essential is that creeping conquests and Communist coups be averted or contained. The dominant power in most Latin-American countries—whether we like it or not—is the army. If the armies of Latin-America turn toward Communism, we are undone. It follows that the close relationships that have been fostered between U.S. and Latin-American armed forces are essential.

Many well-intentioned Americans, including some Congressmen, have deplored this unique closeness; they see military governments in Latin America and the unending coups as enemies of democracy and "progress." But in countries as politically unstable as are most of those in Latin America military government is not necessarily an unstabilizing factor; indeed, it may be the only bar to chaos.[9]

But we must recognize, too, that military governments in some Latin-American countries are assuming new roles. The inequities in Latin-American society and the contagion of foreign ideologies have produced situations in some countries—notably Peru and Bolivia—where military governments no longer represent the ultraconservative right, but retain, or assume, power by espousing (at least in principle) the demands of the left and the cause of the masses. The United States often is caught in the cross fire of the

125

political demagoguery that results, and—as in Bolivia, Peru and Chile—may find the once conservative military leaders of the past endorsing the expropriation of U.S. properties.

This is not necessarily a cause for despair. The United States should insist, of course, upon appropriate compensation. But we must live with the fact that a new nationalism, in some cases with a socialist cast, is waxing in Latin America. It is not necessarily allied with Communism; in fact, true nationalism is the enemy of Communism. We must play it cool: stand ready to assist and advise and invest (with proper safeguards) and remember that "military governments" are not synonymous with a dirty name. The basic problem in Latin America is not the military but the polyglot peoples—what John Mander has described as the failure of European and Indian cultures to "merge in a fruitful symbiosis."[10]

Captain Raymond J. Toner, USN (Ret.), has put the dilemma of Latin America in even clearer perspective:

> . . . during the 19th Century, political power in Latin American countries rested in varying degrees upon a tripod of the oligarchy, the church and the military. . . . In recent years the authority of the oligarchy and the church have decreased somewhat. New instruments of power, particularly the unions, are beginning to make their voices heard. In many countries, the military—and recently the church—are adjusting to the changing needs and pressures to a greater extent than the oligarchy.
>
> Of all the instruments of power, the military still remains the most powerful and possesses the greatest capability to maintain stability against pressures from within and without. . . .
>
> The Latin American military is a part of the social and political body of its State . . . it is reacting *within* the social and political body of its State, not as a foreign and separate entity *upon* it. . . .
>
> Until stable, well-organized political institutions are produced in Latin America, the military will continue to act . . . as "symbols of national sovereignty."
>
> The aspects of the Spanish-Moorish-Jewish-Indian cultures will continue to influence Latin Americans. Their concepts of "democracy" will differ from "democracy" as we of North America conceive it.[11]

In Latin America, as elsewhere in the world, we must stop trying to export democracy after our own image and think, instead, of vital interests. In most of Latin America this means friendly relations, trade, access to the raw materials of the area and, above all, prevention of foreign Communist domination of the area, or, if possible, of any part of it. Indigenous Communists may, of course, assume positions of power within individual countries (as they have already done) and may actually win by the ballot paramount power, as they threaten to do in Chile. This is not comforting, but it need not concern us too deeply unless the country concerned closes its borders to U.S. contacts and permits foreign powers military or base facilities.

The Monroe Doctrine today obviously is not applicable to indigenous Communist agitation, but it is still a bulwark against external conquest.

Thus the prescription for friendly—or at least acceptable—U.S.-Latin-American relations requires, on the part of the United States, very considerable restraint, judgment and patience—a mixture of political sagacity, diplomatic finesse, economic aid (but limited and carefully administered), economic investment (with generous terms to the host country) and political and military firmness. We must not be pushed around, but, on the other hand, we must not throw our weight around unduly. The Alliance for Progress[12] has failed, but the Rio Treaty for mutual defense of the hemisphere is still active and valid and should be developed into a model of regional collective action.

In Latin America the major military danger of tomorrow is internal. Insurgency movements, some of them sponsored by Communist Cuba and indigenous leftists, or by rabid nationalists perhaps indirectly aided by Soviet Russia or Communist China, represent a latent danger in several countries—notably, perhaps, in Bolivia, where Che Guevara died, and in Brazil.

The U.S. attitude toward change in Latin America must not be purely negative and defensive. Change is badly needed, and change in governments, social systems, the military and the church is coming. As many have pointed out, a man is not necessarily a Communist because he longs for change. Latin America is long overdue for change.

The Latin-American military establishments—about 840,000 men under arms in the entire area (including Cuba)—are the key to internal security, but none of the countries has strength enough to repel attack by any major power. Some of them—Brazil, Argentina, Chile, Venezuela and others—do have, however, the capability of providing forces, for instance, for a Dominican force or a Cuban blockade. Their destroyers, frigates and coastal patrol craft and their maritime reconnaissance planes are a small but important adjunct to the U.S. Navy—particularly in the South Atlantic (virtually uncovered in normal times by the navies of any of the Western powers)—in shipping and antisubmarine surveillance. They also have the capability, if their mutual jealousies and suspicions can be eliminated, of aiding each other in the struggle, continuing and unending, against internal subversion.

Brazil, the largest, richest and most powerful (at least on paper) of the Latin-American countries, maintains close to 200,000 men in the armed services and another 120,000 in paramilitary police and security forces. They ride the whirlwind of change, of trouble and dissent, of the "urban guerrillas," Catholic radicals, left-wing malcontents and right-wing vigilantes who today characterize much of Latin America's society. So far they have maintained an uneasy rule, subject, however, at any time to coup or overthrow. But Brazil is only symptomatic of the winds of change that stir Latin America, winds that are forever blowing. Americans who yearn for peace and quiet and stability will not find it in Latin America; we must roll with the punches, protect our really vital interests and judge each situation on its differing merits.

A secure base for the defense of the Western Hemisphere, and particularly of the North American continent and its fringing islands and sea lanes, is a "categorical imperative" of U.S. foreign and military policy.

The bulk of the United States armed forces must be retained in, or based upon, the Western Hemisphere, with land, sea and air units in the United States, mobile and ready for movement to any part of the hemisphere. Normally, the South Atlantic and the west coast of South America require only periodic naval visits, but the important and restless Caribbean must be guarded by an amphibious squadron, with Marines embarked, maritime patrol and reconnaissance and air-defense aircraft in Florida, and by a reinforced brigade of Army troops in Panama.

But Latin America, as a security problem, must be resolved primarily by political means and skillful diplomacy. Insurgency and subversion are the principal threats; the military part of the political-economic-psychological-military team must continue its preventive measures: training, indoctrination, organization, equipment and advice.

Unless this program is continued and expanded, unless we harness well the "national team," Latin America could become the next great arena for Khrushchev's formula for creeping conquest— "national liberation wars."

But our Western Hemisphere strategy—the categorical imperative of defense of the "world island" of the United States and its neighbors—must depend fundamentally upon a clear-cut maritime superiority and unrivaled nuclear strength. Only if we maintain a secure base can we project our strength overseas to protect U.S. interests.

# «« 6 »»
# The Defense of Europe

HORACE WALPOLE'S pessimistic appraisal of Europe's future in 1774 has been repeatedly contradicted by history.

"I take Europe to be worn out," he wrote. "When Voltaire dies we may say 'Good-night.' "[1]

For a "dying" continent, Europe, in the two centuries since Walpole wrote, has demonstrated an amazing vitality. It has survived, and recuperated from, three cataclysmic holocausts—the French Revolution and the Napoleonic era, and World Wars I and II—and many lesser crises.

War and genocide, depression and starvation and tyranny, have indeed slaughtered millions. Europe's children, her former colonies, have grown up and far outstripped her in strength; a Eurasian power—Soviet Russia—towers above the old lands of the West, and Asia, that long-slumbering continent, has awakened and is, slowly but surely, first supplementing, and then replacing, Western Europe as the world's second great-power center.

There are, it is true, signs of deterioration, of degeneration, of weariness, even of decadence and decay, in Europe. Long ago the Romans became Italians, and some of the British reverted from empire builders and world conquerors to, in Napoleon's contemptuous phrase, a "nation of shopkeepers." There are some worrisome signs in Britain of hardening of the arteries—a lethargy, an economic, commercial, technological and industrial backwardness, which has undercut even the shopkeeping skills. The British pound is no longer supreme; the financial and banking capital of the world is no longer London.

Sweden and Denmark, surfeited with the sloth of a stultifying state security and a middleman's wealth protected by others' efforts, present a too civilized society, marred by the overpermissiveness and the indulgence of ease. Greece, uneasy and troubled and volatile, experiences the cyclical government crises that have marred all the modern history of a nation that first gave democracy its meaning.

Yes, Europe can be viewed in one context as sick, as degenerate; some might even conclude that Walpole's prediction was correct.

Yet the pulse of national being beats too strongly; the vital statistics attest Europe's health.

France, long ago written off as a static power, demonstrated a new vitality under De Gaulle. West Germany, broken in defeat a quarter of a century ago, has become one of the world's major industrial powers. Britain, despite her production difficulties and her obsolescent industrial, management and marketing techniques, still nourishes the spark of ancient greatness. Italy, Belgium, the Netherlands, Scandinavia are advanced and ambitious industrial regions. Europe no longer dominates the world, as it did for so many centuries, but the world cannot do without Europe. Collectively, Western Europe is the world's second major-power center, far superior in total industrial production, GNP and aggregate population of educated, technically proficient population to all others except the United States. As Hitler so well understood, Europe represents a rich prize for any conqueror; the subjugation of its peoples, the utilization of its resources by the U.S.S.R., or any other single major power, might well mean ultimate world domination.

The vital interest of the United States in Europe is economic, cultural and geopolitical. The United States has an immense capital investment in Western Europe,[2] and its export and import trade with Western Europe is greater than with any other area of the world. Many of Europe's products—finished and unfinished, such as commercial diamonds—are essential to our economy; in short,

131

Western Europe represents an investment in U.S. prosperity. Its collective military strength and, particularly, its aggregate military potential make Western Europe as an ally an asset to world stability; if it should become an enemy, allied with the U.S.S.R. or any world conqueror, the United States would be forced back across the ocean to a hemispheric defense policy.

In a geopolitical sense Europe is a peninsula of Asia, and the rimlands of Western Europe dominate the heartland's approach to the Atlantic, the most-used ocean. Former Secretary of Defense McNamara once summarized the potential stakes in Western Europe succinctly:

"Western Europe represents . . . after the United States, the greatest aggregation of economic, political and ideological strength in the world. The six Common Market nations, plus the United Kingdom, by themselves, have a total population, military manpower pool and gross national product in excess of that of the Soviet Union."

The geography of Europe dictates its strategy.

The Mediterranean flanks Europe to the south; the North Sea, Norwegian Sea and the Atlantic dominate it to the north and west. Control of these sea approaches by friendly powers is vital to an independent, free Western Europe. Without such control, with the sea approaches to the continent in enemy hands, neither the North Atlantic Treaty Organization nor any other defensive alliance would have any meaning; the rimlands of Western Europe would surely become an appendage of the Eurasian heartland.

For many centuries the classic struggle between the "heartland," the great land powers, and the "rimlands," the great maritime powers, has ebbed and flowed across Central Europe and across its surrounding seas. Invariably, the tide of conquest, surging across Europe from the East, has recoiled short of blue water. But today, the great land power of Eurasia, the U.S.S.R., is becoming a great sea power—the second greatest in the world—and its challenge to the West's traditional control of the sea approaches to Europe is growing.

The defense of Western Europe starts, therefore, far beyond the continental shelf—in the stormy waters of the Western Ocean, in

132

the Mediterranean and at the strategic chokepoints and bottlenecks of maritime trade.

Control of the seas today is a three-dimensional problem, and requires land bases as well as ships. In the North Atlantic, domination of the sea approaches to Europe means control of the base areas of Greenland, Iceland, the Faeroes, Shetlands and Orkneys and the British Isles. The North Cape area of Norway would be untenable against any determined land-amphibious attack from the east, but the Lofoten Islands represent a useful, though not vital, advanced base. In the south, the Azores and, to a lesser extent, Madeira and the Canary Islands are useful outposts guarding the approaches to the Strait of Gibraltar.

Though the sea approaches to Europe from the west can be guarded by ships, ship-based planes and island bases, the defenses of the narrow bottlenecks leading to the Baltic, the Mediterranean and the Black seas are land-oriented. The British stronghold of Gibraltar is protected by distance, the Pyrenees and the Iberian Peninsula from direct threat by land. The Greek and Italian mountain barriers are good defensive obstacles to land attack. The Turkish Straits must be defended by land. Control of the historical sea highway of conquest—the Mediterranean—is therefore, in strategic terms, primarily a sea-air-land problem, with emphasis upon *combined* operations. But in the north, a century-old route of conquest—the flat, relatively featureless North German plain—leads directly from the level fields of Poland across Germany to the base of the Jutland Peninsula and the approaches to the Baltic. In this area designated by NATO as the Central Front, the primary defense of Western Europe is a land defense, with air power a basic supporting arm and sea power in a secondary role.

There are, therefore, two primary and one secondary threats to the maritime nations of Western Europe: the land threat west from Berlin across the North German plain and the sea threat via the Mediterranean and its littoral, and an amphibious and land-air threat to northern Norway.

The chain of command of the North Atlantic Treaty Organization reflects these threats, and the paramount importance of maintaining control of the sea approaches to Western Europe. The

133

# EUROPE AND THE MEDITERRANEAN

✖ Soviet anchorages in the Mediterranean

0      MILES      500

BARENTS SEA

Polyarny
Murmansk
KOLA PENINSULA

WHITE SEA

URAL

Lake Onega

Lake Ladoga

Leningrad

•Moscow

UNION OF SOVIET SOCIALIST REPUBLICS

MOUNTAINS

Sea of Azov

CAUCASUS MOUNTAINS

CASPIAN SEA

ANIA

ucharest

BLACK SEA

Baku

LGARIA
a

Bosporus

Istanbul    •Ankara

SEA OF MARMARA

RACE

Dardanelles

T U R K E Y

•Teheran

GEAN SEA

Mosul

Kirkuk oil fields

✖ GALETA BANK

Kirkuk

I R A N

hens

SYRIA

✖ AMORGOS

Nicosia

Latakia

✖ EAST OF CYPRUS

Baghdad •

✖ EAST OF CRETE

CYPRUS

CRETE

Beirut

Damascus •

I R A Q

Basra •

LEBANON

ISRAEL

Amman •

KUWAIT

PERSIAN GULF

Jerusalem

JORDAN

✖ GULF OF SOLLUM

Port Said

Alexandria

Suez Canal

Cairo •

SINAI

U A R (EGYPT)

Gulf of Suez

Gulf of Aqaba

SAUDI ARABIA

NATO Supreme Allied Commander, Atlantic, with headquarters in Norfolk, Virginia, is charged with maintaining and securing the vital sea communications with the maritime nations of Europe. The Supreme Allied Commander, Europe, with headquarters in Brussels, has three principal subordinate commanders—the Commander in Chief, South, at Naples, guardian of the Mediterranean gateway; the Commander in Chief, Central Europe, with headquarters in Brunssum, the Netherlands, whose divisions and air wings protect the North German Plain; and the Commander in Chief, North, with headquarters near Oslo, Norway, the sentry on the northern flank.

Until the tremendous growth of Soviet sea power and increasing Soviet influence in the Middle East and along the African coasts of the Mediterranean threatened Allied control of that sea, the Central Front was the focus of the major NATO efforts. It presented —and still does, in many ways—the principal strategic threat to the NATO maritime nations. But today NATO is being outflanked from the south. The Mediterranean threat (which will be discussed in the next chapter) is more serious than any immediate threat on the Central Front.

Since the establishment of the North Atlantic Treaty Organization in 1949, its defense concepts emphasized first conventional strength, then massive nuclear retaliation, as a deterrent to attack; then a defense with tactical nuclear weapons; and finally a so-called flexible response with forces tailored to meet in kind any level of aggression. The changing concepts have reflected two fundamental factors: the increasing nuclear power of Soviet Russia and the inability or unwillingness of Western European nations to support and maintain conventional forces strong enough to defeat Communist conventional attack, particularly on the Central Front, menaced by the easiest route of land invasion—the North German plain.

NATO has been impaled on this two-pronged dilemma throughout its history. It still is. The-sword-and-the-shield concept envisaged Europe's conventional forces as a shield to protect Western Europe against physical invasion, while the sword of nuclear retribution would devastate Russia. This concept simply ceased to have adequate credibility in the minds of many Europeans—particularly the French and a large fraction of the West Germans—when the U.S.S.R. acquired a large stockpile of strategic nuclear weapons and the means to deliver them against the United States. Was it likely, Europe asked with some reason, that any U.S. President would undertake massive nuclear retaliation against attack on Western Europe by Soviet conventional forces if he knew such a response would mean devastation of the United States?

The reduced credibility of massive retaliation as a deterrent did not, however, persuade Europe of the feasibility of maintaining enough ready divisions and air wings to turn back a large-scale Communist attack without the use of "nukes." Instead, NATO has fudged the point and slurred its strategy and, in so doing, may have still further reduced the credibility of the deterrent. It has never maintained enough forces-in-being and available for rapid mobilization to insure the defeat by conventional means alone of any large-scale Soviet attack. It has emphasized the technology of tactical nuclear weapons—there are some 7,200 U.S.-owned (plus British and French) nuclear weapons in Europe—but there has been general agreement that any considerable use of such weapons would devastate much of Central and Western Europe and would inevitably lead to a massive exchange of strategic weapons.

Western Europe, like most democracies when political seas are relatively smooth, has simply not been willing to grasp the nettle of high defense costs; consequently NATO has often substituted plans for purpose and hopes for substance.

Thus NATO is an alliance in search of a future; it is too few commanded by too many. It has lost its charisma; to many Europeans and to some Americans, the alliance appears dated and of little relevance to contemporary history. It faces a host of internal problems and contradictions and great and growing external threats.

NATO's internal problems are those endemic to a peacetime alliance of fifteen sovereign states, each with its own parochial interests, each concentrated more upon maintenance of a booming economy than upon defense against "unthinkable" threats.

If fear is the cement of alliances, as John Foster Dulles once said,

137

then the cement of NATO is crumbling today. And European nationalism—some use Gaullism and nationalism interchangeably —rather than integration is the trend today.

De Gaulle broke his integrated NATO ties partially because he felt French sovereignty was impaired by the sheer power of the American partner. His point of view, an underlying psychological factor in many NATO countries, is not without some foundation; the United States, not Europe, is without a doubt the cornerstone of the alliance in physical power and weight of effort. (The U.S. contribution to the staff of the Supreme Commander, Allied Powers, Europe, with headquarters at Casteaux, Belgium, is illustrative. Of the 1,492 officers and enlisted men from 11 NATO nations that were assigned to the international staff at Casteaux in 1969, about 600 were American; the next largest national contingent was from the United Kingdom—about 250.)

This European uneasiness about American "domination," exacerbated by the ever-increasing growth of American business in Europe, is not reflected in widespread popular hostility to the United States. There is, on the contrary, a great body of support, and even of respect and admiration, for American enterprise, technology and power. Nevertheless, organized anti-American demonstrations have become a part of life. The result is bound to be that some of the tarnish rubs off on NATO.

In fact, the principal target of the New Left in Europe is likely to be NATO. The breakup of the alliance is a basic objective of Communism since any alliance of the free nations is an obstacle to conquest. Thus NATO is the target for Communist opposition and for the dissenters against the Establishment, who are so prominent in Europe, as well as in America, today.

Not even the invasion of Czechoslovakia in 1968 really reinvigorated NATO. The somewhat mild political reaction of Washington set a pattern for Europe to follow, and it soothed fears. The invasion was rationalized by many as a defensive Soviet move, and the implied Russian threats to other nations are all but forgotten. In 1968, the year of Czechoslovakia, Allied (non-U.S.) defense expenditures for NATO actually dropped to only 4.5 percent of the booming gross national products.

138

The truth is that NATO is not a part of European life as it was when it was formed. There is no heroic Eisenhower image to personify the alliance; there is more apathy than excitement, as much questioning of its policies as support for them.

Since NATO in December, 1967, approved a strategic concept keyed to an improved readiness for conventional warfare and to a so-called flexible response, NATO's ground and tactical air forces in Europe have actually been weakened, not strengthened. Terms of military service are being shortened (to one year in Denmark); Canada is withdrawing a large part of its forces from Europe; war reserves are low and ill distributed; support and supply forces in many cases are nonexistent.

Norway today maintains some independent battalions and one ready brigade (with one company guarding the Russian frontier in the extreme north). The U.S.S.R. garrisons the Murmansk–Kola Peninsula area with five divisions.

On NATO's vital Central Front in Germany there are theoretically some 23 to 24 NATO divisions or their equivalent. But most of them are divisions in name only. The 12 West German divisions are a faint echo of the German military units of the past. The specter of a Nazi or militaristic renaissance still hangs over Germany—with some reason. But partly as a consequence of past history, West Germany's democratic government, fearful that the Army might once again become a "state within a state," has subordinated the military so greatly in both the social and economic structure of Germany that a career in uniform offers few attractions to German youth. All the German divisions are 15 to 20 percent below war strength; three are missing one brigade, or about one-third of their rifle strength; many have relatively little artillery, and combat support and supply units are lacking. One officer estimated that, in fact, the Germans were maintaining the equivalent of about six or eight good divisions and that the staying power of even these was very limited. German tactical air power, built around the now aged F-104, is being modernized. But the process is just starting.

The U.S. Seventh Army in Germany—once a NATO and global showpiece—lost considerable of its combat effectiveness after the Vietnam war started. It reached a low point in 1967; now its weak-

139

nesses have been partially remedied. But it still has major deficiencies. Its staying power is limited.

Nearly all the rest of the NATO divisions and tactical air forces are much less effective than the Seventh Army units. Constant personnel turnover, inability to recruit enough long-term professionals, equipment obsolescence and shortages, inexperience and understrengths are the rule, not the exception.

This and the practical and psychologically unpalatable facts of life, which make a formula of more divisions politically impossible, dictated the post-Czechoslovakia decision of the NATO Council to concentrate upon improving the quality of existing units rather than creating new ones.

In 1968—partially to provide a sop to Senator Mike Mansfield, who was pressing for U.S. troop withdrawals from Europe; partially to cut down on the gold drain; partially to strengthen the depleted strategic reserve in the United States and to broaden the training base for Vietnam—several fighter squadrons and two brigades (or about two-thirds) of the 24th Division were withdrawn to the United States from Germany. The ground troops left their arms and heavy equipment behind in Europe; the Air Force units flew their planes home but retained at their old German bases stocks of fuel and ammunition.

The withdrawn units continued to be earmarked for NATO and were considered "dual-based" in both the United States and Germany. They were supposed to be ready for immediate return to Germany by air in case of emergency.

But the dual-basing concept, which many Europeans and Americans consider merely a public-relations sugar-coating for the bitter pill of U.S. force reductions in Europe, has already revealed its flaws.

When the Czechoslovak crisis burst on a startled NATO, NATO commanders learned that the two brigades of the 24th Division which had been withdrawn to the United States had been "drawn down," as were all other Army units in the United States and overseas, to provide fillers, replacements and training cadres for Vietnam. It took ninety days to build them up to strength again. Then, in January, 1969, some 12,000 U.S. troops were slowly and leisurely flown back to Germany over a two-week period for a well-advertised maneuver.

Neither the Germans nor NATO were impressed. Had Czechoslovakia led to war, it would have been too little, too late; the United States had plainly "fudged" on its commitments to NATO. Our example was contagious; Canada followed suit and used the same sophistry of dual-basing to justify its pull-out from Europe.

To most NATO commanders, regardless of their national origin, the dual-basing concept, popular with U.S. politicians as a means of saving money, has little military validity. General Lyman L. Lemnitzer, former Supreme Allied Commander, Europe, emphasized the weaknesses of the concept in a speech in October, 1968:

> . . . there can be no major reliance placed upon a Big Lift type of operation to ensure the prompt return of U.S. troops to Europe in a time of crisis. Our reinforcement capability . . . is no substitute for forces actually on the ground. While dual-basing does not reduce the troop commitment to Nato, it docs degrade our "in-theater" capabilities and therefore reduces our readiness to meet an attack with little or no warning.[3]

Dual-basing is no substitute for troops on the scene ready to fight instantly. The large numbers of troops required to maintain, guard and care for the equipment left behind in Europe and the cost of providing two sets of equipment—one in Europe, one in the United States—for the same unit are major disadvantages. More important is the doubtful efficacy of the concept. If a shooting war had actually started, the German air bases used by our flotilla of troop-carrier aircraft and transport planes would not have been usable; they would probably have been bomb-pitted or captured by Russian paratroopers long before the first transport or fighter aircraft could have left American soil. On the other hand, if a mass airlift were carried out in a period of impending crisis, it might well add to tension and provoke war, rather than deter it. Most of the professionals, therefore, reject "dual-basing" as an answer to NATO's needs.

The discredited "dual-basing" concept has been applied, so far, only to try to meet the principal land threat to NATO—an attack across the North German plain. But Germany is not the only ground peril point along the 3,600-mile perimeter of the alliance.

The Turks face seven to eight Russian divisions across the Caucasus and a major and growing Russian fleet in the Black Sea. Most NATO experts believe that the modernized Bulgarian Army, with Rumanian and Russian help, could quickly overrun the indefensible Greek positions in Thrace, and with more difficulty conquer European Turkey.

Thus NATO's forces for conventional war are outclassed, not alone in numbers of divisions but in training, logistics, fire support, experience, equipment and over-all combat effectiveness.

This unpleasant equation becomes even more unpleasant when the reserve forces of both sides, those units that could be mobilized as reinforcements after the start of war, are considered.

The Russian military machine was once geared to a ponderous mobilization cycle that required months of slow build-up. But today the U.S.S.R.'s category 2 and category 3 divisions, those maintained in peacetime at reduced strength or in cadre form, can be fleshed out, equipped and ready for combat, considerably faster than the West's reserve divisions. And the Russians have far more of them—a grand total of close to 100 full or part-strength divisions west of the Urals.

The United States is supposed to be ready to provide within thirty days or so seven more divisions to NATO, in addition to the equivalent of more than five divisions maintained in Europe. This is a "paper" obligation; the United States has not been capable of meeting this commitment since 1965.

The reserves of our European allies are almost nonexistent. Until the British completely withdraw their forces from the Far East and Persian Gulf, the three below-strength British divisions in Germany will have virtually no backup. In 1969 the Northern Ireland troubles virtually denuded the British Isles of troops; the only "reserve" available was the pitifully weak British "Army of the Rhine." *Sic transit gloria mundi;* the power of the British lion, so short a time ago dominant across the globe, is now stretched thin by a requirement for 10,000 troops. German Army reserves exist chiefly on paper.

Today all the European members of NATO (France excepted) muster a grand total of about eighteen reserve divisions or their equivalent, and most of these are Italian, Turkish or Greek.

The diplomats and political leaders of NATO like to point out that a war-strength, fully equipped, fully supported Western division may well be equal in numbers, or combat power, to anywhere from one and a half to three Soviet-type divisions. But this is an equation of small comfort, even if true (which is doubtful), for no NATO divisions, active or reserve, are fully manned, fully supported and fully equipped. NATO's military commanders argue that as of today the U.S.S.R. and her Communist allies could field many more divisions much more rapidly than the West.

Thus the basic dilemma of NATO—one still unresolved—has been, almost from the beginning, the development of a viable strategic concept, or a credible deterrent, to Soviet attack.

European belief in the value of the nuclear deterrent—the utilization of U.S. nuclear weapons immediately against any large-scale Soviet attack on the West—was shaken when Russia acquired a major stockpile of A-weapons and the means to deliver them. The Soviet ability to devastate the United States weakened Washington's will to use the bomb to save Europe. The credibility of the "Big Bang" as a means of defense for NATO was reduced.

The Kennedy administration changed the policy of the United States from past dependence on the "massive retaliation" concept of John Foster Dulles to so-called "flexible response"—a policy of meeting different levels of aggression with variable and escalating force. Former Secretary of Defense McNamara succeeded in selling this strategic concept to NATO.

The new strategic concept envisaged our initial response to any limited Soviet aggression in Europe, such as pinching off a piece of the West German frontier or "rectification" of the borders of northern Norway, with conventional weapons only. This was to be followed, if the Russians persisted, by gradual escalation—first by larger conventional forces, then with extensive use of tactical or small nuclear weapons, with the great strategic weapons targeted against Russia itself as the final deterrent.

"Flexible response" raised the atomic threshold, it was claimed, and gave the West some sanction, short of the immediate use of A-weapons.

But it presented immediately two problems which plague NATO today.

One is the belief of some Europeans that the shift to a so-called flexible response represented a further weakening of will in Washington, an attempt to find a way out. This was the reaction of De Gaulle, shared by Bonn's former Defense Minister, Franz Josef Strauss, who is still a political power in Germany. This school of European opinion has since been strengthened in its convictions by the failure of President Johnson's policy of "gradualism" in Vietnam, which has been equated in Europe with the flexible-response concept.

The adoption of the strategy of flexible response was contributory to the French decision to withdraw from integrated military activities in NATO and to the emphasis by De Gaulle on the development of a French *force de frappe*, or national nuclear deterrent.

Flexible response reinforced the doubts of those who had already questioned America's willingness to exchange Boston for Stuttgart, and, they insisted, signaled U.S. hesitation to the Kremlin. It reduced the credibility of American intentions. "Credibility," as one experienced officer has defined it, "is what you say you are going to do, plus the capability to do it, plus the belief by the enemy (and our allies) that you have the capability and the will to do it."

Today the capability is lacking; there is doubt about the will, and neither Moscow nor our allies completely believe that we will do what we say we will do.

De Gaulle and some of his principal military advisers felt that a small but virtually invulnerable French deterrent force—now planned as 27 land-based missiles in deep mountain silos (each with a 3,000-kilometer range and 300-kiloton warhead) and 5 to 8 nuclear submarines (each with 16 missiles of 3,000-kilometer range and 1-megaton warhead)—would provide a sure national deterrent for France, in place of an uncertain NATO (U.S.) deterrent. Some in Germany, a nation forbidden by treaty from development of nuclear weapons but nevertheless probably capable of producing them within a few months, tended to agree with De Gaulle. To neutralize this school of thought and to give NATO nations a greater sense of sharing in nuclear judgments, two NATO nuclear committees were formed to plan the disposition and utilization of the 7,200 U.S. tactical nuclear weapons now in Western Europe. At the same time a nonproliferation treaty, sponsored by the United States and Russia, was offered to Europe and the world.

The trend toward nuclear nationalism in NATO was thus somewhat dampened (though by no means eliminated), but the fundamental problem of the strategic concept of flexible response remains. For to make it effective, better and stronger conventional and dual-trained forces, capable of making the Russians pay heavily for any aggression, were required. And they would cost more money, considerably more money.

This has been the basic NATO dilemma of recent years, worsened by the partial defection of France, Britain's economic stringency, the Greek-Turkish rift, the political reaction in other NATO countries to the Greek military coup, the drawdown of U.S. forces due to Vietnam, the unwillingness or inability of the rich nations to face the internal political problems that more money for defense would mean, and the unwillingness or inability of the poorer members of NATO to face the economic problems that such a shift implied.

These collective problems, never resolved, have made it impossible to build up a conventional defense of adequate strength. The failure has reduced the credibility of the flexible-response strategy to the Russians (who know NATO's weaknesses well), and to some of the European allies of NATO, yet the attempt to achieve a really strong non-nuclear capability has weakened somewhat the credibility of the nuclear deterrent.

At the same time, the continuing attempt to build up strong conventional forces fosters friction within the alliance and invites invidious comparisons between the inadequate efforts of rich and strong nations like West Germany and defense programs of poor nations like Greece and Turkey. It has also strengthened the hand of the neo-isolationists in the United States, who argue that "if Europe won't defend itself, why should we do the job for them?"

Today NATO's actual strategic plan against Soviet aggression boils down to plans to fight as far forward as possible as long as possible with conventional weapons only ("Which will be very damn short, indeed," one officer has said); then to use tactical nuclear weapons to supplement conventional fire power (an unpopular policy since most of the damage done would be to Allied targets, Allied cities and West European nationals); and finally to invoke against the Russian heartland the strategic weapons of the United States.

"The real deterrent to Moscow today," one official has said, "is uncertainty; the Soviet general staff simply cannot tell the Kremlin what would happen if they used force against the West. The Soviet planner can promise big things up to a point—Berlin probably, perhaps domination of the Dardanelles, a deep penetration of Western Europe—but what then? He doesn't know what those crazy Americans would do, and he cannot promise that his country would not reap a nuclear whirlwind."

This uncertainty should be reinforced—indeed, transformed into a virtual certainty in the mind of the Kremlin that major Soviet aggression against Western Europe would mean nuclear devastation of the U.S.S.R.

"You can't sell the notion, either in Europe or in the United States, that New York and Istanbul are on an equal-risk basis; people just won't believe it," an observer has commented. "We simply have to make it absolutely clear that we *will* use nukes to defend Europe, but we will never use them without consultation with our allies. The answer is 'controlled proliferation,' a European collective control on any level you can get it."

The first steps toward this goal—the establishment of the NATO nuclear committees and a share in nuclear planning for our European allies—have been taken, but they are not yet developed or adequate.

We are still trying to combine incompatibles—equipping, organizing and training the same forces to fight major nuclear and non-nuclear wars. This dual capability may be possible for tactical air

146

forces, but it is almost impossible for ground forces. Nuclear and non-nuclear wars are so different—they are "like Waterloo with machine guns and without them"—that this attempt to neatly capsule a flexible-response strategy in a single-force package is probably doomed to futility.

"Either Europe goes nuclear or, in time, it will accommodate with the Commies."

The concept of a European nuclear force, a favorite of De Gaulle's, still has vitality long after his departure from power. It is, indeed, gaining in strength as Europe realizes that it must provide some of its own nuclear defense and that the U.S. nuclear defense of Europe must be made more credible by a collective European defense, inside or outside NATO. It seems clear that such a force based, at least initially, on French and British weapons is the way Europe is going, and, provided the concept is "collective proliferation," it should increase, not decrease, the credibility of the deterrent.

If Russia were convinced of the capability and the will of the United States to utilize nuclear weapons in the defense of NATO, the NATO strategic concept—regardless of whether it was called "massive retaliation" or "flexible response"—would be more credible all around.

This does not preclude arms-limitations discussions with the Russians, a project Europe (still hopeful of détente) favors. But it means entering upon any such talks from a position of superior strength; the U.S. nuclear armory, which is the ultimate defense of all members of NATO, must be pre-eminent. We must arm to parley.

Emphasis upon a nuclear deterrent does not mean that there is no need for any conventional forces in Europe. Ground units and some supporting tactical air forces, trained in conventional tactics, are needed for four primary purposes:

1. To impose delay, to prevent a Soviet *fait accompli*, and to foil a program of nibbling aggressions such as the biting off of a few hundred yards of West German border territory, aggression in Norway's bleak north, or against Turkish or Greek Thrace. (Berlin is, and will remain, a special case. It is virtually indefensible; the

147

West might answer an initial attack upon it, or its encirclement, with non-nuclear forces, but if Russia persisted, its only defense would be the certain knowledge that the city is regarded by many in the West as a "flash point"—one certain to detonate a nuclear response.)

2. To act as a plate-glass window, or trigger, and to fire the shots that would face the aggressor with the certainty of major war and confront him with the dread specter of nuclear devastation.

3. To maintain a NATO military presence with integrated U.S. units as a visible affirmation of the NATO concept—that aggression against Western Europe would be aggression against the United States, that the United States stands shoulder to shoulder with the West and would inevitably be involved in any defense of Europe against aggression.

4. To exercise political and psychological influence upon West Germany. It is essential to the future peace of Europe and the cause of the West that West Germany remain an integrated member of NATO or of a Western European community of nations, and must neither be neutralized nor come under the control of a Moscow-dominated East Germany.

NATO ground divisions and tactical air forces are needed in the years ahead. But the balance of effort and the disposition of forces require readjustment.

NATO is a political alliance of peoples of approximately common culture and heritage; it still has political and psychological as well as military utility. But it is time to accentuate the positive—to emphasize political and psychological and economic cooperation in Western Europe, to adjust forces to meet the principal and changing threats.

If NATO is to fit the future, it must adapt to change.

It needs better conventional forces—fewer of them, not more, but at full strength, combat-ready, finely equipped and better disposed. The total force-level goals of NATO today, in terms of ground divisions in particular, are unrealistic; they simply will not be achieved, or will be maintained, if at all, only as understrength paper units. The attempt to achieve the unachievable produces a sense of futility and causes NATO to lose face. It is neither necessary nor desirable for the United States to maintain five divisions in Germany indefinitely. One or two good U.S. divisions are enough to make the fundamental point that the United States will not tolerate Soviet aggression against Western Europe; the Germans themselves must fill more of the gap, assume more of the burden of their own defense on the Central Front. Reduction in the strengths of conventional forces should not be precipitate. It must be timed to the political situation in Europe and to arms-limitation discussions, and could perhaps be used to encourage a thinning out on the Soviet side. In any case, reduction in force levels is inevitable and—if it results in smaller but better units—desirable.

The substitution of quality for quantity is not going to solve NATO's military or other problems unless another condition is fulfilled. Reduction of conventional ground forces in Europe without an increase in numbers and improvement in quality of U.S. strategic forces could be disastrous. Ultimately, whether we like it or not, the fate of Europe and the United States depends upon our nuclear capability and its efficacy as a deterrent. A superiority in missiles and bombers and Polaris submarines and in strategic nuclear weapons is *the* indispensable ingredient of any NATO deterrent strategy, and, indeed, of any hope of arms limitation. To attempt the latter without the former invites not only disappointment but also possible catastrophe.

A shift in the basic strategic concept of NATO toward a greater reliance upon a quick use of nuclear weapons in case of major attack on the Central Front; a reduction in numbers, but an improvement in quality, of conventional forces; and more emphasis—now perhaps possible with De Gaulle's passing—on political, psychological and economic commonality in Western Europe may well extend the useful life of NATO for several decades.

But geography does not change. The flat North German plain and the Soviet position in the heart of Europe (at its closest, East Germany is only a hundred miles from the North Sea) represent strategic nightmares to Western planners. The threat of actual armed assault—of the eruption of Soviet divisions (a highly unlikely contingency) into the Atlantic rimlands—must be met by the nuclear deterrent, whether or not NATO persists. But more subtle

149

aggression cannot be coped with by force of arms. A sloughing away of West Germany from the West, a turn by Bonn to neutralism, reunification of West and East Germany on Moscow's terms, would mean, in time, either a major war or the loss of Europe to Communism. In other words, it is the *political* status of Germany (including Berlin) and her relationship to the West and the East that will be the ultimate determinant of future history in Europe.

". . . what may be possible some years in the future is a German effort to make a bilateral deal with the Soviet Union leading to the rejoining of the severed body of the old Reich," George Ball has written. In other words, unification of East and West Germany might, at some future time, be "bought" by West Germany's agreement to provide "large material and financial resources for the modernization and industrialization of the Soviet Union."[4]

Since these words were written, the Soviet Union and her Eastern European satellites have progressed considerably in "modernization and industrialization," and Russia's fear of a united Germany except on Russian terms has not diminished. And to the satellite Communist states—particularly Poland—a united Germany would be a terrible political specter.

Nevertheless, the "pull" of unification and of irredentism—rectification of Germany's eastern frontiers—will continue to be a powerful political factor in the Europe of tomorrow, one that must be reckoned with. That school of German thought which has long felt that Germany's future lies eastward is still strong—latent and submerged in the West,[5] open and powerful in East Germany. An ostensibly neutral and reunified Germany, holding the balance of power in Europe, or a greater Germany allied with Russia, would spell disaster for Europe and the United States alike. Thus the status and the size and the strength of U.S. and NATO forces in Germany (and in Europe) are of far more political and psychological than military significance—particuarly if NATO shifts its defense concept primarily to a nuclear deterrent.

The political status of West Germany will be influenced by its economic well-being, or lack of it, and the military-political decisions of NATO and the West. Thus efforts to improve the combat effectiveness and increase the size of the West German armed

150

forces would inevitably affect the West German budget. And some solution of the problem of Germany's nuclear participation—not yet fully achieved—is essential if Germany is to remain in the Western camp. Both Britain and France are nuclear powers, no matter how small, in their own right. It is impossible to expect Bonn to forgo forever the development of a *national* nuclear capability (regardless of her adherence to the nonproliferation treaty) unless she is included in a *European* nuclear-weapons-control system, or is given a greater share of responsibilty and control over the NATO arsenal. The Franco-German rapprochement, which De Gaulle undertook, but which faltered and faded, should be broadened into a tripartite relationship with Britain, and the atomic capabilities of the three powers melded into a collective whole.

It is impossible to avoid agreement with the large majority of the Assembly of the Western European Union (an influential but nongovernmental group) that realistic contingency planning for what might develop into a European nuclear force is essential. The committees established in NATO to provide some integrated planning for the use of tactical nuclear weapons in case of war might well serve as a catalyst toward broader—and more European—efforts. It is vital for two reasons—to increase in European minds the credibility of the U.S. nuclear deterrent and to meet the national aspirations of European nations—that European fingers join our own on the nuclear trigger. How to do this, to increase the power of the deterrent and to promote stability, rather than to weaken either is one of the great tasks of tomorrow inside and outside NATO.

Any realistic strategy for the defense of Western Europe against land invasion must be built upon maintenance of air superiority over the British Isles and around the coasts and the rimlands of Western Europe. Without the assurance of such superiority neither a limited non-nuclear response nor successful delaying actions of any kind are possible. The capability of Allied air power and conventional ground forces to delay Soviet ground forces until the transatlantic (U.S.) nuclear forces devastate the basis of Soviet power is an important factor in deterrence. For if Soviet conventional forces could seize all of Western Europe rapidly, Moscow could employ nuclear blackmail and hold Paris, London, Bonn as hostages against the destruction of Moscow.

Successful delaying actions can be fought only with the benefit of air superiority. Air superiority in modern terms means an extensive network of early-warning systems and controlling radar, airfields, V/STOL (Vertical Short Take-Off and Landing) fighters, aircraft revetments or shelters, defensive antiaircraft missiles, concealment and dispersal fields. It means the containment, as far as possible, within the Baltic, of Soviet sea power by mining the Skagerrak and Kattegat, and by maintenance of antishipping air and sea patrols. It means the defense of the vital airfields and missile sites of the West against seaborne attack or airborne seizure.

Spain, highly important in Mediterranean defense and in Atlantic maritime strategy, offers a geographical backup position and air dispersal area in the defense of Western Europe against massive Soviet ground attack through Germany. Its airfields are still useful to the bombers of the Strategic Air Command as postrecovery bases, and the U.S. Navy has no comparable alternative to Rota as a logistics and supply base. But its airfields today, in the age of missiles, are of primary importance as dispersal sites for Western Europe's tactical air power. If the whistle blew and Soviet tanks started across the North German plain, Spanish fields might well become the key to the success or failure of Allied delaying tactics.

A reassessment of Spain's political position in Europe and its relationship to the West and to NATO is overdue. It has been too long postponed—Spain has been outside the pale of the liberal socialist regimes of Western Europe—because of the aftermath of the Spanish Civil War and the Franco dictatorship. But the Franco regime is nearing its end, and it should be possible, under a succeeding government, to bring Spain into NATO, or at least to tie her more closely to the fortunes of Western Europe—of which (regardless of politics, prejudice or emotion) she is inevitably a part.

A secondary threat to Western Europe is postulated by the exposed northern Norwegian flank.

The flat tundra of the Arctic offers no major obstacle to the ground invasion of extreme northern Norway by Russian troops, based on the Murmansk-Polyarny area, and Norway's tiny forces, even if supported by airborne troops from NATO's Central Front and by Allied air power, could offer, at best, only delaying actions. The *political* consequences of such a Soviet gambit—the actual invasion of Allied territory—would be ultimately as important, if left unanticipated, as an invasion of the Central Front; but the military consequences would be of far less immediate significance, and hence Western plans should envisage (as they do) initial reactions well below the atomic threshold. In other words, time, an inestimable gift in modern war, should be available to meet any ground invasion of northern Norway before invocation of the ultimate nuclear weapon.

In northern Norway geography provides some advantages to the defenders, despite the flat terrain. There are few surface communications; for considerable periods of the year the ground is a bog; and, above all, there are no major strategic objectives of consequence until one reaches Narvik, with its port and rail communications to the Swedish iron-ore mines and its excellent airfield on the fringing Lofoten Islands.

This area, well above the Arctic Circle and often shrouded in fog, rain, cold, snow and howling winds, is, nevertheless, of strategic importance, as World War II showed. It is the northern gateway to the Norwegian Sea, and to the exits into the Atlantic from the Barents Sea and the Arctic, and in Soviet hands it could serve as a springboard for Russian penetration toward Trondheim and Bergen. Narvik, under the Russian flag, would almost certainly mean the politico-military domination of Sweden, or, at the very least, the reduction of Sweden to the somewhat complacent and docile neutralism that characterized Stockholm's policies during the period of Nazi ascendancy in World War II, and that often seems to characterize them today.

The touchstone of Soviet intentions in Northern Europe is Narvik; almost certainly Moscow would employ combined operations—ground invasions, airborne assault and air operations, and particularly short-range, leapfrog, amphibious operations—to secure such an objective.

153

The capture of Narvik could not be tolerated by the West—if it expects to remain independent and free of conquest—without quick invocation of nuclear retaliation—selected retaliation, perhaps (for instance, the destruction of Polyarny, the Soviet naval complex near Murmansk), but nuclear retaliation nonetheless.

For, given the forces available to the West, and the military strengths the Western nations have shown they are willing to maintain in peacetime, Narvik cannot be held against determined Soviet assault. The best that can be done, as in the case of an assault through Germany, is to delay.

A Soviet drive against Narvik, or any lesser Russian incursion across the Norwegian frontier, would require the same Allied air superiority essential on the Central Front. Immediate, even if small-scale, airborne reinforcements and sizable air and naval reinforcements would be essential to successful Fabian tactics or to any successful non-nuclear reaction to a more limited-objective Soviet move.

NATO controls today what it calls ACE (Allied Command, Europe) Mobile Force, a force composed of earmarked units contributed by the United States, Britain, Germany and five other powers. This is a reinforced seven-battalion airborne force, with supporting aircraft, programed as a ready reinforcement for NATO's southern or nothern flanks. If one can envisage an isolated Soviet thrust into northern Norway, unaccompanied by a major Soviet offensive on the Central Front, then ACE could be useful in supplying the airborne reinforcements that would quickly be needed north of Narvik.

In this Arctic area the weather and the restricted logistics facilities preclude any successful military operations unless a sea supply line is maintained. And, similarly, the easiest way to concentrate Allied air power in the area is by sea, the utilization of carriers. The Arctic, the Norwegian Sea and its fiords are also a happy hunting ground for Allied submarines, and for fast, seaworthy, surface patrol craft. Small but highly trained and well-acclimated amphibious forces should be quickly available.

The importance of Iceland, the Faeroes, the Shetlands and the Orkneys to control of the Norwegian Sea and its maritime approaches is obvious from any map. The defense of Northern Europe is dependent fundamentally upon sea power. It is clear that a military weakness is any area weakens deterrence. Yet it is also clear that NATO will not materially increase the conventional defenses of the northern flank. The north, therefore, like the Central Front, must base its fundamental deterrence upon nuclear weapons and, above all, upon the cornerstone of the whole NATO edifice—that an attack upon one is an attack upon all. In pragmatic terms, the possibility of a limited Soviet attack against northern Norway, or for that matter against Denmark and the entrances to the Baltic, is so remote (because fraught with the same danger and uncertainty for Moscow as an attack upon the Central Front, but with far less hope of any conquest worth the risk) that NATO's precautionary planning seems excessive. To meet the conventional attack the Russians can mount in the area with conventional means requires a disproportionate share of the resources that NATO and the United States are willing to maintain in the years ahead.[6] In the north, as on the Central Front, uncertainty and the fear of nuclear retribution must provide the principal deterrent.

The ground forces required for the defense of Europe and a large part of the air power must be provided by Europe itself; most of the major naval forces and the nuclear deterrent will be a U.S. responsibility.

The dimensions of the Soviet threat to Western Europe, in terms of ground divisions and supporting aircraft, are large but not insuperable. In recent years Moscow has strengthened her military forces in the Far East and in Central Asia to meet a potential Chinese threat. But she still maintains—and probably will long do so—almost 100 divisions west of the Ural Mountains, including about 32 divisions in the satellite states outside the Russian frontiers. The divisions in Eastern Europe are kept at full strength and with full tables of equipment; some of those in Russia are lower-category divisions, which would require additional manpower and equipment after mobilization. The Soviet mobilization system, as Czechoslovakia showed, has a far more rapid capability for "fleshing out" below-strength units than many in the West had believed.

155

Any realistic scenario must envisage a Russian capability something like this: about 35 to 40 Soviet divisions ready for instant action against Central Europe; 2 to 3 against northern Norway; another 70 to 75 deployable within 30 to 90 days after mobilization.

In addition to the Soviet divisions, there are about 60 satellite divisions in Eastern Europe. Some of these, like the 13 Czech divisions, are of very doubtful reliability, but could probably be depended upon for occupation or mop-up duties.

These ground units are supported by very considerable tactical air strength—some estimates give the U.S.S.R. a two-to-one edge —well dispersed and protected by revetments, "hangarettes" or overhead shelters. The limited range of some of the Soviet aircraft, including the Migs, is a handicap to deep offensive operations, but the short distances of Europe do not make this restriction a disabling one.

General Lemnitzer considered these forces, after the invasion of Czechoslovakia, to be "the most formidable conventional armed forces in the world today . . . the largest and most readily usable combat force fielded by the Kremlin since World War II."[7]

These are formidable forces, but they are not impossible to check if one assumes that the primary duty of European ground forces will be to impose delay and that if the bell tolls, nuclear retribution will strike the supporting structure behind the Soviet fronts. Allied ground forces must be keyed to one purpose: to prevent the lightning seizure of Western Europe as a kind of hostage against nuclear retribution.

On the vital Central Front, 12 good, full-strength, well-equipped and well-supported West German divisions, backed by superior Allied air power, could provide the sound nucleus of defensive ground strength needed. In the first stages of any war the Russians probably could not concentrate more than 40 Soviet and satellite divisions against West Germany; the remainder of the ready Soviet units would be required in the Balkans, in the Arctic, against Italy, Greece and Turkey to checkmate Yugoslavia, and to secure Soviet lines of communication through her uncertain Eastern European satellites.

In addition to the 12 West German divisions, the defense should be able to count upon a British corps of 3 well-supported divisions; a Belgian-Dutch corps of 2 to 3 divisions; 1 Danish division (for the German front, plus other small forces for the Jutland Peninsula); and a French corps of at least 2, perhaps 3, divisions—a total of 20 to 22 divisions. One or 2 U.S. divisions, reinforced, would bring the grand total to 21 to 24 divisions—a force which should be able, if well equipped, well trained and well led, and supported by superior air power, to impose the necessary brief delay on Communist ground forces superior in numbers. One cannot possibly foresee, if the NATO strategic concept reverts to a nuclear defense, the need for any larger permanently maintained ground force; indeed, the total might well be smaller. Essential, however, to the success of its mission—delay—is superior tactical air power. The air defense of Western Europe must be able to prevent any quick airborne conquest by Soviet paratroopers or helicopter-borne infantry, and the interdiction and close-support aircraft available to the West must be capable of hampering and cutting Russian communication lines and delaying Soviet armored forces. The present relative strength of Allied to Communist air power—whether reckoned numerically or qualitatively—is inadequate either to the present concept of flexible response or to a nuclear strategy.

The comparative order of battle on the Central Front suggests a course of action for the United States which will support its vital interest in the defense of Western Europe and at the same time reduce its on-the-ground commitment to a supportable level.

U.S. ground strength in Germany should be reduced gradually to approximately one-fourth to one-third its present level—to a reinforced one- or two-division level, instead of the equivalent of more than five divisions that are maintained today. Any such reduction, of course, must be gradual, and integrated with NATO and Allied plans; the political and psychological effects of sudden reductions of U.S. troop strength could be disastrous. But if accomplished slowly over a several-year period, the thinning out of U.S. ground strength might, if well timed, contribute to a thinning out of Soviet strength in East Germany and to arms-limitation agreements.

The reduction of U.S. and, to a lesser extent, of British ground strength in Germany should be accompanied by a build-up of Allied

157

tactical air power. Squadrons withdrawn to this country on the doubtful dual-basing concept should be returned permanently to Germany, and additional increments of strength, not only to compensate for Canadian withdrawals but to increase total Allied air power, must be provided if the concept of brief delay plus quick nuclear retribution is to have its deterrent effect.

The necessary modernization and strengthening of the West German Army that any such formula implies will cost money. West Germany is prosperous enough to assume much more of the burden of its own defense than it has yet assumed. It is time—high time, a quarter of a century after World War II—that the United States reduce materially its annual $12 billion expenditure for our NATO commitments. Our original concept was to help our allies to help themselves; this has deteriorated over the years to U.S. defense of Europe with Allied help. Europe can, and must, assume a much greater share of the burden. Yet it would be unsound to shift the financial burden suddenly and entirely to Bonn's shoulders. The phased withdrawal of American troops should be accompanied by a phased increase not only in U.S. but also in Allied contributions —in barter or other form, arms-aid agreements, tariff reductions, etc.—to assist Bonn's adjustments to its new responsibilities.

The problem of ground defense of Western Europe's flanks is not as pressing or as imperative as the threat in the center; only across, or above Germany, can Soviet forces reach the vital coasts and capitals and the proud cities of Western Europe.

NATO should maintain and strengthen, with U.S. air transport and amphibious help, its capability of moving forces swiftly from the Central Front to the northern Norwegian flank, or the Turkish-Greek front. A U.S. Marine battalion, aboard modern U.S. amphibious ships, might be rotated periodically to Atlantic European waters, to supplement the one normally in the Mediterranean. Available Turkish and Greek forces are inadequate to prevent a quick Communist thrust across Greek Thrace to the Aegean, but these forces, backed by the Sixth Fleet and Allied tactical air power, should be able to impose enough delay to hold the Dardanelles, and Athens and Rome, for instance, against superior Communist ground forces for at least several weeks.

Similarly, in northern Norway a well-devised defense of the Narvik area should be capable of successful Fabian tactics.

The successful defense of Western Europe can no longer be keyed to ground operations; in the age of the missile and supersonic planes and nuclear weapons, the concept has long been outdated.

The United States should not, must not and cannot, for Europe's best interests as well as our own, maintain a five- or six-division force in West Germany indefinitely; this is a policy which some time ago reached a point of no return.

During President Eisenhower's eight years in the White House, he "believed and announced" to his associates that "a reduction of American strength in Europe should be initiated as soon as European economies were restored." In 1963 he wrote that "the time has now come to start withdrawing some of those troops. . . . One American division in Europe can 'show the flag' as definitely as can several."[8]

A frank reversion to a nuclear deterrent offers the only realistic defense concept for Western Europe in the immediate decades ahead.

But that deterrent, in order to deter, must be obviously superior to Communist nuclear power both in quantity and in quality. The complexities of deterrence (discussed in a previous chapter) are so involved and interlocking that margins for error must be generous; the deterrent must be completely credible or it is useless. It must be based at sea, in the form of U.S. and European missile submarines and surface ships, and it must be based ashore, in U.S. and French (and perhaps other) missile silos and bombers.

Two other requirements must be met. The capability of utilizing the seas for Allied purposes and denying, or greatly hampering, their use by an enemy is essential to the interlocked concept of such a transoceanic alliance as NATO. And inferior Allied ground power, acceptable if a concept of nuclear deterrence is adopted, must be backed by superior Allied air power.

This change in concept would mean a shift in emphasis, a change in weapons systems by the United States—not an immediate, but ultimately an eventual, reduction in the costs of our share of Euro-

159

pe's defense, and a slow but gradual increase in West German and European costs. Ultimately, if the policy is successful, we should get more defense, collectively, for less cost.

Such a policy, wisely supplemented by political, psychological and cultural bridge-building between East and West, might "promote the gradual erosion of the partition of Europe." It must be accompanied by a revitalization of NATO, "giving the Europeans a greater voice through a European caucus . . . possibly the appointment of a European as NATO commander . . . movement in the fields of education, technology and science . . . [and] a generally positive attitude toward East-West relations."[9]

The application to Western Europe of an aerospace-maritime strategy would be meaningless unless the United States and NATO maintained superiority in nuclear-delivery capabilities and at sea. Unless these basic requirements are fulfilled, there can be no viable strategy; there is no real alternative.

«« 7 »»

# The Mediterranean
# and Middle East

SINCE THE DAYS of the Phoenicians the Mediterranean Sea has been
man's highroad for commerce and for conquest. Around its shores,
where Western civilization was born, have grown and flourished the
greatest dynasties and kingdoms of history; upon its waters the fate
of nations has been determined.

The strategic importance of the Mediterranean has been obvious
for centuries. It is a great sea passage leading deep (via the Black
Sea) into the southern "heartland" of Eurasia; it outflanks the European peninsula; it offers (via the Suez Canal) the shortest maritime
route to the riches of the Indian Ocean; it dominates the approaches to the Middle East land bridge between three continents;
and it nourishes the maritime arteries of trade between the North
African coast and Europe.

"The main importance of the Mediterranean is that it is the
world's greatest maritime corridor. In any one day, there are usually about 2,600 merchant ships in the Mediterranean. About 1,500
of these [are] at sea and approximately 1,100 in harbour."[1]

Century after century conquerors have come this way—in gal-
leys and triremes, in dhows and frigates, in battleships and carriers,
planes and missile boats. In ancient days command of the Mediter-

ranean went to the strongest fleet; the downfall of Carthage was a triumph of Roman sea power. But since the advent of the plane and the missile, control of the seas—and particularly of the narrow Mediterranean, any part of it easily reached by aircraft based along its coasts—has meant superiority in the air as well as on and beneath the sea's surface. Today the threat of land-based air power, armed with torpedoes, bombs and long-range homing missiles; nuclear-powered submarines; and fast, missile-equipped patrol craft and destroyers challenge the aircraft carrier for sea control.

In fact, World War II forecast the problems of today: the Suez Canal was closed by mining; the British Fleet ran a gantlet of land-based air power and submarine attack from Gibraltar to Alexandria; Malta was beleaguered, and for many hard months naval and commercial operations were possible in the Mediterranean only at the cost of infinite effort and inordinate loss. The Germans accomplished these results—in effect, barring the Mediterranean to free Allied use—with a very limited effort, and with less than half of the Mediterranean coastline under their control.

It is clear that control of this great highway of commerce and conquest cannot be achieved today by surface ships alone. Submarines, above all land airfields, amphibious forces and ground armies —in other words, combined operations—spell victory. Thus any strategy to protect Europe's so-called "soft underbelly" against attack from the south, or to utilize the Mediterranean as a highway to North Africa, the Middle East and India, must ultimately focus upon control of the coasts that border the Mediterranean and the islands that dot it.

Given this context, the dimensions of the problem that face NATO, the U.S. Sixth Fleet in the Mediterranean, and the West are obviously immense. Indeed, as the preceding chapter indicated, the major danger to Western Europe today is around the Mediterranean basin, some of it already under effective Communist control.

Unlike the face-to-face confrontation between East and West in Berlin, where Communist aggression could mean immediate crisis, the Mediterranean has no comparable political fuse, although the Arab-Israeli conflict has ultimate implications of great danger. Rather, the problem around the Mediterranean is the erosion of the

162

West's once powerful political position, and the gradual elimination of U.S., NATO and Western influence from positions and areas of great geopolitical significance.

The problem of control breaks down, geographically, into regional control of the Western and the Eastern portions, and is fundamentally dependent upon the adjacent coastal areas. The narrow bottleneck between Sicily, Malta and Cape Bon in Tunisia is the vital link between the Eastern and Western portions; this strait is a lifeline or a deadly gantlet, depending upon who controls the nearby shores. It is only through this eighty-mile passage that trade and aid can reach NATO's southeastern members—Greece and Turkey. And the Levant—most of the Middle Eastern Arab states and Israel—is dependent upon this passageway for direct and easy access to seaborne lines of communication through the Mediterranean and to the Atlantic.

Sicily, Malta and Tunisia, with its great naval port of Bizerte and its air bases, are thus of key importance in Mediterranean strategy. Planes, ships and submarines based in these areas can monitor and survey all shipping passing through the strait, can harass and shadow any vessels and, deployed in sufficient force, could close the strait to all shipping. Control of these areas in a time of crisis would convey a considerable advantage to the aggressor in the inevitable game of one-upmanship that always precedes any war and sometimes determines whether or not war occurs. Passage of the Sixth Fleet from west to east, for instance, might be contested with harassing tactics and diplomatic protests. Such a gambit is not new, but it would have far greater effectiveness and force if Sicily, Malta and Tunisia were hostile.

There are three other water corridors or passageways that are of primary importance in Mediterranean strategy and two subsidiary ones.

The Strait ot Gibraltar, eight and a half miles wide, is a deep, swift-running entrée from the Atlantic. The Turkish Straits—the Bosporus, the Sea of Marmara and the Dardanelles—are the gateway to the Black Sea. And the man-made Suez Canal is an important maritime short cut to the oil wealth of the Saudi Arabian peninsula, the Red Sea, the Indian Ocean and the Far East.

163

The Strait of Otranto gives access to the Adriatic Sea and thus to the coast of Yugoslavia and the so-called Ljubjana Gap invasion route via Trieste though the mountains to and from the Austro-Hungarian plain. The myriad islands in the Aegean Sea, north of Crete, are potential air and light-craft bases which dominate the Mediterranean approaches to the Turkish Straits.

It is significant that it is around these vital maritime corridors that the latest chapter in man's unending struggle for power is concentrated. The Soviet position in Egypt, Yemen and Aden dominates the Suez Canal and the Red Sea; the improvement in Soviet-Turkish relations and the Russian-backed Bulgarian Army near Turkish Thrace give Moscow considerable influence over the Turkish Straits. And the virulent left-wing nationalism of Arab Algeria, the weakness of Morocco and Spain's quarrel with Britain about the base at Gibraltar have reduced the once dominant Western control over the strait.

Strategically, control of the Western Mediterranean starts in the Atlantic. This is recognized by the NATO command structure. IBERLANT—the Iberian Atlantic Command—is a subordinate command of the NATO Supreme Allied Commander, Atlantic (with headquarters at Norfolk, Virginia). IBERLANT, directed from headquarters at Lisbon, Portugal, is directly charged with defense of the Atlantic approaches to the Mediterranean, and the island commander of Madeira and the naval commander of Gibraltar are under IBERLANT's control in time of war. The weakness of the structure is obvious; NATO does not include Spain, and the great support and logistics base at Rota, on the Southern Atlantic coast of Spain, is under joint Spanish-U.S.—not NATO—control, and Rota's future is doubtful. Spain's claim to Gibraltar, the pressure it has exerted against continued British control there and the uncertain political complexion in Madrid after the death of Franco cloud the political and strategic prospects on the Western approaches.

So does the uncertain future of Morocco and its relationship to the city of Tangier, southern pillar of the "Strait of Hercules." Tangier and Casablanca, together with Moroccan airfields, are important supporting elements in any base structure capable of guard-

164

ing the Western approaches. The United States still maintains a major communications and intelligence facility at Sidi Yahia in Morocco (which covers the Mediterranean area), and maritime patrol plane bases there would be useful in limited war.

Given access to bases in Spain, Portugal, Morocco and the Atlantic islands, a continuing foothold at Gibraltar and the aid of modern electronics, the defense of the Western approaches should be simple. In strategic terms, "defense" means utilization of the Gibraltar approaches for our own purposes, denial of these seas to any enemy shipping in wartime, and the capability of exercising an effective surveillance and/or a blockade over the entire area from Casablanca to Lisbon in cold war or time of crisis. This is obviously a job for air-sea power; land power's sole task is to provide security for the air-naval bases.

The task of monitoring the Atlantic approaches to the Mediterranean is eased by modern electronics. Land-based, ship-based and air-based radar can now be supplemented by a sea-bed cable across the Strait of Gibraltar, capable of monitoring the passage of submarines or surface ships. This underwater surveillance device could provide a "nose count" and directional index—particularly important in determining the numbers of Soviet submarines in the Mediterranean. (The Montreux Convention provides that Soviet submarines passing into the Mediterranean from the Black Sea through the Turkish Straits must cruise on the surface, but Soviet submarines entering the Mediterranean from the Arctic or the Baltic through Gibraltar Strait often proceed submerged.)

In the Western Mediterranean the radical nationalism of Algeria and the increasing Soviet influence in Algiers, as well as wideranging Russian naval activities, have postulated a new threat to a once secure Western control. Visits by Soviet men-of-war to Algiers are commonplace. The important (formerly French) base of Mers-el-Kebir near Oran is protected now by Soviet SAM antiaircraft missiles, and there are some Soviet port authorities and naval advisers. The Algerians operate a small number of missile-armed patrol craft.

Of key importance to the strategy of the Western Mediterranean are the dozen or so Algerian airfields. They have been surveyed with Russian aid, and their runways lengthened to take jets; some Egyptian Tu-16 bombers were dispersed to Algeria after the Six-Day Arab-Israeli War. Several thousand Soviet advisers have been engaged in various economic aid projects and have been helping to train the Algerian armed forces to handle Soviet tanks, Mig-21's and other Russian arms.

The Algerian airfields as a potential base for Soviet bombers represent a pre-emptive threat to the U.S. Sixth Fleet and to NATO. Enemy aircraft based on these fields would transform the Western Mediterranean into a cockpit of conflict. War plans, to be realistic, must be adjusted to such a possibility; the Sixth Fleet's strength would have to be bolstered to meet this contingency. Indeed, the maintenance, under such a situation, of surface naval vessels in the Mediterranean might well become such an expensive exercise that the cost would not repay the advantages.

In any protracted, non-nuclear war, the Soviet logistic supply of these bases would be increasingly difficult—and probably impossible—so long as the West retained control over Italy, France, Spain and Morocco. But such a war is not a probability. A far more likely eventuality is an Arab-Israeli crisis, a crisis in Morocco or elsewhere in Africa, or a small-scale guerrilla war or war of subversion in Africa. And a global crisis, which might even move to the threshold of nuclear threats (as in the Cuban crisis and at Suez, when Khrushchev threatened the use of missiles), is possible. In either case, the Algerian airfields used by Soviet aircraft as staging fields represent an important strategic asset. They not only impose an immediate threat to the Sixth Fleet and the West's maritime lines of communication in the Western Mediterranean, but they also represent a completely new danger to the southern flank of NATO. Since the French and the Italian air-defense systems are oriented to the east and north, the south and west are exposed to sudden surprise attack from Algeria. One may well argue that this will never happen; agreed, it is unlikely to happen, since such attacks would risk nuclear war. Nevertheless, geopolitics means cards, positions, strengths, and the potential threat from Algeria gives the Soviet Union a posture of political strength in the Western Mediterranean it has never before enjoyed. It adds additional pre-emptive power to its diplomacy.

It is a potential threat which can be, to a large degree, contained and countered by two developments: the gradual resumption by France of military participation in NATO, now possible since De Gaulle's retirement, and the participation by Spain in NATO or through a cooperative arrangement (including British-held Gibraltar) in Mediterranean strategy, also possible with the future assumption of power by Don Carlos.

But a converse trend is also possible. Spain has exhibited some anxiety about U.S. intentions in the Mediterranean, and some Spanish-Russian fence-mending appears to have started. A recent report indicated that Madrid and Moscow were considering the establishment of a joint oceanographic station on the Spanish island of Alborán, which lies in the narrow western arm of the Mediterranean, almost in the mouth of the Strait of Gibraltar. The military importance of such a foothold is obvious.

But the expansion of Soviet influence is not limited to Algeria. Some Soviet military equipment has been supplied to Morocco, and Communist attempts to harness the force of Arab nationalism to Soviet purposes continue. Soviet naval visits to Casablanca and Algiers are supplemented, in the Western Mediterranean, by the more or less continuous presence of Soviet naval vessels of various types. These ships habitually use off-shore open-sea anchorages (beyond territorial limits) near Alborán Island; the Banc Le Sec and Galite, off Algeria and Tunisia; Hammamet and the Gulf of Gabès off Tunisia; Terrible Bank, south of Sicily; and Hurd Bank, south of Malta.

The Soviet Navy in the Mediterranean (sometimes numbering more than 60 ships, usually about 35) is today a mixture, as it is elsewhere, of the obsolescent and the most modern. But the obsolescent is rapidly being phased out and is being replaced by the newest ships and weapons systems, the newest techniques and the newest concepts. The Russian Fleet is still weak on logistics; water barges sometimes are brought down from the Black Sea to provide fresh water for its combat vessels. Soviet vessels usually, though not always, refuel and replenish at anchor, or by the awkward and slow astern method. In some ships maintenance and upkeep appear to be grossly deficient. Antisubmarine warfare operations and modern amphibious power are deficient. The Soviet Navy has, as yet, no aircraft carriers. Yet modern, high-speed, missile craft, armed with the Styx and other missiles, light cruisers and destroyers with ship-to-ship missiles which far outrange ours, land-based aircraft with standoff, air-to-surface homing missiles, modern nuclear-powered submarines and helicopter carriers have added tremendous power and versatility to what, a decade ago, was a thoroughly second-rate navy. Today the power of the Soviet Fleet, though it does not match our own, has the respect of all who have studied it. The Soviet Mediterranean squadron represents a "fleet in being," a pre-emptive and inhibiting political factor. Its potential power must be reckoned with in peace and war, and it is a visible evidence of growing Soviet strength.

As early as 1967 the Assembly of the Western European Union was told that the Mediterranean no longer was a "Western lake." "It is no longer correct to speak of the 'danger' of the Soviet Union out-flanking the NATO southern flank," a report to the Assembly stated. "This 'danger' has become a reality which poses members of the Alliance with the problem not of how they should prevent an out-flanking but of how to react to this hard fact."[2]

So far the strategic problem of the Western Mediterranean is largely potential. The problem of the Eastern Mediterranean is actual, and the danger, because of the explosive powder keg of the Middle East, more imminent.

In the Eastern Mediterranean, Soviet naval vessels habitually use open-water, offshore anchorages on the Manfredonia Banks in the Adriatic Sea off Italy; in the Gulf of Sidra and the Gulf of Sollum off Libya; Kithira, just south of Greece; Galeta Bank and Amorgos in the Aegean; shallow-water anchorage east of Crete and east of Cyprus and near Latakia, Syria. But in the Eastern Mediterranean the major Soviet advantage is its increasingly strong position in the contiguous nations.

Russian ships are welcome in many of the principal ports of the Eastern Mediterranean. Yugoslavia is a Communist state—albeit

168

an independent one—which welcomes periodic visits from Russian ships and aids and abets many, though not all, Soviet foreign policy gambits. In strong contrast, there are only two countries, Italy and Greece, where the U.S. Sixth Fleet can be assured of a relatively quiet visit, and even Italy presents a shaky picture, politically and economically. Gradually, the ports of the area have been shut to the U.S. flag.

# Egypt

Egypt's political, economic and military dependence upon Russia is perhaps more complete than that of any of the other major Arab states, more, indeed, than that of any other nation around the Mediterranean basin. One experienced diplomat put it this way: "The Soviet Ambassador in Cairo, who sees Nasser several times a week, probably has slightly less influence than the British Ambassador to Egypt had in the days of glory of the British Raj." Since the British power in Egypt in those bygone days was almost absolute, the dimensions of Moscow's influence are considerable.

Much of Egypt's cotton crop is purchased by the U.S.S.R.; the Aswan Dam has been built with Soviet aid, and there are many other Russian aid projects.

There were in 1969, at least 2,000 Soviet military "advisers" in Egypt and several hundred to 1,000 civilian technicians. In the last months of the year and in early 1970 a considerable number of additional Soviet military personnel were sent to Egypt. They accompanied new shipments of military materiel, including SAM-3 low level antiaircraft missiles, radar and communications equipment to strengthen the pitifully weak Egyptian air defense system. Some additional Soviet pilots and ground crews were reported in Egypt. Russian personnel were believed to be moving into positions of direction and control at SAM sites and in the Egyptian aircraft warning and control system. The Egyptian armed forces are almost completely equipped with Russian weapons, and the Russians control the training schedules and the logistics or supply services. Soviet pilots fly with the Egyptians on training flights, and Soviet-manned Tu-16's with Egyptian markings, based on Cairo West Air

169

Base, regularly overfly the U.S. Sixth Fleet.

The Russian presence in Egypt, though undoubtedly productive of friction, is now so familiar and ubiquitous, and the Egyptians are so dependent upon Soviet support, that Moscow is able to use Egyptian soil for *de facto* (if not *de jure*) air and naval bases. The Russians manage and operate a shipyard in Alexandria, and Soviet naval vessels regularly use Alexandria and Port Said for overhaul and refueling. It appears to be Russian policy to maintain constantly some units of the Soviet Mediterranean squadron in either or both ports to pre-empt, or inhibit, Israeli attack. The Soviet airline, Aeroflot, maintains regular schedules to Cairo and has extended its service to Aswan and to other points in Africa.

Despite Soviet support, the economic situation in Egypt, though considerably stronger than it was, is tenuous; the political situation is calm on the surface but with much opposition to Nasser and considerable frustration underground. But the Russians support Nasser and are trying to maintain possible alternatives. And the indigenous discontent has no internal focus; it has been skillfully directed against Israel.

Thus the emotional trauma of the Arab-Israeli conflict helps Moscow to ride the whirlwind. The exploitation, by Western companies, of oil resources in the Western Desert, the investment of U.S. private development capital in Egypt and the resumption of official relations between Cairo and Washington might help, in time if they occur, to reduce the present tremendous extent of Soviet influence, but not even a settlement of the Arab-Israeli conflict (which is not in sight) will now oust Moscow's influence completely. The Russians are along the Nile and the Suez Canal to stay.

"Peter the Great's dream—a warm-water port—has been realized," a U.S. diplomat has said.

# Libya

Radical Arabism, Egyptian influence and, inferentially, Soviet influence extended its control along the North African coast in 1969, when a Pan-Arab military coup ousted King Idris, the octogenarian monarch, and put the newly found oil wealth of Libya squarely on the side of activist Arab nationalists.

The coup, like the small-scale civil war in Lebanon, was another clear-cut indication that the moderate Arab governments are reaching the point of no return. The Libyan coup immediately exposed President Bourguiba—friendly to the West—to increased pressure from both Algeria and Libya. It left among the so-called moderates only Morocco, ineffectual Lebanon, torn by civil dissent, Jordan and Saudi Arabia. The fate of the moderates, and particularly of pro-Western regimes in the Arab world, is certain if the polarization of the Arab-Israeli conflict continues without settlement.

Libya, like many of the Arab nations, was just emerging from the shadows of feudalism and tribalism when the coup occurred. Tremendous, newly found oil wealth—more than $1 billion of oil revenue went into Libya's coffers in 1969—had exposed its two million people to a social, economic and political revolution. A sleepy, desert country, which may well have a per capita GNP of $1,700 by 1973 (in excess of Britain's), has suddenly found the floodgates of wealth, with all the changes this implies, opened.

The oil concessions are Western, chiefly U.S. (West Germany gets more than 40 percent of her oil from Libya), and U.S.-owned, or partially owned, companies have invested more than $1 billion there. This is both help and handicap to the United States; Libya is dependent upon the marketing facilities these oil companies provide and could not replace them without enormous economic dislocation and a drop in revenue. On the other hand, the U.S. investment and the revenues obtained from it are dependent upon the goodwill of the Libyan Government, and that in turn is certain to be affected by developments in the Arab-Israeli conflict.

In a military sense, Libya's importance to the United States has been concentrated in one large training and staging airfield at Wheelus, just outside Tripoli, a field of potential strategic significance in the control of the Mediterranean, although recently used only for nonoperational flights (training and some staging flights). Wheelus was the last airfield available to the United States for military purposes in North Africa. The coup ended its availability to the United States.

171

# Jordan

Jordan, chiefly because of King Hussein, has been, along with Saudi Arabia and Tunisia and Lebanon, the most pro-Western of the Arab states. But with its long common frontier with Israel, its large Palestine refugee population and the fedayeen guerrillas, it is inextricably involved in the Arab-Israeli conflict, and the King is torn by fierce and mounting pressures. As Hussein said in a recent interview: "It is as impossible for me to openly oppose the fedayeen and their objective of liberating Palestine as it is for the President of the United States to oppose the Negroes."

So far Soviet influence is relatively minor, except among splinter groups of ideologically motivated Palestinian fedayeen. But Moscow's influence is slowly increasing. A recent Soviet plan to extend Aeroflot air service from Moscow to Amman is an index of the trend.

King Hussein, like King Feisal of Saudi Arabia, Bourguiba of Tunisia and all other Arab moderates, is in a more and more dangerous position the longer the Arab-Israeli conflict continues. Today his Jordanian Army can control the fedayeen—though not without concession; tomorrow the balance of power may slowly slip to the activists, the radicals, the Palestinians. Frustration in the Arab world is slowly undermining the position of the moderates.

# Lebanon

Half Christian, half Moslem, its politics delicately balanced between religions and races, this rich little country, traditionally open and neutralist in the conflicts that sweep the Middle East, is immune no longer to the winds of change. Communist influence is still not dominant. The Russians, like the West, find Lebanon at the moment a useful listening post and springboard for the Middle East. Communist money is funneled to some of the leftist papers of the area and to other propaganda activities, and Russian intelligence agents in considerable numbers use Lebanon as a base for information-gathering, pulse-taking and covert activities. As a banking and trading nation, hurt by the Arab-Israeli conflict and the

172

establishment of other banking and brokerage centers in the area, Lebanon could offer in the future fertile soil for Communist expansionism.

The small-scale civil war in Lebanon of 1969 (adjourned, but probably not terminated, by compromise) pushed the little country off its knife edge of moderation toward the Arab—and Russian— cause. The power of the fedayeen guerrillas, based on Syria, of Arab sympathizers and Palestinian refugees in Lebanon, was tested, with some success, against weak Lebanese security forces and a divided government, and the result—as in all Arab countries caught up in the backwash of the Arab-Israeli conflict—was a blow for moderation.

# Turkey

The deterioration in U.S.-Turkish relationships since the early 1960's is one of the shocking facts of life in the Middle East. Leftist student mobs have pushed U.S. sailors into the Bosporus and have practically closed Turkish ports to U.S. naval visits.

The policy of the Turkish Government is officially one of friendship to the United States and of adherence to NATO, but the divisions in Turkey between left-wing groups and extreme right-wing student "Commandos" are so deep and the influence of Communism so strong that the government has been ineffective in maintaining stability and order. Some of the disorders and anti-American manifestations of 1969 were a direct outgrowth of the elections of that year, which resulted in the return of the government and a considerable loss to the left-wing Labor Party. With the distractions of tub-thumping behind them, Turkish politics *should* offer a somewhat more stable prospect in the immediate future. But the Turkish political scene is highly volatile, and the dissenters and the leftists represent a well-organized and vocal minority who will not disappear.

Turkey, moreover, has officially embarked upon a fence-mending policy with all its neighbors, and has deliberately broadened its contacts and improved its relations with Russia. Subtle Soviet support for the Turkish Cyprus position and what is emotionally inter-

173

preted as the anti-Turkish Cypriot policy of the United States have been powerful factors in the realignment of Turkish public opinion. President Johnson's bluntly worded letter, which possibly averted impending Turkish invasion of Cyprus a few years ago, is still quoted or referred to in the Turkish press and is used, often in distorted context, to whip up anti-American emotions. A too pervasive U.S. presence in Turkey, our failure to provide the Turkish Army with the amounts or kinds of equipment the Turks wished, the strengthened Soviet naval presence in the Mediterranean— particularly obvious to Turkey because of the increased numbers of ship sorties through the Bosporus—and the "Big Bully" image pinned on the United States by Communist Vietnam propaganda have all had a deteriorating effect.

The Russians have capitalized on these opportunities but have also undertaken initiatives of their own. Turkish-Russian trade is increasing; Moscow is doing its best to encourage friction, or worse, between Turkey and Greece, both of them essential to the southern flank of NATO. Major Soviet-sponsored aid projects are developing Turkish industry.

Communist "black radios" beam invective and incitement to the left-wing groups in Turkey, and the virulence of the left-wing press, heavily subsidized by Communist funds, equals the worst of the Arab papers.

Turkey, because of its strategic position athwart the narrow sea routes leading from the Black Sea to the Mediterranean, and as one of the "Northern Tier" countries adjoining Russia (Turkey, Iran, Afghanistan), is of major importance in the geopolitics of the Eastern Mediterranean. The Turkish Straits dominate the increasing flow of Soviet maritime commerce to and from the Black Sea. Russian submarines and naval vessels must transit the narrow bottlenecks of the Bosporus and the Dardanelles to sortie to the Mediterranean. The restrictive provisions of the Montreux Convention, which defines and limits the passage of naval vessels through the straits, have so far been observed in general terms by Moscow. But under pressure from the Russians, the Turks have agreed to more liberal interpretations of the provision requiring daylight transits for naval vessels, and as Soviet maritime commerce and naval power increase, there is certain to be increasing pressure to revise the convention.

But air bases in Turkey, the missile-monitoring radars, the communications and electronic-intelligence installations are important to the United States, to NATO and to Turkey. But if these facilities are to be retained, the U.S. image in Turkey must be improved. Our presence should be a low-profile one; U.S. military personnel and U.S. civilian employees should be materially reduced and more and more of the responsibility for operating the facilities shifted to the Turks. The Turkish armed forces—some of the largest in NATO— are more than 16 divisions strong, with a backing of at least 450,000 trained reserves. But weapons and equipment are old, and Army, Navy (highly important in the Black Sea) and Air Force require re-equipment or modernization. Turkey is too important to be neglected. Rapid and strong fence-mending by the United States is an urgent requirement.

The Communists in Turkey are not as strong as they seem. The trends in Turkey of the past few years are plain—toward an independent neutralism. Because of its long history of conflict and friction with its great neighbor to the north and the natural wariness of the Turks of Soviet ambitions, Turkey will not become a Russian stooge or satellite. But it is in strong danger of becoming—from the point of view of the West and of NATO—an unreliable ally.

## Syria and Iraq

These two countries are in some ways more firmly in the Soviet orbit than any others in the Middle East, yet their volatile politics and their internecine quarrels, the highly emotional nature of their peoples and their fractionalized power structure, have made even the Russians despair of exercising rational control. Both countries are almost completely dependent upon Moscow for arms, equipment and military supplies and training, and Soviet economic penetration has made progress. In Iraq the Russians have established their first economic beachhead on the Persian Gulf and their first, though modest, stake in the rich oil resources of the Middle East. Soviet access to an oil concession at Basra and Soviet aid for devel-

175

opment of an unexploited field—plus a Soviet market for the oil—
were part of a series of economic agreements between Moscow and
Baghdad negotiated in 1969, following an earlier agreement in
1967. Soviet aid, including military equipment, probably is now
valued at more than $700 million to each country. There are about
800 to 1,000 Russian military advisers and some civilian technicians in Syria, a somewhat lesser number in Iraq. Large sums of
money help to support the radical press, and Communist leaders
come and go between Moscow and Baghdad, Damascus and various areas of the Middle East. Iraqi-trained Communists, possibly
the most virulent and violent of the Middle Eastern breed, periodically surface as radical labor leaders in the oil fields of Kuwait or
in other potential trouble spots. The violent nationalism and anti-
Zionism of Iraq; the Kurdish rebellion; and Baghdad's differences
with Iran about borders and navigation and sovereign rights along
the Shatt al Arab (the Arvandrood River) estuary at the northern
tip of the Persian Gulf have been exploited by Russia to increase
the military dependency of Iraq upon Moscow.

Iraq, to a considerably greater extent than Syria, has mutual
economic interests with the West; her oil fields have been developed primarily by Western companies, and the oil pipeline from
Kirkuk and Mosul across Syria to the Mediterranean, is still a vital
economic artery to Baghdad. Today, despite Baghdad's strong anti-
Western stance, Iraq has more to gain economically by casting her
lot with the West than with Russia. But tomorrow may be a different story. A new Soviet-financed textile mill in southern Iraq is of
potential importance to the Iraqi economy, and the Baghdad Communist Party, concentrated in a "Red belt" of slums around the
city, is one of the strongest in the Middle East and can probably,
in a crisis, control the street mobs which have so often made or
broken Arab governments.

The Syrian port of Latakia, developed in part by Communist
funds, is visited periodically by Soviet ships. A $150 million Eu-
phrates dam project, financed by Russia, may, in time, greatly alter
the Syrian economy. There is some Syrian dissatisfaction, as there
is elsewhere, with the Russian-supplied arms and equipment; nevertheless the Communist faction in Syria remains strong.

176

The prospect in both countries is continued political instability, factionalism, slowly increasing Soviet economic penetration—particularly in the oil fields of Iraq—and violent and virulent radicalism of the left and the right—a climate fertile for Communist machinations, but uncontrollable and unpredictable.

Russia's great and growing influence around the shores of the Eastern Mediterranean is due, predominantly, to one cause—the Arab-Israeli conflict. Soviet arms and economic aid and psychological and political support for the Arab world have opened gateways to Russian penetration. Washington, too often influenced by the Jewish vote in the United States (and particularly in New York City), has generally tended, until late 1969, to support Israel and has allowed itself to be cast as the villain in Arab eyes. The Arab-Israeli conflict has been polarized in the Middle East into an East-West conflict.

This may be to the advantage of Israel, but it is not to the advantage of the United States. For polarization runs the risk of transforming a regional conflict into a big-power confrontation, and it gives Russia the political and psychological advantages in much of the Eastern Mediterranean basin. For it is in the Arab and Moslem countries (particularly in the Saudi Arabian Peninsula and Iran, which will be discussed in the next chapter), not Israel, that the great oil wealth of the area is found. It is the most cheaply produced oil in the world; it nets the United States about $1.5 billion annually; it fuels Western Europe and Japan; its loss would rock the economy of the Free World; its gain would represent a rich accretion to Russia's depleted Baku fields and to its undeveloped oil reserves. And it is in the Arab and Moslem states, not Israel— in Saudi Arabia, Turkey, Iran, Iraq, Libya, Egypt—that are to be found the staging airfields vital to commercial airlines and to military airlift from Europe to South Asia, and the land transportation routes that connect three continents.

In other words, the *tangible* interests of the United States in the Middle East are in the Arab and Moslem lands, not in Israel. But the *emotional* ties of many Americans, the common basis of the Judeo-Christian religion and the pressure of domestic political con-

177

siderations link us to Israel. The dilemma presented is well-nigh insoluble, yet unless it is relieved—even if unresolved—it could lead to tragedy, not only for Israel but for the United States.

In fact, the United States in the Middle East is between Charybdis and Scylla. Our unbalanced pro-Israel policy has been antithetical to the interests we have in the Arab and Moslem countries. On the other hand, the Moslem world and the Arabs generally represent a culture somewhat alien to American society (the new cult of the extremist "Black Muslims" excepted). And the natural sympathy of a sizable segment of U.S. public opinion for Israel and the political factor of great Jewish influence in the United States might force U.S. intervention in any crisis in which the existence of Israel were threatened. This is an explosive dilemma; it emphasizes the necessity for preventive action before the fuse burns out.

The Middle East has become today what the Balkans were to Europe in pre-1914—a powder keg—and there is no quick end in sight. The creation of the state of Israel—a modern Jewish state, dedicated to global Jewish emigration, a Jewish national home, a growing population and an expanding economy, in the midst of a sea of technologically backward volatile Arabs, many of them living in obsolete social and economic systems and under decadent governments, has created an irreconcilable conflict. A settlement of the Arab-Israeli conflict is unlikely, if only because it is not to Russia's interest: a real settlement would reduce, though not eliminate, her influence. Continuation of the present state of conflict, with artillery exchanges, air duels, terrorism and guerrilla raids across the frontiers, seems inevitable; the tempo may build up rather than decrease. But a "Fourth Round," or another full-fledged, even if brief, war seems unlikely in the *near* future, if only because Israeli combat effectiveness is still far superior to that of her Arab opponents.

This is not true on paper. The Arabs far outnumber the Israelis, though this superiority is far less pronounced when combat effectives are compared. At full strength Israel can put into uniform approximately 300,000 men and women. The combined strengths of the Eygptian, Jordanian, Syrian and Iraqi armed forces may now number about 400,000 men; conceivably by maximum effort these

178

could be increased by another 100,000 or more. To this figure must be added—on paper—the approximately 60,000 troops of Algeria (about 3,500 of them along the Suez Canal); Palestine Liberation Organization, or fedayeen, forces numbering collectively (including all in training) perhaps 20,000; a Saudi Arabian brigade of about 3,500 in southern Jordan; and small detachments of Sudanese, Libyan and other troops—a grand total of more than 600,000 (of which perhaps no more than half at a maximum could be deployed directly against Israel).

The biggest of the Arab powers—Egypt—has about 12 divisions in her order of battle, 7 or 8 of them operational and equipped, the rest being organized and trained. These troops are well supplied with modern Soviet-type arms, and they are supported by about 800 planes and helicopters, about half of them combat types. In comparison Israel could field at maximum strength about 30 to 35 brigades (roughly the equivalent of 9 to 12 divisions), well equipped and well trained, and her Air Force flies more than 300 combat aircraft, including late-model U.S. A4E attack planes and F-4 Phantoms, plus about 80 to 100 logistic, transport and miscellaneous aircraft.

The numerical statistics and the order of battle would seem to indicate a collective Arab superiority. But this is apparent rather than real. There is no Arab unity; in fact, one of the dangers of the Middle East is Arab disunity, expressed often among the Arab states in violent words and deeds. Israel occupies, geographically, a central, compact position; she can concentrate air or ground power against her neighboring foes far more easily than they can concentrate against her. Her mobilization potential and war reserves are far superior to that fraction of the Arab total that can be brought against her. And in leadership, morale, professional skill and training Israel is much stronger than her enemies—particularly in the air. The air raids of 1969 showed conclusively that Arab air power, despite some slight improvement since the Six-Day War, was no match for Israel's.

The Eygptian armed forces, with massive military aid and under Soviet tutelage, are improving slowly; their aircraft dispersion and protection and, to a much lesser extent, their air-defense system make a repetition of the Israeli air blitz of the Six-Day War very unlikely—though not impossible. But the great weaknesses of the Arab states are technology and, above all, leadership and sound governmental structures. From behind defensive positions the Arabs can fight a fairly effective static battle; they cannot wage mobile warfare. And their lack of an officer corps, which cannot be created quickly, condemns them for years to come to inferiority to Israel. The only way in which this inferiority can be overcome in the near future is the reinforcement of the Arab forces with Soviet "volunteers" in large numbers or combat units. The Israelis believe that such a reinforcement, to tip the balance, would have to be fairly massive and hence obvious; the participation of a few pilots in a kind of unacknowledged proxy war would be insufficient, they believe. Washington and other Western capitals have emphasized far too much the importance of Soviet weapons and equipment in the equation of power in the Middle East, and have under-estimated the importance of Israeli personnel—leadership, training, teamwork, technology. With some exaggeration, it has been said that "you could give the Israelis bows and arrows, and they could still lick the Arabs." It is true, of course, that in a purely passive sense, the Arab air forces are more secure and better protected against destruction than ever before. But unless the aircraft can be used effectively to win air superiority they are merely symbols of power; so far the Arab interception capabilities, ground support and interdiction and offensive effectiveness—though improving—are weak. The skills of sizeable numbers of Soviet pilots, flying in Arab planes, would help to redress the balance, but, alone, would not compensate for the marked Israeli superiority. For air power means ground crews, mechanics, radar operators, aircraft warning and control systems, and a whole complex of advanced military technology.

Such open intervention by Russia in the near future is unlikely as long as the United States retains ties and positions with the moderate Arab states and maintains the Sixth Fleet in the Mediterranean. The risk of great-power confrontation would probably be too major to risk in Kremlin eyes. Yet the possibility of some Soviet involvement—particularly on a small scale and with enough increment of Russian power to result in at least an Israeli repulse—is a definite danger tomorrow. One cannot forget that Soviet pilots intervened in the Yemen civil war, and one must always remember that the Soviet leadership is uncertain and insecure and foreordained to sudden change.

And there were ominous signs in early 1970 that Russia was grasping the nettle of danger and had decided to strengthen Egyptian air capabilities with Soviet personnel. This does not necessarily mean open confrontation; Soviet military men—bolstering Ho Chi Minh in North Vietnam—were killed and wounded by U.S. bombs, without a word from Moscow. But it does increase the risks. And Moscow's action was clearly reaction to the wide-ranging Israeli air raids over Egypt, which struck targets near Cairo and dramatically exposed Egyptian weaknesses. Tragically, many of the deeper-penetration raids were made with U.S. supplied F-4's—a fact which widened the gulf between Washington and Arab capitals. The aggressive Israeli attacks which have accomplished little of permanent military significance forced Russia to back her Arab proteges and more than match the U.S. aid to Israel. Moscow's stakes in the Middle East are now too great to permit her to stand aside if her Arab proteges should face another humiliating defeat. Thus U.S. and particularly Israeli policies, as well as Russian policies, have forced a further polarization in the Middle East.

One cannot predict the policies of a future Soviet Government, though it is certain that increasing Russian power will permit increasing boldness. But today and for the foreseeable future Russia wants controlled chaos in the Middle East.

An important element of the "controlled" part of this formula is, at the moment, reduced tensions. The U.S.S.R., like the United States, is worried about the inflammatory situation in he Middle East (though not enough to change her basic policy), for she cannot control either Israeli reactions to Arab actions or the fedayeen. And Israel, though stung by the slow attrition of the endless guerrilla fighting and the economic drain it represents, knows that the capture of Amman, Damascus, Cairo—though probably entirely feasible from a military point of view—would create a major political crisis and accomplish little. Her armies would suffer sizable casualties from street fighting, and above all she would be unable to hold her positions. Israel, with 2.5 million Jews, now controls territory with a population of 1.5 million Arabs inside her expanded frontiers. She is already attempting to assimilate the unassimilable; further conquests would lead inevitably to acute indigestion.

Thus, though no final solution of a problem which only history will resolve, is foreseeable, an easement of tensions—a kind of *modus vivendi*—in the area is essential if the fuse to the powder keg is to be cut or even lengthened and, particularly, if the deterioration in the U.S. position in the Middle East is to be halted. There should be no doubt about it: the Middle East *is* a powder keg, and the U.S. interests in the area *are* major. Israel is already the world's sixth atomic power; she has nuclear weapons, or the capability of assembling them quickly. She has rockets of sufficient range to reach from her borders to the major Arab capitals. And her peoples and her government possess the ruthlessness and the determination to use —*in extremis*—any and all means to survive.

But Israel's basic problem is not immediate but long-term, and it is far more subtle than the military problem of survival. It is demographic and passionate, and there is no clear end in sight. As Michael Howard and Robert Hunter have written:

> Israel . . . [is] confronted with all the problems of a multiracial society, in which the minority group is potentially hostile and sustained by powerful consanguineous supports beyond the frontier. . . .
> Israel thus faces a dilemma to which her military talents provide no solution, and to which even nuclear weapons will be irrelevant. A strategically secure frontier, in the south and east, will give her a strategically insecure population. . . . The Israelis can congratulate themselves on their success in reconciling the small Arab population for twenty years within their borders, but the change [since the Six-Day War] in the dimensions of their task is likely to transform its entire nature. It is hard, indeed, to see how it can be accomplished at all, unless the Israelis abandon many of their Zionist ideals and revert to the older concept of a Palestine shared peacefully between Arab and Jew.[3]

Over any long-term period it is clear that Israel cannot survive in an Arab sea completely dominated by Russia and her satellites.

*for the conclusion!*

Without U.S. power to balance Soviet influence, without the U.S. Sixth Fleet in the Mediterranean, Israel is ultimately doomed. Yet, to check the spread of Soviet power, Israel herself must be checked; the polarization of the area must be halted, a better balance between the protagonists maintained. The Zionists and Israel have been, too often, the tail that wagged the dog of U.S. foreign policy in the Middle East; no *modus vivendi* or easement of tensions is possible given the frozen positions of the past, now seemingly, but belatedly, more flexible. The first requirement is the exercise of U.S. power and responsibility; the utilization of pressure against Israel; the utilization of pressure against Russia and her Arab clients to force, not settlement, but easement. And the second requirement is strengthening what remain of the moderate regimes in the area— Tunisia, Jordan, Lebanon, Saudi Arabia, some of the Trucial States along the Persian Gulf, and Iran—to offset the power and militancy of the Russian-backed Arab radicals. Our diplomacy has been unimaginative, timid; the old clichés echo in a new era. Yet the hour is late in the Middle East; the knell of American power may be sounding there.

A political policy is no stronger than the power that supports it; for the United States there is much fence-mending needed in the Eastern Mediterranean.

The first requirement is the strengthening of the Sixth Fleet. It has become a prestige and political symbol that considerably transcends its military importance. The Russians are determined to force its withdrawal from the Eastern Mediterranean basin, if possible from the entire Mediterranean Sea. Such a withdrawal would now have catastrophic consequences; it could only be interpreted as a signature to defeat, a concession that the Mediterranean had become a Soviet *mare nostrum*. As long as the Sixth Fleet remains in the Mediterranean it epitomizes U.S. power and U.S. interest, and it represents—just as the Soviet Mediterranean squadron does —a "fleet in being," a pre-emptive and inhibiting force, which acts as a checkrein to Russian freedom of political action.

The Sixth Fleet, like most of our forces overseas, has been allowed to deteriorate in combat power as the United States focused its efforts upon Vietnam. Old ships, inexperienced men, old planes,

183

lack of spare parts, have too often hobbled its power. It is a sad commentary on U.S. policy in the Mideast that in the winter of 1969 the *Shangri-la* and the *Forrestal*, the two carriers then assigned to the Mediterranean were flying planes (A-4 attack aircraft and F-4 fighters) very considerably older than the models Washington was supplying to the Israelis. The newest ships, the newest aircraft, plenty of spare parts and some of the Navy's most experienced personnel should be assigned to the Mediterranean; the Sixth Fleet should have an A No. 1 priority equal to that of the Seventh Fleet in the Western Pacific.

But qualitative strengthening of the fleet might be accomplished by a change in concept. The Sixth Fleet must remain in the Mediterranean, but in the future it need not be a fleet of fixed composition as in the past. A certain minimum force should always be assigned to the Mediterranean, but it might be useful to vary the fleet's strength, as the Russians have varied theirs. Periodic cruises by large units could augment the permanent strength, and perhaps might be more welcome to some of the nations that are now lukewarm, at best, to the fleet's presence. Certainly, no sizable quantitative increase in the Sixth Fleet's present power—about fifty ships —is now indicated, though in the future the intermittent assignment of an additional carrier (normally there are two attack carriers in the Mediterranean) and/or of an antisubmarine warfare carrier on a full-time basis may be needed, and at times the Marine amphibious landing team should be doubled to two battalions. Improved antimissile defenses and better antishipping missiles are needed.

The fleet's greatest need is for improved reconnaissance; in time of crisis the Commander, Sixth Fleet, must know where Soviet and satellite ships are at all times. A detachment of a few U.S. patrol planes, based on Rota, and a squadron in Sicily are now the only U.S. maritime-air capability in the Mediterranean; it is augmented by small British and Italian and Greek contingents. At least 2 squadrons—from 18 to 24 land-based maritime patrol aircraft, about double the current figure—are needed in the new conditions in the Mediterranean. ASW capabilities, which would be strengthened by such an augmentation, also require the assignment of

184

newer and better-equipped ships. More U.S. nuclear-powered attack submarines—there are normally 2 or 3 assigned to the Mediterranean—are needed to checkmate increasing Soviet submarine strength (normally, there are about 8 Soviet submarines in the Mediterranean; at times there have been as many as 14). And new technological developments—variable-depth sonar, mobile arrays of deep-water listening devices, infrared sensors—should be deployed quickly to the Mediterranean. But in a sea as narrow and as canalized as the Mediterranean, land bases are the ultimate key to the exercise of power. The fewer land bases the United States retains, the greater the restrictions on the freedom of action of the Sixth Fleet.

From the Central to the Eastern Mediterranean the land bases essential to U.S. power are the Italian peninsula, Sicily and Malta (the latter now independent of Britain, economically unstable and wooed by Russia) and Greece, Crete and Cyprus. The modest U.S. air installation at Athens, used by the Navy for its maritime patrol craft, is well-nigh indispensable if any system of surveillance over the exits from the Black Sea, the myriad islands of the Aegean and the Eastern Mediterranean is to be maintained. The British bases on Cyprus are all that is left in the Eastern Mediterranean of the once powerful British position in the Middle East and are an important facility for both NATO and the United States.

Turkey is often viewed as the strategic pivot point in the Middle Eastern area. Its geographical position, astride the exits from the Black Sea, facing Russia across the Black Sea and the Caucasus, dominating the northern shores of the Eastern Mediterranean, and, as a member of both NATO and CENTO (Central Treaty Organization), linking Europe and Asia, does bestow upon Ankara a geopolitical importance that transcends the country's actual power. To the United States it offers important land bases, not only for control of the Mediterranean but also as staging fields to the Middle and Far East, and facilities for technical-intelligence-collection of great importance (giant radars that monitor the flights of Soviet ballistic missiles and space probes launched from Russian test sites; communications stations and electronic "eavesdropping" stations that record Soviet radar pulses and internal communications). Turkey also has the strongest army on NATO's southern flank—one which suffers from all the problems of a relatively undeveloped nation, but one capable of future development and imbued with a fighting heart. Turkey is certainly an ally worth having, and every effort—political, diplomatic, economic and military—should be used to halt the recent deterioration of U.S.-Turkish relations.

Yet Turkey's relationship with Greece, still acute because of the unresolved Cyprus issue, weakens NATO, and any realistic assessment must calculate the likelihood of Turkish neutrality in any conflict or confrontation between the United States and the U.S.S.R., except one involving actual invasion of Turkish soil. The Turks will fight, but not for someone else. The days of Korea are over, and the U.S. rejection, during the Vietnam war, of a Turkish offer to send a division to South Vietnam (the price, in modernization of the Turkish Army, was considered too high) probably marked the end of an epoch and the return of Turkish policy to an uneasy balancing act.

Thus, though Washington should try to retain Turkey as an active member of the Western alliance, the United States cannot count with real certainty upon Turkish soil or Turkish facilities in any Mideast or great-power crisis.

This makes all the more imperative the retention of land airfields in Italy, Sicily, Malta, Greece, Crete and Cyprus, and the exercise of U.S. economic and diplomatic power to open Beirut in Lebanon, to visits by ships of the Sixth Fleet.

In addition to the qualitative upgrading and slight strengthening of the Sixth Fleet, U.S. and NATO land-based tactical air power in the Mediterranean basin must be modernized and strengthened, not only in anticipation of Soviet exploitation of Algerian airfields, but also in answer to the *de facto* use of proxy bases in Egypt and Syria by Moscow. The Italian air-defense system—particularly in Sicily—should be strengthened and reoriented as needed, and emphasis in both Greece and Turkey should be upon a modest build-up of tactical air power and maritime patrol aircraft. U.S. land-based air power in the area (acting as part of the NATO forces) is normally 3 squadron detachments (20 to 30 planes) on rotation to Italy and Turkey. The deteriorating situation may re-

186

quire a slow increase to 2 or more squadrons (a maximum of about 50 to 75 aircraft) based on Italy, Sicily, Greece and perhaps Turkey, with the maintenance facilities to sustain them.

To NATO nations and to U.S. interests around the Mediterranean rim, the threat of actual land invasion is minimal. Outright invasion by large armies would ring the gong of general war; neither NATO nor the United States could look the other way if Soviet forces moved from Hungary and Austria into Italy. No major increase in *nominal* NATO land strength seems necessary or desirable; what is needed is the fleshing out of existing units to full strength, and their modernization.

No permanently assigned U.S. ground forces are required in the Mediterranean region (except for the embarked battalion of Marines with the Sixth Fleet and the Southern European Task Force in Italy), though highly ready reserve units should be available in the ACE Mobile Force in NATO and in the United States for quick transportation to the area for maneuvers or emergency.

The northern shores of the Mediterranean from Spain to Turkey are held by Allied or friendly land forces with U.S. aid and support. Communist Yugoslavia and Albania represent a potentially dangerous enclave in this NATO crescent, but for ideological reasons this is not an immediate danger. Since the Soviet invasion of Czechoslovakia there has been an implicit threat that megalomaniac men in the Kremlin might be tempted to bring Yugoslavia to heel by overt force. Such action would confront NATO and the West with a major crisis. Intervention by NATO in behalf of even an independent Communist state might well split NATO, but lack of action could doom NATO's Mediterranean front. Any such crisis would be acute, for the Yugoslavs would never yield to overt force easily, and their guerrillas in the hills and mountains would surely call on the West for aid.

A more subtle crisis could come with the death of Tito, who in 1970 was nearing eighty. Pro-Moscow, anti-Tito elements in Yugoslavia could be expected to make a bid for power. At the same time, the territorial ambitions of some of Yugoslavia's Balkan neighbors, tacitly encouraged by Moscow, could lead to external crisis. Some fear that this combination of external and internal pressure could

187

led to a breakup of the Yugoslav state with incalculable consequences.

Other than staff and command elements, the only U.S. land combat unit in the area is SETAF (Southern European Task Force) at Vicenza, Italy, which is supposed to provide artillery, rocket and atomic support to the more than seven Italian divisions assigned to NATO. SETAF, with 3,000 men, exists now in reduced strength, ostensibly capable of being fleshed out quickly in time of war. The Italian Army, of more than 300,000, augmented by an Air Force of about 450 combat aircraft (in need of modernization) and by a sizable and relatively modern Navy, provides adequate protection to Italy against land attack, except in case of all-out assault. But both the Navy and the Air Force need modernization and ultimately augmentation to meet the Soviet challenge in the Mediterranean and to keep open the sea lines of communication that are vital to Italy.

The Greek armed forces of about 160,000 men maintain only about 4 divisions at close to full strength; the rest of the 12 divisions exist in reduced or cadre strength only. The Air Force, with more than 200 combat planes, is in fair shape; the Navy, weakest of the services, operates old ships. The Army badly needs modern equipment and the arms aid halted or reduced by the Greek military coup, and all three services have been racked and weakened by political purges of the officer cadres.

Turkey, with almost 500,000 men under arms, is in better shape, but like all the southern flank members of NATO, its armed forces require new equipment. On the whole, however, any land threat to the northern shores of the Mediterranean does not appear to be an imminent or serious one.

There is, however, one peculiarly sensitive land frontier in the region, which requires modest strengthening. The long and narrow finger of Greek Thrace, in some places only thirty miles wide from the Bulgarian frontier to the Aegean Sea, is peculiarly vulnerable to conquest—down the valleys of the Vardar and the Struma to Salonika, or farther east. The region could be cut in two with minimum force, and today the Greeks have little with which to prevent it. Though full-fledged invasion by the modernized Bulgarian Army (4 armored divisions plus 6 or 8 mechanized ones), backed perhaps by Rumanian or Soviet troops, might result in a quick victory, it is unlikely because of the unforeseeable political consequences. But Bulgarian infiltration, provocations, political agitation and the familiar technique of inspired revolution, backed, at the right time, by small Bulgarian Army forces, could offer a potential threat to Thrace. The reward from the Russian viewpoint might be high: the immobilization and neutralization of Turkey, the outflanking of the Black Sea exits, an entrée to the Aegean. This is an unlikely eventuality (though considered by one recent NATO ambassador as the most possible of several improbable scenarios of NATO conflict), but the temptation needs to be removed. Strengthening the Greek Army—fleshing out its brigade of tanks to at least one full armored division, modernization of weapons, a modest increase in infantry strength—would be a relatively easy accomplishment, once we stopped cutting off our nose to spite our face, and decided to resume full military support to the Greek Government, support which was virtually halted when the military junta took over.

Thus the fundamental requirement in the Mediterranean basin is a basic revision of politico-economic and psychological policies in the area. Strategically, geopolitically, the United States and NATO can place their main reliance upon modern sea-air power, but only if it is heavily bolstered by land-based air power around the Mediterranean's rim. The erosion of the Western, and particularly of the United States, position in the entire region and particularly in the Eastern Mediterranean must be halted; we are reaching a point of no return.

The southern shores of the Mediterranean, which once protected NATO's southern flank, have been largely neutralized or lost. And the northern shores, from Spain to Turkey, are threatened. Dr. Alvin J. Cottrell summarized the conclusions of a conference at Georgetown University in the following terms: ". . . there appears to be a clearly developing trend away from association with Western Europe [in the Mediterranean]. . . . West European nations are tending more and more to dissociate themselves and their security from that of Greece and Turkey."[4]

Italy is still linked to the West, but the violent strikes and political agitation of 1969 exemplified the great strength of the left and the polarization of Italian politics; even Italy is shaky, and, as Dr. Cottrell pointed out, "U.S. influence in the Mediterranean is steadily deteriorating."

A modified air-maritime strategy in the Mediterranean can have no pertinence if land bases are not available to the West. Loss of many more land areas around the basin will mean neutralization and political nullification of the Sixth Fleet, yet withdrawal of the Sixth Fleet would symbolize a signal Soviet victory of tremendous consequence to the future.

The hour is late.

And nowhere later than in the Arabian Peninsula and around the shores of the Persian Gulf—the "heartland" of Middle Eastern oil deposits and the focus of Russian ambitions.

<<< 8 >>>

# East of Suez

*"Ship me somewheres east of Suez,*
*where the best is like the worst,*
*Where there aren't no Ten Commandments,*
*an' a man can raise a thirst."*

KIPLING'S SOMEWHAT arbitrary dividing line between the Good
and the Bad finds its parallel today in the struggle between "The
Good Guys" and "The Bad Guys" for control of the oil of the
Middle East and of that vast coastal littoral extending from the
Cape of Good Hope to Burma.

The Indian Ocean basin is the newest stage in the modern drama
of world politics; it may become, as the years pass, an area vying
in importance with the Atlantic and Pacific.

It is not an area where actions and reactions occur in isolation.
Suez—particularly since the closing of the canal, following the
Six-Day War in 1967—is a convenient demarcation line, but what
happens in the Mediterranean will intimately affect what happens
in the Red Sea, Arabia and the Persian Gulf, and the Arab-Israeli
conflict casts its shadow at least as far as Pakistan.

Thus political policy and military strategy must be considered
whole; the Middle East—as discussed in the previous chapter—in
a geopolitical sense includes all of the Arab and much of the Moslem world, and, most importantly, Saudi Arabia and Yemen, the

small states and sheikdoms along the Persian Gulf, Iran and, to a lesser extent, Pakistan.

But the Indian Ocean area also poses two other interlocking strategic questions: access to, and development of, the resources of Africa and the security of the maritime trade routes around the Cape of Good Hope; and the India-Burma problem.

In the entire area the politico-military equation is complicated by vast distances and vast differences; by a struggle for survival; by the projected British withdrawal (by 1971) from the Persian Gulf; by backward economies and political systems; by maximum aspirations and minimum power; by anticolonial and, in many cases, anti-Western ferment; by ancient territorial, economic and religious rivalries; by the dead hand of obsolete traditions and outmoded customs; and—everywhere—by the expansionist ambitions of Communism.

But in this area, far more than in Europe or the Mediterranean, the picture is clouded by the Sino-Soviet conflict and the disparate ambitions of Moscow and Peking.

As far east as Afghanistan and Pakistan—to approximately the banks of the Indus River—Soviet policies appear to be keyed primarily to the oil wealth of the Middle East, the Arab-Israeli conflict, NATO, the Mediterranean and Africa; in India-Burma they are plainly oriented primarily against Peking, secondarily against the United States. The Chinese Communists, on the other hand, though they have dabbled in revolutionary politics in Africa and Arabia, are as yet too weak to project major power overseas, but they are able, by proximity and the mass strength of their ground armies, their guerrillas and propaganda, and the threat of nuclear power, to exercise a profound, if sometimes underground, influence in India and Burma and Pakistan.

The United States, which has no historical experience of much importance or continuity in the Indian Ocean, is thus faced with a dilemma: What should our policy or policies be in the area?

Consider, first, Arabia and the Persian Gulf.

Here, U.S. interests are patently great; U.S. companies own about 47 percent of the oil concessions in the area. The world's largest

192

*known* petroleum reserves (possibly excepting the newly discovered fields north of the Brooks Range in Alaska and unknown resources in Russia) are in the Middle East, and it is the most readily accessible and by far the cheapest to produce.[1] Western Europe, Japan, Australia and Africa import most of their oil from the area, and U.S. forces in Vietnam have been fueled primarily from the Middle East. U.S. oil companies earn between $1.2 and $1.6 billion annually from their investments, and five Middle Eastern countries—Iran, Iraq, Kuwait, Qatar and Saudi Arabia—are dependent upon the almost $3 billion (1967 figure) earned annually from oil revenues. The undeveloped states of the area have commenced to move rapidly, and with consequent social and economic dislocations, from feudalistic societies into the twentieth century; their progress is largely dependent upon oil. Yet there is a fly in the ointment. The need for increased revenues for development—as in Iran—comes at the very time when Middle Eastern oil fields are beginning to feel the competition of newly developed Japanese sources and particularly of North African fields (Libya and Algeria, primarily), which are much closer to Western European markets. They may, in time, meet further indirect competition from Alaska.

The oil companies are not, therefore, inclined to expand Middle East production as rapidly as many Middle Eastern governments would like; thus the stage is set for some incipient friction with Western interests.

Thus, to the destabilizing and highly emotional factor of the Arab-Israeli conflict is added potential economic friction.

In addition to the oil stakes of the area, and the Suez Canal–Red Sea–Strait of Bab el Mandeb sluiceway is of high strategic importance—the shortest maritime route from Europe to the Indian Ocean, a gateway to East Africa and, to the U.S.S.R. in particular, a shipping short cut of considerable political and military, as well as economic, importance.

The Arabian (Persian) Gulf, bordered by weak nations, with a heritage of ancient rivalries and conflicting claims, is another rich prize. An average of about 58 ships, most of them tankers, flying the flags of all the world enter or leave the gulf every twenty-four hours in transit to the great oil refineries or oil-loading terminals at

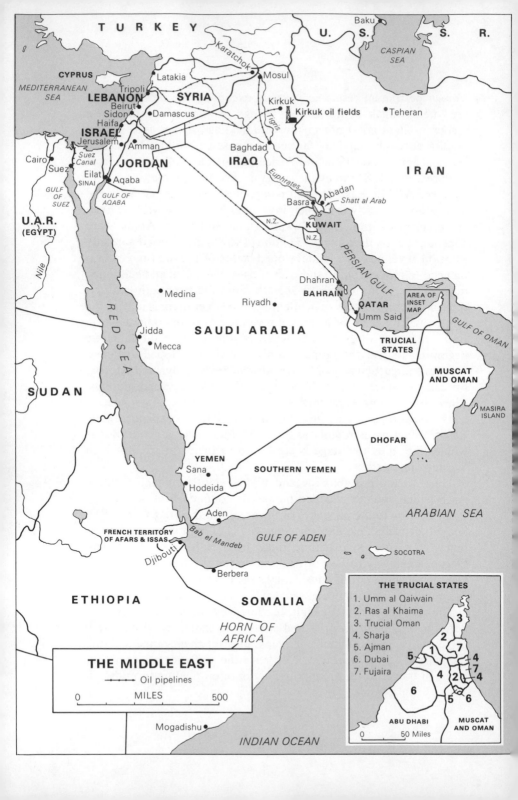

TURKEY · U. S. S. R.

Baku

CASPIAN SEA

CYPRUS
Latakia
Mosul
MEDITERRANEAN SEA
Tripoli
LEBANON
Beirut
SYRIA
Karatchok
Kirkuk
Kirkuk oil fields
Teheran
Sidon
Damascus
Haifa
ISRAEL
Jerusalem
Amman
Baghdad
Tigris
IRAN
Cairo
Suez
Suez Canal
JORDAN
IRAQ
Euphrates
Eilat
Aqaba
SINAI
GULF OF AQABA
Abadan
Basra
Shatt al Arab
U.A.R. (EGYPT)
GULF OF SUEZ
N.Z.
KUWAIT
N.Z.
Nile
PERSIAN GULF
RED SEA
Medina
Riyadh
Dhahran
BAHRAIN
AREA OF INSET MAP
QATAR
Umm Said
GULF OF OMAN
SUDAN
Jidda
Mecca
SAUDI ARABIA
TRUCIAL STATES
MUSCAT AND OMAN
MASIRA ISLAND
DHOFAR
YEMEN
Sana
Hodeida
SOUTHERN YEMEN
ARABIAN SEA
Aden
FRENCH TERRITORY OF AFARS & ISSAS
Bab el Mandeb
GULF OF ADEN
SOCOTRA
Djibouti
Berbera
ETHIOPIA
SOMALIA
HORN OF AFRICA

THE MIDDLE EAST
↤──↦ Oil pipelines
0    MILES    500

Mogadishu

INDIAN OCEAN

THE TRUCIAL STATES
1. Umm al Qaiwain
2. Ras al Khaima
3. Trucial Oman
4. Sharja
5. Ajman
6. Dubai
7. Fujaira

3
2
7
5
1
7
4
4
7
2
4
6
5
6
ABU DHABI
MUSCAT AND OMAN
0    50 Miles

Kharg Island, Abadan, Kuwait, Bahrain and elsewhere.

Commercial and military air routes from Europe and the United states to the Indian subcontinent and Southeast Asia also funnel through the Middle East. These round-the-world routes have already been interrupted, in times of crisis, in the Middle East bottleneck. Soviet airline routes, on the other hand, pass above client states—Syria, the United Arab Republic and the Sudan—into the heart of Africa.

To the West, the strategically placed airfields at Dhahran, Saudi Arabia, and at Teheran, Iran—as well as overflight rights—are essential to any rapid commercial or military air transport from Europe to South Asia.

United States interests, particularly long-term strategic interests, are major, and they are definitely threatened.

## The Arabian Peninsula

The tremendous oil wealth of the peninsula, and its geographic location, commanding the Red Sea and the Persian Gulf, make the desert kingdom of Saudi Arabia and its fringing ministates natural targets for Soviet ambitions. Saudi Arabia, under King Feisal, with Aramco (Arabian American Oil Company) as the principal concessionaire, is a conservative nation which rigidly adheres to the ancient precepts of the Koran. (The right hand of a thief is chopped off; an adulteress is stoned to death.) Mecca, the center for all the world's Moslems, attracts a million or more pilgrims annually, who represent some of the most volatile and easily inflamed peoples of the world. Communism is officially detested, but so is Zionism, and the turbulence of the Arab-Israeli conflict is reflected in the scarred furniture and battered baracks of the U.S. Army training mission at Dhahran, where Arab mobs ran wild after the Six-Day War.

Saudi Arabia is a wealthy conservative monarchy in a sea of Arab radicalism, and each resurgence of the Arab-Israeli conflict has its repercussions in Riyadh and Jidda. Feisal has no use for Communism, but Soviet Communism backs the Arabs, and Feisal, like Hussein of Jordan, is trying to ride two wild horses. As long as he lives he will probably keep a relatively stable Saudi Arabia free from

195

major Russian influence; after his death stability will depend upon the strength and character of the successor selected by the numerous Saud family.

Today there are two factions vying for power, each bitterly opposed to the other. Nominally, Crown Prince Khalid, an amiable but unimpressive man, is slated as Feisal's successor, with Prince Fahd, a strong and able man, earmarked as Deputy Prime Minister. Presumably, this faction can count upon the Saudi Arabian regular army, commanded by Khalid's rival for power—Prince Abdullah, who commands the tribal militia and King's guard, the so-called White Army. The two armies—typical of the intricate balancing act that has been a part of Saudi Arabian politics for years—are about evenly matched in numbers (about 20,000 to 30,000 men each), and nominally in equipment, but the militia, the White Army, is superior in morale and will to fight. Thus a political crisis, perhaps even a kind of civil war, could add to Saudi Arabia's troubles after Feisal's death; certainly the rivalries provide Russia with an opportunity for its typical divide-and-conquer techniques. The problem of the succession—always a major problem in Arab countries—and the transition of Saudi Arabia from a tribal desert economy to the twentieth century are certain to provoke friction and dissidence.

Today serious Communist inroads in Saudi Arabia itself appear to be conspicuous by their absence, though there are hidden sympathizers, and—covertly—latent anti-American feeling. Like the iceberg—the bulk of its vast expanse hidden beneath the surface— there may be in Saudi Arabia more underground subversion than is allowed to surface by an efficient police force and rigid controls. Saudi Arabia has already agreed to oil exports to Rumania. In 1969 Saudi security forces made a widening series of arrests—including some students, a few Army, police and Coast Guard officers—and guards around the royal residence were strengthened. At the same time King Feisal's anger at what he considers to be a "wholly biased" pro-Israel American policy and the Saudis' frustration at Washington's futile efforts to achieve an Arab-Israeli settlement reached a new peak. The two incidents may well be related. Russian policy is undoubtedly attempting to tear open the deep scars in the Arab psyche, and Jewish control of the Dome of the Rock, and

196

other Moslem religious shrines, in East Jerusalem represents a continuing affront. And those who count Saudi Arabia as securely within the Western camp should never forget that as part of the anti-Israel Arab coalition, Riyadh has maintained a brigade of about 5,000 men in southern Jordan for many months.

Saudi Arabia is probably the most orthodox of the Moslem countries, and religious hatred is becoming a more and more important factor in the irreconcilable Middle Eastern clash. Although the Moslem world is too divided and backward to permit effective united action, and although it lacks a leader with international charisma and oustanding political-military capabilities, the call for Jihad or a holy war against Israel, sounded again by both Feisal and Nasser in 1969 (following the burning of the Al Aqsa Mosque in East Jerusalem), is one which may well have an increasing appeal.

The ultimate Communist objective in the kingdom is clear—to sever the strong religious ties of the people, to obscure their moral values and to promote the same crisis of values which has shaken the West and helped to prepare the way for Communist ideology.

But so far, Russian ambitions in the peninsula have been concentrated in far more profitable areas—in the rich but weak and often primitive border states, once dominated by the British, now independent or soon to become so. The Communist contagion started years ago in the primitive kingdom of Yemen on the Red Sea, where until recently civil war, between a republican government backed by Egypt and Russia and a royalist government backed by Saudi Arabia, was bitterly waged. The active war has ended; the conflict continues, though the two sides are at least to some extent reconciled. Russian influence, a few years ago almost dominant in the area, has been reduced in Yemen proper. But the Soviets still maintain a presence, with about 200 Russians, including a number of pilots, in the little state. The improved base and harbor and airfield at Hodeida on the Red Sea is virtually Russian-controlled. About half a hundred Soviet aircraft represent a potential threat to neighboring Saudi Arabia, and a new arms-aid agreement with Moscow appears to have been reached recently. Disorder and instability are still "normal," and Soviet ambitions in Yemen are unrelinquished.

197

The focus of Soviet activities seems, however, to have been shifted to Aden and Southern Yemen since the British withdrawal in 1967 and the installation of a violently anti-American radical government. The Russians maintain a fifty-man embassy in Aden; Soviet men-of-war have visited the port, and early in 1969 Soviet aircraft delivered a squadron of Mig-17 fighter planes. Tanks, rockets, antiaircraft guns, artillery and other arms have also been delivered. A small training advisory mission has started to strengthen the combat effectiveness of Southern Yemen, and radar and other equipment are improving the facilities of the strategically located airfield near Aden and the port. The radicalism and aggressiveness of the government have already led to small-scale clashes with Saudi Arabia along the ill-defined frontier of the Hadhramaut (identified, in the British era, as the Eastern Aden Protectorate).

But the People's Republic of Southern Yemen, which includes Aden, appears doomed, like its sister country, Yemen, to continued border clashes, internal conflict, economic and political instability and perhaps to civil war. The plague of the Arabian Peninsula— tribal animosities—seems certain to bedevil the Soviet efforts to maintain a subservient puppet government in Southern Yemen, and the dissident Aulaqis and Audhali tribes could make a common cause with the small army against the most extreme leftists in the Aden government. Nor will Aden's economic ills soon be cured. Since the British left in November, 1967, the population of the city has dwindled by about one-third, and the port, once an important fueling and ship-repair point when Suez was opened, is nearly empty. Soviet economic aid to date has been of an emergency nature; Moscow is obviously wary of the republic's future. Nevertheless, Aden is almost completely dependent upon the Soviet Union: the People's Republic of Southern Yemen and the National Liberation Front based there have no alternatives.

Potential Soviet domination of the Strait of Bab el Mandeb and the southern entrance to the Red Sea is being further strengthened by Russian Communist political, economic and psychological encroachments in Somalia, Ethiopia and the Sudan, the latter now controlled by a leftist government. The Russians have built a modern port, often visited by Russian warships, at the best natural

198

harbor in Somalia—Berbera—and it is linked with Moscow by powerful radios. This port, near the "Horn of Africa," and Aden control the Gulf of Aden and provide springboards for penetrations along the East African coast and into the Indian Ocean.

From Southern Yemen and Aden as a base, the Soviets are mounting an increasing offensive against one of the most primitive of the Arab countries—the Sultanate of Muscat and Oman, a large, rugged, little-known land in southeastern Arabia. Sultan Said ibn Taimur, who has kept his kingdom isolated and as far as possible insulated from the outside world and the twentieth century, is now faced with active revolt—a small shooting guerrilla war, sponsored by the Russian-backed Omani Liberation Front, recently merged into a so-called Popular Front for the Liberation of the Occupied Arabian Gulf.

These guerrilla fighters have as their immediate targets the British-officered force of the sultanate, composed largely of Baluchis. Some Baluchis and some British have already become casualties in this unnoticed little war, one complicated in a small way by the Chinese Communists, who are training at least fifty revolutionary Dhofaris and who have been backing with small quantities of small arms and automatic weapons a so-called Dhofar Liberation Front (Dhofar is a part of the sultanate). The miniwar in Muscat and Oman is of considerable potential importance to the West, since the British, still committed to withdrawal from other parts of the Persian Gulf area by the end of 1971, plan to retain a foothold in Muscat and Oman and a staging airfield on the island of Masira off its coast.

Agents are infiltrated by dhow from Aden to Muscat, and thence to the small sheikdoms of the gulf. The same pattern of backwardness and instability, complicated in many instances by fabulous newly discovered oil wealth, facilitates Communist inroads along most of the eastern, or Persian (Arabian) Gulf, coast of the Arabian Peninsula.

From Muscat and Oman, northward along the western side of the Persian Gulf, nine small states—little British protectorates, or emirates or sheikdoms—reach northward almost to oil-rich Kuwait at the head of the gulf. Some of them, like Abu Dhabi, with a native

199

population of about 16,000 people, have recently made incredible oil discoveries; Abu Dhabi will have from its initial year of oil royalties the highest per capita income in the world. Since the announcement of the impending British withdrawal these nine little states have been trying to form a Federation of Arab Emirates to provide greater collective strength than any single one of them can muster. But their frontiers are inadequately defined, there are conflicting territorial claims, and the differences, jealousies and conflicts between the states are many. The Federation, so far, has made little progress, and in each state Arab extremists are organizing, planning, plotting and, with Soviet help, are sponsoring cells and formulating plans for riot, disturbance and revolution.

The island of Bahrain, strategically located in the gulf near the great Saudi Arabian airfield at Dhahran, has been the British headquarters for the whole area since their withdrawal from Aden, and the United States Navy has used Bahrain for the past twenty years as the headquarters for its small Middle East Force of three ships. The Middle East Command, headed by a rear admiral, is a political and psychological, more than a military, force. It has consisted of two destroyers, with a converted seaplane tender as a flagship, and its ships periodically visit ports in many parts of the Indian Ocean basin to show the flag, to maintain a U.S. presence and to feel the pulse of the area. Ostensibly it has no fixed base, but it has been using small British warehouses, docks, office space, barracks and recreation facilities at Bahrain for years. British ships based in the gulf—chiefly mine sweepers and patrol craft—are to be withdrawn, or turned over to Bahrain or other amirates, and the United States has been negotiating with the British to take over some of their land facilities at Bahrain. Such a facility, modest though it is, is particularly important since the closure of the Suez Canal and the severance of the normal supply lines for the Middle East Force. A limited stockage of spare parts and ships' stores is essential if any real operational capability is to be maintained.

The ruling family in Bahrain—headed by Sheik Isa bin Sulman Al-Khalifah—is solidly pro-American and pro-Western; it is anxious to maintain an American presence. But even here the winds of change are stirring the gulf's calm waters, and Bahrain, like other

Trucial States, is attempting hastily to form and train local militia or national guards to try to replace the stabilizing power of the British. And the ruling family knows that in many ways their monarchical privileges represent an anachronism in the twentieth century.

Kuwait has a special stature among the small Persian Gulf enclaves and in the Soviet plans for conquest. It is one of the richest of all the oil areas in the Middle East, and its oil production costs are fantastically low. The so-called Popular Front for the Liberation of the Occupied Arabian Gulf has so far ostensibly excluded Kuwait from its planning—perhaps because Kuwait is a sovereign state, represented in the United Nations, and most particularly because the Russians maintain a sizable and active embassy there. Kuwait, controlled by the British until 1961, paid a high price for her UN membership in 1963 when the Russians lifted their veto in return for recognition. Seven Russians were on the original diplomatic list of the Soviet Embassy after recognition. All seven were Soviet intelligence personnel, and they initiated, through national liberation fronts, left-wing splinter groups of the Arab nationalist movement and other means, the initial and considerable Communist penetration of the Persian Gulf area, now to a large extent— but not exclusively—directed and promoted from Aden.

Kuwait, with a population of only 600,000 people—approximately 60 percent of them foreigners, many of them Palestinians —is one of the most Pan-Arab of the Arab states. It is inflexibly anti-Zionist, has never declared a cease-fire with Israel, and will not, according to some well-informed diplomats, accept a peaceful settlement. Kuwait has been one of the great bankers of the Arab cause, and has been helping to subsidize Egypt and Jordan since the Six-Day War and the closure of the Suez Canal, and has financed health and education projects for the other Arab states, including an $84 million loan to Iraq, a country which once threatened Kuwait territory in a dispute, now quiescent but still unsettled, about sovereignty and borders.

Despite all this, despite the leaning toward political extremism, Iraqi Communist agitators, apparently acting with Soviet encouragement, are organizing the oil workers into radical Communist-influenced unions, and the danger of internal subversion—particularly by that large portion of the population that is non-Kuwaiti—is viewed as a real one. The Soviet Embassy in Kuwait, headed by an Ambassador trained in intelligence-collection and subversion, is still active, covertly in some of these organizing efforts, and openly in sponsoring trade agreements of many kinds. Chinese, Bulgarians, Hungarians, Poles, Czechs and Yugoslavs are all present in a small way in Kuwait, attracted by its immense wealth and, like Russia, determined, if possible, to take over part of Kuwait's international trade.

The Western concept and the regional concept of how to replace the vacuum left by the withdrawal of British power from the Arabian Peninsula is a simple one: in unity there is strength. But the difference between the states of the area—the many conflicting territorial claims, the suspicions, jealousies and political, personal and economic rivalries—appear to be far stronger than the common interests.

Howard Cottam, for more than six years the U.S. Ambassador to Kuwait, imported a National Geographic globe for his office. For more than six weeks it was held in a Kuwait customs office while the official demanded, politely but insistently, that the state of Israel be scratched from the map and that the name of the Persian Gulf be changed to Arabian Gulf.

In short, Soviet Communist penetration of the Saudi Arabian Peninsula capitalizes on local conflicts, but its program is long-term, definite and deliberate. As one diplomat put it, "The Russians have a positive expansionist policy in the gulf and the Arabian Peninsula, while the British are pulling out and the Americans are doing nothing."

# Iran

Iran, once centuries ago the great power of the Middle East and still conscious of its glamorous past, is Moslem, but not Arab—aloof, except for the passions of religion, from the Arab-Israeli conflict, but embroiled nevertheless in regional conflicts. Iran has restated, though with restraint, an old claim to Bahrain Island, has

202

only recently agreed with Saudi Arabia to a median boundary line in the gulf, is in sharp conflict with Iraq, and has some touchy relationships with the Arabs in general and Nasser in particular. Nevertheless the Shah insists there must be regional solutions to regional problems, and he professes to believe that Iran and her neighbors—particularly Iraq and Saudi Arabia—can replace British power in the gulf.

But Iran's military capabilities are very limited. She has a very small but very efficient Air Force (150 to 200 combat aircraft, including U.S. F-4's), which is probably, plane for plane and pilot for pilot, the best in the Middle East. But like most of the Middle Eastern air forces it is a "one-shot" force and has no capability for long-sustained combat operations. And the Iranian surface components are weak. The Navy has been building up a small but relatively modern squadron of frigate types and coastal patrol craft for service in the gulf. The Army's seven divisions and one airborne brigade are understrength and in process of reorganization; some exist only in brigade strength. Some 50,000 well-trained gendarmery, loyal to the Shah and particularly useful for internal security, bring the total personnel strength of the military forces to about 200,000. The Shah is anxious to strengthen and expand his armed forces—particularly his Air Force—as rapidly as possible, and says that he will take equipment and arms where he can get them—from Russia if the United States cannot, or will not, provide them. He believes that cooperative action by Middle Eastern countries, particularly by Saudi Arabia and Iran, will enable them to solve their own security problems without great power forces in the area. Implicit in this belief is Iran's improved relations with the U.S.S.R. This represents a deliberate Iranian (and Russian) policy; like Turkey, Iran has been mending her fences with her great neighbor.

Iranian trade with Russia, and through Russia to the Eastern European satellites and Western Europe, is increasing; excluding oil, which so far goes largely to Western markets, 27 percent of Iran's exports now go to the Soviet bloc. A gas pipeline from Iranian wells is being built into Russia, and Teheran has agreed to supply Russia with almost exactly the same amount of gas that Russia is exporting from her own wells to Western Europe. But in

STRATEGY FOR TOMORROW

the case of Iran the gas is paid for by barter deals; Russia gains in hard currency. Soviet aid projects valued now, though uncompleted, at more than $1 billion will be paid for over the next fifteen years by Iranian gas. In return, the Russians are building a steel mill near Isfahan, and a machine plant, and they have furnished Iran with about $100 million worth of "unsophisticated" military equipment—principally military trucks, armored personnel carriers, jeeps and light antiaircraft guns. The Iranians reason they are the gainers by these deals, since the exported gas has been flared, or burned, in the past, and therefore was a wasted asset; other observers fear the deal is a foot in the door for Russia, and a potential Soviet mortgage on Iran's future. Many think that where a gas pipeline has led, an oil pipeline will follow, and that ten to fifteen years from now the U.S.S.R. will be tapping the oil wealth of Iran and perhaps of other Middle Eastern countries.

There is, indeed, good reason for this belief: Moscow has told her satellites to seek oil from sources other than the U.S.S.R. The Soviet Black Sea–Caspian (Baku) oil fields apparently are being depleted, and it would be far cheaper for the Soviets, particularly if they can arrange barter deals, to utilize Iranian and Middle Eastern oil in this southern Russian industrial region and possibly to sell it to their Eastern European satellites than to transport it from Siberian or other reserves. And the same potential gain in hard currency for Russia, made possible by the gas pipeline, is in prospect if an oil pipeline is constructed from Iran into Russia, and at the same time a branch of the Soviet "Friendship" line to the satellites (tapping the Volga-Urals wells) is extended to West Germany. Such an arrangement is, in fact, in the first stages of implementation, and the West Germans, who would supply the necessary pipe, have been active both in West Germany and in Iran in promoting it.

A similar and perhaps even more important deal between the Russians and the Italians has been initiated. A barter arrangement to sell Russian natural gas from the Ukraine and Siberia to Italy in return for pipe, pumping stations and other equipment is projected for a twenty-year period starting in 1972. The gas will initially flow over an existing line to Bratislava in Czechoslovakia, which will be

204

extended through Austria to northern Italy. Also projected is a pipeline from Iran through Turkey to the Mediterranean. Iran has already agreed to export oil to Rumania and Bulgaria, and a long-term deal with Czechoslovakia, involving some 20 million tons of Iranian oil, is being arranged. The Soviet Volga-Urals area, now the main source of Russian oil production, will probably be superseded by the vast deposits in Siberia in the 1980's, but the extended pipeline costs may make Middle Eastern oil considerably cheaper for the satellites. In any case, there is no doubt that Russia plans to utilize and market Middle Eastern gas and oil. Clearly, the old and comforting shibboleth about Middle Eastern oil –that the Communist world could not supply the markets—will not be true tomorrow.

Politically, Moscow is discreet and quite cautious and proper in its official relationships with Teheran. The Tudeh (Communist) Party is outlawed in Iran, and there appear to be few overt Soviet attempts to revive it, other than the fulminations of the Communist radios that beam invective against the Shah into Iran. But there are still many cells in Iran—"discussion groups," which professedly follow no political ideology, but actually are ghostly carry-overs from the days of the Tudeh Party's power.

The Russian Embassy maintains an active presence in Iran, collects statistical and economic information, pushes cultural exchanges—a Russian circus, a few musicians —and supervises the activities of about 1,300 to 2,000 Soviet civilian technical advisers in the country.

Perhaps most important in the long-term view is the continuing development of communications between Iran and Soviet Russia. The increased railroad traffic is being expedited at the frontier, where there is a change of gauge, by shifting wheels and axles of the railroad cars instead of transshipment of the contents. Road traffic is increasing and roads are being extended and improved.

Shah Mohammed Reza Pahlevi, who has done much in a short time to modernize his country, and his top advisers appear to have no illusions about Communism, and they know the whole history of their country is one periodically punctuated by conflicts with their big neighbor to the north. But the Shah, like King Hussein and

King Feisal, is trying to ride several wild horses simultaneously: to force Western oil concessionaires to increase Iranian production to provide increased development revenues at a time when Middle Eastern oil is encountering competition from North African and other fields; to remain on good terms with Soviet Russia and to accept her aid, yet to resist the hidden encroachments of Communism; to strengthen bonds of friendship with the West; to modernize his nation without mortgaging its future; to remain aloof to great-power conflicts; to attempt to settle regional conflicts by regional means; to meet Arab threats yet to satisfy Moslem demands; to arm his country with the help of any and all countries, including Russia, without impairing its sovereignty. It is a large order, particularly since the Russians have made it clear they will maintain an active presence in Iran.

And, as one authority put it, "The problem is you have only one Shah, and I can't see much of a supporting structure beneath him."

Thus the stakes are huge in the Arabian Peninsula–Persian Gulf area, and the differences are many. Both the Shah and Feisal have taken the first steps toward some kind of accommodation of their ancient differences; both say they believe in regional solutions; both insist they do not want the British to maintain their small forces at Bahrain or elsewhere in the gulf region after their scheduled withdrawal date at the end of 1971. But the competition for the market in oil is divisive, and long centuries of rivalry must be bridged in a year. The prospects are that with the British withdrawal a vacuum of power will invite Soviet penetration in the gulf region in 1972.

## Afghanistan—Pakistan

In a sense, these countries are the geographical and political connecting links between the twin problems east of Suez—Russian Communism and Chinese Communism. Afghanistan, a strategic country, which controls the important Kyber Pass from Kabul into the plains of West Pakistan, and thence to the Indian Punjab, is a buffer state, largely under Russian domination, but Pakistan has welcomed Chinese and Russian aid and, with U.S. help, hopes to balance Moscow against Peking. Pakistan, a Moslem country, also has important links to the Middle East; some of her territory borders the approaches to the Persian Gulf, and Pakistani pilots have been assisting the Saudi Arabians in the development of a small air force. She has also been providing modest military-technical assistance to Jordan.

Afghanistan communication routes and supply facilities have been developed by Russia at the cost of about $750 million in Soviet aid; intelligence officers estimate that today the U.S.S.R. could support about 22 divisions there, as compared to an estimated 5 or 6 in 1951. Afghanistan occupies a key geographic position, on Pakistan's flank, near the disputed Jammu-Kashmir area, and close to the wild Chinese province of Sinkiang, with its nuclear test facilities, its oil and uranium.

Despite the rugged terrain, overland communication routes from the Central Asian area to South Asia and the Indian Ocean littoral have been intensively developed by both Russia and China. The old approach, via the Kabul River valley and the Khyber Pass to the Grand Trunk caravan route from Peshawar to Calcutta, has been improved and hard-surfaced for part of its length; the massive barrier of the Hindu Kush Range has been pierced by a tunnel, and a small network of connecting roads are tied into Russia's river and canal transportation system. The North West Frontier, fabled in British tradition, has been "tamed"; Soviet trucks with bridge girders and steel now roll southward toward the sea.

In the past few years, the Chinese and Pakistanis have built a jeepable road following the old historic "Silk Route" of the caravans, which is usable most of the way by heavy trucks in good weather—between Sinkiang (Lupgaz via the Mintaka Pass to Misgar and Gilgit) and Rawalpindi, paralleled by another road, from Lhasa in Tibet to Katmandu in Nepal, the Hindu border state between India and China.

This development of north-south communication routes, paralleled in some cases by air routes, is one of the more significant recent developments in South Asia; it both reflects and enables the extension of Communist power.

Afghanistan is a kind of Russian protectorate; Pakistan is still part of the third world—clearly aligned with neither the Communists nor the anti-Communists. Its attempted neutralism—a devel-

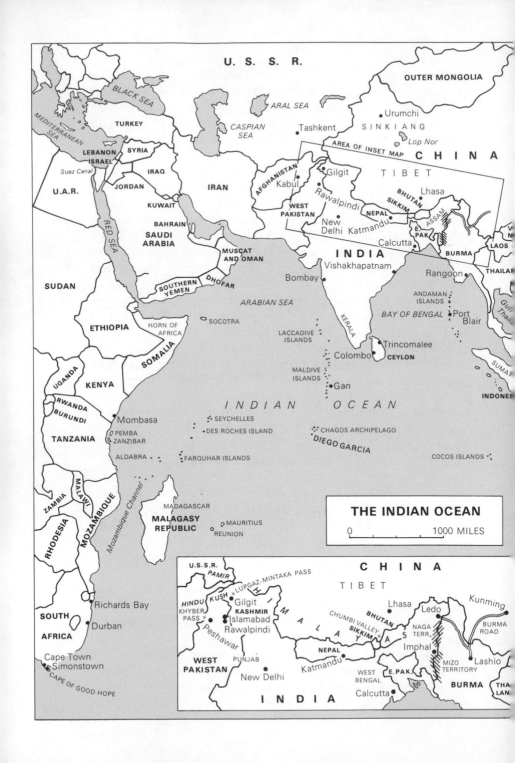

THE INDIAN OCEAN

0 _____ 1000 MILES

opment since the short-lived India-Pakistan war of 1965, and the consequent stoppage of U.S. military aid—is beset with difficulties. The Moslem religion is not receptive to the godlessness of Communism, and the Pakistanis have few illusions about the purity of Chinese intentions. Yet Pakistan's unsettled quarrel with India over Kashmir and her feeling that she has been wronged and let down by the West is a pervasive political factor, and it seems clear that she will take arms and aid from any source. Her dictatorial political system, her high illiteracy, her chaotic economy and her limited resources mean no end to instability. The geographic separation of East Pakistan from West Pakistan is a divisive factor of major importance. East Pakistan earns most of the nation's hard currency, yet is more crowded and less developed than West Pakistan. The feeling of neglect in the East is paralleled by a natural attraction—a common language plus geographical propinquity—between East Bengal (Pakistan) and West Bengal (India). The West Bengal Government is a Communist and left-wing coilition, with strong Chinese, as well as Russian, influences; thus the Communists hold a political card in their dealings with either Rawalpindi or New Delhi by their ability to foster or dampen trends toward separatism.

The Pakistani trend toward neutralism has ended Pakistan's usefulness—if, indeed, it ever existed—as a member of the South-East Asia Treaty Organization, an organization that has always been stronger on paper than in the field. Because of her geographical location, her religion and her interests Pakistan was in any case always an artificial member of SEATO; her natural interests lie more with the Middle East than with Southeast Asia. And the privileged position of the United States in Pakistan, which reached its peak in the earlier days of the long rule of Ayub Khan, has also ended. In 1969, at Pakistan's insistence, the United States evacuated its important airfield facilities and communications installations at Peshawar, the same airfield from which Gary Powers started his ill-fated U-2 flight over the Soviet Union. The abandonment of Peshawar should not be exaggerated or underestimated. It marks another stage in the slowly rising tide of Communist expansion in the Middle East and South Asia, but it does not mean, in any sense, the loss of Pakistan. And Pakistani airfields, though useful, are not essential to U.S. military or commercial air routes. The revolt against Ayub Khan in 1969, and the installation of military rule, probably marked the low point in U.S.-Pakistani relationships; President Nixon's brief visit started a much-needed thaw. It seems likely that the improvement will continue, though slowly, if only because the Pakistanis are realists and they are trying to balance the competing great-power influences on their country one against the other. Like many of the third-force nations, they will accept arms from whatever source proffered. U.S. arms aid to Pakistan, except for spare parts in limited quantities, was halted after the short war with India. Communist China filled the gap (and trade between the two countries quadrupled in the five-year period 1962–63 to 1967–68). Now Soviet Russia is providing some arms and increasing trade.

Pakistan's armed forces are considerably smaller than India's; there are only about 12 nominal understrength divisions, all infantry, except for a brigade-size armored "division." The Army, the obsolescent Navy, and a small Air Force of about 200 to 300 planes have old equipment, few spare parts and an inadequate logistics base to support any protracted intensive fighting. The 300,000-man armed forces, supported by approximately 200,000 paramilitary frontier and police forces, are the key to internal security, and might well repel any Indian assault, but could play only a delaying or guerrilla role in any major conflict against China or Russia. Pakistan for a long time to come will be more preoccupied with her internal instability, destabilizing social, economic and political problems, and her feud with India than with external factors.

Pakistan remains strategically, and particularly politically, important. Its great port at Karachi dominates—along with Indian Bombay—the Gulf of Oman and the Arabian Sea; its territory provides Russia with her only land communication routes to South Asia. Instability and disorder in Pakistan, as the largest Moslem country in the world, can influence Iran and the whole Middle East. A Communist takeover or attempted takeover would probably mean the fractionalization of the country; if it should succeed, Iran, India, all South Asia might be doomed.

Today Communism has not reached the sea in Pakistan, but it

has pierced the great mountain barrier—the Hindu Kush—which once held conquerors at bay.

## India—Burma—Ceylon

A weak and fragmented Congress Party, which has been dominant in Indian politics since Gandhi and Nehru, and the menace of Chinese Communism, plus large sums of money and an Indian predilection for socialist slogans and sophistry, have helped Russia make deep inroads into India—a country with 535 million people and immense problems.

India faces in the next two to three years another major political crisis—perhaps a dissolution of central power. In most Indian states, especially in the North Indian heartland (including the rich Punjab), there is chronic political instability, in many of them economic stagnation or chaos and the erosion of some old social values. Two key states, Kerala and West Bengal (which includes the city of Calcutta), are under Communist-dominated governments, entire newspapers are supported by Soviet funds, and the Indian military establishment—particularly the Air Force and the Navy— is becoming increasingly dependent upon Soviet aid. There are 300 or more Russian military advisers in India and an additional 150 to 200 civilian technicians. Moscow has provided about $2 to $2.5 billion for all projects, including at least $750 million in military aid.

Steel mills, a Mig-21 plant, more than 100 Migs, at least 127 Su-7's, helicopters and transport aircraft have been provided by Russia, and Indian pilots have been trained in Soviet schools. Russia has furnished the Indian Army with some antiaircraft missiles, artillery and tanks and some air transport essential to supply Indian outpost lines along the Himalayas. More and more the Army appears to be dependent for some types of spare parts and ammunition on Russian supply. The Indian Navy, which has one old British 16,000-ton aircraft carrier, the only carrier in an Asian navy, has received initial substantial deliveries of a programed total of 4 Soviet submarines, 11 Soviet patrol craft, 2 landing craft, some naval helicopters and 2 submarine tenders. The Soviet naval contribution appears to be so major that two distinct fleets are being

211

developed. The Russian-furnished ships are being based at Vishak-hapatnam on the Bay of Bengal side of the peninsula, where there are perhaps 20 to 30 Soviet naval advisers.

The Indian Government maintains that it provides the same facilities to all visiting naval craft of all nations, but there appears to be some legitimate doubt about this statement. The Indians are constructing in considerable secrecy some naval facilities in or near Port Blair in the Andaman Islands, which dominate the principal maritime route from the Pacific through the Malacca Strait into the Indian Ocean, and there and at Vishakhapatnam, also under major development as a ship-repair and submarine base, it is believed Russian naval vessels have access to refueling, and perhaps to docking, facilities.

Ceylon, with strong Communist influences in its political life, has been beset by considerable economic instability and fratricidal strife since its independence, and the important ports of Colombo and Trincomalee offer potential friendly havens for visiting Soviet warships. But the country's economy, so far, is dependent upon Great Britain and the West, and the island is overshadowed in strategic importance by the Indian subcontinent, with whose fate it is almost certainly identified.

Soviet and Indian trade is increasingly interlocked; Moscow, for instance, has agreed to procurement over the next decade of about $750 million worth of Soviet-type freight cars manufactured in India. India has been subjected to considerable pressure to buy Soviet commercial aircraft; she has already saddled herself, in the words of one expert, "with one hell of a debt to Russia."

All this Soviet effort has not persuaded New Delhi to relinquish —at least in policy statements—her policy of nonalignment. But actually the first steps have been taken in the integration of the Indian economy—and the Indian military establishment—with the Russian. In 1969 Moscow proposed publicly the establishment of an Asian security organization and suggested privately to New Delhi the integration of Soviet and Indian strategic planning.

Moscow's interest in India is clearly twofold: its primary and immediate objective is defensively anti-Chinese, but the main thrust of its propaganda is offensively anti-U.S.[2] In part, the heavy-handed anti-American attitude is simply an Indian adaptation of a global Communist "pitch"; in part, a recognition of the realities of Indian politics. The Mao influence in Indian Communism is rather strong, despite, or perhaps because of, the proximity of the Chinese Communist menace, particularly in such states as West Bengal. So far left-wing coalitions of various Communist and non-Communist factions have been essential to the maintenance in power of Communist regimes. Moreover, Russia realizes there is a built-in ideological bias in the political life of India that is anti-Western and pro-Marxist. Few at the top level in the Indian establishment are Communist or unalterably Russian-oriented, but at the second or third levels of government there are many Communist, or Communist-oriented, civil servants, and some of the younger officers in the military services appear to have been impressed by Soviet equipment and Soviet training and indoctrination.

Even more important, it is clear that New Delhi's policies since the Chinese incursions across India's mountain borders in 1962 have regarded Moscow as the "Big Brother" protector of India. What Delhi once saw as a kind of Moscow-Delhi-Washington axis became predominantly, in the Indian mind, a Moscow-Delhi axis, especially after the short war with Pakistan in 1965, and the consequent ending of U.S. military aid.

Today, the nightmare of Indian foreign policy is the specter of a U.S. rapprochement with China; even the slightest hint of a desire, on the part of Washington, for better relations with Peking causes great ground swells of perturbation in Delhi.

Yet Indian policy is, in many ways, ambivalent. There is, despite the disparity in size and armaments, almost a pyschosis about Pakistan, and about 9—including 3 in Kashmir—of the Indian Army's 29 divisions are deployed opposite the Pakistan frontier.[3] The frontier with China has been considerably strengthened since 1962, the Army greatly expanded; troops have been acclimated, weapons, communications and logistics improved. Today about 9 or 10 divisions, plus supporting units, are deployed near the northern frontier with China, and the equivalent of about 2 others are in Assam and near the Burmese border, which represents a flank threat to India.

Today there appears to be no great land threat to India from

213

China; tomorrow could be a different story. The high Tibetan plateau, 1,000 miles or more from the nearest Chinese railhead, and the great barrier of the Himalayas offer tremendous obstacles to the massing and movement of major forces. Estimates of Chinese troop strength in Tibet vary between 80,000 (U.S. estimates) to 120,000 (Indian estimates)—about 4 active divisions, plus separate units. Logisticians believe that a maximum of 12 divisions could be supported there until the whole supporting infrastructure, roads, airfields, depots, etc., were greatly improved.

There are a number of sensitive points along the Indian frontier, in addition to the almost inaccessible border along the Jammu and Kashmir portion.

There is considerable Chinese Communist influence along the rough mountain road from Tibet to Katmandu in the independent Hindu kingdom of Nepal. The Indians have until recently kept some border watchers and intelligence teams—one of the many causes of friction with the Nepalese—along the Tibetan-Nepalese border. But Delhi's relationships with Nepal are frequently irritated; the Indian Army has no reserves and no line of defense south of the Nepalese border, and the Nepalese Army is inconsequential. The terrain is tortuous, and though the Chinese have the capability of seizing Katmandu quickly with an airborne assault, it would be difficult to supply more than two or three divisions along the Tibet-Katmandu road.

Perhaps the most sensitive and most dangerous point along the Chinese-Indian frontier is the Chumbi Valley, where a finger of Tibet thrusts southward between the princely protectorates of Sikkim and Bhutan toward East Pakistan. In this area the pass rises from 10,000 to 15,000 feet, and the high ground is held by the Indians. But once clear of the mountains, the going is all downhill, the prospects inviting, with Darjeeling and the tea regions of Assam as prizes, and a broad access route down the rich plains of the Ganges and the Brahmaputra toward Calcutta. A successful Chinese thrust in this region could conceivably cut off the entire North East Frontier area from India.

The valley is well guarded; so, too, are Bhutan (where an Indian military training and advisory team is maintained) and its southern

214

border. Primarily because of the logistic difficulties, it is doubtful that the Chinese have a present capability for a deep penetration of India. But if Peking should achieve such a capability, the Indian Army probably could not fight successfully for more than three weeks to a month; their deficiencies in reserves, replacements, ammunition supply, spare parts and logistic support are so major that for India a long war is virtually impossible.

A flanking threat through Assam and Burma must also be countered. Indians consider this potentially a greater danger than a direct thrust southward from Tibet, and the Indian military estimate the old Burma (Ledo) Road could be rehabilitated and prepared for at least rough military traffic by Chinese engineers within about three months.

The Burma threat is complicated by the existence of long-term rebellions and guerrilla movements in Burma and in bordering Indian territory. In India, the Nagas in the Naga Hills southward almost as far as Imphal, and the Mizos farther south have been trained and armed and aided by China, and, until 1966, by East Pakistan. The Indians have been forced to maintain about 80,000 military and paramilitary forces in the Naga area (including the 8th Mountain Division) and another 30,000 in the Mizo area to fight guerrilla forces that have probably never totaled at maximum more than 6,000 to 10,000 men. In 1969 the Indian campaign, with Burmese cooperation and by divide-and-conquer techniques among the various tribes, resettlement, and major economic development programs, achieved sweeping successes. The guerrillas were split up and heavily reduced in number by casualties and capture. The Naga-Mizo threat reached the end of a chapter, but it is probably not the end of the book, for dissident factions in Burma are still supported by China across the ill-defined frontier, and Rangoon's control over northern Burma is at best tenuous.

Burma itself, a potentially rich rice bowl of Asia, is attempting to maintain a precarious and isolated neutralism. Its economic life has virtually stagnated; its governmental processes are distinguished, even among Asian nations, for bureaucracy, red tape, nepotism and inefficiency; and at least two minor Communist factional rebellions, an ethnic Chinese movement (with Kachins,

215

Shans and Burmese) with headquarters near Bhamo and the important Kachin independence movement among the hill people of the
north, in addition to the transfrontier activities of the Nagas and
the Mizos, have defied liquidation. The Burmese Army of about
125,000 is tied down in, and capable of, internal security duties
only. The prospect is for more of the same. The slow, almost imper-
ceptible improvement in Burma noted in 1969 may continue, but
for years to come Burma will be more or less of an international
cipher with at least its northern and mountain regions a cockpit of
conflict and dispute, more and more influenced by China.

The potential ground threat of the Chinese Communists to the
Indian subcontinent is latent. Today it has an immediate threefold
importance: the forced diversion of much of India's marginal economic resources to the military budget; the support and stimulation
of small-scale but unending rebellion in Assam and Burma; and the
increasing dependence of India upon the U.S.S.R.

What many in New Delhi regard as an even more serious threat,
that of air power, from Chinese fields in Tibet and from Pakistan
accentuates the strain upon the Indian budget and emphasizes the
dependence upon Soviet aid. With Soviet aid India is building a
small but rather modern air force, as far as planes and pilots go. But
it has major deficiencies. A very limited early-warning and ground-
control intercept radar network with interlocking communications
is being improved slowly, but any really effective air-defense system, as we know it, is virtually nonexistent. American experts
believe the Indian Air Force would be able to fight an air war for
no more than three days to a week before most of its surviving
planes would be deadlined for lack of spares.

But the mushroom clouds from the Chinese nuclear test site at
Lop Nor in Sinkiang Province overshadow New Delhi and pose
the great unanswered questions in India's future military policy.
Each nuclear test in China has its underground political reverbera-
tions in India. The specter of Chinese missiles with nuclear warheads targeted against Calcutta, Bombay and New Delhi
preoccupies the thoughts of many Indian strategists and if Chinese
ICBM's should be test-fired across India into impact areas in the
Indian Ocean, the resultant shock wave might forever destroy the

216

strange blend of Marxist philosophy, pacifist slogans, nonalignment mysticism and Gandhian "passive resistance" that has distorted Indian thinking. India as a nuclear power is becoming more and more a probability with each Chinese test at Lop Nor, and most experts believe New Delhi could develop a nuclear weapon within a year.

But joining the nuclear club would not greatly diminish the Indian inferiority complex, which is "sicklied o'er with the pale cast" of arrogance. New Delhi and the Indian military have plainly pinned their hopes for nuclear security on Russia, and secondarily and wistfully on the United States. New Delhi officially opposes the deployment of U.S. Polaris submarines or naval forces in the Indian Ocean, but any talk of improved relations between Washington and Peking sends shivers down the backs of the Indian Defense Ministry, and many Indians hope that if the crunch came, Russia and the United States would jointly provide India with nuclear security.

But India's future is more likely to be determined by its own internal contradictions than by external threats. It is a massive colossus, in terms of population, but with feet of clay. It is not so much a nation as a conglomerate of peoples of different races, languages and religions, with inadequate resources and insufficient food, at perpetual war among themselves. The once desperate food scarcities in India have, it is true, been somewhat relieved, by U.S. and other help, with the remarkable development of the Punjab and other grain-growing regions, but population growth, checked for a time by birth-control measures, continues;[4] the economy is far from promising, political stability is threatened. Perhaps the best that can be hoped for in the foreseeable future is that the New Delhi Government will stagger on, but somehow survive one crisis after another; a darker possibility is a continuing swing to the left and fractionalization of central power, with all the chaos that would accompany such a process—a process that might be checked for a time by a right-wing backlash and the imposition of a military government.

Certainly the prospects in India are not bright; it was—and is— nonsense to envisage India (as it was fashionable to do a decade ago) as the hope of Asia and the kingpin of any U.S. geopolitical

217

policy in Asia. India is a weak reed; the United States would be ill-advised, indeed, to lean upon it.

## Africa

The long closure of the Suez Canal, the importance of Middle Eastern oil, the rise of Communist China and the new Soviet naval interest in the Indian Ocean have all focused increased strategic attention upon Africa south of the Sahara, and particularly upon South Africa, which dominates the Cape of Good Hope maritime route.

Central Africa (south of the Mediterranean states and north of South Africa and Rhodesia) is a region rich in raw materials and weak in peoples—a vast underpopulated area of some 32 so-called nations, 2,000 tribes and 4,000 languages and dialects.[5] This vast region, cut loose precipitately from its past colonial ties, has no real indigenous military or political strength; it is comprised of un-developed economies and educationally and technically backward peoples with weak leaders, venal governments and little sense of national unity.

It is, in the words of Ernest Lefever, "a partial power vacuum, largely underpopulated and, in educational, economic, and political terms, underdeveloped. Its economic potential invites the attention of the more advanced industrial powers and its instability and chaos tend to play into the hands of external militant forces seeking to alienate Africa's political leaders from their traditional Western ties."[6]

Partially to counter these trends and to increase internal stability, the United States has provided limited military and training assist-ance and some public health and safety funds to many of the Cen-tral African states. The bulk of these funds have gone to Ethiopia, where the United States operates a military communications facility at Kagnew. Except for the economic importance of its raw-material resources Central Africa offers little of strategic impor-tance to the United States.

Southern Africa (including the Republic and Rhodesia) by any geopolitical standard has a far more important place in the global

218

equation of power. Its dominating geographic position, on the Cape of Good Hope maritime route, is "dramatically illustrated by the fact that an estimated 1.5 million tons of shipping passes around the Cape every day, over half of it being oil for Europe."[7]

The South African Republic has by far the most developed economy on the continent, produces some 43 percent of all the minerals of Africa and 73 percent of the gold supply of the non-Communist world. It also has the strongest and most stable government on the continent, built on white supremacy and the separation of the races.

Most of Africa's military strength south of the Sahara is concentrated in South Africa. The Republic maintains almost 40,000 men in its regular armed forces, and manufactures most of its own light weapons, but must import tanks and heavy arms. The Navy, built around two ASW destroyers, is small but efficient; the Air Force, equipped primarily with French Mirage planes, has about 200 combat aircraft. An efficient, tough South African police force, almost as large as the armed forces, is trained and equipped for riot control and paramilitary duties, and there is a large, but as yet scarcely trained, European militia.

Rhodesia deploys about 30,000 military and paramilitary forces, including the police. It has, despite an economic boycott by much of the Western world, a viable and going economy. The Portuguese colonies of Angola and Mozambique are sparsely populated and underdeveloped, with considerable potential wealth. They are both roiled by externally supported insurgencies against Lisbon's rule, and Portugal maintains about 55,000 Portuguese and African troops in Angola and 40,000 in Mozambique. The future of the Portuguese colonies is clouded by the end of Salazar's rule and tomorrow's uncertain policies in Portugal. But Rhodesia and South Africa retain major strategic and economic importance. The economic embargo against Rhodesia—a nation far more moderate in its racial policies than South Africa—has already hurt, not Rhodesia, but the United States. Rhodesia is an important source of high-grade metallurgical chrome; since the embargo, our need for this metal has made us dependent for the majority of our supplies upon the U.S.S.R., which has already taken advantage of our dependence by increasing the price. Such a policy as that which we have applied to Rhodesia is strategically, politically and economically a policy of no-return.

The African continent, as Henry C. Wolfe once put it, is "a major economic prize . . . because of its wealth of raw materials . . . almost 25 per cent of the world's manganese, more than 50 per cent of the gold, 70 per cent of the palm oil, 75 per cent of the sisal, 80 per cent of the columbium." Its raw materials, including the diamonds, antimony and gold of South Africa, the beryl of the Congo, the chromite of South Africa and Zambia, the columbium of Nigeria, Angolan and Nigerian oil, rubber and manganese and uranium, are of considerable importance to the United States and to the Western world's reservoir of raw materials.

But, except for the white-supremacy nations of South Africa and Rhodesia, Africa's politics and its economy are tribal and disparate, feuding and divisive; it is a complex of "nations" that are not nations in any modern sense of the term, and for some generations its backwardness and its problems are likely to defy solution. Access to the raw materials of Africa—a rich storehouse of untapped wealth—and uninterrupted use of the Cape maritime route represent our major strategic interest south of the Sahara. But for protracted periods the United States, by stockpiling and the use of substitutes, could do without most African resources, though perhaps at the cost of increased prices. The danger in Africa is not immediate, but long-term: the danger of much of the continent's being gradually unified ideologically, politically and economically under an alien concept.

The new "nations" of Africa are inclined, in any case, toward the shibboleths of Marxism and socialism, and both the Russian and the Chinese brands of Communism are active in many regions of Africa with propaganda and limited arms and economic aid. The Chinese have established a foothold in strategically located Zanzibar (Tanzania) and are aiding Zambia to build a railroad to Dar es Salaam. Chinese weapons and agitators have made fairly frequent appearances in small numbers in the heart of Africa. But to both Communist states—and particularly to China, which has no deep-sea Navy —Africa south of the Sahara is too difficult of access to permit easy

220

support for revolutionary movements. And the cultural ties of the colonial past—particularly in the former French colonies—still represent an important anti-Communist influence. More important is the continent's divisiveness and instability and even the color bar; black may be beautiful, but yellow is a shade less so, and white is perhaps suspect.

Africa could well be a major problem in the distant future, but the present danger is the gradual pre-emption or closing off of raw-material sources. But even that is a long way off; today Africa needs the West more than the West needs Africa, and the extreme separatism, regionalism and backwardness defy any quick melding of rival tribalisms.

The only military facility the United States maintains in Africa south of the Sahara is an important communications station in Ethiopia, which will continue for some years to have major interim usefulness. But it may perhaps be replaced by the time the U.S.-Ethiopian agreement expires in 1978. Space-tracking stations are maintained at other localities. It is noteworthy that the United States has no bases as such in Africa, nor does it now have the vital interests there that necessitate bases. Its interests, except for continued access to raw materials, are essentially contingency ones—staging fields, overflight rights and naval refueling facilities and maritime patrol bases in time of war. Such facilities would be convenient but not vital; hence no high price—political, economic or military—need be paid to assure them.

It is anomalous and faintly ironic that the most strategic, and at the same time the most stable, areas of sub-Sahara Africa are the extreme southern portions, where the southward-thrusting tip of Africa dominates the South Atlantic–Indian Ocean sea route. "In any 10-day period, there are almost 2,000 ships traveling the sea routes off South Africa's shores."[8] This is anomalous and ironic because this area—in which strategic interest must focus—is comprised, with the single exception of Zambia, of white-dominated nations. South Africa and Rhodesia, the most developed and most pro-Western of its nations, are in no way immune to the problems of black versus white which beset most of the former colonial areas of Africa and of the United States itself. But they have been free

221

from the vicious tribal wars and factional feuds—black against black—which have sapped the energies of most of the other new states. And even the Portuguese colonies of Angola and Mozambique, though roiled in parts by desultory guerrilla warfare, have escaped the horrible traumas of Nigeria and the Republic of the Congo.

The rebellions in the Portuguese colonies, aided, of course, with arms and training by Communist China and Eastern European satellites, are an incipient source of danger. In Mozambique the rebels probably control (in the countryside and at night, but not in the towns or in daylight) most of two provinces, and the intermittent, small-scale warfare drags on after more than five years of fighting. But the Portuguese control the main political, communications and economic centers, and there appears to be no quick end in sight.

But neither the Portuguese "wars" nor the newly established "front" that is commencing to operate against Rhodesia is the torch that will set Africa aflame, unless the major Communist powers opt for increased risks and greatly increase their aid. Even then the tribalism of Africa defies any quick unity, and the specter of the black peoples cooperating to push the white man from the continent seems far off.

The ineluctable facts of geography place Simonstown, Durban and a new port of Richards Bay high on any list of focal ports and air bases. The maritime route around the Cape of Good Hope is a far easier route, from the point of view of both weather and distance, than the route around Cape Horn. The Suez Canal will in time be reopened, but the great tankers will not be able to use it. Thus a port near the Cape of Good Hope will continue, for an indefinite future, to have a contingent importance to the West.

A British–South African letter exchange of 1955 permits continued British naval use of South African-controlled Simonstown in time of peace and its use by Britain and her naval allies in time of war. Thus an important base on a key maritime route is presumably available to the West—so long as the Afrikaner Government of South Africa, irked by Western pressures against its racial segregation policies, does not renege.

222

The contingency utilization of this base by the Western maritime powers is mutually important to Britain, to the United States—particularly if we strengthen our forces in the Indian Ocean—and to South Africa.[9] In South Africa and Rhodesia the pragmatic needs of strategy and the facts of geography are clearly at odds with the politics of passion.

The emotionalism and divisiveness that complicate the racial problems in the United States and in South Africa will prevent positive measures to meet strategic needs near the Cape of Good Hope. But Washington can certainly refrain from exacerbating the problem by pressures which irritate feelings and freeze positions and by such feckless and useless acts as arms embargoes against South Africa and the cancellation of visits of U.S. warships to South African ports.

"I see no evidence at all," George Ball has written, "that the policies we are now pursuing towards South Africa are promoting beneficent change; instead, they appear to be retarding it."[10]

## The Indian Ocean

There can be no doubt that the vast Indian Ocean area—that immense seascape extending from the Cape of Good Hope to the Red Sea, the Persian Gulf and the Strait of Malacca—is the stage for the newest drama in world politics. New actors have entered from the wings of history: Soviet Russia; less obviously, the Chinese Commmunists; and, hesitantly, still half-hidden by a curtain of indecision, the United States.

In the age of the missile and of space voyages, the Indian Ocean has acquired a new strategic importance. Utilization of its vast water areas by sea-based missile-launching systems greatly strengthens the power of the U.S. nuclear deterrent. Submarines or surface missile ships cruising the Indian Ocean add new dimensions to dispersion—always an important factor in the degree of vulnerability of missile systems. Their mobility would increase the enemy's problem of locating them to such a degree that it would be well-nigh impossible to ensure their destruction. Missile ships cruising in these waters would be on station in some of the least-populated

223

regions of the world, well removed, if desired, from normal maritime trade routes. And they would expose the heartland of Asia—Singkiang Province and the Chinese nuclear installations as well as Soviet Central Asian military and industrial complexes—to attack from a new direction, from the south. Similarly SABMIS, or antiballistic missile ships, cruising south of the Indian coastline, could provide at least nominal military, and even more important, political, protection to the Indian subcontinent in case of the threat of Chinese nuclear missile blackmail.

In addition to the newly acquired potential of the Indian Ocean basin as a gigantic and invulnerable missile pad, men-of-war cruising in these exotic seas have a psychological and political effect, often disprotionate to their actual power (as Soviet ship visits have shown), on the far from stable lands of Africa, the Middle East and the Indian subcontinent.

And modern technology has placed a new emphasis upon the broad reaches of what is, to Americans, the world's least-known ocean. The advent of the missile and the range and power of land-based aircraft have made the Mediterranean a lake rather than a sea. In time of war or crisis it offers at best a precarious maritime passage, and since the closure of the Suez Canal—a completely undependable strait during any threatened or actual belligerency—the shortest approach is around the Cape of Good Hope. The Persian Gulf, the Arabian Peninsula and the Middle East can no longer be defended from the Mediterranean alone; these facts stress the necessity of developing an Indian Ocean strategy.

Russia has shown an awareness of the significance of the Indian Ocean much more discerning than the nation which produced Alfred Thayer Mahan, the apostle of the *The Influence of Sea Power upon History*.

Soviet maritime and oceanographic activities in the Indian Ocean are, in the words of an expert observer, "increasingly impressive," and it is now apparent that the relatively recent Russian naval advent in the area is a permanent feature. Soviet freighters carry sheep and goats to Saudi Arabia from East African ports for sacrifice at Mecca, and trade with lettuce, cucumbers and Coca-Cola along the African coast. Soviet fishing fleets have made their debut east of Suez and Russian men-of-war—surface ships, submarines, auxiliaries and space-recovery vessels—now more or less continuously cruise from Ceylon to Mombasa. Since 1968 more than thirty Soviet naval vessels have been at times in Indian Ocean waters; during the late 1960's for the first time in a century Soviet naval forces have paid repeated visits to Persian Gulf ports. Russian ships rotate—from Vladivostok, the Arctic Fleet and the Baltic—to the Indian Ocean, but a naval presence of some sort, varying from a few ships to many, has been maintained there continuously ever since 1968, and one Soviet admiral has described the Russian naval forces as "The Russian Strategic Indian Ocean Fleet."

This strategic innovation is more impressive and more important since it has been maintained without any fixed bases in the area, over vast sea distances around the Cape of Good Hope and through the Strait of Malacca.

The Suez Canal is the shortest sea route from Europe to the Indian Ocean, and one which, until its closure in 1967, was increasingly used by Russia. Tankers from the Black Sea carried oil through the canal; Soviet merchant ships and occasional warships used the canal with increasing frequency.[11] At the time of its closure it was becoming almost a Soviet lifeline to Russian Indian Ocean ambitions, and there can be no doubt that (with the possible exception of Egypt) Russia would probably profit most—logistically, politically, economically and militarily—from its reopening. Communist support of the liberation fronts around the Arabian Peninsula would be materially facilitated, and the opportunity for incitement of Communist-sponsored revolutionary movements all over Africa would brighten.

A possible scenario in the Middle East–Arab–Israel–U.S–Russia crisis is therefore some compromise arrangement which would permit the reopening of the canal. The Israeli price would be high; it could be compensated in the Arab mind—if at all—only by much-increased Soviet aid. Any such arrangement would not be a settlement; it could represent a *modus vivendi*. The reopening of the canal is to Russia's interest; a complete settlement is not. And the reopening would intensify and abet Soviet expansionism in the Arabian–African–Indian Ocean area. But in spite of the long clo-

225

sure of the canal, the Russians have made their debut east of Suez, and they appear to be there to stay; Soviet expansionism is not just temporary and vacillating; it is planned, directed and purposeful. What should we do about it—if anything?

To anyone who has visited the Middle East–Indian Ocean–African area, the lack of a comprehensive and coherent U.S. policy is striking. Nearly every ambassador has an astigmatic view; the nationalistic blinders of the problems of the country in which he serves tend to restrict his horizons. This is an old diplomatic danger; so, too, is the propensity of some ambassadors to identify so completely with the nation to which they are accredited that they forget their primary obligations as ambassadors of the United States. These dangers are peculiarly significant in the Middle East, where the isolation and insulation of many embassies, the continuous high tensions, the pressures of domestic factors in the United States and the high propaganda content of the atmosphere all contribute to subjective judgments.

Our policies, such as they are, have been fractionalized. The U.S. Government's organization—specifically the State Department system of distinct and separate North African, Middle East and Southeast Asia areas, and the Pentagon's military command system —contribute to disparate, and sometimes conflicting, judgments and actions. Both should be modified.

One possibility would be the establishment of a roving ambassador, or "super" ambassador, accredited to all the Arab countries and to Israel, as well as to Pakistan, Afghanistan, Turkey and Iran. He should be a figure of national and international standing, whose reputation, seniority and tact would minimize the ruffled feelings inevitable in various embassies incident to the establishment of such a special envoy. He should be based in Washington, a right arm of the Secretary of State, but should travel frequently from the Maghreb and the western end of the Mediterranean to Pakistan. At the same time the desk system and the Assistant Secretary chain of command in the State Department might well be altered to produce a more unified policy.

In Africa, too, policy requires clarification. "American policy toward black Africa has been characterized by ambiguity because of the race factor in domestic and international politics. Consequently the United States has tended to be more 'friendly' toward black-ruled states than to white-ruled states, often without due regard to the larger strategic significance of the state in question."[12]

Nevertheless strategically and economically the Republic of South Africa is, to us, the most important nation on the African continent, and it holds a corner on the Free World's gold supply, on which the stability of Western currencies to a large extent depend.

The military command system east of Suez, in some ways a product of service rivalries, is now an anachronism in view of the new and ever-growing Communist expansionism.

In 1969, Shah Mohammed Reza Pahlevi of Iran, who has a mastery not only of the English language but also of its vernacular, said in an interview: "You know you had a lot of whiz kids in your administration [the Kennedy-Johnson administrations] who thought they could run the world with a couple of airborne divisions." His comment was particularly pointed at the time since the commander of the U.S. Strike Command, based in the United States but responsible for Iran and much of the rest of the troubled areas as far east as India, had just visited Teheran.

Present military command structure divides the water areas of the Indian Ocean (excluding the Persian Gulf–Red Sea) between the Commander in Chief, Pacific, based in Hawaii, and the Commander in Chief, Atlantic, based in Norfolk, Virginia. The U.S. Sixth Fleet in the Mediterranean reports to the Commander, U.S. Naval Forces, Europe, in London, and he, in turn, to the Commander in Chief, U.S. Forces, Europe, in Germany. But all the land areas—Africa, the Middle East, the Indian subcontinent—and the small Middle East Force of the Navy, based on Bahrain, report to the U.S. Strike Command, based in Florida. Thus one of the most important areas of the world is under a kind of "absentee ownership"; U.S. forces, except for the Middle East Command, are conspicuous by their absence, and contingency planning is based—in the last analysis—on a "couple of airborne divisions" to "run the world."

The swift movement of airborne troops to threatened areas to

227

meet an incipient crisis is a valid and essential part of modern mobility. This airborne mobility is particularly important in any area where direct confrontation with Soviet or Chinese forces is impossible or unlikely and in any area where the principal threat is small-scale guerrilla war. But air mobility is limited by the availability of staging or terminal airfields and overflight rights, and it cannot cope with the vast ocean areas of the Indian Ocean, or with the threatened direct great-power confrontation in the Middle East. And the hybrid, divided command system contributes to de-emphasis of the area at the very time when emphasis is needed. Serious consideration should be given to the establishment of an Indian Ocean command, to include all water and land areas, including the East African coast, east of Suez to the Burmese-Thailand border. Strike Command should retain its cognizance over West Africa south of the Sahara and its important joint training function in the United States.

In addition to a modernization of the U.S. diplomatic and military command structure, the international functions of CENTO should be continued as long as the member nations—Pakistan, Iran, Turkey and the United Kingdom—find it useful. CENTO is a paper military organization—in this sense of very doubtful utility—but it has sponsored important economic and logistic improvements, particularly in communications, in all the member countries.

The question of a U.S. military presence east of Suez will become one that is more and more pressing to answer as U.S. involvement in Vietnam is phased out and the Soviet-Chinese challenge becomes stronger. Two immediate possibilities should be examined.

The Navy's Middle East Force, a flag-showing and fact-finding unit, based at Bahrain, is now more than twenty years old. It does not require any immediate major augmentation, simply expansion of its present three-vessel strength to its authorized five ships, and the provision, on rotation, of modern, large vessels. Arrangements for indefinite small-scale utilization of the facilities at Bahrain should be completed, and the Commander, Middle East Force, who must travel thousands of miles annually, badly requires the provision of a far more modern transport aircraft for his use.

228

Some American experts believe that retention of the small naval facilities at Bahrain after the British withdrawal would be counter-productive politically and would establish the Middle East Force as a target for Communist agitation. These observers argue that the Shah's formula for regional solutions of regional problems should be tried, and that, instead of permanent base facilities in the gulf, periodic visits by modern U.S. naval task forces should be scheduled.

Such a course of action is, indeed, an alternative to taking up the burden of the British Raj, though it is not likely to be an effective one. Certainly a low-key, low-profile presence is essential, but on the other hand, in the turbulent regions around the Arabian Gulf, where the United States has such large oil interests, a ready, on-the-scene force would appear to be essential.

As a complement to Bahrain, the planned British retention of Masira Island, off the coast of Muscat and Oman, as a staging base for aircraft is important to any Indian Ocean policy that the West may adopt. Unlike mainland footholds, island bases often enjoy a certain immunity from the political contagion of large land areas.

In addition to these gulf outposts and to South African ports, a transit airstrip and small fuel installations on the island of Gan, in the Maldive group, which is, however, "politically sensitive," will presumably remain available to Western planes. Farther east, the Cocos Islands (800 miles southwest of Singapore), administered by Australia, offer a cable station, modest refueling facilities and an airstrip.

To supplement these inadequate existing facilities and to provide support for any increased Western presence in the vast areas of the Indian Ocean, the possible establishment of a small naval-air facility at Diego Garcia has been under discussion for several years. Diego Garcia is part of a new British colony, established in 1965, under the title of B.I.O.T.—British Indian Ocean Territory.

The B.I.O.T. includes the Chagos Archipelago, near the center of the Indian Ocean, 1,200 miles northeast of Mauritius. It also includes the tiny, low-lying coral atolls of Farquhar, Aldabra and Des Roches, north of Madagascar. The British Royal Air Force has expressed interest in this group—against the opposition of natural-

229

ists—as potential refueling or air-staging bases. Some strategists, who rule out the possible use of South African ports or black African airfields as sea-air routes to the Indian Ocean, believe these islands, near Madagascar, plus small refueling facilities (for both ships and planes) on Ascension Island and/or St. Helena in the Atlantic, would offer emergency military alternatives around the Cape of Good Hope.

Diego Garcia, though undeveloped and subject to rough weather and high seas in the northwest monsoon, offers a number of natural and political advantages.

Like Ulithi Atoll in the Pacific, used by the U.S. Navy in World War II, it offers a natural anchorage and facilities for a small advanced base. It has virtually no native population (the archipelago itself has about 900 people), and hence none of the incipient problems inherent in the establishment of a foreign base in the midst of an alien people. The atoll of Diego Garcia has a potential anchorage area about 10 miles long by 7 miles wide, with an average depth of 80 feet. There is ample dry land area for an airstrip, small communications facilities, a fuel tank farm, and quarters for a station complement, if needed, of 200 to 300 men. Funds for initial development —dredging and blasting of coral heads, construction of a small airstrip—have been requested. Diego Garcia, as a small advanced base in standby condition, could be an important ace-in-the-hole if future political and strategic developments required assignment of U.S. forces to the Indian Ocean on any permanent or semipermanent basis.

One must recognize, of course, that modest military establishments tend, sometimes, to grow into unnecessarily large behemoths, and that Washington must carefully consider—particularly at this time of reduced commitments—the pros and cons of a U.S. military-political involvement in the Indian Ocean area. But strategically it is clear that a small air-staging facility and naval anchorage and refueling station such as Diego Garcia would be of great utility if any permanent U.S. unit or squadron were to be assigned to the Indian Ocean. Bahrain, in the Persian Gulf, is too far away and too much involved in the regional problems of the gulf area. Diego Garcia, along with the British island of Masira, in the

Arabian Gulf, east of Muscat and Oman, are almost essential staging fields and air bases if Western power is to be exerted for any continuous period in the area.

Future developments may well lead to the conclusion that a permanent military establishment in the Indian Ocean area, other than the Middle East Command, is not desirable. A planning command may be all that is now required, with occasional rotational visits by units and squadrons detached from the Pacific and the Atlantic. The maintenance of a permanent fleet or permanent tactical air forces in the area has many disadvantages. Because of the long supply lines and the logistics problems, it would be extremely expensive. It might have—certainly would have with the strong left-wing parties—an adverse effect in India. The sultry hot climate would require modern, carefully air-conditioned ships, designed for the tropics; even so, frequent drydocking would be necessary. Morale, over any long-term period, would be a mounting problem; there are few places in the entire area where an amphibious force could even practice landings, and the crews aboard ship, and the personnel of tactical air squadrons based possibly at Masira, Diego Garcia or Bahrain, would be cooped up inside steel walls or in tiny bases far from the multiple recreational facilities most Americans have come to associate with civilization.

But the arguments for a deterrent submarine and perhaps surface-ship *missile* force are cogent; sooner or later, if the credibility of the deterrent is to be maintained, and particularly if it is to be applied to China, such a force will have to be established in the Indian Ocean.

As Admiral John S. McCain, Jr. and a few other percipient naval officers pointed out long ago, the Indian Ocean has become the newest stage for great-power rivalries, and it offers, to the power that dominates it, potential control over the rimlands of Africa, the Middle East and the Indian subcontinent.

And it can be dominated only by a maritime strategy—a strategy of ships.

231

# «« 9 »»
# Asia and the Broad Pacific

LENIN ONCE WROTE that the way to Paris led through Peking.

Thus he expressed in ideological terms his innate understanding of the geopolitical importance of the Asian heartland to control of the world.

Mao Tse-tung voiced the same fundamental concept in different terminology when he spoke of "a countryside of the world," a tide of peasant revolution—launched in China—gradually isolating, inundating and overwhelming the great industrialized metropolitan "island" power centers of the world.

And Admiral Arthur W. Radford, USN, then Chairman of the Joint Chiefs of Staff, once stressed that a unified China, under no matter what form of government, would represent a potential threat to the United States.

The central fact of Asia, and of the Western Pacific, today is China—that vast, inchoate, sleeping giant, now awakening from the lethargy of centuries. Her development, under a strong Communist central government, into an industrial nuclear power has changed the history of the world.

But China's development is not the only factor that will affect tomorrow's Asian policies. Another great Asiatic and Pacific power —Soviet Russia—vies with Peking for dominance in Central Asia and Siberia; armed clashes, increasing in size and reminiscent of the undeclared war between Japan and Russia prior to World War II, have already emphasized one of the major determinants of future history.

And Japan, a virile island nation, has become far more powerful in industrial and economic strength than she was, as an empire, prior to World War II. Today Tokyo potentially holds the balance of power in the Orient—balance between East and West, between Russia and China, between left and right.

For the United States, the development of new and tremendous power centers in Asia, by far the world's most populous continent, cannot be ignored. Americans may not like to fight thousands of miles from home and blueberry pie, but what happens in Asia may well determine the question of life or death for American generations yet unborn.

The Pacific, the world's greatest ocean, is both a broad highway and a defensive rampart for all of East Asia, the Western Hemisphere and Australia and New Zealand. The world's leading technological and industrial powers border it, the world's most populous nation faces it. Its island-speckled surface provides facilities and bases for offense and defense. Its bordering continents, its myriad islands and its deep seas contain the wealth of empires, the stuff of power. And the Pacific maritime approaches lead to the Indian and the Arctic oceans, and, around Cape Horn and through the Panama Canal, to the Atlantic.

To the United States the defense of the Pacific today is no longer a matter of choice. The broadened U.S. political responsibilities of the past decade—particularly the inclusion of Hawaii and Alaska as states of the Union—mean that U.S. vital interests, the defense of American territory, now extend to within two miles (the distance in the Bering Strait between U.S.-owned Little Diomede Island and Russian-owned Big Diomede Island) of the U.S.S.R., and out into mid-Pacific at least 2,000 miles from our continent. In addition, the U.S flag flies over American Samoa, deep in the South Pacific, 2,771 miles southwest of Honolulu, over a whole complex of tiny islets extending from 150 degrees west longitude to about 165 degrees east longitude; to Guam, only 1,500 miles east of Manila; and to all those sun-dappled little islands of the U.S. Trust Territory of the

233

Pacific Islands—once the so-called Japanese Mandated Islands. In no other ocean, in no other area, is the United States so definitely committed by territorial imperatives to political and geographical defense commitments so far from our continental shores.

There is, too, in the Asian-Pacific area another vital interest: the erection of a defense against the aggressive, expansionist ambitions of Mao Tse-tung's Communist China. Whether we like it or not, as long as Peking pays obeisance to Mao's concepts, our vital interests will be involved. As Coral Bell writes:

> ... there could hardly be a more thorough-going claim to universality than that made for the thoughts of Mao Tse-tung. The strategic doctrine of the "country-side of the world" is not a doctrine for expanding China's power in Asia. It is a doctrine about how "the cities of the world"—i.e. the industrialized states, including those of Western Europe as well as North America may be subjugated or undermined by the subsistence peasantries of Asia and Africa and Latin America. It is a doctrine which looks to bringing down the entire present structure of the society of states. . . . Thus . . . the dominant powers of the central balance will automatically find themselves involved.[1]

This involvement may well occur first along the eastern rimlands of Asia, for in Southeast Asia and in some of the island archipelagoes fringing the coast there is little indigenous strength to oppose the outward thrust of the "countryside of the world."

The Pacific maritime routes are essential arteries of U.S. industry and economy. Beryl (for beryllium, used in alloys and nuclear chemistry and physics), imported from India and Australia; columbium and tantalum from Malaysia; copper from Chile and Peru; fibers (hemp, sisal, henequen) from the Philippines; lead from Australia; rubber from Indonesia and Southeast Asia;[2] sugar; thorium (a form of fission fuel used in nuclear reactors) from Australia and Malaysia; tin from Malaysia; tungsten from South Korea; zircon, a corrosive-resistant metal of great importance to nuclear development[3]—all these and many other raw materials essential to advanced technology are imported by sea from nations around or near the Pacific basin.

The capital investments of the United States in Asia and in the

Pacific countries, though small compared to U.S. investments in Canada and Europe, are important and growing rapidly.

These, then, are the interests of the United States in Asia and the Pacific—some of them vital, others merely important; some of tremendous immediacy, others long-term.

The strategy of the Pacific is the strategy of great distances and narrow straits. In no other ocean are the distances so great; in no other ocean are the continental land masses so hemmed in by fringing islands; the East Asian rimlands and their coastal seas are screened from the broad Pacific by a chain of islands, stretching from Alaska's Aleutians and the Kuriles to Indonesia.

For centuries the epic struggle of heartland versus rimlands has been more graphically demonstrated in the East Asian–Western Pacific area than in any other region on earth; here through history the power of the land has met the fury of the sea.

This island chain, as the late General Douglas MacArthur emphasized, has long been rightly regarded by Washington as the key to U.S. interests in Asia and the Western Pacific. The denial of these islands to any actual or potential Asian continental enemy, or, alternatively, the use of some of them by the United States for military facilities, has been a cornerstone of U.S. policy. They have represented, in a sense, the U.S. frontier in the Western Pacific, an outpost line of defense.

The Korean involvement in 1950 and the Vietnam involvement in 1965 extended U.S. "salients" to the continental land mass of Asia.

The importance of the island chain is twofold: in the control of the narrow straits and maritime passages debouching from the coastal seas into the broad Pacific and as springboards for operations against the continental land masses.

A chain, of course, is no stronger than its weakest link, and any break in the island chain weakens materially the entire outpost line. However, geographic and economic factors make some portions of the island chain more important strategically than others. These factors permit the convenient grouping of Pacific-Asian strategic problems under several subsidiary headings; none of these prob-

235

lems, however, is insulated or isolated; one affects the other; all are interrelated.

Geopolitical imperatives emphasize the following interrelated areas: Bering Strait–Bering Sea–Aleutians–Kamchatka–Kuriles; Japan–the Ryukyus–Korea; Taiwan; the Philippines, Indonesia; Southeast Asia; Australia–New Zealand–Micronesia; the Sino-Soviet conflict and the Asian heartland.

## The Northern Sector

The Alaskan-Aleutian area, an imperative of continental defense, and of great economic importance, has a great pre-emptive value to Pacific strategy. Great-circle airline and shipping routes across the Northern Pacific pass above, or close to, the state's shores. Its land mass dominates the narrow Bering Strait and Bering Sea—the passage into the Arctic Ocean, used in most summers by Moscow to reinforce its Pacific Fleet and to resupply its Arctic settlements and bases. This inhospitable maritime passage, closed during much of the year by ice or weather, is nevertheless of increasing importance to both the United States and the U.S.S.R.—to the United States as a possible route for tankers to new-found oil deposits in northern Alaska, to the U.S.S.R. for its Arctic naval and commercial convoys.

The Aleutians serve the United States as outposts for reconnaissance and intelligence purposes. Communications intelligence facilities which monitor Soviet traffic, giant radars which measure the parabolas and record the flights of Soviet long-range missiles impacting in the Kamchatka missile range or in the Pacific, and maritime patrol aircraft which skirt the shores of Alaska and provide surveillance of the Soviet submarine base in Kamchatka are key elements in the U.S. global-surveillance capability.

Petropavlovsk is the only Soviet submarine base that fronts upon the open oceans; its submarines sortie into the broad Pacific. Its harbor sometimes freezes, but channels are kept open the year round, and, once freed of the land, the Soviet squadrons can seek immediate anonymity in the broad reaches of the sea, unconfined by narrow straits or choking ice fields. For these reasons Petropavlovsk, despite its remoteness from the main Soviet logistic centers in Siberia, is inherently the most important single submarine base under the flag of the U.S.S.R. Thus our monitoring positions in the Aleutians have major importance.

The mist-shrouded Kurile Islands, bleak dots of land in a frigid sea, are of peculiar strategic importance. They were owned by Japan until the Japanese defeat in World War II led to their seizure by Russia. Today the Russian flag flies over these little islets, and thus Russia dominates the maritime passageways into the Sea of Okhutsk, to the oil deposits of Sakhalin, and to the important Soviet industrial-military bases on the Siberian mainland at Magadan, Nikolayevsk, Sovetskaya Gavan and Vladivostok. It is through these passageways in the Kuriles, or, alternatively, via a longer distance through the Sea of Japan and other narrow straits, that Soviet merchant ships, tankers and surface men-of-war of the Soviet Far Eastern, or Pacific, Fleet must sortie.

Russia's recognition—increasingly emphasized since Moscow's decision to achieve global maritime capabilities—of the importance of the Kuriles means that Japan's hopes of regaining some or all of these islands is doomed to failure in any foreseeable future. Nevertheless they could serve as bargaining counters, with Russia holding the political chips, in any broad politico-economic negotiations between the two countries. They are also an ace-in-the-hole for the Communists in the psychological and political infighting that will certainly mark Moscow's attempts to strengthen the Russian-brand Communists in Japan.

Despite the geographic importance of the Northern Pacific sector, it is of subsidiary political and economic importance in the broader picture of Pacific-Asian strategy. The principal protagonists in this area are Russia and the United States; neither is likely to step directly on the toes of the other, and, except for Japan's claims to the Kuriles, the area is not roiled by the regional and national problems and the instability which provide a springboard for Communism elsewhere.

## Japan

Japan is the Germany of the Orient; as Japan goes, so may go much of Asia.

237

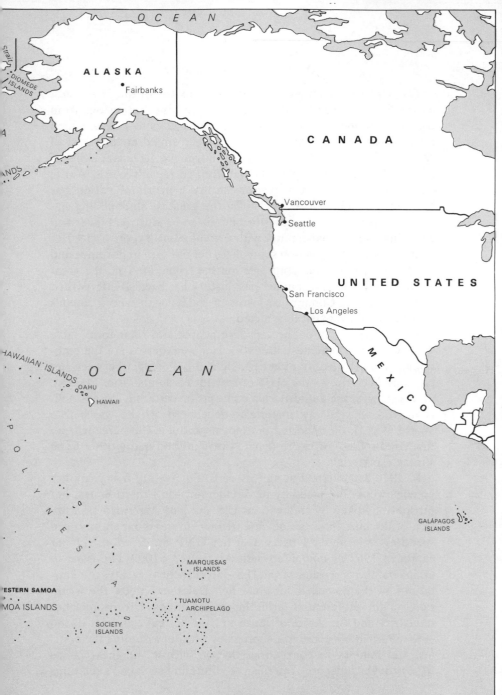

OCEAN

Strait

DIOMEDE
ISLANDS

ALASKA

Fairbanks

CANADA

NDS

Vancouver

Seattle

UNITED   STATES

San Francisco

Los Angeles

HAWAIIAN ISLANDS

OCEAN

MEXICO

OAHU

HAWAII

P
O
L
Y
N
E
S
I
A

GALÁPAGOS
ISLANDS

MARQUESAS
ISLANDS

ESTERN SAMOA

MOA ISLANDS

TUAMOTU
ARCHIPELAGO

SOCIETY
ISLANDS

THE PACIFIC OCEAN

The Japanese main islands and the Ryukyus to the south shut off the Sea of Japan, the East China Sea and the Yellow Sea from the open Pacific and dominate the sea-air routes to Korea, which many Japanese once considered a "dagger aimed at the heart of Japan." The tremendous energy and advanced technical skills of Japan's 100 million people have transformed Japan's World War II defeat into victory; in a quarter-century a prostrate nation has become self-sufficient in foodstuffs, the greatest shipbuilding nation, the world's third greatest economic and industrial power and a leading commercial country with a tremendous export trade. Her central geographic position symbolizes her military importance and her future destiny: she confronts, on the fringe of Asia, the great Pacific powers with whom her past history has been so intertwined and both of the Communist giants of today, with whom Japan's tomorrows are inextricably mixed.

The homogeneity of the Japanese people and their formidable spirit are Japan's greatest strengths. Her weaknesses are the emotionalism and volatility of her people and the conflict between her past and her future—the clash of new ideas, democratic, Marxist, nihilistic, with the authoritarian concepts of yesterday. She is deficient, too, in vital raw materials—dependent, as she was before World War II, on imported petroleum products (90 percent from the Middle East), iron ore (from Australia) and many other basic strategic materials.

In 1970 Japan stood at a crossroads. For twenty-five years her policies were dominated by her conqueror, the United States, her prosperity stoked by tremendous U.S. aid and American assumption of the burden of her defense. (In recent years Japan has been spending only about 1 percent of her GNP on defense; $11 per capita in 1967 as compared with Australia's $109.) The issue of Okinawa, the extension of the U.S.-Japan security treaty, the limitations of the so-called Japanese Self-Defense Forces, the irritations of the preferential tariffs Japan has imposed to protect her industries and the desire of Japan to have her cake and eat it, too —to maintain her economic supremacy without assuming the political and military responsibilities that go with it—all these issues have brought Japanese-American relations, in fact Japan's relations with the rest of the world, to a head. The so-called client-sponsor psychology that has marked U.S. relations since the end of World War II is definitely being replaced, and as Japan assumes the obligations of power, she will become more and more independent and less and less dependent upon U.S. power and influence.

This transition from the "do-as-we-please" of the past to "damned-if-we-do, damned-if-we-don't" of the future will present major difficulties for Washington and immense dangers for both countries and for Asia and the Western Pacific. For Japan is the major strategic link in the island chain fringing Asia, and her policies will, to a considerable degree, determine Korea's future.

Japan's internal, interlinked problems are political and military.

The introduction to Japan by the occupation forces of General Douglas MacArthur of free labor unions and the leavening of old Japanese political institutions (including the concept of the Emperor's divinity) with democratic, one-man-one-vote ideology has encouraged a ferment of ideas in Japan today and a basic conflict between right and left. The radical or left wing of Japanese thought —student organizations, labor unions, etc.—is well organized and thoroughly entrenched. It has small but probably increasing political power. But it is riven by the same differences that mark the radical left everywhere; Japanese leftists pay obeisance to the same multiplicity of strange gods as do other radicals—Mao Tse-tung; Brezhnev; Stalin; and Marxist nihilist-anarchists. This split, which seems likely to increase as the rift in the once monolithic façade of world Communism widens, weakens the left.

Right-wing Japanese thought, on the other hand, has centuries of tradition and environment behind it. A quarter of a century of Western influence has made at least a superficial impression on the Japanese psyche—chewing gum, strip-tease and neon lights—but the spirit of Bushido, the lore of the samurai still linger, and a fervent—indeed, fanatic—chauvinism still exists. Much of this is embodied in the driving energy and radical concepts of what Kei Wakaizumi has called "the disproportionately influential Zengakuren,"[4] the militant right-wing blend of religious mysticism and political action. Composed primarily of students and the younger generation—who now represent about 57 percent of the voting

241

population—this group is essentially negative in approach; in Wakaizumi's words, "it rejects the present system and seeks its downfall" (a goal curiously similar to many of the activists of the American radical left). The present younger-age voters will assume power in the later part of the 1970 decade; the maturation of their thought may well determine the future of Japan.

It is clear that in Japan, as well in the United States, political thinking is tending toward extremes of the right and left; whether the sound center will be able to resist and reverse this polarization will depend largely upon the ability and charisma of leaders yet unknown, as well as upon external pressures.

A key issue in the ferment of political thought through which Japan is passing is the role that Japan should play in the world, particularly in the Western Pacific–Asian area.

The constitution imposed upon Japan by MacArthur forswore armed forces for Japan in perpetuity, but the prohibition has been evaded—with the encouragement of the United States—by the creation of so-called Self-Defense Forces, limited to the defense of Japanese territory and unavailable for military operations elsewhere. In actuality even these forces were, until recently, minimal, and unable to provide protection for Japan. Even today Japan's defense against external aggression is dependent upon the U.S. nuclear umbrella, U.S. air defense and U.S. maritime protection, as well as upon the U.S.-supported shield of South Korea. The defense forces of Japan are incapable—as some Japanese have lately been pointing out—of safeguarding the vital tanker supply route from the Middle East to Japan through the Strait of Malacca, or of meeting any external overseas threats.

Today Japan's armed forces—in transition, like the rest of the country—number about a quarter of a million men, about 175,000 of them in the Army. The framework for 12 small infantry divisions (7,000 to 9,000 men), 1 mechanized division and an airborne brigade are maintained, supported by medium artillery, old tanks and a few aircraft and helicopters. The Air Force of 40,000 has between 500 and 600 combat aircraft, the great majority of them F-104 or F-86 interceptors. Most of these are obsolescent by today's standards, and collectively they are about equal in quantity, though not

242

in combat capabilities, to North Korea's Air Force. This force is in the process of modernization with the F-4E Phantom, which can be employed both as a fighter and a fighter-bomber, scheduled to replace the F-86 by 1976 (too late to permit Japan to achieve technological parity with the new generation of Soviet tactical aircraft). The Japanese Navy has a present strength of about 40,000 men, who man 8 submarines, 40 destroyers, frigates and escorts, and about 165 smaller ships and auxiliaries, a total of about 130,000 tons. The Navy flies almost 200 land-based maritime patrol and ASW aircraft.

The next five-year defense plan, starting in 1972, is scheduled to increase defense outlays slightly and to emphasize the Navy. A 100,000-man reserve force for the Navy and Air Force (which now have no reserve strength—the Army has 30,000) is scheduled.

Japan's future political and security policies and her relations with the United States will be profoundly affected by decisions future governments may make about the development of nuclear weapons. The trauma of Hiroshima still influences Japanese public opinion profoundly, and it will be years before the hidden conflict between "progress" and "revulsion"—between those few who now favor a national nuclear deterrent and the many who reject all things nuclear—is finally resolved. Technologically, Japan today has the capability to produce nuclear weapons within a year or less, and the inevitable development of nuclear reactors for commercial uses suggests that someday Japan may grasp the nettle and move from commercial to military exploitation of the atom. But that is some way off, and in the 1970's Japan will probably depend for her deterrent upon the nuclear defense provided by the United States. Ultimately, however, there will be powerful forces working toward a national nuclear deterrent—the threat of Chinese missiles and nuclear weapons and the increasingly uneasy relationship between the U.S. need for military facilities and base rights in Okinawa and Japan and Tokyo's insistence upon complete sovereignty and control.

The Okinawa issue, now pushed for a time off the front pages by 1969's uneasy compromise, is nevertheless an acute indication of change. It has broad implications to U.S. strategic policy in the

Western Pacific, and its solution demands the quick formulation of alternatives. It is impossible to avoid the conclusion that political and psychological factors in the Ryukyus and in Japan, and an indecisive U.S. policy about Okinawa during and after World War II, have made that island today a wasting military asset from the point of view of the United States.

The desire of the Japanese Government to subject Okinawa to the same restrictions that now govern the hundred-odd[5] small U.S. military facilities in Japan proper will mean ultimately—no matter how delayed—the reduction of the extensive Okinawa facilities to an outpost or forward position, still of some importance in the purely national defense of Japan, but of limited usefulness in Western Pacific–Asiatic strategy.

No nuclear weapons can be stored or brought into the Japanese installations in the main islands, and these installations have become more and more limited in their usefulness by resurgent Japanese nationalism. Tokyo's ambivalence—her desire to have U.S. protection but to control and limit the bases essential for such protection and to prohibit their use in support of any other military mission (unless first specifically approved by the Japanese)—is reducing the strategic importance to the United States of the Japanese link in the chain of fringing Asiatic islands to a negative one. The bases have—and will have as long as they are retained—the important capability of denying Japan and the Ryukyus to hostile continental powers. But they will have a very limited positive function in dampening war, or supporting U.S. military operations elsewhere in the Western Pacific. The exception—an important one if it continues—is the limited logistics role the bases can still continue to play, particularly in ship, automotive and aircraft repairs, hospital facilities and manufacture of noncombat material under U.S. contract, such as trucks. To Japan, this role is of some economic importance; it represents "money in the bank" without real involvement, and this was essentially the most important function of the Japanese bases during the Vietnam war.

The Ryukyus, under U.S. administration since World War II, have had a broader military importance. Okinawa has been used freely by American forces, though not without an increasing outcry and political turbulence. It was a supply and logistics base of major importance during the Vietnam war; it has been a staging base or alternate base for B-52's and their refueling tankers; and it has served as a storage area and base for nuclear weapons. The U.S. Okinawa installations include winged missiles, with nuclear warheads, emplaced in heavily protected launching pads, one of the largest airfields in the Far East, a fine naval anchorage, and very extensive supply, repair, training and barracks installations. Okinawa has been, since World War II, *the* principal U.S. base in the Western Pacific; it has been used freely—in contrast to the Japanese bases—in direct support of the Vietnam war and of our own forces in Korea and Taiwan and as a strategical pivot of the entire U.S. position in the Western Pacific. Except for the weather menace—it lies in typhoon tracks—it is ideally located between Japan and Taiwan. It is far enough from the mainland to strengthen materially its defense against a China weak in sea and air power, yet it is close enough to dominate the approaches to Wenchow, Shanghai and to all of north China.

The U.S.-Japan agreements of 1969, which automatically extended the treaty and promised the return of Okinawa to Japanese administration, eased the immediate problem but simply postponed the long-range one. Automatic extension reduced the political risks inherent in renegotiation of a new treaty, but it merely delayed the inevitable; certainly by or during the latter half of the 1970's, when the now "younger generation" assumes political power in Japan, the political outcry for complete sovereignty over all bases on the main Japanese islands and in the Ryukyus may become irresistible. If the United States chose to maintain the status quo in Okinawa, a stance that is highly unlikely in view of the Vietnam war reactions and the 1969 agreements, it could perhaps retain its virtually sovereign rights, but only at the price of very strained relations with Tokyo and the danger of bringing into power governments of right or left inimical to the United States. Both in the Japanese main islands and in the Ryukyus the conclusion is inevitable: U.S. military facilities will become more and more restricted and less and less useful in the application of power to the Western Pacific. Indeed, it appears likely that in the distant future United States armed forces will be withdrawn from Japan and Okinawa altogether. However, in the short-term transition—in the early 1970's—U.S. forces will still utilize some of the main island bases and Okinawa, with Japan assuming *all* sovereign rights and, gradually, the responsibility of protecting her own territory against any *conventional* attack. In this context Okinawa will serve for some years as a military asset, not only negatively in defense of Japan but also positively, as a supporting base for all military operations in the Western Pacific, though only with tacit or actual Japanese Government approval, and with Tokyo in charge of the Ryukyus civil administration.

The effect of these changes upon the validity of any strategy based upon the fringing Asiatic islands, and particularly upon the future of Korea, is one of the most important issues of our day.

Withdrawal from Japan and Okinawa must mean, if the United States is to exercise its power effectively in the Western Pacific, the gradual establishment of alternative bases.

But there is a more immediate and more difficult problem, the problem of Korea, which is intimately and unavoidably associated with the future of the U.S.-Japan security treaty and with the Japanese bases.

To the United States, South Korea represents a continental salient in what is essentially a maritime strategy in the Pacific. We have been committed *de facto* since World War II, and particularly since the invasion of South Korea in 1950, and *de jure* since our bilateral treaty with Seoul in 1953 to a recognition that an "attack on either of the Parties . . . would be dangerous" to our own "peace and safety." The commitment promising action in accordance with our "constitutional processes" is vague but definite, and it has been fortified for two decades by the maintenance of U.S. armed forces in South Korea.

These armed forces and these of South Korea have been supported and backed up by U.S. air power, naval power, some ground forces and supply and logistics facilities in Japan and Okinawa.

There is a long history of mutual antagonism and dislike between the Japanese and the Koreans, a fact which handicaps any rational solution of the strategic problem of Korea. Yet since Japanese

246

strategists have long considered Korea a "dagger aimed at the heart of Japan," certainly all of Korea under a Communist flag could be of little comfort, politically, economically and militarily, to Tokyo. The conclusion is unavoidable that as long as U.S. troops are maintained in Korea, U.S. forces in Japan and Okinawa must be free to support and reinforce them in case of crisis. At least tacit understandings with the Japanese government must be reached in any discussion of the future of the U.S.-Japan security treaty that this special three-cornered U.S.-Japan-Korea relationship must be maintained during the interim period while the United States is establishing a new base structure in the Western Pacific. Even after U.S. displacement from Japan and Okinawa it would be to the mutual interest of all three countries to reach some formula which would permit at least emergency use of Japanese ports and airfields for Korean support in time of crisis. For no other bases are as close to Korea as the Japanese facilities. Geography makes such arrangements well-high imperative if military aid to Korea, in time of war, is to be prompt and effective—particularly if that aid is to be conventional in nature. Indeed, an argument that might be persuasive to Tokyo is the nuclear one; if Japan will not permit the use of her territory for the support of Korea, then the United States will inevitably be forced to revert, as in Europe, to the nuclear deterrent. It is of vital importance that all the governments and peoples concerned have a clear understanding of these issues; otherwise the United States (and, inferentially, Japan) will find themselves bound by commitments on the Asiatic mainland which they do not have the means to support effectively.

The Korean commitment is, in any case, one of the most difficult problems U.S. strategists face. We have the bull by the tail and do not know how to let go. South Korea represents both triumph and despair—triumph in the creation of a highly prosperous, energetic, strong and politically fairly stable nation from the ashes of a bitter and bloody war; despair in that there is no end in sight: the volatility of the people insures some periodic political unrest, and an unsettled war, with a border seamed by fortifications and guarded by watchful armies, means an ever-present threat.

North Korea, perhaps the most savage, ruthless and primitive of

247

the Communist powers, is openly dedicated to the conquest of South Korea and is backed (though factionally) by both Russian and Chinese Communism. "North Korea has been preparing its people for a renewal of war. . . . Kim Il-sung's . . . willingness to risk war with the United States in pursuit of his goals has been demonstrated in recent crises."⁶ Another divided country, another of the unresolved problems of World War II, threatens tomorrow's history.

Yet Korea must be seen in perspective if we are not to turn our back on two decades of gargantuan effort and major sacrifice. Some 35,000 Americans died in the Korean War to turn back blatant and overt aggression; Communism *was* halted. The same prophets of doom were prominent then as now; precisely the same shibboleths used now to describe South Vietnam were employed then to denigrate South Korea. The South Koreans "wouldn't fight"; they "ran faster than they did anything else"; they "couldn't govern themselves"; they "couldn't support themselves"; they were a "corrupt, hopeless mess."

Yet today South Korea is a going country; billions of dollars in American aid and the faith of the few have paid off. South Korea supports itself and has even contributed a reinforced corps—two and a third divisions—to South Vietnam. Left with virtually no industries after the war, it has established them and has a growing export trade. It is far more prosperous than the North and far more free; the student riots and the protests in the Korean parliament would never be tolerated in the North. There is still some corruption, and Seoul is not a democratic society in any Western sense and probably will never be. But it is precisely because South Korea stands out so starkly above the morass of most of the Asiatic continent that it is a prime target of Communism; disadvantageous contrasts with the "perfect society" of the Oriental Marxists cannot be tolerated.

South Korea is worth saving, but how to save it?

South Korea is subject to two threats: internal subversion and external aggression, both based in North Korea.

The threat of internal subversion is, at the moment, secondary and is likely to remain so as long as South Korea remains economically prosperous and has a relatively good government. There are unquestionably Communists or fellow travelers indigenous to the South, organized and unorganized. They are not large in number but could become so, with political troubles or economic reversals. Pyongyang's attempts to assassinate South Korean officials and to establish guerrilla war cadres in the South, as well as the continuous infiltration of agents and harassment along the truce lines, are portents of the future. These attempts will continue sporadically and will require a disproportionate effort on Seoul's part to counter them, for a few rural or urban guerrillas, if successfully established in South Korea, could greatly weaken the government.

The threat of internal subversion in South Korea, given the political volatility of the people and the persistent Communist attempts to encourage a coup or revolution, will be a constant one and can be met only by constant vigilance, economic and social progress and political stability.

The American role in countering internal subversion is purely a supportive and advisory one, but a role which calls for the best talents of our foreign service. Seoul should be a post for our ablest and strongest ambassadors, and their guiding policy must be the development of political maturity and stability, continued economic prosperity and encouragement of a South Korean–Japan rapprochement.

The United States maintains in South Korea two reinforced divisions, part of the Fifth U.S. Air Force (most of it based in Okinawa and Japan), and an over-all command structure (with two hats, both the U.S. and United Nations commands, worn by the same U.S. general). Total strength of U.S. forces is less than 60,000 men, the great majority Army troops. The combat effectiveness of these forces was materially reduced during the Vietnam war by the "drawdown" of inventories, and the assignment of priorities in weapons, technicians, men and so on to Vietnam, The *Pueblo* incident and the increased aggressiveness of the North Koreans, however, forced the strengthening of the U.S. ground and air elements during 1968 and 1969.

The Republic of Korea maintains very large armed forces, which have some major strengths and some key weaknesses. The Army

249

totals more than 555,000 men, the Marine Corps 30,000, the Navy 17,000 and the Air Force 23,000, with an additional 10 reserve divisions organized in cadres only, and a projected 2,000,000-man paramilitary militia for antiguerrilla and local defense purposes. The grand total is more than 620,000 men (2,620,000 if the militia is included) out of a total of population of 31,000,000. Including the South Korean units serving in Vietnam, Seoul maintains about 22 divisions, or their equivalent, all of them infantry, except for 3 armored brigades. They are supported by artillery, rockets and surface-to-air missiles.

South Korea's ground forces compare favorably with North Korea's Army of about 345,000 men, organized in 1 armored division and 18 or 19 infantry divisions, plus independent units (each smaller in size than the South Korean divisions). The North Koreans are well equipped with Soviet-type light and medium artillery, medium and heavy tanks and missiles, and they are backed by a sizable reserve force.

The North Korean Navy of about 10,000 men has one element lacking in South Korea—4 submarines of the Soviet long-range W class, and a number of fast, missile-equipped patrol boats. But it operates nothing as large or with as much fire power as the 11 South Korean destroyer and frigate types.

North Korea's major and key advantage is in the air, a superiority which was emphasized dramatically during the *Pueblo* incident. Almost 600 combat aircraft—all Soviet types—are flown and maintained by some 30,000 men. These include Il-28 light jet bombers—old in vintage but with enough range to reach all of South Korea—close to 100 Mig-21 and Mig-19 interceptors, and more than 400 older Mig models. North Korea maintains an impressive early-warning and ground-control intercept system, dramatized shortly after the *Pueblo* was captured when U.S. radar showed the tracks of about 100 Migs just north of the 37th parallel, rising to intercept American aircraft flying over South Korea. The detection and shooting down in early 1969 of a Navy reconnaissance plane well off North Korea's shore was another evidence of an effective and extensive North Korean air defense.

South Korea has no such indigenous capability; in case of war in the near future any air support capable of matching North Korea would have to be supplied in large measure by the United States. Seoul counts about 200 combat aircraft in its order of battle, most of them old F-86 interceptors or reconnaissance planes. In 1969 the United States started to furnish modern F-4 fighters to South Korea, but equality in the air between North and South Korea is some years off.

External aggression from North Korea in the form of border incidents, sabotage and infiltration by espionage and assassination teams will be unremitting, and requires, to be met, closely patrolled frontier and coastal zones and the establishment as rapidly as possible of an antiguerrilla internal security militia.

Large-scale invasion from North Korea alone is unlikely as long as (a) U.S. forces remain in South Korea and/or (b) South Korea maintains political, economic and social progress. But if Seoul falters and if there should be, for instance, sizable internal dissidence in South Korea, Pyongyang's temptation to invade might be great.

The ultimate threat is Chinese- or Russian-assisted invasion of the South, also an unlikely eventuality, as long as China is riven by the dissidence and factionalism that have marked much of Mao's rule and as long as the Sino-Soviet split is so obvious. But this is not a threat that can be ignored, and the Seoul Government can never forget that in the easy coastal invasion corridor, just north of the Han River, a relatively few miles away, Communist hordes can be concentrated almost overnight.

This invasion route from Kaesong toward Seoul, with a subsidiary corridor farther east in the peninsula, presents a strategic problem that Seoul—and Washington—will have to live with for an indefinite future. It is also a problem that a developing Japan will have to face.

A closely guarded frontier, fortifications and carefully surveyed fields of fire, plus preparations for demolitions and obstacles, provide a considerable military deterrent to Pyongyang's threats of conquest. But the ultimate deterrent is a U.S. presence in South Korea and the commitments the United States has made to Seoul.

Whether we like it or not, there is no quickly foreseeable end to this commitment—no easy U.S. extrication from involvement in the continent of Asia. Political, moral and military commitments are all involved; and rapid and complete pull-out by U.S. forces might precipitate a Communist attempt at conquest, and would certainly undermine the South Korean Government. And any U.S. indication that we intended to renege on our past and to fashion a new future independent of South Korea might well be equally disastrous. An independent South Korea is not vital to the United States, but the United States is vital to an independent South Korea. And abandonment of South Korea to its fate would certainly influence —adversely from Washington's point of view—the future of Japan. The art of politics and the art of strategy are the art of the feasible; a complete severance of our commitments to Korea is not within the art of the feasible.

But a reduction of those commitments and a gradual shifting of some of the burden to Japan and to Seoul itself are possible and desirable. After the end of the Vietnamese war and the return to South Korea of R.O.K. divisions serving in Vietnam, the U.S. ground strength in South Korea could well be cut in half—reduced to a maximum of one reinforced division, instead of two. For some years logistics and support facilities capable of sustaining a rapid expansion of American troops in emergency should be maintained in South Korea. And until such time as the South Korean Air Force has achieved at least parity with the North in combat capabilities the U.S. Air Force must maintain instantly ready units in South Korea, and these units may well have to be increased in size as future restrictions hamper the use of Okinawa and the Japanese bases. Ultimately Japan itself must shoulder some of the burden of providing immediate air and naval support to South Korea in case of unprovoked invasion; it is in Japan's own interests to do so.

The United States can initiate a limited disengagement in Korea, but always with the clear understanding that there is no complete disengagement in sight. Unlike Europe, wheıe our allies have not provided the ground strength necessary to repel major conventional ground attacks, South Korea has built up an army capable of meeting the North Koreans on equal terms. But threats from Russia and/or China are a different order of magnitude. The deterrent to these maximum threats is South Korean and Japanese strength plus a small but continuous U.S. presence in South Korea, backed by U.S. air and naval power deployed from bases in the Western Pacific, and a military aid program keyed to modernization and expansion of the South Korean Air Force. Unlike in Europe, the nuclear deterrent cannot be really credible when applied to the defense of South Korea, for the risks and the costs—to Japan and the United States—of the use of nuclear weapons would be greater to the United States than the vital interests involved. And, unlike in Europe, an alternative is available, for the indigenous ground forces are strong enough to meet most conventional threats by conventional means.

## Taiwan

Taiwan, site of the Chinese Nationalist Government and focus of the so-called two-China situation in the Western Pacific, is an important link in the strategic island chain that hems in the Asiatic rimlands. Chiang Kai-shek's government and Taiwan itself have been much criticized and our support of this government maligned. Yet the politico-strategic advantages to the United States of a strong ally in Taiwan are major.

The United States does not require—in normal times—permanent base rights in Taiwan. U.S. patrol and reconnaissance aircraft are intermittently based on Taiwan and the nearby Pescadores. During Vietnam, Taiwan has provided a variety of support activities, including air transport staging fields and repair and reworking facilities for aircraft. Taiwan is also of major importance in intelligence-collection. Chinese Nationalist reconnaissance vessels and aircraft, U.S. pilotless reconnaissance drones, high-flying "spy" planes, electronic and communications-monitoring stations, and agents infiltrated into the mainland from Taiwan or the offshore islands provide tremendous amounts of pertinent military, economic and political data about the fortunes of Chinese Communism. Together with Hong Kong, Taiwan and its subsidiary islands represent by far the most important intelligence outposts in the Far East. Nor can the analyses of all the data gathered by the Chinese Nationalist intelligence experts be derided—as it has so often been

253

in the past—by American "experts" who have dismissed Taipei's estimates as self-serving and biased. Some of them have been thus colored, but it is well to remember that the Chinese Communist order of battle in North Korea and Manchuria was first furnished, in precise detail, to the United States from Taiwan in 1950 *before* U.S. and South Korean forces had encountered the Chinese Communists in the field. Taiwan's facilities, and the knowledge that Taiwan's ports, airfields and ground area could be used if needed in time of emergency, are helpful, useful and comforting. But these facilities are not essential as U.S. bases. What is essential is the denial of Taiwan to any enemy or potential enemy. For Taiwan, under the Chinese Communists, would mean a break in the island chain; it would threaten the Ryukyus to the north and the Philippines to the south, and its loss would have a profound political influence over the rest of Asia far more adverse to our interests than any possible gains in our relations with the China mainland.

Recognition of a *de facto* two-China situation, resumption of diplomatic relations with Peking and the entry of Communist China into the United Nations must not be paid for at the cost of Taiwan. The gains would be nebulous, the costs, strategic, political, economic and moral, disastrous. Chinese Communist ambitions, keyed to a "countryside of the world," will never be sated by the seizure of Taiwan.

In a strategic sense Taiwan represents an important flanking threat to the Chinese Communist mainland positions. Taiwan and the Nationalist-held offshore islands of Quemoy and Matsu dominate the Chinese coast from Swatow through Amoy to Foochow and control the hundred-mile, wind-swept Taiwan Strait, which links the East China and South China seas. Because of its geographic position, the Nationalists' wishful but avowed intent to "return to the mainland" and the considerable strength of the Nationalist forces, Peking's military freedom of action has been considerably limited, even during the Korean and Vietnam wars. A very sizable part of the Chinese Communist Army—totaling probably 600,000 to 800,000 men out of a total ground strength of more than 2,500,000—has been constantly deployed opposite Taiwan. Recently, when the Sino-Soviet split led to shooting affrays with the

Russians on the Manchurian and Sinkiang frontiers, it was the Chinese concentrations near North Vietnam that were thinned out and shifted northward, not those opposite Taiwan. To Peking, Taiwan represents, strategically, a deadly potential peril—a small but definite psychological and political peril to the façade of monolithic Communism on the mainland, but a major military threat.

The Nationalist forces in Taiwan total more than half a million men of all services, with a militia and reserves (poorly trained, organized and equipped) of another million. The Army order of battle includes the equivalent of about 24 divisions, but only about 16 of these are full-strength and fairly well equipped—most of them with World War II infantry weapons. A limited number of surface-to-surface and antiaircraft missiles, including the Nike-Hercules, which can carry a nuclear warhead, have been furnished the Nationalists by the United States to strengthen their defensive capabilities. The Nationalist Navy of about 35,000 operates 5 destroyers, 6 frigates, many patrol boats and a sizable number of landing craft, including 27 LST's. Its training and morale can only be classified as fair to indifferent. A well-trained two-division Marine force is an amphibious spearhead. The Air Force, proven in combat in battles over the Taiwan Strait, has some highly experienced and well-trained pilots among its 85,000 personnel and, man for man, plane for plane, has considerably more combat effectiveness today than the Chinese Communist Air Force. But its aircraft are tactical, not strategic; it has defensive, but very limited, offensive strength, and more than 200 of its less than 400 combat aircraft are old and obsolescent F-86's and F-100's.

The limited offensive capabilities and strong defensive strength (the latter also a result of the formidable barrier of the Taiwan Strait) represent a deliberate policy on the part of Washington, which, when the policy was formulated, was seriously concerned about Chiang Kai-shek's constantly voiced promises to return to the mainland. A return to the mainland since China's consolidation under the Communists has actually been possible only with the help of U.S. naval, air and possibly other support. The U.S. policy of strong defensive, but limited offensive, strength for Taiwan was (and is) sound, in that it is calculated to prevent the tail from wagging the dog—to insure the United States against being dragged by its heels into a war on the mainland.

But the implementation of the policy and the priority demands of Vietnam have led to a gradual deterioration of the Nationalists' defensive strength. Much of their equipment—ground, air and sea —is old, almost unserviceable and definitely obsolescent; spare parts for many World War II items are being manufactured, at considerable cost, in Taiwan. If the island and the Nationalist forces are to retain their strategic viability as a strong flanking position, opposite the heart of mainland China, it is essential that a new aid program be initiated to re-equip, in particular, the air, antiaircraft and naval forces. Taiwan must be retained as a bastion of Free World strength.

The offshore islands, which lie close to the China mainland (Quemoy is separated by a strait only one or two miles wide), are held by about 80,000 Nationalist troops, who have tunneled deeply into the native rock and heavily fortified the islands. The United States Government has correctly retained its flexibility of action and diplomatic maneuver about these islands; our commitment to Taiwan does not necessarily extend to Quemoy and Matsu. In case of Chinese Communist assaults against those islands the action that Washington might take would almost certainly depend upon the circumstances and the context of world events. During the Eisenhower administration the Communist blockade, by artillery fire and naval and air attacks, of Quemoy was broken by the rather simple expedient of furnishing to the Chinese Nationalists medium artillery capable of firing nuclear shells. The shells were *not* provided, but Peking understood the lesson; one plane could transport to Quemoy enough ammunition to doom any Communist amphibious assault. Today there probably could be no such simple answer to Communist attempts at conquest of the offshore islands. For the Communists now possess nuclear weapons and could retaliate in kind. The eventuality, for the immediate future, is unlikely, for Quemoy, in particular, is so strongly held that a Chinese Communist assault upon it—in addition to creating a political crisis in the Orient—could succeed only at the cost of thousands of lives. Ultimately, if the Chinese mainland increases in strength, these island positions—very close to the mainland, and hence vulnerable to many forms of assault—will represent a wasting asset.

But there is no such prospect for Taiwan, one of the largest islands in the Western Pacific, buttressed against attack from the mainland by many leagues of blue water. Its position has been weakened, it is true, as have all other positions in the Western Pacific, by Peking's development of nuclear weapons and particularly the mating of nuclear warheads to medium-range missiles. But active nuclear attack by Peking against Taiwan would instantly invoke nuclear retaliation, or its threat, by Washington. Taiwan, like Japan, is sheltered under the U.S. nuclear umbrella. And overt conventional attacks can be defeated, in the foreseeable future, by the Nationalists, provided their weapons systems are modernized and maintained on a basis of qualitative parity or superiority with those of the Chinese Communists. This is particularly true if the Nationalists are furnished a sufficient number of dual-capability (conventional and nuclear) defensive weapons, such as the antiaircraft missiles, Nike-Hercules, and air-to-air, nuclear-tipped missiles. The defense of an island position, such as Taiwan, against an overt enemy assault from sea or air provides one of the few scenarios in which tactical defensive nuclear weapons can be used to strengthen the defense without any considerable danger of extending the conflict.

No immediate military threat to Taiwan thus appears to exist, and U.S. efforts should be keyed to maintenance of the present strategic status quo. This means, in addition to a reasoned program of arms modernization, continuance of the economic prosperity and political stability that Taiwan has enjoyed for the past decade. It means, too, the orderly transfer of power when Chiang Kai-shek dies to his successors (his son is the present heir apparent) without any major internal disorder or attempted coups.

This is less easy than it sounds. Some in the West fear that Chiang's successor might be tempted to make an "arrangement" with the Communist ruler on the mainland, or that "silver bullets" (bribes) might help to organize a Communist coup. Over the years, however, it is more likely to be the pull of pride, the ties of race and the chauvinism which so many Chinese—even overseas Chinese—

257

feel that will influence Taiwan's political arrangements with the mainland. These internal dangers, which could conceivably lead to the loss of another key position in the island chain, can only be met by a clear manifestation by Washington of support, political and military. This is one reason why a military modernization program for the Nationalist armed forces is such a great psychological as well as military requirement.

There looms, too, another danger for Taiwan—now only a speck on the horizon. Worried by the Chinese rift, Moscow has permitted unofficial "feelers" in Taiwan. It is conceivable that if a Sino-Soviet war developed, Taiwan might be tempted and persuaded to undertake limited intervention, an eventuality which might involve, and would certainly worry, Washington.

## Philippines—Indonesia

These islands represent the Southern pivot or anchor of the island fringe that contains the rimlands of East Asia.

They are important raw-material sources; their geographic position dominates many of the narrow straits into the South China Sea and the Indian Ocean, and they represent maritime outpost lines in the defense of Australia.

And to the Philippines the United States has a historical "Big Brother" obligation, a kind of commitment by tradition.

The context of the Philippines in Western Pacific strategy was illustrated by the Vietnam war. Clark Air Force Base and Subic Bay —both in Luzon—were important supporting bases for U.S. combat forces in Vietnam, particularly for air and naval units. Today, and in the future, neither is indispensable, both are useful—more and more so as the now inevitable U.S. withdrawal from Okinawa accelerates. Other U.S. installations in the Philippines, such as Sangley Point, are redundant and should be eliminated. In the Philippines, in particular, the U.S. presence should be as unobtrusive as possible; the lower the profile, the better.

For the Philippines are not a shining jewel in the diadem of U.S. colonialism. Perhaps because of the islands' long history of subjugation, Filipino politicians are peculiarly sensitive about their "rights" and their "sovereignty"; the slightest indiscretion or misstep by Washington or its representatives makes Uncle Sam a whipping boy. And the internal problems of the Philippines are major. The economy is marginal; governments are inefficient and many of their members are often corrupt. The Hukbalahap Communist movement, organized around some of the poor peasants in Luzon—which once was a threat to stability—still exists and recently has had a minor revival, although today it is difficult to distinguish between ideological motivation, organized brigandage and officially sanctioned corruption.

The Philippines have little defensive strength; a constabulary of almost 20,000 is probably better trained than the armed services, totaling some 30,000. The Army has one organized division, plus some training divisions, and a reserve—on paper—of about 200,-000. Its most important and its most efficient units are some 10 engineer construction battalions, one of which has served in Vietnam. The Navy has a few coastal patrol craft, which are more useful in antismuggling duties than in military operations. The Air Force, with a total of about 60 combat aircraft—most of them obsolescent—is a token force.

These forces are so small and ineffective that they could offer no real defense to any sizable attack from nearly any quarter. More important—since the threat is present and actual, not distant and potential—they cannot even patrol the vast indented coastlines of the myriad islands in the archipelago against gun-runners and the infiltration of agents.

In effect, the Philippines depend for their security upon their insular position and their membership in SEATO.

The South-East Asia Treaty Organization[7] may be a political—and certainly is a military—euphemism for the United States. But the Philippines shelter under its somewhat vague and embracing phrases, and the island archipelago is not the only state which finds SEATO more politically palatable, internally, than Uncle Sam. SEATO has, therefore, a definite usefulness psychologically and politically, and it offers a mechanism—particularly important to the undeveloped countries of the area—for discussion, consultation and joint action.

259

The rich Indonesian Archipelago stands alone, something of a maverick but now a friendly one, in the complex politics of the area. Under Sukarno, it was almost, but not quite, delivered into the Communist camp; U.S. bayonets in Vietnam may well have made possible the counter-Communist coup. Today, though hidden dissent and Communist cadres still exist, its government is friendly to the West and trying desperately but inexpertly to restore an economy shattered by decades of misrule and corruption.

The importance of Indonesia is strategic and economic. Its geographic position makes the archipelago both an Indian Ocean and a Pacific power; Sumatra lies athwart the vital narrow shipping passage, the Strait of Malacca, and its myriad islands and the passageways among them are both barrier and access to the rich continent of Australia. In a strategic sense a Communist Indonesia, particularly an Indonesia strong at sea and in the air, would outflank, as history already has shown, the Philippines and would menace, particularly on the island of Borneo, the Federation of Malaysia. Indonesia is of major importance and has great promise as an important source of rubber and oil, and its great population —112 million people, larger even than that of Japan—make it potentially a great power.

But the potential is far from fulfillment, and Indonesia is far from a unified nation. Its widely disparate peoples—varying greatly in ethnic origin, religious beliefs, social customs and political persuasions—and the somewhat indolent lethargy of both governors and governed make it unlikely that Indonesia will play any significant international political role in the area in the near future.

It has, on paper, some of the strongest forces in Southeast Asia, totaling almost 350,000 men in the regular services, plus another 130,000 in the police and paramilitary forces. Its Navy, in particular, fostered and nourished by Russia in the days of Sukarno, appears fairly formidable, with some 12 Soviet W-class submarines, an ex-*Sverdlov*-class cruiser; 18 former Soviet destroyers or frigates, a dozen *Komar*-class missile patrol boats and many mine sweepers, patrol and coastal craft. But numbers are deceptive. The end of Soviet aid, the lack of adequate training, the effects of the hot and humid climate on ships that were not air-conditioned and

260

were not built for tropical service, and the purge of the services following Sukarno's fall have all combined to make the combat effectiveness of the Navy extremely low. Many of the radars and much of the electronic and electrical equipment are believed to be inoperative, and corrosion has had its effect on engines and ships' hulls. The Air Force, probably at one time more influenced by pro-Communist leaders than the other services, has a total of about 550 aircraft, most of them obsolescent and many of them unserviceable. Except for about 25 Tu-16 Soviet-model medium jet bombers, and 16 Mig-21's—many believed to be inoperative because of lack of spare parts or adequate maintenance—its combat planes are obsolescent. The Army, equipped with both Soviet- and Western-type weapons, is organized in about 16 infantry brigades, backed by a number of battalions of tanks and armored cars. Much of its strength is tied down in internal security duties.

To the United States the Indonesian Archipelago is of more negative than positive strategic importance. It is essential that this rich, populous island group retain its independence and be denied to Communist conquest. But the United States does not need military facilities on Indonesia's territory. American capital investments and Indonesian raw materials are important but not vital.

The U.S. cue in Indonesia should be unobtrusive helpfulness. The island archipelago will need all the economic help it can get simply to break even with its expanding population. But this must take the form of technical assistance and productive capital, very rarely of grants in aid. Rubber, oil and tourism—the latter largely undeveloped in some of the most picturesque islands in the world—offer hopeful possibilities. In some future time, but not soon, Indonesia might wish to become a member, or associate member, of SEATO, in order to participate in the combined opportunities the alliance could offer—not primarily for military security but for economic opportunity and political cooperation.

## Southeast Asia

Southeast Asia, like the Middle East, is a crossroads of commerce and of history. The Strait of Malacca is a sea bridge between

261

two great oceans, and the peninsula—Thailand-Indochina-Malaysia—is, for Indonesia and Australia, an outpost line against aggression from the Asiatic heartland. This entire region has been for centuries a kind of border area, where the tide of Chinese expansionism has ebbed and flowed and left its mark, and where the sea peoples of centuries past have met the land peoples.

The shadow of China looms over the governments and the peoples from north Thailand to Singapore. Chinese influence is a consequence of geographical propinquity and physical power and the large Chinese ethnic content of the populations. The so-called "overseas Chinese"—industrious, homogeneous, thrifty—control a disproportionate share of the banking, commercial and economic life of the region, and sometimes their hidden political ties to their homeland and the ancient prejudices that always exacerbate racial and ethnic differences make some of them ideological instruments of Communism and many of them—probably most of them—proud to be identified with the new, strong and expanding China.

The area, with the exception of a few pockets of enterprise, has been marked by political instability and corruption, authoritarian governments, a peasant economy with very little industry, nineteenth-century social and health conditions, and primitive agricultural practices. A medley of religions, a mixture of races, and loyalties that often are more village and tribal and religious than national, as well as the penalties exacted by a tropical climate, add materially to the problems.

The strategic importance of the area is its location as a peninsula appendage of Asia, which dominates the key water routes from the Pacific to the Indian Ocean. Nature has richly endowed some of these countries, with actual or potential wealth. This is a highly important rubber-producing region, and Thailand and the lush green aqueous environment of the Mekong Delta in South Vietnam are normally rich rice-exporting regions, a fact of high importance to overpopulated China.

To the United States, the area cannot possibly be termed vital after the Vietnam war is ended. Japan controlled it in World War II and lost the war. But it is important, and our major interest focuses on the Strait of Malacca and its freedom from Communist control.

262

## South Vietnam

The U.S. involvement in South Vietnam has resulted, like our presence in Korea, in the establishment of a continental salient on the mainland of Asia. It is a salient that is more dificult to hold and maintain than the Korean one. Korea is a relatively narrow peninsula hemmed in by the sea, with few good north-south communication routes and adjoined only on its northern frontier by territory under another flag. South Korea also has a more homogenous people, with fewer ethnic, religious and regional differences than those of South Vietnam. South Vietnam, though inherently far more richly endowed by nature than South Korea, is bordered by Cambodia and Laos as well as North Vietnam. Approach roads and access routes to the south from the Chinese frontier are many, easily concealed, well dispersed. The Mekong River valley and innumerable canals and water courses, as well as a long indented coastline, offer countless approaches for infiltration. And, like South Korea, South Vietnam is close enough to Communist China by "shank's mare" to make its defense against a persistent and insistent enemy difficult.

Whether or not one believes in the domino theory for Southeast Asia—that if one government topples to Communism, all will topple in a kind of chain reaction—it is clear that a U.S. unilateral pull-out, a scuttle-and-run policy which abandoned Saigon to Communism, would have profound effects in many parts of Asia. The Communization of South Vietnam could not now occur—after all the years of war, the thousands of casualties, the heavy expenditures and the major effort—without its being characterized as an outright American defeat, the first in our history as a nation. It could not now occur without the execution or exile of thousands —perhaps hundreds of thousands—of non-Communist South Vietnamese who have fought long and hard against the Vietcong. It could not now occur without a tremendous loss of confidence by Asia and the world community in the effectiveness of U.S. power and the value of American commitments. It could not now occur without shock waves in Cambodia, Laos, Thailand, Malaysia, Singapore, the Philippines, Indonesia and Japan. There is no doubt that the imposition of Communism by force on the people of South

Vietnam would represent another battle lost in the struggle for the world, and in the long view of history would almost certainly mean less stability, more conflict, perhaps in time major war. In this sense, only, Vietnam is vital.

It is idle to argue that the United States would not now be faced with such appalling consequences if it had not become involved in Vietnam in the first place. This may well be true. But it is an argument in a vacuum; we cannot be concerned now with the "might-have-beens," the "ifs" of history; we must face things as they are.

There is no easy way out of Vietnam, no quick "solution" in sight. We are probably inextricably involved in Vietnam for a considerable time to come; the problem is how to reduce our forces there as rapidly as possible without turning Saigon over to the Communists. It is not a problem that will be solved by anyone but us. Russia will give us no help; it is not in her interest to do so. It is to Moscow's interest to extend the war; a large segment of U.S. power is tied down far from Soviet vital interests, and as long as the war continues, Hanoi's dependence upon Russia, and hence Russia's influence in a country bordering Communist China, is insured. The Soviet formula in Southeast Asia is the same formula used in the Middle East—controlled chaos, with emphasis on the word "controlled"; Russia wants no direct involvement.

China will certainly give us no help in ending the war. She vies with Russia for influence in North Vietnam; Peking consistently has urged a completely intransigent line on Hanoi and her arms aid has equipped the Vietcong. No Saigon government will willingly make the kind of accommodation our liberals have been urging to end the war. For most anti-Communist South Vietnamese know that the establishment of a coalition government with the Communists is the "kiss of death"; it is their throats that would be slit, their property that would be confiscated, their families' lives that would be at stake.

We must chart our own course and hold it true, despite dissidence on the home front, if the end in Vietnam is not to be worse than today.

The course already has been charted, but it is full of shoals and only a strong captain can guide us through them. The gradual reduction of U.S. troop levels in Vietnam, already well started, must continue, with more and more of the burden of the war transferred to the South Vietnamese themselves. Yet troop withdrawals, once started, cannot be halted; they represent—militarily and politically —a slippery slope. Nor do we any longer retain the options of 1965 —bombing and blockade of North Vietnam. Our means of persuasion have been reduced. The enemy, badly hurt by the Tet offensive and his huge casualties, nevertheless retains a capability for extensive terrorism and small-scale guerrilla attacks, supplemented by larger "surge," or so-called high-point, low-point, efforts, including assaults by fire against U. S. bases and South Vietnamese units and cities. The conflict in Vietnam—always, as we have fought it, a war of attrition—has now become a war of wills, with Hanoi still counting heavily upon its chief ally in its drive for victory—war weariness in the United States. No matter what we do no quick end can be counted upon. The Vietnamization program must, inevitably, be a protracted one. As in Korea, some U.S. forces must remain for an indefinite future, and for a long time to come air and artillery and helicopter and heavy naval support and logistical backup must be provided by the United States.

The process of Vietnamizing the war must involve, first, far more emphasis upon strengthening and broadening and making more effective the South Vietnamese Government and police forces; second, it must reduce far more effectively than it has yet done the power of the underground Vietcong infrastructure—the secret government—in the South. And, third, the military strengthening of South Vietnam—the regional and popular forces and the regular services—must include not only more modern arms but better leadership. All of these are lengthy, time-consuming processes—all of them started, in some cases well started, but very far, indeed, from finished. South Vietnam, assailed, it should always be remembered, by a North Vietnam fully supported by the world's two greatest Communist powers, is not yet ready to stand on its own feet.

The prospects, then, are that some American forces must remain in Vietnam for years to come. The problem is to reduce this number to a minimal figure as rapidly as possible, and to do this, the fighting must be minimized and, if possible, contained chiefly in the largely uninhabited mountainous, jungled, border areas or seacoast swamps.

But two must play at this game; to reduce the tempo and extent of the fighting, the enemy must be willing; or, alternatively, he must be unable to maintain the past tempo. That he has been hurt, badly hurt, there is no doubt, but that he can continue, with Russian and Chinese aid, the tempo of 1969 for an indefinite period there is also not much doubt. Thus the tapering off of the war would appear to depend more upon unforeseeable political events than upon any present planned use of military power. The death of Ho Chi Minh, for example, could, in the long view, lead to a crisis of succession in Hanoi and a split in North Vietnam's leadership. And an exacerbation of the Sino-Soviet conflict could affect Vietnam.

South and North Vietnam are approximately matched in military potential. South Vietnam has a population of about 17 million, North Vietnam of 19 million. Normally North Vietnam was the more industrialized part of the country, South Vietnam the very rich granary. But the bombing of the North and the extensive military construction program in the South, including tremendous port improvement programs at Camranh Bay, Danang and Saigon, road-building, the establishment of rock quarries, airfield construction, improvements in agricultural practices, medical facilities, etc., and the establishment of all kinds of small industries have made South Vietnam probably the best-developed country in Southeast Asia, with (when the fighting stops) a sound economic base for a promising future.

The total armed forces of South Vietnam now approximate 1 million, but the army of about 425,000, organized in 11 divisions and other smaller units, is still in some respects outgunned by North Vietnam's 450,000-man Army, plentifully supplied with Soviet-type small arms, rockets, missiles, antiaircraft guns and light and medium tanks. North Vietnam's air defense, with more than 6,000 guns of 37 mm. and above, and hundreds of SAM missiles plus an extensive and effective radar and communications network, provided the first combat example of how effective modern air defense could be. South Vietnam is also weak in air power; she has only about 125 combat aircraft, of which about 15 are fairly modern F-5's. As U.S. forces leave Vietnam, the South Vietnamese Air Force will receive more modern planes, including F-4 fighters, which should help to restore a more even balance. North Vietnam operates about 130 combat aircraft, including some 8 or 10 Il-28 light jet bombers, capable of reaching any point in South Vietnam, 21 Mig-21 interceptors—far more effective than any plane South Vietnam now has—and about 100 Mig-15 and Mig-17 fighters.

South Vietnam has a distinct advantage in naval power and operates river forces, mine sweepers, coastal patrol and escort vessels, gunboats and hundreds of motorized armed junks.

There are extensive paramilitary forces (militia-type units) in both countries. In South Vietnam the regional and popular forces, the civilian irregular defense groups and the national police—all of them key factors in pacification and antiguerrilla war—total almost 600,000. All badly need better organization and equipment.

There is, thus, an extensive job to be done, a task started but by no means finished, to help the South Vietnamese assume the burdens of their own defense. It will be a hard job but not a hopeless one, a problem comparable to, though not identical with, the one Washington faced in Korea in 1953.

The United States' long-term strategic interest in South Vietnam is a stable, prosperous, viable country with—at least for the foreseeable future—a non-Communist government, a government that, at a minimum, is neutral in fact, not merely in theory. We do not require, and should never retain, permanent bases there; in fact, it is to our own interest to reduce the size of our continental salient in Southeast Asia and our commitment to that salient as rapidly as possible.

## Laos and Cambodia

These countries have been inextricably involved, along with South Vietnam, in the Communist–anti-Communist–civil-guerrilla war that has raged in the area for the last two decades. The so-called Ho Chi Minh trail, a devious complex of jungle paths and roads that has been used so effectively by Hanoi to supply its forces in the South, traverses hundreds of miles of Laotian territory, and Cambodia has been used as a port of entrée, a supply and recuperation base, and a point of attack against Saigon and its environs.[8]

Cambodia and Laos, along with South Vietnam, are the three so-called "protocol states"—not members of the South-East Asia Treaty Organization, but supposedly protected by its terms. Both Cambodia and Laos have disavowed this protection; nevertheless, Laos, at least, has been helped in its fight against about 30,000 Pathet Lao indigenous Communist forces (equipped by the Chinese and North Vietnamese) and some 40,000 to 50,000 North Vietnamese regulars (guarding and developing the Ho Chi Minh trail and supply routes to South Vietnam) by ground and air forces in Thailand, by powerful U.S. air support and covert U.S. Army and CIA-directed trail watchers, raiders, guerrillas and advisers. Cambodia has been powerless to prevent the use of its territory by thousands of North Vietnamese and Vietcong. Cambodia's sticky and volatile relationships with its neighbors include territorial, ethnic and economic disputes with South Vietnam and Thailand.

The Royal Laotian forces, including some so-called neutralist troops, number about 65,000, a few of them fairly well equipped by the region's standards. But one of the more important factors in Laos is the hill tribesmen of the north and northeast, who have been generally unfriendly to the Communists and, as guerrillas, trail watchers, etc., have played a large role in the harassment of the North Vietnamese supply routes. All these forces have been stiffened by Royal Thai troops, often wearing Laotian uniforms, by U.S. advisers and special warfare experts and by extremely heavy tactical bombing.

Cambodian troops number only about 45,000, with mixed equipment from many sources and very little combat capability.

The future fate of both these countries depends to a very major extent upon the outcome of the Vietnamese war. But no outcome that can possibly be envisaged will basically alter in our favor the *de facto* situation in Laos, where the King rules over only a portion of his domain. Northern Laos is, and long has been, an area of Chinese influence, particularly in the province of Phongsaly, next to the Yünnan frontier. Route 19 from Hanoi, through Dienbienphu, traverses this province, and Chinese road-building crews are completing a new road, which will eventually extend southwestward from Route 19 toward the Burmese and Thailand borders. Another spur extends northward to the Chinese border. Chinese influence is also felt in other parts of Laos, even, at times, as far south as the Plaine des Jarres, important to the North Vietnamese–Vietcong supply routes to the south. This influence is almost certain to continue and, if it remains restrained to the northern provinces, represents no great threat to anyone. At the same time, Laos itself will long exist torn by internal dissidence, with a kind of ideological war-lordism dividing the country. Again, this represents no profound threat so long as Luang Prabang, Vientiane and the western sections of Laos along the Mekong remain under the King, or under non-Communist forces.

Cambodia's future problem is simply survival as a nation.

Its fate, and that of Laos, are linked to the fortunes of Saigon and of Hanoi. Indochina, despite its disparate peoples and tribal factions, is a strategic whole. The effective neutralization of the entire area would be to our interest. Our vital interests in the area are negative, rather than positive—to avoid defeat, to turn back the Communist bid for conquest.

The United States has no vital interests in these countries. Strategically, these countries represent a land route to the Malaysian Peninsula and a gateway to the rich Mekong Valley. To rich Thailand, they are important as buffer states against North Vietnamese–Chinese Communism; if they can be kept so, Thailand's principal purpose—and our own—will be served.

# Thailand

The ancient kingdom of Siam, unlike the other countries of Southeast Asia, has no colonial past, and thus, until recently, it had little anti-Western bias, none of the sense of psychological inferiority which has caused in so many undeveloped countries an over-compensation of prickly arrogance. Its natural wealth, its weak neighbors and its relative remoteness from China also contribute to

269

its well-being, and its government—often criticized by Western liberals as dictatorial—has, nevertheless, the advantage of political stability and relative efficiency.

Thailand's happy times, however, have been rudely interrupted by the wars in Vietnam and Laos, the incursion of North Vietnamese refugees, some of them Communist subversives, in the northeast provinces just across the Mekong from Laos, and the development of small-scale guerrilla movements, principally astride the Malaysian frontier in the south and in the northeast. Its somewhat somnolent, easygoing existence has been rudely shattered by the construction of six large U.S. air bases and military facilities throughout the country and by the incursion of thousands of U.S. soldiers. Bangkok has become a boom city, its streets as jammed with new automobiles as its canals are jammed with klong boats, and the evils incident to quick money—profiteering and corruption, a moral letdown and a sense of political uneasiness in the cities as well as in the countryside—have corrupted Eden.

Thailand is nevertheless probably the single most enthusiastic member of SEATO, and has assigned planes, special units and Thai artillerymen to back up the Royal Laotian forces. Its 120 combat aircraft include counterinsurgency planes. The Communist guerrilla movements, particularly the one in the northeastern part of the country, represent more of a latent than a present threat. They are small-scale, and, measured against the daily history of Asia, where life is cheap and violence common, the casualties are minuscule. So far, the Thais, with U.S. guidance and material aid and training, have been able to contain, though not to conquer, the guerrillas.

The future history of these guerrilla movements—and, indeed, of Thailand—will depend upon the outcome of the Vietnam war. Communist victory in South Vietnam and Laos would almost certainly lead, sooner or later, to intensification of Communist activities in Thailand. On the other hand, a Communist repulse would not necessarily spell the end of the Thai insurgencies; more likely they would continue, but at a somewhat desultory and bearable level.

To the United States, Thailand has particular political, and some strategic, significance. It is the centerpiece of Southeast Asia—

270

independent, anti-Communist, relatively stable and prosperous, with none of the difficult colonial heritage of its neighbors. If it should fall to Communism, there would be little hope for the smaller and more troubled states of the area. Thailand's southern appendix, forming a common frontier with Malaysia, near the Kra Isthmus, fronts on both the Gulf of Thailand and the Andaman Sea, and provides a land gateway to strategic Singapore.

There have been, intermittently, for the past few years more than 40,000 Americans in uniform stationed in Thailand, most of them Air Force personnel manning the planes and the great bases developed to support the Vietnam war. Force reductions, already started, will continue, and ultimately, when the Vietnam and Laotian wars have ended, or settled into some kind of uneasy stalemate with a low level of combat operations, virtually all U. S. forces in Thailand can be, and should be, withdrawn. The process may, however, have to be gradual—as gradual as the withdrawal from Vietnam, and for a long time to come there will be need for U.S. advisers and U.S. aid and for a few small special units—Army Special Forces, Navy Seabees, logistical units and medical units and perhaps some engineers who have been engaged in road-building and public health.

For a long time, predating our combat involvement in Vietnam, the United States has maintained a prepositioned stockpile of Army equipment in Thailand, enough for approximately one brigade. It has been cared for and maintained by U.S. service troops and Thai civilian labor, and though some of it is undoubtedly obsolete or unserviceable, much of it could be useful in an emergency. However, the concept of prepositioning heavy equipment on land in various areas of the world, to be available to troops flown out from the United States, has political liabilities, and it is expensive. And unless the equipment in Thailand is fully replaced with more modern items as they become available, it represents a wasting asset.

In the long-term view, more important, to both the United States and Thailand, than prepositioned equipment is U.S. access in peacetime maneuvers or in crises to one or more of the Thai bases. This complex of port facilities, airfields and storage areas has been built up with U.S. dollars by U.S. and Thai contractors. Many of these facilities add sizable capital investments to Thailand's eco-

STRATEGY FOR TOMORROW

nomic infrastructure and represent important peacetime assets, as well as potential military bases. This is particularly true of the complex near Sattahip, on the Gulf of Thailand coast, south of Bangkok. Docks, ammunition and oil storage, barracks and warehouses, one of the finest airfields in Asia and naval facilities are included in this complex. An agreement to permit U.S. military use under certain conditions and to include a limited amount of U.S. aid for maintenance would be to the interest of both countries.

Thailand is a good friend and good ally; no matter how desirable or necessary it may be to reduce our continental salients in Asia, precipitate pull-out could lead to political disaster. Our policy in Thailand must be one of support and encouragement, the build-up of indigenous forces, the increase of Thai capability, a gradual drawdown of U.S. forces and direct U.S. military support. Economic aid, particularly in the form of technical advice and development aid, keyed to a Mekong River development project (linked with Vietnam, Laos and Cambodia), will be an essential bridge between the inflation of war and the deflation of peace.

## Malaysia

This is a country with a very short past, a mixed present, a doubtful future—and a key strategic position. It is an artificial conglomerate, both ethnically and geographically, and it suffers from all the evils of its somewhat artificial birth. The Malay States in the important mainland peninsula have now been linked with Sarawak and Sabah (Borneo), hundreds of sea miles away, in a Federation of Malaysia, yet contiguous Singapore, natural capital and key strategic point, is a separate city-state. In Malaysia a very large Chinese minority, the banking and commercial sinews of the state and the ethnic group from which most of the Communist guerrillas who fought the British for twelve years were drawn, are in riotous confrontation with the ruling Malays. And the accession of Malaysian sovereignty over Sarawak and Sabah has caused friction with both the Philippines and Indonesia.

Malaysia maintains small armed forces, almost completely inadequate to face any sizable external threat, marginally strong

272

enough, so far, to maintain internal security. They total about 44,-000 military personnel and another 25,000 police, some of them with light field equipment. The Army of about 38,000 is organized in 20 infantry battalions, supported by a few armored cars and some 105-mm. howitzers. Some of its units are fairly well trained in counterinsurgency and jungle warfare. The government has been attempting to modernize its Air Force—it numbers only about 20 combat planes—in order to have some means of extending at least symbolic power across the South China Sea to Borneo.

In addition to the very major strains in its mixed society, Malaysia faces, still, an insurgency threat. An estimated 1,000 Communist guerrillas, perhaps still led by Chin Peng, the Communist leader who fought the British to a standstill for twelve years, still lurk in jungle hideouts along the 361 miles of Thai-Malaysian border. In recent years the activities of these ideological outlaws have been sporadic and small-scale, but they have occasionally ambushed Malaysian security forces, they control a few villages, and their future will wax or wane dependent primarily upon two factors—the Chinese-Malay confrontation in Malaysia and developments in Vietnam and Thailand. In fact, there is a close liaison between Thai and Malaysian guerrillas; the fate of both are interdependent.

Strategically, mainland Malaysia is important chiefly as a land isthmus between the South China and the Andaman seas and as a land bridge between Southeast Asia and Singapore and the Malacca Strait. As the Japanese demonstrated in World War II, Singapore is dominated, strategically, by the fringing Malay States to the north.

Yet the "thin red line of Empire" will be very thin, indeed, after the British departure in 1971. Present British plans contemplate the maintenance of a jungle warfare training school in Malaysia, periodic training in Far Eastern waters for four ships of the British Navy four months of each year, and occasional training exercises by the Royal Air Force in Asian skies. An airlift of troops from Britain to Singapore and combined maneuvers with Australia, New Zealand, Singapore and Malaysia will provide some slight political and psychological—but little military—assurance to the peninsula that London will not entirely abandon the regional responsibilities inherited from its days of glory.

To the United States, Malaysia has been, and still should be, chiefly a British and British Commonwealth commitment. We cannot, in any case, save Malaysia solely within Malaysia; its defenses lie in Thailand and are also indivisibly associated with Singapore's. Some economic and technical aid, military and technical training and a clear assurance that a U.S. presence will be maintained in the Western Pacific–Southeast Asia area are about the best we can do now. And, even so, it is quite possible that the future of Malaysia may depend more upon the price of rubber than upon U.S. aid programs.

## Singapore

The focus of strategy in Southeast Asia is Singapore—that *rara avis* in modern political groupings, a city-state. Singapore's defection, in 1965, from the Federation of Malaysia, formed only two years earlier, has complicated political and economic relationships, but as the British, Australians and New Zealanders have emphasized, Singapore and Malaysia are indivisible in a defense context.

Singapore's great importance is primarily geographical; it is one of the finest ports in Asia and a major port of the world, and it dominates the maritime "Main Street" of Asiatic waters—the Strait of Malacca—as well as the broader passage (leading to Sunda Strait) between Malaysia and Borneo. Its facilities, built up under 150 years of British rule, are the finest in the East, and include great drydocks and ship-repair facilities, miles of docks, three airfields, tremendous workshops, warehouses, schools, hospitals and housing, as well as radar and communications installations. The British have occupied about 16 percent of the island's 224.5 square miles, and directly and indirectly some 87,000 people, out of Singapore's total population of 2 million have been dependent on British payrolls.

To replace this tremendous economic loss is the challenge of Prime Minister Lee Kuan Yew, who has used the British withdrawal as a means of fostering national unity in the diverse, polyglot population. About three-quarters of Singapore's population are ethnically Chinese; the balance Malaysians, Indians, some British and many mixtures. Communist-dominated labor troubles and ethnic riots have marred the brief modern history of Singapore, and the plain-spoken but somewhat enigmatic Mr. Lee is well aware of the problems he faces.

Singapore and the Federation of Malaysia, as well as Thailand, have followed the course of American policy in Vietnam and U.S. fortunes there more closely than nearly any other Asiatic power— for good reason: they know that U.S. troops in Vietnam are their first line of defense; a U.S. pull-out or defeat would expose them to imminent peril.

Yet they are hedging their bets. Singapore's efforts are both military and economic. The military efforts focus on regional arrangements with Malaysia, Australia and New Zealand, with backing from Britain. A ten-year defense program to produce 45,000 trained soldiers has been started, and two infantry brigades and an armored unit are scheduled to be ready when the British withdraw in 1971. An Israeli defense mission and Israeli military schools are participating in the training program. The ultimate goals of the Singapore defense force are somewhat uncertain, but they have been defined by Singapore's Foreign Minister as "enough of a force to make anyone who might want to swallow Singapore think twice." The regular "standing army," under this concept, would apparently number about 8,500 to 10,000 men, with 70,000 trained reserves, about 25 jet fighters, and small naval coastal patrol forces, specifically earmarked to keep the Strait of Malacca open to shipping.

These forces would be dovetailed, if current thinking is implemented, with Australian, New Zealand and British forces in Singapore and in the Federation of Malaysia. Australia and New Zealand now plan to maintain 2 infantry battalions and some 8 jet fighters on Singapore, an infantry company and about 40 more fighters at Butterworth airfield in northern Malaya and 2 frigates or destroyer types in nearby waters. A number of British technicians and officers have been assigned to the great naval dockyard in Singapore to help operate and maintain it, and British plans for the

275

Malaysian jungle warfare training school contemplate the rotation of British infantry battalions continuously through the school. Tengah Air Base in Singapore is to be maintained as an operational field ready to receive airlifted troops from Britain.

All these somewhat tenuous plans are still chiefly on paper, and there are a lot of holes in them. For instance, the major British radar complex on the island of Penang is essential to any sound air-defense system, yet plans to train Malaysian technicians or to transfer responsibility for this unit are still ephemeral, and no effective joint air-defense system for the whole peninsula is as yet programed.

Economically, programs for replacing the British investment appear to be somewhat more advanced. Industrial parks have been prepared in Singapore, and by tax incentives and other efforts several hundred new companies have been induced to move to the city-state. The great naval facilities are being adapted for commercial purposes, and numerous merchant ships have been drydocked and repaired. Improved relations with Indonesia and with Malaysia have boosted trade, and military procurement contracts for the Vietnam war have provided much-needed aid. But the future is still, at best, uncertain. Major unemployment and its dangerous political and social consequences in a city riven by ethnic and religious differences and with the labor unions controlled by the Communists could have disastrous consequences. Singapore, to have a future, must establish itself as a trading, commercial and industrial hub of Southeast Asia.

To the United States, Singapore's basic importance is as the guardian of the maritime gateway, the Strait of Malacca. It is not, for us, an indispensable base. Some U.S. experts have argued that the United States should establish a multilateral Indian Ocean command with headquarters at Phoenix Park (the British HQ) in Singapore. But such a peacetime commitment would mean the creation of another U.S. salient on the continent of Asia, and inevitably Singapore would come to be known as an American base, no matter how disguised in multilateral colors. The disadvantages of political friction and high expense would follow, without any great concomitant gain. For it can never be forgotten that the real de-

276

fense of Singapore against external threat, or internal subversion supported from beyond its frontiers, lies to the north. The United States is already committed in Vietnam and in Thailand, probably —despite a policy of disengagement—for some years to come. In Singapore we should definitely exhibit a low military profile, and the Commonwealth nations, with British help, should show the flag.

And an Indian Ocean command on the continent of Asia would be a shining target for charges of Western imperialism. Nor can we possibly play such a leading role when the powers with primary interests—Britain, Australia, New Zealand—have specifically disavowed any automatic defense commitment to Malaysia and Singapore.

A low U.S. military profile does not preclude periodic visits by U.S. military aircraft and units of the U.S. Seventh Fleet. Overhaul and repair contracts for some naval vessels might well be transferred from Japan to the Singapore dockyards. And contingency plans should make Singapore's facilities available in an emergency. Tourism and U.S. investment capital can help Singapore's economy. And, in time, there may well be a role for SEATO in Singapore, if and when a broadened and modified alliance including Singapore and the Federation of Malaysia, with much of its orientation economic as well as military, can be established.

# Australia, New Zealand and Micronesia

The ANZUS Treaty of 1951, in addition to SEATO, links the defense interests of Australia, New Zealand and the United States in a common front. But the treaty is merely recognition of a strategic common interest in the South Pacific–Indian Ocean–Western Pacific–Southeast Asia area.

To the underpopulated, rich continent of Australia and to New Zealand, land of milk and honey, the pressure of overpopulated Asia and the threat of Chinese expansionism are ever-present dangers. The bonds of Empire have been severed and the protection of the British fleet has gone; Australia and New Zealand are de-

277

pendent today and for the foreseeable tomorrows upon the power of the United States.

But this is not a strategic one-way street. In strategic terms, as World War II showed, Australia (in particular) and New Zealand provide the major land masses, the essential support bases for all forward positions in southeast Asia, and, indeed, throughout most of Micronesia. They are the dominant links between the South Pacific and the Indian Ocean; Australian bases at Perth, and the U.S. Navy's major communications facilities on Australia's northwest cape are essential to naval operations in the Indian Ocean.

The defense of Australia and New Zealand must clearly be based on control of the air and the sea; they are far enough from the mainland of Asia and from any major threatening island archipelagoes to permit maintenance of small ground forces. But both nations have realized their outpost positions today must be further extended than in the past, and both recognize it is to their own interest to help Southeast Asia defend itself. Australia also has a major defense interest in eastern New Guinea, the Bismarck Archipelago and some small island protectorates—none of them of major importance in peacetime, all of them individually and collectively a protective screen in time of war.

The effective military power of both nations is small. New Zealand has a regular Army of about 6,000 men, with about 12,000 in the organized reserves, which form the nucleus of 2 brigade groups with supporting forces. A Navy of 4 frigates and several mine sweepers and miscellaneous patrol and small craft is supplemented by a small Air Force of about 30 obsolescent combat aircraft, plus a number of more useful maritime patrol planes and transports. Australia, like New Zealand, utilizes a limited form of conscription, but her total armed forces number only about 88,000 men in all regular services, plus a militia-type reserve of about 40,000. The Army numbers about 47,000—8 infantry battalions in Australia, 1 in Malaysia, 3 with supporting services, in Vietnam. It is well equipped, and its professional soldiers are well trained. The Citizen Military Force—the militia-reserve—is organized in about 25 infantry battalions, plus supporting forces, with 1 battalion each in Papua and New Guinea. The Navy's 17,000 regulars man 1 light

ASW aircraft carrier, 10 destroyer or frigate types, 3 submarines, mine sweepers and various miscellaneous and support ships. The Air Force has 230 combat planes with French Mirage III jet fighters for air defense, old Canberra jet bombers, and more than 20 U.S.-type maritime patrol aircraft. Modernization of the Air Force with the controversial swept-wing F-111 US. attack bomber is scheduled.

To the United States, tied by bonds of a common language and to a large extent a common heritage, as well as by common interests, with Australia and New Zealand, military aid—even grants in aid—to these small forces is well worth the cost. Essentially U.S. sea and air power provide the backbone of the defense of Australia and New Zealand; what the United States requires to strengthen the common defense, a requirement which faces few difficulties, is military access to Australian–New Zealand ports, bases and airfields in time of emergency. Of all the available sites, the great roadstead of Manus in the Admiralty Islands and the west coast Australian bases appear to have the greatest geographic importance in the context of tomorrow's problems.

To the north of Australia and squarely athwart all the maritime and air approaches to the East and South China seas lie the so-called Trust Territories of the Pacific Islands—the former Japanese Mandated Islands—where so much American blood was spilled in World War II. These tropical dots of land—the Marshalls, the Carolines and the Marianas—can provide both barriers and bases for any Pacific strategy. Guam, 3,300 miles west of Honolulu, 1,500 miles east of Manila, is the only island in Micronesia that is under complete U.S. sovereignty. All the rest, including nearby Saipan and Rota in the Marianas group, are under United Nations trusteeship, with the United States as the trustee.

If the United States is to maintain any forward position in the Western Pacific, retention of these Trust Territory islands—indeed, their outright ownership by the United States—is essential. Australia and New Zealand could, though with difficulty, be supported, even if the Trust Territories were under an alien flag, but by a more circuitous route via American Samoa. But if the United States loses

279

the right to utilize some of these islands for military facilities, the cost would be high if U.S. power again has to be projected across the Pacific. This will be far more true tomorrow than it is today. For the limitations that will hamper our future utilization of Okinawa, and our inevitable ultimate withdrawal from the Japanese islands and the Ryukyus, mean fallback, and alternate positions must be made available. In fact, the time is short, and very few political or military preparations have as yet been made.

The political requirement is simple: some formula—plebiscite, local self-government, commonwealth status—must be found to bring these island groups completely under the U.S. flag. In some ways they have been somewhat neglected orphans of Uncle Sam; there is dissatisfaction, some yearning for the "good old days" under the Japanese, and it is quite conceivable that unless positive U.S. action to assure a better future is taken soon a plebiscite tomorrow would register a vote favoring a return to Japan. These overriding political considerations mean that this is a problem for the President and the Department of State, not the Department of the Interior.

Guam, with its fine harbor of Apra, and its well-developed airfields and ammunition storage facilities, is the natural focus of U.S. military facilities in Micronesia. U.S. Polaris submarines in the Pacific utilize Apra as a forward base, and B-52 bombers used Guam during the Vietnam war. Guam has drawbacks as a key military base; like Okinawa, it lies in the typhoon belt, and it is too small to accommodate all the facilities that might be displaced from Okinawa. Tentative plans for development of the island contemplate, in addition to warehouse and other construction, a new form of floating drydock for Apra Harbor. Ultimately Rota and Saipan will be required to accommodate the airfields and storage areas needed, and there may well be need for development of staging fields or refueling or communications facilities at Ulithi Atoll and in the Palau group.

Formalization and perpetuation of U.S. sovereignty in the Trust Territories is one of the strategic imperatives we face in the Pacific unless we are prepared to withdraw our defense line to Hawaii. Because of the Japan-Okinawa situation the need is acute and the time is short. The United States can never forget that any Pacific-Asiatic strategy is fundamentally dependent upon our capability to traverse the vast distances of ocean between San Francisco and Hong Kong—i.e., sea and air power and the forward bases to support them.

## The Asiatic Heartland— Sino-Soviet Rift

The enormous and remote frontier between China and Russia, extending from the Pamir Mountains and Sinkiang to Manchuria, poses only one great problem for the United States—the threat of nuclear war. The ideological polemics, the bitter verbal attacks and, more important, the frequent border incidents, shooting affrays and occasional minor battles between the two Communist giants hold both promise and threat to the Communist and non-Communist world.

The promise is of a further weakening of the once monolithic structure of world Communism. There is no doubt that mutual fear in Peking and Moscow has diverted attention and strength to the Asiatic heartland from Free World areas threatened by Communism's expansionist philosophy. There is no doubt that both powers have strengthened their common frontiers at the expense of increased economic costs, and their combined efforts to promote world revolution and achieve economic and political domination have been weakened and fractionalized. We no longer face a united front of the world's most populous nation and the world's second greatest industrial power. And the end to this conflict is not in sight.

The threat of the Sino-Soviet rift is perhaps more remote, but, if realized, incalculable. The use of nuclear weapons by Russia or China or both would inevitably produce, like most drugs, a side effect of international proportions. If weapons of large size were used in large numbers, the prevailing winds could carry radioactive particles across Japan and to the Western Hemisphere. The extent, the nature and the consequences of such fallout would depend upon so many variables that any accurate forecast is unpredictable, but, at the minimum, the political and psychological pressure of public

281

opinion upon the U.S. Government to "do something" would probably be irresistible. Small weapons used in small numbers would
have only local or regional effect, but even so their use would cause
a global tremor of anxiety and fear.

The Sino-Soviet rift has a built-in permanence. It started as an
ideological split, each side claiming to be the one true god of Communism. But fundamentally and basically it is a power conflict.
China is intent upon becoming a unified, industrialized nuclear
power, and Mao Tse-tung has been using Communist nationalism
to eliminate opposition and weld the country into a monolith. Nos-
talgia for vanished Chinese greatness, chauvinism, the deliberate
build-up of an external threat—Russia—and history—Russia's an-
nexation in the nineteenth century of almost 800,000 square miles
of Chinese territory in Central Asia, around the Amur and along
the northern part of the Sea of Japan—have been used to inflame
Chinese public opinion.

This deliberate excitation can, of course, be turned on or off in
a dictatorial Communist society—though not without some convulsions. And when Mao dies and some of his older associates pass
from the scene, a new deal in China may produce leaders anxious
to reduce the ideological conflict with Moscow. The crack, the rift,
could, indeed, be papered over; in fact, it is likely that sometime
before the year 2000 there will be another period in Sino-Soviet
relations of amity and agreement, of a seeming concert of Communist views. And this will represent a period of considerable danger
for the United States and the West.

But basic factors insure over any long-term period the recurrence
of friction between Russia and China. Moscow, like the United
States, cannot view without some concern the development of a
strong China under centralized leadership. (To this extent U.S. and
Soviet interests in Central Asia coincide.) Even more important to
Moscow is the potential threat to the relatively empty lands of
Siberia and Central Asia of China's bursting population. The conflict for land—land China claims and Russia holds—is a conflict as
old as man, one that becomes more and more acute as the global
population explosion increases world pressures. Inherent in this
threat, in Moscow's view, is the development of China as a modern

industrial power, armed with a plentiful number of missiles and nuclear weapons. This nightmare causes sleepless nights in the Kremlin—all the more so since it is becoming reality.

Today China has some A-bombs, a few thermonuclear weapons, short-range and a few medium-range missiles (up to 1,800 miles), and may at any time commence production of ICBM's and submarine-launched missiles. These weapons, coupled with the huge hordes of Chinese manpower along the somewhat thinly held Russian frontiers, have a decided deterrent and pre-emptive effect upon Soviet actions and Soviet diplomacy, and force the United States to "face two ways" and prepare against two threats.

Today, and for some decades to come, Soviet Russia has, and will maintain, a great advantage over China—particularly since China's fight for unification and against war-lordism in any form is not over.[9] In fact, China's attempts to become a great power conceivably may never succeed in our lifetime. Her difficulties are immense; her impressive nuclear technological progress has been due to selective emphasis and does not reflect an across-the-board advancement. Today Soviet power far exceeds Chinese power. But this general superiority varies in local geographic regions; it cannot be applied everywhere. Russia's weakest, and therefore more strongly held, area is along the Amur River Valley and the Manchurian frontier, where the Trans-Siberian Railroad—the Soviet lifeline to the Far East—runs, in places, within a few miles of the frontier. Mongolia, with primitive armed forces of about 30,000 men (heavily supported, however, by Russians), is virtually a Russian protectorate and, for Russia, an important buffer state. For if it were lost to China, which once dominated it, the Chinese pressures against Siberia would be extended so far to the west that the Russian positions in the Maritime Provinces from Khabarovsk to Vladivostok might be difficult to hold.

In Central Asia itself, the geographic advantage along the frontier lies with Russia. Singkiang is remote and with few communications to eastern China. The U.S.S.R. has a railroad to the frontier and a natural gateway through the so-called Dzungarian Gates near Yümin to Urumchi, Singkiang's capital, which is the terminus of a railroad from Lanchow, an important Chinese atomic and industrial center in the northwest. The Dzungarian Gates, which are passes through the high Ala-Tau Mountain range along the frontier, are some 270 miles from Urumchi, 100 miles from some of the principal Chinese oil fields at Karamai, and about 500 miles from the Chinese nuclear test sites near Lop Nor. The vulnerability of these areas to a quick Soviet armored thrust has apparently been recognized by Peking; a supplementary or alternative nuclear test site is being prepared to the south, farther from the frontier, in Tibet.

There are advantages and disadvantages for both powers along their 2,500-mile common frontier, and both China and Russia number among their peoples many ethnic minorities—some unhappy under alien rule or susceptible to subversion.

Today and for the immediate tomorrows Russia has, not an ideological advantage—for the Kremlin leaders have been branded with the label of "conservatives" and "stand-patists" by those who read the little book of Comrade Mao—but an immense military advantage. Chinese numbers, formidable under some situations but "cannon fodder" against modern fire power, have been overemphasized. A human tide can infiltrate and overrun weak spots, but its sheer mass reduces momentum, creates major supply problems and invites slaughter, as Korea showed.

To the United States, conflict between the two Communist giants presents opportunities, difficult to exploit, for political advantage, particularly in the world Communist movement. It may also present opportunities to promote, deftly, solutions to political problems in areas far removed from Central Asia.

How Washington should capitalize upon this gift from the gods of Communist dissension is a key problem for the State Departments of tomorrow. There are limits to any positive actions we can take; in fact, our prudent course is watchful waiting. Two imperatives should govern. Outside pressures—Vietnam, the Middle East, Berlin—are not likely to heal the rift; increased pressures might, indeed, extend it, as Vietnam showed.[10] But it is probable that the conflict is independent and self-perpetuating. It is also clear that talk of a U.S.-Chinese or a U.S.-Russian détente is largely misplaced. We may be able to improve relations with either or both powers, but when the chips are down, it is highly improbable that either Communist power would fight with us against the other. William E. Griffith, Professor of Political Science at M.I.T. Center for International Studies, summed up the fundamental realities as follows: "... Russia remains our immediate concern. The Kremlin is not suddenly going to be friendly with us simply because of the Chinese threat. Rather, the Soviet Union, like China, is an expansionist, imperalist power basically hostile to the United States."[11]

We have two enemies in Asia.

For the United States, a sound Pacific strategy must be built around unrivaled maritime-air superiority, based, in forward positions, on the island chains that fringe the Asiatic land mass, in Australia and New Zealand and Micronesia, and with main bases and backup positions in Hawaii. Korea and Vietnam and Thailand represent continental enclaves, with ground commitments, on the Asiatic continent. These salients cannot be liquidated or eliminated overnight; the military and political consequences would be far too acute.

Nor can air and sea power alone maintain a balance of power in Asia. Ground forces—U.S. or Allied or indigenous—will be required but any U.S. commitment to the Asiatic mainland must be carefully evaluated from the point of view of U.S. immediate and ultimate interest, strength of position and chance of success.

Maintenance of the Seventh Fleet in the Western Pacific, with strong supporting land-based air power on island bases is essential to U.S. interests. Some ground power must be maintained in Vietnam, Thailand and Korea, as well as in island positions for some time to come, but it can be reduced, slowly but surely.

In 1969 U.S. forces in forward positions in the Pacific included about 390,000 men in the entire Pacific Fleet; almost half a million men in South Vietnam; 55,000 in South Korea; more than 40,000 in Thailand; 40,000 in Okinawa; 40,000 in Japan; 30,000 in the Philippines; 14,000 in Guam; and 10,000 in Taiwan—a total of about 1,110,000.

Readjustment and redeployment and reductions in the post-Vietnam period could in time about halve this number; there would be a gradual but major reduction in Japan and Okinawa and Vietnam, reductions in Korea and Thailand and the Philippines, perhaps a slight increase in Taiwan, a major build-up in the Marianas and Micronesia.

But the United States cannot go it alone. Japan must, and will, play an increasing role in the security of Asia, as well as in its economy. The Russian attempts, so far stillborn, to form some sort of an Asiatic security grouping may not be entirely antithetical to our interests—depending, of course, upon the character and the extent of such a group. And SEATO can be reshaped and revitalized and broadened, and other regional organizations, such as the informal and embryonic ASEAN (Association of Southeast Asian Nations), can be encouraged to deal with common economic problems. Nor need we object in time to the development of a group of neutralist buffer states in former French Indochina.

But there is one indispensable and vital requirement for American security in the world's greatest ocean and along the coasts of the world's most populous continent. We must command the sea and its depths and the skies above it.

# «« 10 »»
# Strategy for Tomorrow

IT IS TIME for a change, time to tot up the balance sheet of commitments versus resources, time to redefine our vital interests, time to determine how we can protect those interests, at, in Sir Robert Thompson's words, "a cost acceptable to the United States."

In his book, *No Exit from Vietnam*, Sir Robert has clearly sketched the "two unpleasant options" the United States faces in Vietnam—defeat or continuation of the war. Negotiation, as conducted by the Communists, is merely part of the conflict utilizing different means. Defeat would have such catastrophic consequences to the future that Sir Robert rejects it as simplistic and unrealistic. He believes that the U.S. war aim—an achievable one —must be to "establish, at a cost acceptable to the United States, South Vietnam as a free, united and independent country which is politically stable and economically expanding,"[1] an aim that would block Hanoi's designs for conquest without the liquidation of Hanoi or its form of government.

The outcome of Vietnam, the course the United States follows there, will determine the immediate history of Southeast Asia and will have global repercussions.

But the need for modified international policies and a new or modified strategic concept is not based on Vietnam alone; Vietnam has simply emphasized the limitations, the dangers and the costs of the policies and concepts followed since World War II. They were, for their era, fairly effective policies. We have made mistakes, but we preserved much of the world for freedom. Now it is time for a change.

The policies of tomorrow and the strategy the nation adopts to support them must stem from the past, and the imperative guidelines of technology, geography, politics and economics will insist upon retention of many of the objectives and goals, methods and means of the past. But not, by any means, all. The emphasis will change, but the fundamental purpose—maximum security for the United States in a stable world—will remain the same.

There is, of course, a contradiction in terms even in this basic aim, for a world without change is a world man has never experienced, and change means instability. Thus security policies attempt continuously to stabilize unstable situations; they must be broad in principle, flexible and adaptable to many variant situations in application.

To the geopolitician of tomorrow there are only a few courses of political policy available, and pragmatically some of these are inapplicable.

Isolationism, once in our past a defensible strategy, is no longer a practical policy. Some Americans, emotionally distraught at the frequency of our overseas wars, outraged and frustrated by Vietnam, forgetful of history, deny this statement. A Fortress America, it is said, heavily defended on our own soil but with virtually no forces overseas, would be insulated from foreign wars. Those Americans who accept this technological and economic heresy presumably base it upon the narrowest possible definition of our vital interests; they would defend the United States, but nothing else.

In the days of the sailing ships—indeed, until the Spanish-American War—this was a valid concept. The broad seas were barriers; the British Navy dominated them. We were, in economic terms, a "have" nation, with a frontier to conquer and most of the raw materials we needed for our industries available within our own borders.

But all this has irrevocably changed. The ramparts we watch

288

today must be far extended from our shores to insure even a moderate security. The jet plane of globe-girdling range, the nuclear-powered, missile-launching submarine and, above all, intercontinental missiles and space vehicles with nuclear warheads have altered forever the dimensions of the old geography; we are, today, in geographical terms, no longer an isolated continent, but a continental island in a very small world. Any sound security system in the nuclear age requires early-warning positions and outpost lines —and first lines of defense—far from our shores, at sea, in the air and space and on land. And the military costs of a defense based only on our own soil would be prohibitive. We would become, indeed, a "garrison state." Technology has not eliminated geography, but it has effectively nullified isolationism as a pragmatic security policy.

The industrialization and urbanization of the United States and the tremendous growth of our economy have also forever altered the comfortable facts of the past—"unconquered open spaces," "unlimited wealth," "all we need." We are today, in raw-material terms, a "have-not" nation; we require access to raw-material resources outside our frontiers. We must, indeed, *import* some sixty-six critical and essential commodities, or about 80 percent of our strategic raw materials, from beyond our own borders. And we *export* more than two-thirds of the world's coal shipments and more than half of its grain. If we are to sustain an expanding economy, this dependence upon overseas sources and markets will increase, not decrease, and even today we could not indefinitely sustain our prosperity, or even maintain a reasonable military security, without the raw materials of South America, Africa, Europe, Asia and Australia.

Ian MacGregor, chairman of American Metal Climax, Inc., has pointed out that the impending "doubling of the world's population, development of the poor nations, rising incomes and modern technology will place a tremendous strain on the earth's available resources."[2] He noted the decreasing U.S. control of the world's supplies of vital minerals, and urged a national minerals policy for the years ahead. Today, the United States, with a population of about 200 million people, uses about 20 pounds of copper per capita or 2 million tons. The rest of the world uses about 3 pounds per person or 4.5 million tons. By the year 2000, Mr. MacGregor estimated, the United States, with a population of 300 million, may need substantially more than 20 pounds per capita of copper, while the world's needs could reach 15 times the amount consumed today.

Indeed, one can logically argue that any strategy for tomorrow must be keyed to what Brooks Emeney thirty-five years ago prophetically called "The Strategy of Raw Materials."[3]

Access to raw materials, overseas trade and overseas investments are essential to the viability of the U.S. economic system and to our prosperity. We cannot, literally, live without the world.

Many military isolationists acknowledge the logic of the economic arguments but insist that in the space age there is no reason why a strong America, with its defenses withdrawn to its own shores, could not maintain an alert satellite "spy" system in space and its economic interests overseas. They see the United States as a sort of a giant neutralist Sweden, friendly to all, trading with all, allied with none, immersed primarily in commerce and in developing that better mousetrap which leads the world to your door.

It is a poor parallel. Sweden is a minor power, which, like Switzerland, has stayed out of war for many decades because of geographical position, the self-interest and tolerance of the great powers, and the concessions (for instance, during World War II) made during crisis to great-power demands. Today Sweden, without accepting any of the responsibilities of alliance, is sheltered by NATO, and even more by the United States. But there is no one to shelter the United States, the world's greatest power. And the United States has global interests and global investments far greater than Sweden's. Great-power neutralism is in any case a fiction; if neutral, the great power would cease to be "great"; its appetites and ambitions would turn inward upon itself (as in Sweden); its morality would be suborned, its horizons diminished, its decline certain. The nibbling conquests and expansionist drives of Russia, China and other powers would gradually conquer the nation's interests overseas; more and more, our future would be restricted, our prosperity reduced.

290

Those who argue for a completely isolationist course—no more alliances, no more commitments, no more overseas wars—are not only dated; they completely ignore the lessons of the recent past. The objective of any security policy is to protect the nation, to keep war as far as possible away from our shores. It is far better to fight overseas than in the California mountains or in New York streets; it is still better to deter war by projecting our strength to forward positions.

How can Americans so soon forget the youth of yesterday's England who thought of Czechoslovakia as a "faraway place" and cheered Chamberlain's fatuous "peace in our time," who in 1938–39 did not want to "die for Danzig," but who died instead in 1939–40 for an England beleaguered and beset?

An isolationist Fortress America is not a pragmatic policy in the latter half of the twentieth century.

Many of the new breed of internationalists advocate a diametrically opposed but equally utopian and impractical policy—a world state, founded on world "law" (an undefined and indefinable term). They envisage a kind of parliament of man, an international organization, with national arms outlawed or curbed, and an international police force, lending allegiance to some kind of superadministration. Such a world order could be developed, it is argued, by modification of the United Nations, by the forswearing of national sovereignties, by the conveyance of power to the "Brotherhood of Man."

In a postcolonial era and a revolutionary age when we are witnessing the Wilsonian concept of the "self-determination of peoples" gone wild, when village, tribal and regional loyalties have fractionalized even common area interests, the possibility of any such development is ephemeral; the relatively few but unduly influential, sophomoric do-gooders who seriously advocate it are positive dangers to the slow progress of man.

For centuries men have dreamed of a United States of Europe; it is an unrealized dream, and it is not imminent today, or tomorrow —if ever. How far more difficult a parliament of the world, embracing all the disparate races, creeds and colors! What possible mechanism can be organized to assume the powers of the nations? Never,

291

in human history, has a large power entity voluntarily conveyed its power to a nonexisting, or smaller, power entity; there is no foreseeable way that such a voluntary grant of power can be conveyed. Any such world organization, to be effective in peace-keeping and in stabilization (viz., security), would require power, great power, power that in the ultimate could not be challenged successfully by regions or nations. And it is altogether questionable whether or not any such absolute power would, ultimately, redound to the good of man. Rather than a Golden Age, such a utopian attempt to achieve a world government might result in world tyranny, or in civil war.

If not world order by world government, why not world order by U.S. fiat? Domination of the world by direct power and indirect influence—but American rather than Communist domination—has been offered, in the past, as a possible alternative policy. What the late Henry Luce called "The American Century" may be well named, but it is already evident that the U.S. legions, like the Roman legions of yesterday, are overextended. Conquest of the world, or its domination by U.S. power, is no longer a possibility, if it ever was, even in the short-lived era of our nuclear monopoly. We cannot now bend Russia and China to our will, eliminate them as threats to world peace, without unacceptable cost and damage to ourselves and to the world around us. World domination is not possible without world war—all-out war (the very development we are trying to avoid)—and even then the outcome would be sackcloth and ashes.

Nor can the United States continue indefinitely in the role of "world policeman"; the costs are too high. This is the service that Vietnam has done; it has exposed the high cost of universally applied containment to keep the peace; it has forced a reappraisal of our overseas commitments and our vital interests. It should be obvious, without argument, that the demands on the U.S. economy, the U.S. taxpayer and the U.S. patience in the decades ahead are too great to support a global policy of intervention.

There is, then, only one viable policy available to the "continental island" of the United States in the latter half of the twentieth century. It is a policy all U.S. administrations have endorsed since World War II, but one which requires considerable modification today. It is a policy of international cooperation and regional alliances and groupings, of combined effort backed by superior U.S. strength. It is a policy, in the last analysis, of balance of power, best defined, perhaps, in the words of Paul Scott Mowrer, as "the instinctive tendency of free nations to combine against that one or group . . . that seems to be expanding so aggressively and exerting such domination as to endanger the liberties of all."

It is, in other words, a reasonable internationalism, but it is neither imperialism nor a world state. It implies active participation —political, economic and military—in the world community in defense of our own *vital* interests and in the interest of global stability. The important word is "active." Reasonable security cannot be achieved purely by negative methods; the U.S. presence must be felt around the world as long as we have the responsibility of power.

In political and military terms any attempt to maintain a balance of power in the world—to maintain stability against aggressive expansionist powers—must mean a flexible political and diplomatic policy. It must mean some commitments overseas, some alliances or groupings, some organized cooperative efforts with other nations in mutual self-interest. But these groupings are certain to change; some will outlive their usefulness and new ones must be formed. The enemies of yesterday may be the friends of tomorrow. We cannot therefore forge unbreakable alliances immune forever to change. Too often—for instance, today—the diplomatic carryovers from the past limit the dimensions of tomorrow.

A reasonable internationalism, a policy of maintaining the balance of power, need not exclude the United Nations—regional groupings are specifically provided for in its charter—but it cannot depend upon it for security or stability. The United Nations has very definite utility, particularly in the economic and public-relations fields, but it is virtually powerless in great-power confrontations and has been able to apply only tangential pressure even in conflicts involving the smallest powers. Neither Biafra nor Vietnam, Israel nor the Arab states can depend upon it for security. The veto power and the proliferation of small and powerless states each with a vote equal to the most powerful make the settlement of any

293

major, or even minor, political problem in the United Nations almost impossible. Political, and particularly security, problems must be settled, for the most part, through the age-old methods of bilateral or multilateral diplomacy. The UN can provide facilities and a forum and encouragement for arms-limitations discussions, for instance, but little more.

But the UN does have utility, limited but definite, in psychological, economic (including relief) and what might be called "watchdog" functions. As an international forum it is unrivaled; the sound of Khrushchev's shoe-thumping was heard around the world. It can be a safety valve, and the blowing off of steam may sometimes prevent small frustrations from becoming big ones. It can also mobilize pressure—by means of that somewhat ephemeral factor often described as "world public opinion." Economically it can, with other more specialized international agencies, be of great usefulness, and its children's fund and relief and rehabilitation operations are a blessing to the sore-distressed and weary. Its most important military, and parapolitical, function is its "watchdog" activities—the Cyprus force, the observer teams along the Suez Canal and elsewhere in the Middle East. These could have far greater importance in the future, particularly in small-power disputes in which the great powers are either not involved or only remotely involved—as truce teams, border watchers along disputed frontiers, keepers of the peace.

But fundamentally our new internationalism, an off-shoot of the old, must depend first upon U.S. power, second upon various groupings, alliances and cooperative endeavors—shifting and flexible, both in composition and concept over any long-term period, but constant in the short view.

What, then, should be the strategic concept—the grand strategy —to implement America's world role in the last half of the twentieth century?

There are really only three major alternatives (with numerous variations of each); there were only two until the advent of the long-range plane and the missile.[4]

The first is an oceanic, or maritime, strategy—traditional with Britain until World War I.

294

The second is a continental strategy, a strategy that, to a large extent, dominated Russian military thinking until the late 1950's, and that ever since World War II has committed large U.S. ground forces to the continental land masses.

The third is aerospace strategy, a concept that had its beginnings in the strategic bombing campaigns of World War II.

Each of these strategies has its assets, each its limitations, and there is dependence and overlap, one upon the other.

But the shape and size of our future military forces, the nature of our commitments and perhaps the future of the nation will depend upon the concept we *emphasize*.

In World War II the "bomb-'em-out-of-existence" school of strategists were before their time, technologically. There was never any possibility of achieving this aim or of winning victory through air power alone until the development of the atomic bomb, and even Japan's surrender was the result of a complex of causes, with Hiroshima as the straw that broke the camel's back. But today long-range missiles and nuclear weapons have the power to liquidate any nation as a going, organized, national entity. The threat is so major that beside it all others pall into insignificance.

Today the answer to this threat is deterrence—the maintenance of a force powerful and effective enough to deter any enemy from launching a nuclear attack. Today the primary implements of deterrence are offensive weapons, but, more and more in the years ahead, technology will develop defensive weapons and damage-limiting methods and means.

But until the sword of Damocles is forged into plowshares in some future paradise, the threat will be forever present, and thus the first and absolute requirement for any grand strategy tomorrow is "sufficiency" in strategic weapons. Since deterrence is a knife-edge formula—easily upset, easily changed—and since the political and psychological results of inferiority would be highly dangerous to the United States and destabilizing for the world, "sufficiency," in this context, must mean a clear-cut and visible U.S. qualitative and quantitative superiority. Equivocation on this issue risks the life of the nation.

In this sense, an aerospace strategy for the 1970–80 period has the A No. 1 priority. But nowhere is the blending of strategies, necessitated by the influence of technology, more apparent than in the field of strategic weapons. Sea-based missiles are a major and increasing element of deterrence; thus oceanic strategy complements and merges with the strategy of aerospace.

The ability to exercise control is the function of strategy. But how you exercise control determines defense priorities and costs.

The examination, in this book, of the complexion of tomorrow's world and the nature of the nation's security problems emphasizes as a second fundamental priority the capability of oceanic control. There is no doubt that an oceanic or maritime strategy, modernized technologically and modified regionally to meet special needs, is best suited to U.S. capabilities, exploits our strengths rather than our weaknesses, is more likely to secure the American future and preserve the American dream, is achievable at less cost, reduces political and psychological frictions, and is far more flexible politically and militarily and psychologically than is a continental strategy. But this said, it must be emphasized that military force in the modern age is indivisible and that more and more its various forms are being blended by technological advance.

Continental strategy basically is a strategy geared to land power, to the control by ground armies of the continental surfaces of the world. It is geared to, and it requires, great numbers of men—the *levée en masse* of Napoleon, the conscription-produced forces ever since. The heartland powers—the great land powers of history, whose frontiers could be threatened by powerful land neighbors—have, perforce, keyed their security policies to continental strategy.

Maritime or oceanic strategy is basically a strategy geared to sea power—now sea-air power—to the utilization of the seas for commerce and supply, and to the control of the seas and their vital geographic bottlenecks by naval vessels, surface and submersible, by land-based and ship-based planes and missiles, by amphibious forces and by strategically placed island bases. The rimland powers—the great sea powers of history—whose defense and prosperity depended primarily upon the oceans, have traditionally utilized an oceanic strategy.

296

Historically and technologically there are compelling arguments for the United States which favor an oceanic, and oppose a continental, strategy.

The decline of the British Empire dates from Ypres and the bloody holocaust of the trench lines of World War I. In World War II the Churchillian propensity for peripheral strategy—utilization of the Allied command of the sea and the air to strike with combined forces at weakly held points around the perimeter of Europe —was strongly opposed, indeed ridiculed, by U.S. strategists. And even at the end of the war in the Pacific—a war clearly keyed to an oceanic strategy—a tremendously costly and totally unnecessary invasion of Japan, and even of Japan's conquests on the Asiatic mainland, was being pressed and prepared by ground and continental strategists.

And ever since World War II, in part because we won the war but failed to win the peace, the United States has been committed to maintenance of large ground forces on continental land masses. As in Russia, until Khrushchev's time, the ground army generals have played a dominant role in strategy formulation.[5]

Yet there are strong technological as well as historical arguments for change.

The United States is the most advanced and developed industrial and technological nation on earth, yet our population is small, indeed, compared to the Communist heartland powers and the masses of Asia. Life is cheap in Asia, and, indeed, in many other parts of the world; it is expensive measured by the values and mores of Western civilization. Continental strategy, a conventional ground war (without the use of nuclear weapons), implicitly involves too much of a man-against-man equation, to our disadvantage. In both Korea and Vietnam our weapons systems were superior quantitatively—in many cases qualitatively—to the enemy, yet the fundamental burden of the war rested upon the foot soldier. Washington politically hobbled and deliberately restricted, particularly in Vietnam, our greatest natural elements of superiority —sea power and air power and technological superiority. In response to enemy build-up we limited our technological escalation, but practiced manpower escalation. At the infantry battalion level

297

U.S. casualties in Vietnam have been extremely high—possibly, per actual combatants engaged, higher than in any of our other wars. The enemy does not measure victory or defeat by body counts. Yet to the United States, casualty statistics—particularly in any long war of attrition—represent a powerful political factor which favors the enemy.

The arguments, therefore, for leading from strength to the enemy's weakness, of exploiting our superior sea and air and technological power, and of avoiding, wherever possible (*and then only in defense of U.S. vital interests*), large-scale, long-drawn-out ground conflict, are overwhelming.

A modernized, modified oceanic strategy should provide the general guidelines for the development and application of U.S. military power through the rest of the twentieth century.

The late President John F. Kennedy epitomized the need in an address aboard the carrier *Kitty Hawk:*

> Control of the seas means security. Control of the seas can mean peace. Control of the seas can mean victory. If there is any lesson of the twentieth century, especially of the last few years, it is that in spite of the advancement in space and in the air, this country must still move easily and safely across the seas of the world. Knowledge of the oceans is more than a matter of curiosity, our very survival may hinge on it.

In Britain's heyday, the "Empire upon which the sun never set" maintained relative global stability and protected her far-flung interests chiefly through an understanding of what Alfred Thayer Mahan called the "influence of sea power upon history." In the age before the plane and the guided missile her supremacy at sea enabled her to take as much or as little of a war as she wished. Those "far distant, storm-beaten ships" that stood between Napoleon and the dominion of the world at Trafalgar protected Britain's island base from invasion and enabled her to carry any war to an enemy far distant from her own shores. Her naval power, of course, was backed by a judicious use of the British pound and British maritime power to support friends, punish enemies and hire mercenaries, and by a small professional army capable of limited intervention in

298

strategic areas at times and places of Britain's choosing. And her control of key nodal points along the world's maritime arteries—Hong Kong, Singapore, Aden, Suez, Malta, Gibraltar, Bermuda and her West Indian possessions—multiplied her strength and maximized her influence. This military strategy was tied to a diplomatic policy dedicated to maintenance of the balance of power; i.e., to a system of shifting alliances that would balance or more than balance any one power or combination of powers that might threaten Britain's vital interests.

Today, with the technological revolution still unfinished, today in the era of supersonic planes and missiles any application of the maritime, or oceanic, strategy of yesterday to the problems of tomorrow obviously must be undertaken with care.

Nevertheless, the essential geopolitical parameters of today's confrontation are still the same as those of yesterday. We are faced basically with the outward thrust of what Mackinder called the great "heartland" of Eurasia toward the "rimlands," or coastal areas; it is these areas that require support; it is this thrust that must be countered.

This thrust, in the past limited to the mass movements of vast hordes by land, has assumed new dimensions with new technology. In most of Asia it is still, largely, a ground threat. But since World War II, Soviet strategy has changed from the defensive, landlocked concepts of the past to an offensive global goal. Soviet missile power, now superior in many aspects to that of the United States, has a world-wide capability. And one of the most important developments of our time—little noticed in the preoccupation with Vietnam—has been the massive development of Soviet naval and maritime power and its breakout from the narrow seas to the oceans of the world.

Thus the type of military threat confronting the world in the immediate future ranges from the sophisticated technology—naval, amphibious, air, missile, ground—of the Russians in the European Middle Eastern and Siberian areas to the massed ground armies—rapidly being modernized—of the Chinese Communists in the Far East.

The adaptation of an oceanic or maritime strategy of the past to

299

the technology of the present and its molding to fit the special security needs of the world of tomorrow unquestionably require careful planning, technological imagination and innovation and a redistribution of the defense budget with emphasis upon new naval construction.

A modernized oceanic strategy means air power and missile power as well as a nuclear-powered navy and a larger and more modern merchant marine and secure bases for all forms of military power. The mobile floating-base techniques, developed in World War II, modernized in the Vietnamese war, copied by the Russians, enable fleets to remain at sea for long periods, with the help of ammunition ships, tankers, stores ships and other replenishment vessels. These techniques improve combat effectiveness and extend range, but they can be no full substitute for forward land bases. And land bases are, per se, highly important elements in maritime control. Logistically, fleets are more independent than ever before of the tether of the land, but technological advances are making the projection of air power and missile power from land bases more and more important factors in control of the seas—particularly of the narrow seas.

Thus if the Sixth Fleet is to remain in the Mediterranean, retention of some peripheral land bases will be essential; in the Western Pacific, island bases must be retained, improved and made secure; and if United States power is to be substituted for British power in the Indian Ocean, a new base must be developed.

To be secure in the uncertain tomorrows, island bases must have adequate defenses against air-missile and amphibious attacks from ships or continental positions. Modern technology strengthens considerably the defensive advantages of positions surrounded by the sea. Surveillance and detection are eased, isolation and interdiction of the battlefield are practical, and some warning time is available. Even more important, the utilization of *defensive, tactical nuclear weapons with localized effects* could doom nearly any conventional attack against an island base.

Nuclear weapons of limited power and range—weapons such as the Nike-Hercules antiaircraft missile, air-to-air missiles launched by interceptor aircraft and artillery shells or rockets with nuclear

300

explosives—are peculiarly suited to defensive purposes. Their power could doom virtually any assault through the air or any amphibious attack launched against island positions from continental bases. Such bases could be eliminated, or crippled, of course, by sudden surprise assault by missiles with hydrogen warheads, but such an assault would inevitably risk an all-out nuclear war, and in such a war our forward-base positions—except those equipped with strategic missiles—would be, in any case, secondary targets.

The probable dangers to advanced-base positions close to continental land masses are all associated with attacks by conventional means—the bombardment and blockade of Quemoy, for instance, the gun-running and infiltration of Communist agents into the Philippines. The latter tactic—the utilization of guerrilla or insurrectionary war applied to insular positions—cannot, of course, be met by purely military means, but any overt enemy military offensive or threat, short of the use of nuclear weapons, against island positions can be parried with relative ease by the use of tactical nuclear weapons.

In such a contingency there is no reason why such weapons should not be used, provided the case of aggression is clear-cut and overt. Indeed, the defense of island positions is one of the few contingencies in which such weapons might be used defensively without any considerable risk of touching off a nuclear war, or even of encouraging undesirable escalation. For the effects would be localized, confined to the skies and the seas near the position defended, and no offensive weapons would need to be utilized against mainland positions. In fact, all forward island positions under the U.S. flag, and all such positions used by the United States under foreign flags where the host country is willing, should be equipped with defensive tactical nuclear weapons. Such weapons insure the security of the base against conventional assault.[6]

Secure forward bases in various parts of the world are part of an oceanic strategic concept. But they must never become too great a part. A base for air and sea power exists only to enhance the mobility and flexibility of aircraft and ships. The tremendous advantage of oceanic strategy is that it utilizes to the full the freedom of the seas; it reduces to a minimum the dependence—with all the consequent political, psychological and economic liabilities—upon the land. The United States must use the base, not let the base use us. If the political and psychological liabilities of the use of an island base become too great—as has happened in Okinawa, as may happen in the Philippines—the base must be abandoned, a substitute found or more advanced "floating base" techniques developed.

Those techniques are available to a degree undreamed of a decade ago.

Secretary of Defense Robert S. McNamara sponsored one development—the FDL–C-5A concept—during his tenure of office. The proposed FDL (Fast Deployment Logistic Ship) was to be a floating, mobile warehouse, air-conditioned and temperature-regulated, for stockpiles of arms, ammunition and equipment. The C-5A (heavy logistic transport aircraft) was developed as a companion piece to the now abandoned FDL. The concept envisaged a reduction in reaction time by prepositioning arms and equipment aboard logistic ships, in forward positions in critical areas of the world and then transporting the soldiers by the C-5A to be mated with that equipment in the area of conflict. The concept, superficially attractive, was intended to complement to best advantage the heavy-lift capability of the ship with the speed of the plane, and it represented a sea-based variation of the dual-basing concept tried in Europe.

Its disadvantages, however, have, so far, killed the idea a-borning. Costs would be extremely high; dual sets of equipment would have to be provided for the same unit—one set in the United States, another aboard the FDL's. Both sets would have to have constant replacements and modernization; both would require detailed maintenance and upkeep; hence the costs might well become prohibitive to an economy-minded Congress in times of reduced tension. More important, the FDL concept has a built-in strategic inflexibility. To mate the men and the equipment, advanced airfields, ports or beaches near, or in the area of, operations would have to be available, and the airfield would have to be close enough to the maritime unloading point, and yet secure enough from enemy attack to permit matching of men and equipment and their organization for combat before their exposure to battle. There are relatively few places in the world which satisfy these requirements, and most of these are not in potential trouble areas. There is, moreover, an economically more attractive and strategically more flexible alternative, which was persuasive to Congress. The same amount of money proposed for the FDL invested in modern merchant ships would tremendously advance the much-needed modernization of the merchant marine. Roll-on and roll-off ships with specially built stowage for motor vehicles and tanks and with ramps and heavy-lift cranes; container ships; vessels equipped with their own lighters; ships designed to unload cargo with the aid of heavy-lift helicopters—these and other high-speed vessels have already proved their commercial practicability. The renaissance of the American merchant marine—an essential part of any maritime concept—requires the development of the latest technology. Today the United States is in a dangerously vulnerable position, with some 95 percent of our imports of critical and strategic commodities carried in foreign flagships. Modern merchant vessels, used for commercial purposes in normal times, can be tagged for immediate availability as heavy-cargo carriers in time of crisis. Reaction might not be quite as rapid as the FDL–C-5A concept, but it would be more certain and more flexible and far less costly.

In any case, to utilize to the optimum the availability of the seas, the initial forces of intervention and their logistical backup must be sea-based. Air transportation of troops has the great advantage of speed, but it is becoming less and less dependable as available overseas bases are closed to the United States and overflight rights curtailed. And air transports cannot compete with ships as heavy-weight lifters. The fuel required by cargo and transport planes must be transported to forward fields by ships, and heavy aircraft consume enormous amounts of fuel. The C-5A, for instance, would require, in flights to Asia, about 1.82 tons of fuel per ton of cargo at advance bases in the Western Pacific. Thus the speed and mobility of the plane are limited, strategically, by the inflexibility of its needs for forward fields, overflight rights and immense amounts of prepositioned fuel and spare parts.

This does not mean that airborne troop lift is obsolete or undesirable. Air-transported ground power is here to stay. It could be a determining factor in certain situations (the Dominican Republic intervention; trouble in Cuba or Panama). It will always be necessary. But generally it should be regarded as a supplementary or backup force to reinforce and build up beachheads established from the sea. The tried-and-tested techniques of amphibious warfare and the utilization of landing craft and helicopter assault, supported by ship-based guns, rockets and aircraft, provide a global pattern of maritime power applicable to the rimlands of the world. Assault forces, already mated with their weapons, supplies and equipment, aboard landing craft and amphibious ships, not only have a unique strategic flexibility; they eliminate the requirement for the complex, expensive, prepositioned, dual-basing system.

But optimum advantage of the mobility, flexibility and what might be called the "political chastity" of sea power cannot be insured unless advanced techniques in sea-basing for both combat operations and logistics are developed. Naval logisticians have estimated that some 36 CH-54B heavy-lift helicopters, each with a payload of 18 tons, could handle all cargo from some 125 ships per month in a ship-to-front line transfer, which could bypass ports, airfields and beaches and could extend well inland far beyond the high-tide mark. A sea-based logistics system—with "ammo," food, POL and other supplies afloat in ships' hulls rather than ashore— could certainly satisfy all initial needs for an assault landing anywhere in the world (provided the modern ships and techniques were available) and could—the Navy thinks—utilize far less manpower than a land-based system. These estimates may be optimistic, but the feasibility of a sea-based logistics system is clear; it was proven, with the means then available, in World War II; and the Navy and the Marines utilized such a system at Danang in South Vietnam in all the early years of the Vietnam war.

To achieve the maximum capability of sea power, more research and development funds must go to new ship designs, new propulsion systems (gas turbines, water jets, hovercraft, hydrofoils, lightweight nuclear engines), surface-to-surface missiles and cargo-handling equipment. If only a fraction of the funds available for the development of new types of aircraft, such as the C-5A and the supersonic transport, had been made available for new types of ships, the Navy today, and, above all, its indispensable logistics consort, the merchant marine, would be in a far better position to meet the greatest challenge in its history—Russia's surge toward maritime supremacy. Since World War II the Russians have constructed about 170 million tons of naval ships as compared to the U.S. 150 million tons; by 1975, if current construction rates are a guide, they will have the most powerful navy in the world and the world's most modern merchant fleet.

Sea power, a maritime strategy, must be built around ships—modern ships—and ship construction and design has had too low a priority.

For successful application, an oceanic strategy demands not only a Navy second to none but also one clearly superior to all. It must be a Navy quickly able to project U.S. power anywhere in the world, supported by a modern, quickly responsive merchant marine. And it must be backed, wherever forward insular positions are available, by land-based air power.

The formula requires a balanced fleet—aircraft carriers, cruisers, missile ships, antisubmarine warfare and escort craft, minecraft, supply ships, amphibious ships, helicopter carriers and submarines. It requires more and more the transfer of a considerable portion of the nation's strategic nuclear-missile deterrent force from fixed and vulnerable land bases to mobile, sea-based launching "platforms" in both submarines and surface ships. The tremendous and growing advantages of the sea-based system so far outweigh the disadvantages[7] that any oceanic strategy must include putting a much greater proportion of our missiles at sea.

Naval fleets and task forces, supported by long-range, high-speed, land-based bombers as well as by tactical air power, could provide visual evidence of ready support for rimland nations, and could help to maintain the balance of power. At some bases—Hawaii, Guam—small airborne units, perhaps of brigade strength, should be available for rapid reinforcement of amphibious forces.

And behind these sea-based and island-based outposts of American power, there must be maintained in a central strategic reserve in the United States a highly mobile, professional Army—relatively small in size[8] but unequaled in quality, with overwhelming tactical air support, and quickly available as a ready reaction force. The

305

spearhead of this army—at least two divisions—should be instantly ready for air transportation to any threatened area; the remainder available for rapid sea reinforcement.

Such an oceanic concept frees us from some of the rigidity and entanglements of a continental strategy, but it cannot insure the security of the rimland nations against aggression from the heartland. Dr. Coral Bell, an Australian scholar, in a paper published by the Institute for Strategic Studies, believes that such a policy would have to be supplemented by mainland "redoubts," held by friendly or allied forces, areas, hopefully, with enough economic and political strength and social stability to warrant U.S. aid and military support.[9]

No oceanic strategy—nor any other strategy—can completely free us from the land, least of all since many of our major interests are associated with the continental positions of the coastal nations.

Dr. Bell has correctly noted in her recent paper that "no one has ever produced a convincing demonstration—or even a convincing theory—of precisely how influence may be wielded over the sort of small-scale actions which actually change the pattern of power in Asia, by lurking near the coast in the Seventh Fleet or equipping the island chain with Minuteman missiles."

As a matter of fact, it was the inability of sea-air power to meet successfully the Communist threat to South Korea and South Vietnam that led to the commitment of United States ground combat units in both places. It can, and should be, emphasized that air-sea power was called upon late in the game and, at least in Vietnam, was heavily restricted by political considerations.

Nevertheless it is *ground power that ultimately controls land area;* sea and air power can devastate and to some extent can deny and inhibit and blockade, but they cannot, per se, control peoples or areas—least of all in insurgency-type wars, where guerrillas move among the people as fish swim in the sea.

Hence a modernized maritime strategy is not adequate *alone* to support a stable balance of power in Asia, or anywhere else in the world. At times and in places it may be necessary to commit United States ground power to meet what Dr. Bell describes as the "real problem on the mainland . . . military-territorial attrition."

This is merely another phrase for describing the basic problem which we have not yet successfully resolved—the problem of nibbling Communist aggression, of insurgency and guerrilla wars. John F. Kennedy recognized the significance of the "war of national liberation," as Khrushchev euphemistically dubbed concealed Communist aggression. But the late President vastly overemphasized the Green Berets and classroom studies as "answers" to the enemy tactic; he was far too cautious—in the Bay of Pigs, the Cuban missile crisis, Vietnam—at times when bold but wise action could have changed the course of history. Neither he nor any subsequent President has yet demonstrated the art of restraint coupled with action—of choosing with the utmost care the time and place and cause of intervention.

The Army is the military service with primary responsibility for nipping insurgencies in the bud. The lessons of Vietnam and the limitations of our capabilities so graphically revealed there have led to intensive study and tentative plans for new post-Vietnam organization. Regional assistance commands, each consisting of civic action and nation-building components backed by combat units, tailored to specific areas of the earth are contemplated. Fluency in the language, knowledge of the terrain and of social, political, health and agricultural problems would be stressed, and experts in engineering—road-building, well-digging, sanitation, health, education, etc.—would be included in such groupings. The concept is useful and potentially important, but fundamentally the answer to insurgency must be envisaged in the broadest possible terms—political, economic, social and military—and the "country team"—the embassy and all its divisions—must be responsible for execution of a carefully formulated policy.

In the past, our failure to resolve the dilemma of creeping Communist aggression has been due in part to our predilection for a continental strategy, to what some wags have called "prepositioned intervention"—not at times and places carefully chosen, but more or less as a matter of routine, as if, indeed, there were no other choice.

A maritime, an oceanic, strategy permits us the luxury of choice; we can choose the time and place of ground intervention; we can take as much or as little of any war as we wish. And it goes without saying, as Vietnam has proven so heart-breakingly, that any continental areas chosen for intervention should offer, in Dr. Bell's words, "favourable conditions for resisting further encroachment . . . diplomatically, politically and morally, as well as militarily." The dollar may substitute for the soldier if a decaying economic situation, for instance, is met in timely fashion. Or, if troops are needed, a thousand men in the very early stages of an enemy insurgency are worth twenty thousand two months later. If Vietnam has proved anything, it has proved that time lost is irretrievable in war and that a policy of overcaution, of "gradualism," of "too little and too late," can doom the highest endeavor.

In developing a global strategy, therefore, one must modify the desirable but pragmatically impossible goal of the "Never Again" school to "Never-Again-except-under-carefully-chosen-conditions-and-at-times-and-places-of-our-own-choosing-and-even-then-within-limits."

The problem is to choose the times and places and to set the limits. The places must be where our vital, or highly important, interests are involved, or where there is a strong probability that they will become involved. Strategic areas—strategic by virtue of geographic position and economic domination—are of key importance; an oceanic strategy, keyed to forward-island positions and to maritime freedom of access to ocean bottlenecks like the Strait of Malacca, for instance, cannot tolerate the loss of the British Isles, of Japan, of Singapore, to a potential enemy. And one does not ever completely wipe the slate of history clean, no matter how thorough the reappraisals of commitments, the evaluation of interests. We can reduce our commitments, but we cannot possibly afford, from either the political or the military point of view, to eliminate *completely* our continental salients in Europe or in Asia (Korea, Vietnam, Thailand) in the near future.

The time for continental intervention, if it should come again, must clearly be what the British would call "early on." The old "ounce-of-prevention-pound-of-cure" cliché is as valid in politics as in war. Signs of trouble in any country or area usually are visible

308

long before the eruption; political, economic and psychological action then may obviate military action later.

The first line of defense is diplomatic and political—the "image," the will, the policy of the United States; the second is the dollar; the third, United States naval and air power; the fourth, troops of our allies and indigenous forces; and the last, the United States soldier.

Wherever U.S. aid of any sort is given, particularly to under-developed countries, it must be closely supervised by the United States. The "cumshaw" is a way of life in much of the world; the morass of corruption in Vietnam, where we have monitored but not tightly controlled our own economic aid, has tremendously re-duced, if not nullified, the effectiveness of the aid.

The power of the U.S. dollar—*if we keep the dollar sound*—can be a major stabilizing agent and a deterrent to war. But it must be used for that purpose, not merely hitched to some utopian ideal. The dollar can be used pre-emptively, in cold war, as the pound was used by Britain in the Napoleonic era, to deny products to the enemy, to equip allies or to pre-empt strategic materials; it can be used to strengthen weak, underdeveloped nations, and as a carrot of incentive. Technical aid and long-term, low-interest loans for specific and well-vetted projects offer the greatest hope of greatest return; military aid, carefully and specifically applied, can be useful, but much, in the past, has been wasted, and general economic aid, not tied to any project, is often wasteful.

The Commission on International Development, chaired by for-mer Prime Minister of Canada Lester B. Pearson, presented to the World Bank in 1969 a lengthy report on international aid programs. It represented admittedly a kind of utopian concept—"the aware-ness that we live in a village world, that we belong to a world community"—which carried with it a "political and social impera-tive for governments" who have, to provide aid to governments who have not. The aid suggested would approximate for the United States a program of more than $8 billion to underdeveloped coun-tries annually.

One can agree with the Commission's statement that "interna-

309

tional development is a great challenge of our age" without either endorsing the Commission's philosophy or its pragmatism. An annual $8 billion aid program would certainly utilize the dollar, but at considerable risk to the dollar's stability, and at the cost of more important priorities, both domestic and foreign. And one must face the fact that, given the world's presently inadequate mechanisms for analysis of projects and supervision of aid, any such expenditures as these would probably result in considerable diversion and waste. In other words, it is very doubtful that any such aid program would contribute ultimately to a greater degree of world stabilization; it is even more doubtful that it would contribute to the national security of the United States. Practically, there is no likelihood that tax-weary citizens and a cost-conscious Congress, eager to divert a larger portion of U.S. revenues to domestic needs, would vote in any foreseeable future for a foreign aid budget more than five times larger than the 1970 aid program. The Pearson report is neither hardheaded nor realistic; aid is a tool, but it must never be a "giveaway" program.

The dollar is not elastic; neither our political, economic nor military commitments can be open-ended and limitless. Our own fiscal situation today is the best possible argument for dollar conservatism tomorrow—judicious use of it to accomplish our political purposes in the world abroad, but never again an attempt to have our cake and eat it, too, to provide both guns and butter without the necessary controls, to wage a first-class war with "business as usual," to aid the world with no value received. This way lies disaster; the dollar can be a second line of defense tomorrow, but it must be conserved.

If the crunch comes and military power is invoked, it must be used to maximum effectiveness, not handcuffed and hobbled, as it has been in Vietnam. Naval blockade, for instance, is an optimum cost-effectiveness type of military pressure; it costs us little and the enemy heavily. If it had been utilized long ago against Haiphong and the ports of North Vietnam, the United States would be today in a far better military position.

If all the first lines of defense fail and the United States should again become involved in a continental ground war, there must be a limit to our own self-imposed limitations. This is not to say that there must not be limits; one cannot justify today—if indeed, one ever could—a war without limits, and too often—in World War II, in Vietnam—the image, the idealistic character of the United States, has been marred by the means adopted to achieve an end. We cannot descend to the levels of our enemies; the ends in limited war do *not* justify any and all means.

But the political purpose of war is to achieve by force what could not be achieved by peaceful means; that purpose, therefore, must be well defined, and the means of achieving it must stem from it. There is a caveat: in war one persuades an enemy by superior power; there are many methods of persuasion, and some, but not all, of them are justifiable; some, but not all, of them contribute to the ultimate purpose of a more stable peace. Victory in limited war is nevertheless not only feasible but essential if limited wars are to be fought at all. One cannot possibly accomplish any worthwhile purpose by self-frustration.

The self-imposed limitations that the United States, in the interest of its own stability and its future, must accept in continental war are limitations upon manpower escalation, accompanied by far fewer technological restraints. In Korea and Vietnam, and to a certain extent in World War II, we increased our commitments in numbers but (particularly in Vietnam) limited our policy and strategic options, and hobbled our technology. The misguided liberals and Congressmen who so bitterly opposed the bombing of North Vietnam, who were quick to oppose the use of chemical defoliants and tear gas, appeared to forget that limitations on superior U.S. technology meant open-ended bloodshed—greater casualties for the United States. One limitation we must impose in any future continental war—particularly in Asia—is a limitation on manpower commitments; one limitation we must oppose is a limitation on our technology. We must never adopt an open-ended escalation of manpower while accepting limitations upon the escalation of weapons and options.

This said, it should be added at once that no thoughtful military strategist advocates unlimited *Schrecklichkeit,* or no restraints whatsoever. The proper amount of force to achieve an end, and no more, is justifiable, and weapons and options to match the amount of force required. But this does not mean, in limited war, *any* weapons; the United States should never be the *first*, in a continental war, to utilize nuclear weapons against enemy troops or cities or inhabited areas; we should never be the *first* to utilize lethal chemical agents; we should *never* use biological agents against *human beings.* [10]

The end cannot possibly justify *any* means; otherwise we have sunk to the level of the evil we fight. War brutalizes some men, ennobles others. Some men like to kill, others to heal. In all wars there are atrocities by all combatants. Vietnam has been no exception. As a nation we have tended ever since World War I to justify in the name of victory more and more extreme means. In World War II we utilized against the Japanese the same unrestricted submarine warfare tactics that the Germans used against us in World War I—tactics that in an earlier war were a primary reason for U.S. participation. In World War II we dropped A-bombs and killed thousands in Tokyo fire raids. Some of the tactics and techniques used in Vietnam were morally repugnant and of doubtful military expediency. War does brutalize too many men, and long-continuing conflict does tend to dull the idealism and the better instincts of man.

Yet the over-all instincts, the basic policies of the United States, in Vietnam as in World War II, were ranged on the side of good, not on the side of evil; never did we condone or utilize as part of our pattern of operations the mass terrorism and wholesale murder employed by the enemy. There were atrocities by Americans, but they were outside the law, forbidden and, when discovered, punished. It is well to keep in perspective the relative values: to the Communists life is cheap, to the United States it is precious.

And that is why we cannot—must not—sacrifice our manpower in endless continental wars, while restricting our technology.

If the United States cannot, in the future, bolster governments under attack and secure them against creeping Communism with a United States troop commitment of, for instance, less than 100,-000 men, then it had better do one of two things: either call it quits or escalate technologically rather than with manpower. Certainly any direct involvement with massed Chinese Communist ground forces on the Asiatic mainland should imply immediate technological escalation. Such escalation might involve the use of exotic new conventional weapons (a *sine qua non* of any future security policy is primacy in military research and development) or the utilization under carefully restricted conditions, where targets and geography are favorable, of small, defensive nuclear devices.

The use of such devices obviously involves risks—the risk of an undesirable escalation of the war, the risk of a burgeoning nuclear conflagration. It could mean that the enemy would retaliate in kind. However, in the immediate future, this would represent an improbable risk, whereas the use of such weapons would certainly cause adverse political and psychological consequences. It will be some time before Communist China develops tactical nuclear weapons in any quantity, and it is highly unlikely that Soviet Russia would entrust such weapons to the Chinese, or to Communist insurgents in Thailand.

But the careful and precise use of an atomic shell, fired from an 8-inch howitzer, the utilization of atomic land mines to guard a frontier (as proposed by Turkey), the creation of a restricted and carefully controlled radioactive belt in virtually uninhabited country through which any aid from outside the country would have to pass, or the use of atomic demolition devices in thick jungle areas or in precipitous defiles to cause tangled "blowdown" or landslides to block trails, roads or natural approach routes can substitute for manpower and add great power to the defense.

The use of tactical nuclear devices, even for very limited defensive purposes, is impossible in thickly settled Western Europe or in most continental areas without great damage to nonmilitary targets and to civilian populations and without increasing the risk of escalation to large strategic weapons to a virtual certainty. But these disadvantages and risks are far less evident in parts of Asia, or in any uninhabited, or very sparsely settled, jungle and mountain area such as the frontier regions of Vietnam and Laos. "Clean" nuclear devices can be carefully controlled as to yield, place and height of detonation, to localize the efforts and minimize radioactive fallout, and yet their use can make jungle trails—like the Ho Chi Minh

313

complex—a maze of cratered and tangled debris and can add greatly to the difficulties of an infiltrating enemy.

Obviously the use of nuclear devices of any sort represents a last resort. Today even those in the Pentagon who hold that the atomic bomb—at least in its tactical version—is "just another weapon" agree that its employment postulates unknown dangers, and might invite response in kind. No one of responsibility advocates the use of any such weapons lightly, but on the other hand no one advocates wars of attrition on the Asiatic mainland.

Lieutenant Colonel Prentice G. Morgan, USA (Ret.), has eloquently summed up the disastrous consequences of unwise limitations in the waging of limited wars:

> It is held, for instance, that limited war must be fought without victory. History shows that indecisive wars breed more wars as, cite the English-French wars of our colonial period. Victory, of course, does not mean the enemy's unconditional surrender but attainment of our own clearly held war aims.
>
> Apparently we believe that limited war may be limited in area— that it need not be carried to the enemy's country but can be fought defensively on friendly territory. Acceptance of this by our Confederacy ruined the South for generations.
>
> We seem to think force should be applied gradually in limited war, but this denies the classical principles of the offensive and surprise.
>
> In the name of limited war uneducated public opinion decries the use of weapons peculiar to our advanced technology, i.e., napalm, nontoxic gases, etc. It should be understood that the limitation of weaponry should be dictated by self-interest alone, that, for instance, we limit ourselves to non-nuclear means only so as not to invite reprisal. This is certainly what governs the enemy.
>
> We seem to believe that limited war may be fought without marshaling public opinion at home by explaining the objectives and the consequences of failure. It was this attitude on the part of Prussia that almost caused the Germans to lose the Franco-Prussian War. Here, I think, we have erred most gravely in the current situation and that the danger is great that the greatest casualty of the Vietnam War may be the very concept of limited war, leaving us at some future date with no alternative but inaction until we are faced with a choice between defeat and mutual destruction.[11]

314

Tactical atomic weapons and other new arms cannot be automatically forsworn if Asia is to be stabilized, for even their tacit invocation contributes to the "balance of terror" which—whether we like it or not—now governs the world we live in. And it is only by technological escalation, rather than by manpower escalation, that United States military forces can without excessive cost in United States blood redress within the immediate time frame of the near-tomorrows the unfavorable manpower balance in Asia. And only thus can the power of the deterrent to aggression be maximized.

In the long view, there is and must be a finite limit to United States overseas commitments—political, economic and military. In the long view, as Asia grows in relative power and importance, a greater proportion of our total commitment must be applied to the Middle and Far East, less to Europe. In the long view, as Gunnar Myrdal, the Swedish economist, has pointed out in his monumental report on eleven nations from India to the Philippines, ultimate help for Asia must come from Asia itself; the major need is for a sweeping change in Asia's own attitudes and institutions. And, in the long view, the United States must make it clear that involvement with its own men in a continental ground war, particularly in Asia, will not be unlimited and open-ended as to numbers, but at the same time restricted as to weapons and methods.

An oceanic strategy, modified to permit continental intervention but at times and places of our own choosing, is the concept best suited to America's tomorrows. It leads from strength. It protects the continental island of the United States. It secures the vital maritime sea routes to other continents and to our Free World allies around the rimlands of the world. And, if war should come, it enables us to take as much or as little of it as we please, to harass the enemy around the wide sea rims of the continents, to blockade by air and sea, to hold continental redoubts, to establish beachheads in weakly held areas, to exploit the tremendous mobility and flexibility of oceanic power. But above all it should minimize the terrible bloodletting of continental wars, and it makes a reasonable security feasible at reasonable costs.

315

The strength and the type of forces required to support an oceanic strategy must be determined by a global assessment of the capabilities of the enemy, the nature and probability of the threat, the extent of our commitments and the priorities of interests. Force levels must be flexible, force composition subject to change with change in the world political and military situation.

Any investment—in national security, as in stocks or bonds—involves risks. Any national security policy worth the name can only be formulated by the calculation of risks. No matter what management technique is applied to this process, some risks are—and always will be—incalculable; such is the nature of man.

But the fundamental requirement for a sound security policy is that the risks be clearly faced—as far as they can be foreseen. Minimizing military risks, which means maximizing the military budget, may well increase the nation's economic risks. In fact, in part because of the continental strategic concept that has dominated our military establishment since World War II, in part because of failures to make sound political and economic policy decisions, the nation has increased considerably its economic risks in recent years. An imbalance in payments, the outflow of gold and sizable inflation, plus greatly increased direct and indirect taxation (federal, state and local), have reduced the buying power of the dollar and increased the strain on every taxpayer's pocketbook.

The balancing of national risks—the military against the political and economic to achieve a reasonable over-all risk—cannot be accomplished except at Presidential level. The Pentagon, the military, the Joint Chiefs of Staff are claimants; they must advise and protest; they must assess in stark terms the risks involved in reduction of force levels, in elimination of certain commitments, in adoption of specific concepts, but only the President can balance their evaluations against the needs of the domestic economy, and domestic and foreign political risks.

The formulation of a defense budget, therefore, is an intricate balancing act, which must, and does, start with some Presidential guidelines. The validity of these guidelines depends essentially upon the President himself and his manner of doing business. The input into the decision-making process from all sources—the utilization, or lack of utilization, of the State Department, the National Security Council, the Central Intelligence Agency and other agencies—and the thoroughness of the evaluation procedure strengthens or weakens the assessment of the risks. The Presidential procedure can, indeed, make the process simply an offhand gamble, or as rational a process as is possible.

Too often, it has been the former; nearly always decisions which have led to major reductions in defense budgets, weapons systems or ready forces during or just prior to crisis have been disguised and sloughed off by self-serving politicians in Washington as a "bigger bang for a buck," "cutting fat out of the Pentagon" or providing more effective defense with less money. The famous economy program of President Truman, which Secretary of Defense Louis Johnson eulogized, led to the debacle of the early days of Korea. Secretary McNamara early in his administration adopted what he called a "flexible strategy," and modified most of the nation's tactical air power for conventional, as well as nuclear, bombing. But, as Vietnam so bitterly illustrated, he refused to face publicly and squarely the costs of his policy. A conventional air war—in contrast to nuclear bombing—requires many more planes, many more pilots, many more spare parts and bombs and weapons and the production line to sustain them, consequently more money. Mr. McNamara's refusal to face the increased dollar costs of his "flexible strategy" caused plane, pilot, spare parts and armaments shortages and handicapped our effort through much of the war. It is refreshing, therefore, to note that Secretary of Defense Melvin Laird has taken a less political and more realistic stance than most of his predecessors. The heavy cuts made in the military budget in 1969 and the consequent reduction in the ready armed forces of the United States during the first year of the Nixon administration— an unprecedented reduction of our defense structure during an actual war, and in a time of crisis—was not lauded by Mr. Laird; he called them what they were, a weakening of our defense structure. These cuts were made as a result of the President's balancing of risks, his belief that domestic political and economic factors required them. Only history can assess whether or not this Presidential calculation of risks was sound, but the process of risk calculation should never be obscured by political shibboleths.

The budget guidelines furnished by the President must be matched in the Pentagon against the strategic concept and our global commitments and the subsequent force levels accommodated to all factors. The strengths of the services are the ultimate output, and their total manpower and their degree of readiness must be weighed against research and development funds for future weapons systems, construction for bases, military housing and other purposes, and so on.

The results of this complex analysis involve multiple judgments, which can be helped by quantitative and qualitative analyses, but which ultimately are the responsibility of men's minds. The consequent force levels are never what the generals ask for; few generals have ever had enough. There must be, inevitably, a system of priorities, and the lowest priorities suffer. But what is essential is to red-flag the calculated risks in each category, to determine clearly the highest priority of needs, and to insure that the risks and the needs are clearly understood at all top levels of government and in Congress.

What can we afford to spend for defense? Edwin L. Dale, Jr., the *New York Times'* economic and financial expert, believes that "we can 'afford' any figure at all, in the economic sense . . . strictly speaking any damn figure you want, without inflation or disruptive economic consequences; all that is required is the right level of taxation and domestic spending to keep the budget balanced." A $90 billion national defense budget in 1975 would represent 7.5 percent of our estimated GNP for that year, as compared to about 8.5 percent in 1969, and Mr. Dale believes "we can have a very potent defense with a G.N.P. percentage gradually declining (with the end of the Vietnam war), to between 6 and 7 percent."

Mr. Dale's estimates will be supported by many, debated by some. But the size of our future defense budget, in proportion to the GNP, will depend to major degree upon the state of the world around us, and the enemy threat. The former is not stable; the latter is not static. Modern weapons systems are tremendously expensive; yet without them no global power can long remain one.

Yet the modern American soldier, the product of the highest standard of living in the world and to some extent of a pampered environment, is also expensive; about one-third of our defense budget goes for manpower—salaries, etc. It costs in peacetime about $10,000 per man per year to maintain (feed, house, clothe, pay and care for) one GI overseas; about $7,000 annually at home.[12] Thus we cannot have both new weapons systems and mass manpower if there is to be any military budget reduction, post-Vietnam (in terms of percentages of GNP).

Continental commitments and large armies require mass manpower; oceanic strategy does not.

The clear priorities in any defense budget tomorrow must be: (1) unexcelled weaponry; (2) command of the air and of the oceans and of aerospace; (3) small, ready but modern and mobile ground forces, backed by an administrative structure and mobilization potential capable of providing sizable reserves.

This concept requires emphasis on long-term professional forces rather than on short-term draftees. There are disadvantages and dangers to volunteer professional forces, which must be overcome in the interest of both combat effectiveness and democracy. Large professional forces sometimes have a tendency to develop apart from the country for which they fight; this separatism, this growth of power in a vacuum, must be compensated for. There must be close ties to the civilian community; ROTC and OCS must continue to provide short-tour junior officers to the armed forces, and universities and academic institutions must preserve their ties to the Pentagon. The surest means of fostering a "state within a state" is to isolate and insulate the military. But the transition from the draft to the volunteer must be slow and orderly; one cannot know, with certainty, whether or not military needs can be met fully by volunteers until our international commitments are readjusted, a new strategic concept evolved. Few serious students of security policies have ever advocated in the past twenty years the complete elimination of the draft; the retention of some, if only stand-by, administrative machinery is essential. A crisis which demands far more manpower than can be furnished by volunteer recruiting alone, a crisis really involving the nation's vital interests, must be met by the mobilization of manpower as well as industrial power.

But there is a deep-seated, historical and long-lived American bias against a peacetime draft—a residue of the sentiments expressed by many of our ancestor immigrants who fled Europe to escape conscription. This instinctive American dislike for compulsory soldiering was brought to a head by the Vietnam war. The draft became the focus of opposition to "the Establishment." Some who faced the penalty for their convictions were sincere and honorable in their opposition. But some used draft opposition to try to ennoble their essentially selfish and ignoble aims.

The draft clearly requires modification to reduce, as far as possible, its inequities, and eventually bring about its replacement—entirely or largely—except in time of major crisis, by a volunteer, professional force. The modifications required have been clearly charted. One-time "jeopardy," based on a random lottery system for all nineteen-year-olds (now in effect), with almost complete elimination of past grounds for deferment, is a far fairer system than the one in use for almost two decades. There is no reason why lottery numbers, which would determine priority of induction, should not be drawn and assigned, at least a year before draftees reached their nineteenth birthdays (or high school graduation, whichever came first); they could plan accordingly. There should be no college deferments; we cannot afford a special white-collar elite exempt from the obligations of citizenship. Already, far too many of our troubles, too much of our anguish, has been caused by the intelligentsia of laboratories and classrooms who have never emerged from their ivory towers and who cannot see beyond their narrow horizons. If a young man was not drafted during his nineteenth year, he should henceforth be exempt from a military call-up except in time of major national emergency; then any age group, up to thirty-five, would be subject to call.

Transition to this system might well be followed, after the reduction of combat in Vietnam to a low level, by a trial period—for one or two years—of an all-volunteer system or one with minimal draft inputs. No one can know whether such a system, with proper incentives, will meet our needs until it is tried, and until our needs are measured, more realistically than they can be today, against a

320

new strategic concept and revised global commitments.

The disadvantages of an all-volunteer, professional force have been overemphasized by some commentators. Increased incentives for service careers, if they took the form entirely, or largely, of increased pay, could result in what some might call an "army of mercenaries." But the real danger of such armed forces is not Bonapartism, of a uniformed "man on horseback" prepared to take over the government, but of inadequate combat effectiveness. There is little real militarism, in the Prussian sense, in the American armed forces, in part because our system of manpower recruitment draws from all social classes, in part because there is far less rigid class autocracy in our officer hierarchy than in other armies, and in part because of our well-developed military educational system, which draws so heavily upon the educational system of the nation.

Prussianism, the danger of a "state within a state," is not necessarily encouraged by a professional, all-volunteer force. But combat ineffectiveness—a reduction in will and capability to fight—is a real danger if the government substitutes only dollar incentives for the glories of yesterday. A mercenary can fight, but soldiering then becomes nothing but a job, not an honorable career, and the pride of service, the ideals and traditions which make men willing to die for their country, are of more importance than dollars to many men, particularly to the type who make professional soldiers. The services quite clearly have failed to emphasize adequately the psychic incentives of the past when the Army was a "home" and the services a proud career. We have ignored tradition or ignobled it; the flag in Memorial Hall at the Naval Academy that Perry flew at the Battle of Lake Erie, with the emblazoned dying words of Lawrence, "Don't Give Up the Ship," is now known, sardonically, by the midshipmen as the "Bucher flag," a commentary on the capture of the *Pueblo*, without a fight, by the North Koreans. And too many officers, among them those who enjoyed the privilege of high rank, have degraded their profession, and undermined the "special trust and confidence" bestowed in them by the President, by shady transactions or moral cowardice, or a descent to the doctrine of the enemy—that the end justifies any means.

If proper career incentives—dollars, advancement, responsibility

321

—plus psychic rewards, and restoration of sound traditions and service morale were the guidelines rather than increased pay alone, a volunteer professional force would prove far superior in effectiveness in normal peacetime to a part-draft army. Its turnover would be less, its skills greater, its leadership more developed. And there is no doubt that such a professional long-term force meets the needs of the technological age.

Whether or not such a force can be developed in the milieu of today one cannot know with certainty. The armed services of any nation are bound to reflect the problems of that nation. Ours are great. The homogeneity and the "band-of-brothers" concepts, which were part of the bone and muscle of the much smaller services of thirty years ago, have gone, probably never to return. Integration has caused basic problems in the services which can never be easily resolved; it has impaired the common concept of a common purpose and the unit integrity which once existed. The racial frictions which still exist are far more serious and violent than the services will admit; they could, indeed, particularly in a time of domestic crisis, lead to the unreliability of some units.

Such basic problems must be overcome if dependable armed forces—and particularly volunteer professional forces—are to be maintained. Some critics believe an all-volunteer force would inevitably become an army of the poor and the black. It could, indeed, become that—particularly if pay were the sole incentive, and if the social reformers and politicians continue to dictate personnel policies. One of the basic reasons there is such a disproportionate number of Negroes at the cutting edge of the sword—in rifle platoons and companies, particularly in airborne units—is that the Negro in today's Army has never had it so good; soldier's pay, plus the extra pay of the paratrooper, attracts him, and he enlists and re-enlists. Yet his lower educational qualifications usually fit him only for the MOS (Military Occupational Skills) of rifleman, and inequitable draft deferment policies have tended to draft first those who do not go to college. But this situation need not occur if the politicians and the sociologists will leave the services alone. The services themselves can control both the ratio of races and their assignments if they are allowed to. The problem is not new; after

322

the Korean War the Army had a disproportionate number of Negro noncoms and long-term enlisted men, who had enlisted and re-enlisted, who had been promoted for reasons of seniority rather than ability, and who did not in many cases have the minimum qualifications necessary for retention. The problem was eventually solved by retirements, reassignments and control of enlistments.

This problem cannot be allowed to recur if the nation wants combat-effective, truly professional forces. Too often the sociologists, the professional reformers and, above all, the politicians—looking for minority-group votes—have tried to use the services for their own self-serving experiments. During one recent administration some of the reformers in the Pentagon actually proposed that the next entering class at the Naval Academy be one-third to one-half black, regardless of standards. But low standards for a minority group—or any preferred group—and high standards for the rest will prevent professionalism, and above all will exacerbate the severe racial frictions that now rack the armed services. There cannot be two standards of qualification or two standards of discipline. That the U.S. Marine Corps, in attempts to alleviate such friction, should permit a special style of haircut (the Afro haircut) for blacks is an admission that double standards and two kinds of discipline might be permitted. And this could be the kiss of death. The insistent political pressure to water down discipline, to favor minority groups, to "take it easy" with draft dissenters and with the "soldier-lawyers" who run the close-to-the-borderline-of-subversion "underground military press" and "coffeehouses" is the biggest single danger to combat-effective professional forces. It cannot be tolerated. As the late General George C. Marshall once said, "We cannot have a political club and call it an army." But it need not doom any such force. A return to old standards, and administrative, disciplinary and enlistment controls—if the services were allowed to use them—could prevent the development in volunteer services of "the poor man's, black man's army," or the "political club" which some observers fear.

There are certain to be problems—severe problems—in the transition from compulsion to inducement, from services supported in considerable part by the draft to volunteers. One will be the recruitment of officer candidates of high standards. The principal officer sources for the armed services are the service academies, who must provide the long-term professional "hard core," and ROTC and Officer Candidate Schools. By far the greater number of younger officers who serve for a time and then return to civilian life is provided by OCS and ROTC and by various aviation cadet programs. Yet even the service academies, affected by the loud and vocal anti-Vietnam claque and the new antimilitarism, have found their selectivity reduced, the number of qualified applicants narrowed. The so-called "revolt" against ROTC is but a symptom of a malaise, but it is a symptom that has been especially pronounced in the liberal and somewhat effete East—in the Ivy League colleges in particular. Yet these colleges—Harvard, Yale, Princeton, Dartmouth, Columbia—have not really paid their way for a decade or more, from the point of view of the government, as far as production of significant numbers of high-quality ROTC officers is concerned. Their withdrawal from, or limitation of, the program does not fully reflect the national norm; it may, indeed, in the long run, hurt the Ivy League considerably more than it hurts the ROTC. There is a need for reform of some ROTC programs but never for elimination. To secure qualified professional officers of the highest caliber for long-term professional armed forces, there are three fundamental essentials:

1. Maintenance of high physical, mental and moral standards at the service academies and retention of their basic purposes as school of the soldier, school of the sea, school of the air.

2. Maintenance and perhaps expansion of ROTC for all services to provide the "civilian soldier," the "civilian sailor," the "civilian airman" who are essential—particularly in a long-term volunteer force—to maintain the link between the services and the society they serve, and to provide some of the career professionals for the regular services and the reserve officers required in national emergencies.

3. Maintenance of OCS at a flexible level, reduced when officer needs can be reduced, expanded in times of emergency, to provide junior officers for the services and a commissioned career for enlisted men.

The size of the U.S. armed forces in tomorrow's world will fluctuate with the winds of change. But, within the political and economic guidelines established by the administration in power, they should be strong enough to meet brush-fire situations, to control the vital sea lanes and air space, and to handle continental emergencies around the rimlands involving up to 100,000 ground troops. Any war that requires a greater commitment than this must not be fought by the professionals alone. Professionals can and should meet emergency situations; they are the first line of defense. But, as the French experience in Indochina showed, political alienation of the armed forces from the body of the nation is a very likely result if the professionals are forbidden the aid of the citizen soldier and if the services fight a long and wearing war without the backing of the nation. Executive action, with or without Congressional sanction, is imperative in the age of space-annihilating weapons to meet crises, but Congressional approval—a declaration of war—is equally imperative for any large-scale or protracted conflict if the armed services and the nation are to avoid fractionalization.

The organization of the Department of Defense and of the armed services has evolved in the past thirty years from uncoordinated, loosely organized services under the policy direction and strategic control of the President to a highly overcentralized, overstaffed bureaucracy. The elimination of the traditional military checks and balances of the past,[13] the concentration of policy-making power, administrative and management power and command power in a few hands in Washington; the close and detailed monitoring of procurement, planning and operation and of tactics and training as well as strategy; and the far-flung command and control networks made possible by modern communications have often made the operational analysts and management experts and staff generals in the Washington command post the architects of our history. Our recent wars—particularly the Vietnam war—have been run from Washington; sometimes the President and the Secretary of Defense have become platoon commanders, wing commanders, destroyer skippers; once during the Dominican crisis a four-star general in Washington ordered the U.S. commander on the scene to move one tank one block.

The result of this overconcentration of power, the centralization

325

of control and the proliferation of staffs, agencies, committees and bureaucrats has been to dull the cutting edge of the sword—the fighting forces. And this same trend, coupled with Secretary McNamara's veiled contempt of what he thought of as "military minds," his lack of loyalty down, his propensity to be a one-man band, and his swift retributive actions toward any officer who he thought opposed his policies have reduced initiative and flexibility and have hurt service morale.[14] Today's officer, schooled for many recent years that the best way to promotion and pay is to report first and to take action afterward, often tends to pass the buck upward —to report to his seniors and let them make the decisions. The *Pueblo* case symbolized this trend. There are certain immutable and inviolable rules which are well understood by all in the service: a captain is responsible for his ship; he cannot allow it, while he has any means of resistance, to fall into enemy hands—"Don't Give Up the Ship." Yet not only Commander Lloyd Bucher but almost the entire chain of service command during this incident was indecisive, slow in reaction, lacking initiative.[15] A fundamental reason was the tendency to "buck up," to refer to higher authority for decision, and the complex and cumbersome bureaucracy now established in Washington and extending its tentacles to subordinate commands all over the world is often incapable of swift decision.

The development of the organization of the armed forces has moved almost full circle since the days when Jim Forrestal, the first Secretary of Defense, attempted to control policy-making in the Pentagon. Only in recent months have some of the faults of overcentralization and overcontrol been partially corrected: whether or not the correctives are sufficient only another war or crisis can demonstrate.

The reduction in initiative, which once used to be an outstanding American characteristic, and the slowness in decision-making in times of crisis have been paralleled in the modern Pentagon— particularly since 1963—by slowness in procurement and in translating blueprint dreams of new weapons into "hardware." The short "lead time"—or lapse between idea and operational product —which used to characterize our arms production has been gradually lengthened until the U.S.S.R., for instance, has been able, in

326

many cases, to design and produce a new weapon or weapons system in shorter time—and of course at far less cost—than we can.

When Mr. McNamara took office, he instituted a system of review and analysis of development projects and a planning, programing and budgeting cycle which involved numerous reviews and justifications to prevent unnecessary duplication and unnecessary cost. Like many ideas that are tried out in Washington, the concept was sound, and initially it prevented some waste. But so many echelons of authority were involved, and management gradually became so centralized in the Secretary's office, and both the Pentagon and Congress required so much monitoring of, and so many reports from, contractors, that the whole process slowed down, and "lead time" lengthened. The so-called "total package procurement plan" for weapons systems, with competition on paper between contractors, was intended to save money, but it not only failed to do so in certain conspicuous items—like the F-111—but it, too, lengthened "lead time."

A definite amount of service competition is healthy; such competition between the Army Air Force and the Navy produced both the air-cooled and the liquid-cooled aircraft engines, both essential to victory in World War II; the F-4 fighter, produced by the Navy, but now used by both Air Force and Navy; and many other items. The old system of contracting—the development of prototype weapons systems by various bidders, in accordance with common specifications—leads to the procurement of the best weapons and, in many cases, may save money. The Navy and the Air Force used to specify the kind of plane they wanted and the missions they wanted it to perform; then each interested contractor would build several of these aircraft for competitive testing, and the contract award would go to the winner. This system may well be too expensive nowadays to use in major weapons systems; certainly cost was the rationale of the system introduced by McNamara, in which components were tested and built and the contractors competed *on paper* in a design competition before any metal was bent. But the new system has had some conspicuous failures, and it certainly has not produced the best weapons possible in the shortest time possible.

327

Both in the operational and in the administrative and procurement field, there has been a concentration of power at the top, and the establishment of echelon after echelon of reviewing authorities along the chain of command and administration, nearly all of whom have the power either to delay or to deny but who lack the power to affirm. Under the concept of common-usage items, a plethora of defense department agencies—supply, intelligence, communications—has evolved. There has been no reduction in numbers; in fact, the new superagencies require more personnel, not less; men and women have simply shifted their office space and their designations from service departments to the Defense Department. It is doubtful, too, except in communications, that the result has been greater efficiency. The organizational pyramid, indeed, has been inverted; probably never in the history of human conflict have so few been commanded and managed by so many.

Greater organizational efficiency in Washington can undoubtedly save money and speed decision-making, but it will not work miracles, and if it is to be translated into improved combat effectiveness on the battlefield, the services' command and staff systems and chains of command must be improved and made more responsive.

The transition, in the unification process after World War II, from the two services, Army and Navy, coordinated but under no common commander short of the President, to the present system of four services (five, in time of war, with the Coast Guard), commanded by unified theater commanders in various parts of the world and by the Secretary of Defense through the corporate organization of the Joint Chiefs of Staff, has led to swollen staffs and unnecessary expense. The shibboleths of standardization and of unification have led to "laws," often unwritten, which are, nevertheless, as rigorous as the immutable laws of the Medes and Persians, that each service must have approximately equal representation on every unified staff, and that every unified commander must have separate but equal component commanders under him. The result has been, in many ways, to change the so-called duplication of the old Army-Navy system into triplication. There is no doubt whatsoever that the establishment of a separate Department of the Air Force, in this technological era of aerospace, has helped to provide a mechanism for the imaginative development of weapons systems, concepts and ideas that may be vital for tomorrow. On the other hand, there is no doubt either that it has cost the nation many added billions, purely because of the triplicate and quadruplicate form of organization that has developed, not only in Washington but throughout the world.

Decentralization in Washington, reduction in the enormous numbers of bureaucrats at the top, the concentration of more authority and more responsibility upon lower echelons and particularly upon the Secretaries of Army, Navy and Air Force, and elimination of the requirements that have spawned bloated triservice staffs around the world will reduce expense and promote efficiency. Many commands are essentially one-service, or two-service, in nature; in South Vietnam, for instance, General William C. Westmoreland quite correctly believed the war was essentially a "ground show."

In addition to command and staff reductions in Washington and in the field, a clearer delineation of authority is vital for successful command and control and for rapid decision-making. A great many superagencies have grown up in Washington that now have a finger in the Pentagon pie, and their operations often influence or confuse operations in the field. Shadowy lines of responsibility or dual or triple reporting chains have grown up which, as both the *Pueblo* case and the Vietnam Green Berets case demonstrated, can complicate a crisis and confuse or delay its resolution. The Central Intelligence Agency, the National Security Agency (communications intelligence, codes and ciphers, etc.) and many other agencies work with the military forces, and sometimes it has not been clear who is commanding whom. In part, the confusion is the military's own responsibility. Their attempts to increase security and to isolate much information on a so-called "need to know" basis have compartmentalized military staffs and chains of command. A little less security, particularly in the present age when modern technology makes complete security impossible, might make for greater efficiency.

329

One organizational trend in the Department of Defense, which must be halted and reversed, has dangerous implications. It is the trend toward centralization of power in the hands of a few and the accompanying divorcement of responsibility from authority.

Since the first days of unification a beguiling and superficially appealing "solution" to interservice conflicts and dissenting opinions has periodically surfaced. The "solution" has been concentration of power at the top of the organizational pyramid, the establishment of a kind of greater general staff divorced from their services and of a kind of Super Chief of Staff over all the armed services. This pattern, no matter how gilded, is a close replica of the pre–World War II German system, and of both the German and the Japanese general staff systems. In both systems general staff officers occupied preferred positions and exercised enormous and well-nigh unchecked powers; their authority was great, their responsibility hazy at best. The system led to development of "military party lines"—a single concept of military doctrine—to encroachment upon, and finally usurpation of, the civilian authority, and to catastrophic defeat in war.

The U.S. military organizational concept has gone far—in some ways, too far—toward this extremely dangerous pattern; the Chairman of the Joint Chiefs of Staff, for instance, has, *de facto*, tremendous authority but limited responsibility. Both the Chairman and an all-powerful Secretary of Defense have been interposed between the President as Commander in Chief and the responsible uniformed heads of the services. Yet, as Vietnam has shown, it is vital for the President to receive undiluted military advice; it is vital to guard against the burgeoning of only one school of military thought; it is vital that no "state within a state" be allowed to develop in America. Authority and responsibility must go hand in hand; checks and balances within the Pentagon as well as outside it must be maintained; the roles of the individual service departments enhanced; the Chiefs of Staff must wear two hats—service and corporate—and there must be free and easy communication upward from uniformed personnel to the Commander in Chief.

There will always be in any organization as big as the Department of Defense and the military services a certain amount of waste and inefficiency. Bigness and complexity—and both are an inevitable part of the armed services of tomorrow—involve an unavoidable degree of expense; this is, indeed, one argument for a reversion, as far as possible, to the smaller, simpler, more elite services of the past, which were at once more manageable and had higher standards of duty, discipline and professionalism. But fundamentally force reductions mean reductions in total power; the old siren call of the politicians that billions can be saved by greater efficiency in the Defense Department simply is not true—millions, yes, but billions, no. We may reduce the budget by billions in the years ahead; if so, we will do it at the cost of total power. Every defense budget represents a calculated risk; we may increase the military risk (by cutting the budget) because the political risk has decreased, or the economic risk demands it, but we *must* squarely face these trade-offs. It is the height of hypocrisy to claim that we can maintain the same defense posture for much less money.

There is, too, a lower limit, a floor, to the force levels we must maintain if we are to remain a global power. An oceanic strategic concept will enable reductions, but no concept, no world strategy, no possible scenario for the world of tomorrow, can justify the kind of pre–World War II force levels this country maintained. An oceanic strategy will require the largest and most modern Navy in the world; a Marine Corps of three full divisions, with at least three battalions embarked upon amphibious craft, and one or more at forward-island bases; land-based air power unexcelled by any; leadership in space technology; a modern professional Army, qualitatively the best in the world—all backed by a ready reserve. For the regular forces the minimum force structure possible in the next decade will appear to be at least 1.5 million men, more probably 2 to 2.25 million.

And no single strategic concept can meet all challenges and all needs; military force is indivisible, and military power of all types from all services will be required in the years ahead. We must accentuate a maritime concept; it should be the basis for future planning and force composition, but land power and aerospace power are essential to national power, and the man on the ground with the gun in his hand is still the ultimate weapon.

The maintenance of forces such as these, far from dooming international cooperation and the limitation of arms, can encourage both. Too often the United States enters upon negotiations with other nations like a naïve college freshman playing poker. We cannot achieve our aims, we cannot promote arms reductions, if we disarm unilaterally, if our own liberals and woolly-minded politicians hobble our technological progress.

Yet there is danger—grave danger—that we have started down a slippery slope. We have entered upon—indeed, begged for—peace negotiations in Vietnam, but have forsworn the pressures that might make a negotiated peace possible. We have stopped bombing North Vietnam, abandoned victory, are withdrawing our troops. And we have started arms-limitations discussions with Soviet Russia from a posture that is rapidly becoming one of military inferiority. We have allowed Moscow to overtake and surpass us in major elements of strategic power—numbers and size of land-based ICBM's, antiballistic missile systems, medium- and intermediate-range missiles, numbers of bombers. We still retain an equivocal lead in sea-based missiles, but it may be short-lived; the Russians launched an estimated 10 to 20 new submarines in 1969, the United States 5. By the end of 1970, Moscow will have a larger fleet of nuclear-powered submarines than the United States. By 1975, if present programs are maintained, the United States may well be in second place in sea-based missiles and in over-all nuclear striking power. Washington has already started a kind of unilateral arms-limitation program; for the first time in history major force reductions and cuts in the defense budget have been effected before a war was finished.

The limitation of armaments and some reduction of the costs and the tensions that arms races help to cause are highly desirable goals. But we may already have doomed our efforts; one cannot bargain successfully—or at least safely—from a position of actual or potential inferiority. Arms races are dangerous, but arms inferiority even more so; any agreement which would freeze the United States in an inferior position could well doom us to war or to loss of the things we hold dear. The alternatives offered so glibly by the liberals —a halt in technological developments, a reduction of arms or

332

annihilation—have never been realistic ones. Greater strength, new developments do not spell disaster; deterrence has been maintained through a quarter-century of the atomic age; it can be maintained in the dangerous tomorrows. But not from a position of inferiority, not by unilateral arms limitations, not by faith alone, not by one-sided acceptance of the mythical notion of some kind of "technological plateau."

Restraint—yes! Wisdom—yes! But never a refusal to face facts, ugly facts, as they are.

Arms races may gather a mad momentum, which should and can be checked, but essentially they are the result, not the cause, of world tensions. Fundamentally, those tensions are generated by the expansionist Communist societies and by a host of other problems —political and economic and social. And until those problems are resolved arms and armaments will play a large part in the history of man.

If the United States is to survive the dangerous last third of the twentieth century without becoming "Red or Dead," it must keep its powder dry.

In modern military terms this translates into six overriding priorities:

1. Superiority in strategic weapons. Nuclear inferiority dooms the deterrent, dooms the possibility of success in any kind of conventional conflict, dooms our diplomacy.

2. Maritime superiority—the capability to use the seas for our purposes, and, if necessary, to deny their use to an enemy.

3. Research and development across the board. The age of miracles has not ended; technological surprise is still possible. Active basic and applied weapons research for both offensive and defensive weapons and in mobility is a fundamental requirement of security. Dr. John S. Foster, Director of Defense Research and Engineering, told the Armed Forces Management Association in 1969 that "the Soviets have been expanding their research and development efforts for space, defense and atomic energy during the past few years by an average of about 10 percent a year. During the same period American defense R & D spending has gone up about 4 percent a year, not quite enough to cover the inflation rate for

technology; and atomic energy and space spending, together, have actually diminished." The results have been apparent in the new and formidable Soviet ships in the Mediterranean, the new Soviet-type weapons in Vietnam and the Middle East, and—in the form of technological surprise—in the Czechoslovak invasion. In Czechoslovakia the Russians introduced a new form of chaff, which had been hitherto unknown in the West, as a means of blanking out the Prague radars. The chaff, described by some sources as "gaseous," but more probably a much refined form of the metallic strips dropped by aircraft in World War II, was highly effective over a wide area.

4. Intelligence—a knowledge of the enemy and of the world around us—is the bedrock upon which all policy must be built.

5. The shortest possible "lead time"—the interval between blueprint concept and finished hardware—for all weapons systems.

6. The pre-eminence of man as the king of battle; upon his will and skill hangs the future of America. The armed forces of tomorrow must maintain a school for leaders.

Force levels can and must be flexible; weapons change and leaders wax and wane. Domestic needs can and must at times supersede foreign priorities; calculated military risks may have to increase to reduce economic or political risks. But if we neglect any of the six priorities listed, we shall be undone.

A maritime strategic concept is best suited to the U.S. geographic and strategic position and to the peculiar brand of American genius which has made our nation the most advanced industrial and technological power in the world. It offers the optimum framework for accommodating incompatibles, of meeting with the resources available and finite funds both domestic and foreign needs, of providing for external security while remedying internal ills. It guards our interests overseas, but minimizes the likelihood of undesirable involvement.

Today the United States is again at an historical crossroads.

We are entering an era of negotiations. The United States and Russia, the Warsaw Pact and NATO discuss arms limitations and the thinning out of forces in Europe. This can be a hopeful development in the epic of man. But it can also be a snare and delusion.

We must remember that no system of arms inspection that can be devised by man is, at one and the same time, technically certain and foolproof, and politically feasible. Trust is a necessary ingredient of agreement, and actions speak louder than words.

If hope is to be translated into even a moderate achievement—a short climb up the long slope from the abyss in which we began—we must use our own power to force the limitation of power.

There can be, realistically, no other way. We must arm to parley. Or there will be no meaningful parley. Or we shall enter an era of incalculable risk.

We *must* keep our powder dry. And if we do, there will not be a global Utopia; it will be the same old world with all the problems of man. But it will be a livable world, a world in which U.S. national security is—*not* guaranteed, for there is no absolute security, no infinite guarantee—but reasonably insured. One way lies hope; the other, decline and fall.

# Appendices

## «« Appendix I »»

## INDUSTRIAL PRODUCTION

|  | Steel<br>Ingots, Castings | Aluminum | Electric Power<br>(1967) |
|---|---|---|---|
| U.S. | 134,101,000* | 2,968,366* | 1,317,300* |
| U.S.S.R. | 110,000,000<br>(1967) | 1,430,000 | 556,855 |
| Japan | 52,673,000 | 371,778<br>(1968) | 237,168 |
| West<br>Germany | 38,929,000 | 268,839 | 172,250 |
| U.K. | 27,233,000 | 40,934 | 196,187 |
| France | 21,589,000 | 400,701 | 111,637 |
| China† | 17,600,000 | 110,000 | 36,000 |
| Czechoslovakia | 10,062,000 | 68,000 | — |
| India | 7,198,000 | 91,803 | — |

*Steel figures in long tons; aluminum in short tons; electric power in millions of kilowatt-hours.
All figures for 1966, except as noted.
†Communist China—mainland only.

SOURCES: *Minerals Yearbook*, Vols. I and II, U.S. Department of Interior, Washington, D.C., Government Printing Office, 1968; *World Almanac*, 1970, p. 140; Federal Power Commission.

## «« Appendix II »»

## GNP AND FORCE LEVELS

Comparative Data on Share of Population
and Gross National Product Dedicated to
Defense in Selected Countries

| GNP Per Capita | | Percent GNP for Defense | | Percent Population in Armed Forces* | | Index of Resources Dedicated to Defense | |
|---|---|---|---|---|---|---|---|
| U.S. | $3,796 | Israel | 10.5 | Israel | 2.7 | Israel | 28.4 |
| Canada | 2,658 | U.S.S.R. | 9.0† | R.O.K.‡ | 2.0 | U.S. | 13.6 |
| Australia | 2,178 | U.S. | 8.5 | U.S. | 1.6 | U.S.S.R. | 12.6† |
| France | 2,052 | U.K. | 5.8 | U.S.S.R. | 1.4 | R.O.K. | 7.8 |
| W. Ger. | 1,990 | France | 5.2 | Turkey | 1.4 | Turkey | 6.6 |
| U.K. | 1,924 | Turkey | 4.7 | France | 1.1 | France | 5.7 |
| ENATO§ | 1,570 | ENATO | 4.6 | ENATO | 1.0 | U.K. | 4.6 |
| U.S.S.R. | 1,531 | Austral. | 4.2 | U.K. | 0.8 | ENATO | 4.6 |
| Israel | 1,454 | W. Ger. | 4.1 | W. Ger. | 0.7 | W. Ger. | 2.9 |
| Japan | 986 | R.O.K. | 3.9 | Austral. | 0.6 | Australia | 2.5 |
| Brazil | 310 | Pakistan | 3.6 | Canada | 0.5 | Canada | 1.5 |
| Turkey | 295 | Brazil | 3.1 | Thailand | 0.4 | Brazil | 0.9 |
| Thailand | 141 | Canada | 0.3 | Brazil | 0.3 | Thailand | 0.8 |
| R.O.K. | 131 | Thailand | 2.1 | Japan | 0.2 | Pakistan | 0.7 |
| Pakistan | 115 | Japan | 1.0 | Pakistan | 0.2 | Japan | 0.2 |
| Warsaw Pact totals (less U.S.S.R.) $1,208 | | 4.4 | | 1.1 | | 4.8 | |

*It is theorized that the proportion of people in the armed forces of a country multiplied by the proportion of their GNP spent on defense could be an index of the country's military power.
†No expenditures for space R & D and exploration included in the defense budget figures used

for this table, although application of space resources for military purposes by U.S.S.R. is considerable.
§European members of NATO.
‡South Korea.

SOURCE: Arms Control & Disarmament Agency Report #68-52, of December, 1968; based on 1966–67 figures.

## «« Appendix III »»

## SOURCES OF ESSENTIAL RAW MATERIALS

| | U.S. Domestic Production (Percentage) | Imports (Percentage) | Principal Foreign Sources (in order of importance) |
|---|---|---|---|
| Antimony | 47* | 53 | Mexico, South Africa, Bolivia, Yugoslavia, U.K. |
| Asbestos | 14 | 86 | Canada, South Africa |
| Bauxite | 13 | 87 | Jamaica, Surinam, Dominican Republic, Haiti |
| Beryl | 11 ('63) | 89 | India, Australia, Brazil, Congo |
| Chromite | None | 100 | South Africa, Zambia, Rhodesia, Malawi, Philippines, U.S.S.R., Turkey |
| Cobalt | 11 | 89 | Congo, Belgium-Luxembourg, Norway, France, West Germany |
| Columbium-Tantalum | None | 100 | Nigeria, Canada, Brazil |
| Copper | 72 | 28 | Chile, Peru, Canada, South Africa |
| Fibers | None | 100 | Philippines, Brazil, Mexico, Tanzania, Haiti |
| Iron Ore | 66 | 34 | Canada, Venezuela, Liberia, Chile, Brazil |
| Lead | 46 | 54 | Mexico, Australia, Canada, Peru, South Africa, Yugoslavia |
| Manganese Ore | 1 | 99 | Brazil, Gabon, Ivory Coast, Congo, Ghana, India, South Africa |

STRATEGY FOR TOMORROW

| | U.S. Domestic Production (Percentage) | Imports (Percentage) | Principal Foreign Sources (in order of importance) |
|---|---|---|---|
| Mica Sheet | 6 | 94 | India, Brazil, Malagasay Republic |
| Nickel | 9 | 91 | Canada, Norway |
| Petroleum | 86 | 14 | Venezuela, Canada, Saudi Arabia, Iran, Sumatra, Kuweit |
| Rubber | None | 100 | Indonesia, Malaysia, Liberia |
| Sugar | 51 | 49 | Philippines, Mexico, Dominican Republic, Peru, Brazil |
| Thorium Ore | —† | — | Australia, Malaysia |
| Tin | 1 | 99 | Malaysia, Bolivia, Nigeria, U.K. |
| Tungsten | 68 | 32 | Bolivia, Canada, Peru, Australia, South Korea |
| Uranium | 80 | 20 | South Africa, Canada |
| Zinc | 52 | 48 | Canada, Mexico, Peru |
| Zircon | — | — | Australia |

*All figures are for 1965 and in round numbers unless otherwise noted.
†Blanks indicate information unavailable.

SOURCES: *U.S. Life Lines—Imports of Essential Materials—1963, 1964, 1965,* Washington, D.C., Office of the Chief of Naval Operations, Department of the Navy, December, 1966.

«« Appendix IV »» (*over*)

## U.S. COLLECTIVE DEFENSE ARRANGEMENTS

For details see: "Worldwide Military Commitments," *Hearings Before the Preparedness Investigating Subcommittee of the Committee on Armed Services, United States Senate,* 89th Congress, 2nd Session, Part I, August 25 and 30, 1966. Washington: U.S. Government Printing Office, pp. 13-29. Compilation prepared by Department of State, August, 1966.

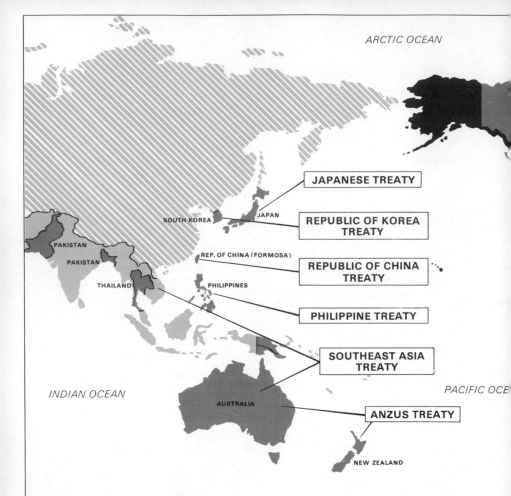

ARCTIC OCEAN

JAPANESE TREATY

REPUBLIC OF KOREA TREATY

REPUBLIC OF CHINA TREATY

PHILIPPINE TREATY

SOUTHEAST ASIA TREATY

ANZUS TREATY

JAPAN
SOUTH KOREA
REP. OF CHINA (FORMOSA)
PAKISTAN
PAKISTAN
THAILAND
PHILIPPINES
INDIAN OCEAN
PACIFIC OCE
AUSTRALIA
NEW ZEALAND

**REPUBLIC OF CHINA (Formosa) TREATY (BILATERAL)**

UNITED STATES
REPUBLIC OF CHINA (FORMOSA)

A treaty signed December 2, 1954, whereby each of the parties "recognizes that an armed attack in the West Pacific Area directed against the territories of either of the Parties would be dangerous to its own peace and safety," and that each "would act to meet the common danger in accordance with its constitutional processes." The territory of the Republic of China is defined as "Taiwan (Formosa) and the Pescadores."

**SOUTHEAST ASIA TREATY (8 NATIONS)**

UNITED STATES    AUSTRALIA
UNITED           PHILIPPINES
KINGDOM          THAILAND
FRANCE           PAKISTAN
NEW ZEALAND

A treaty signed September 8, 1954, whereby each Party "recognizes that aggression by means of armed attack in the treaty area against any of the Parties . . . would endanger its own peace and safety" and each will "in that event act to meet the common danger in accordance with its constitutional processes.

**ANZUS (Australia—New Zealand—United States) TREATY (3 NATIONS)**

UNITED STATES
NEW ZEALAND
AUSTRALIA

A treaty signed September 1, 1951, whereby each of the parties "recognizes that an armed attack in the Pacific Area on any of the Parties would be dangerous to its own peace and safety and declares that it would act to meet the common danger in accordance with its constitutional processes."

**PHILIPPINE TREATY (BILATERAL)**

UNITED STATES
PHILIPPINES

A treaty signed August 30, by which the parties reco "that an armed attack in th cific Area on either of the F would be dangerous to its peace and safety" and eac agrees that it will act "to the common dangers in acco with its constitutional proce

**UNITED STATES COLLECTIVE DEFEN**

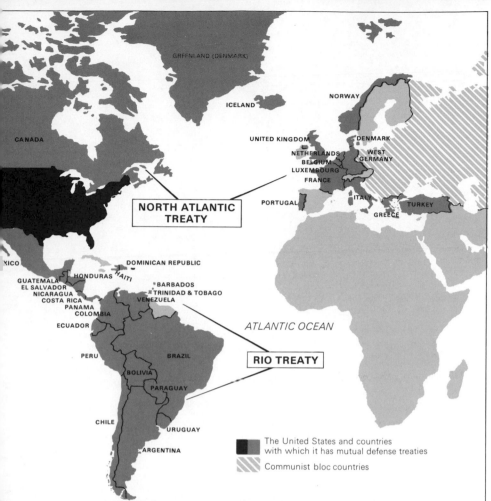

NORTH ATLANTIC
TREATY

ATLANTIC OCEAN

RIO TREATY

GREENLAND (DENMARK)

NORWAY

ICELAND

CANADA

UNITED KINGDOM          DENMARK
        NETHERLANDS    WEST
        BELGIUM        GERMANY
        LUXEMBOURG
           FRANCE

PORTUGAL                ITALY     TURKEY
                          GREECE

XICO           DOMINICAN REPUBLIC

GUATEMALA    HONDURAS
EL SALVADOR         HAITI
NICARAGUA                  BARBADOS
COSTA RICA              TRINIDAD & TOBAGO
    PANAMA         VENEZUELA
      COLOMBIA

ECUADOR

PERU              BRAZIL

    BOLIVIA

        PARAGUAY

CHILE

        URUGUAY

    ARGENTINA

■■ The United States and countries
   with which it has mutual defense treaties

▨ Communist bloc countries

| | | | |
|---|---|---|---|
| **NESE TREATY TERAL)** | **REPUBLIC OF KOREA (South Korea) TREATY (BILATERAL)** | **RIO TREATY (22 NATIONS)** | **NORTH ATLANTIC TREATY (15 NATIONS)** |

| | | | | | |
|---|---|---|---|---|---|
| **UNITED STATES JAPAN** | **UNITED STATES REPUBLIC OF KOREA** | UNITED STATES | COLOMBIA VENEZUELA | **UNITED STATES** | LUXEMBOURG PORTUGAL |
| | | MEXICO | ECUADOR | CANADA | FRANCE |
| | | BARBADOS | PERU | ICELAND | ITALY |
| | | HAITI | BRAZIL | NORWAY | GREECE |
| | | DOMINICAN | BOLIVIA | UNITED | TURKEY |
| | | REPUBLIC | PARAGUAY | KINGDOM | FEDERAL |
| | | HONDURAS | CHILE | NETHERLANDS | REPUBLIC |
| | | GUATEMALA | ARGENTINA | DENMARK | OF |
| | | EL SALVADOR | URUGUAY | BELGIUM | GERMANY |
| | | NICARAGUA | TRINIDAD AND | | |
| | | COSTA RICA | TOBAGO | | |
| | | PANAMA | | | |

ty signed January 19, 1960,
by each party "recognizes
armed attack against either
in the territories under the
istration of Japan would be
ous to its own peace and
and declares that it would
meet the common danger in
ance with its constitutional
ons and processes." The
replaced the security treaty
September 8, 1951.

A treaty signed October 1, 1953,
whereby each party "recognizes
that an armed attack in the Pacific
area on either of the Parties . . .
would be dangerous to its own
peace and safety" and that each
Party "would act to meet the common danger in accordance with its
constitutional processes."

A treaty signed September 2,
1947, which provides that an
armed attack against any American
State "shall be considered as an
attack against all the American
States and . . . each one . . . under-
takes to assist in meeting the
attack . . ."

A treaty signed April 4, 1949, by
which "the parties agree that an
armed attack against one or more
of them in Europe or North America
shall be considered an attack
against them all; and . . . each of
them . . . will assist the . . . attacked by taking forthwith, individually and in concert with the
other Parties, such action as it
deems necessary including the use
of armed force . . ."

RANGEMENTS

# Notes

## 1» Man and Power

1. Colonel Amos A. Jordan, Jr., ed., *Issues of National Security in the 1970's.* New York: Praeger, 1967, from chapter by Lieutenant Colonel Paul F. Gorman, "Internal Defense and the Less Developed Countries," p. 127.

2. Quincy Wright, *A Study of War.* Chicago: University of Chicago Press, 1942, Vol. II, p. 1284.

3. *Ibid.,* p. 1285.

4. Robert Ardrey, *African Genesis.* New York: Dell (paperback), 1963, pp. 323, 324, 348.

5. Robert Ardrey, *The Territorial Imperative.* New York: Dell (paperback), 1966.

6. Konrad Lorenz, *On Aggression,* New York, Harcourt, Brace & World, 1966. For an opposite point of view, see *Man and Aggression,* edited by M. F. Ashley Montagu, New York: Oxford University Press, 1969. The contributors emphasize "the unique importance of human history and cultural institutions." But in this author's opinion, history would appear to emphasize the importance, as outlined by Ardrey and Lorenz, of instinctual behavior.

7. Robert Leckie, *Warfare.* New York: Harper & Row, 1970, p. 182.

8. William R. Kintner, *Intercollegiate Review,* March-April, 1967. There are, of course, some things worse than war (the Nazi concentration camps,

for example). Wars *do* settle problems (i.e., the elimination of Hitler). Robert Ardrey's eloquent passage in *African Genesis, op. cit.*, p. 324, is illustrative:

> Let us not be too hasty in our dismissal of war as an unblemished evil. Are you a Christian? Then recall that Christendom survived its darkest hour in the fury of the Battle of Tours. Do you believe in law? The rule of law became a human institution in the shelter of the Roman legions. Do you subscribe to the value of individual worth? Only by the success of the phalanx at Marathon did the Greeks repel the Persian horde and make possible the Golden Age. Are you a materialist? Do you regard as a human good the satisfaction of economic want? The Pax Britannica, made possible by the unchallengeable supremacy of the British fleet, gave mankind the opportunity to lay the broad foundations of the Industrial Revolution.

John Stuart Mill put it more baldly over a century ago:

> War is an ugly thing, but not the ugliest thing: the decayed and degraded state of moral and patriotic feeling which thinks nothing worth a war is worse. . . . A man who has nothing which he cares about more than his personal safety is a miserable creature who has no chance of being free, unless made and kept so by the exertions of better men than himself.

And, in a famous Memorial Day address at Harvard, "The Soldier's Faith," Justice Oliver Wendell Holmes spoke, (*Speeches*; Boston: Little-Brown, 1913- p. 56-66.) in 1895, in much the same terms:

> What kind of world do you want? War . . . is horrible and dull. . . . But some teacher of the kind we all need. . . . We need it everywhere and at all times. . . .. In this time of individualist negations . . . revolting at discipline . . . denying that anything is worth reverence. For high and dangerous action teaches us to believe as right beyond dispute things for which our doubting minds are slow to find proof. Out of heroism grows faith in the worth of heroism. . . . In this snug, over-safe corner of the world . . . our comfortable routine is no eternal necessity of things, but merely a little space of calm in the midst of the tempestuous untamed streaming of the world.

348

# 2» Of Recent History

1. Lyman B. Kirkpatrick, Jr., *Captains Without Eyes.* New York: Macmillan, 1969, p. 270.

2. Sir Robert Thompson, "The Strategy of Intervention," paper delivered at the seminar on "Vietnam: Lessons and Mislessons," Adlai Stevenson Institute, Chicago, 1968. This and other papers delivered at the same conference were edited by Richard M. Pfeffer, conference director, and published under the title *No More Vietnams?* by Harper & Row, New York, 1969. I am indebted to the publisher for permission to utilize excerpts from the conference and the book.

3. *Ibid.* Stanley Hoffman has described the process, in a paper delivered at the same seminar, as "a copulation with statistics."

4. *Aviation Week and Space Technology,* September 1, 1968.

5. See *Economic Impact of the Vietnam War,* a prescient study of the dangers of trying to have your cake and eat it, too, published by the Georgetown Center for Strategic and International Studies, Special Report Series No. 5, June, 1967—a panel report, with the background paper by Dr. Murray L. Weidenbaum. The underestimate of defense spending and a sharp rise in inflationary pressures were noted, and the report recommended (a recommendation that went unheeded) that "should another major escalation occur in the level of the U.S. commitment in Southeast Asia, it would be important to promptly develop the restraining fiscal measures needed to offset the inflationary impacts."

6. In Korea and to some extent in the later stages in Vietnam attempts were made to "ration" casualties, i.e., to limit the numbers of U.S. killed and wounded by prescribing the kind and size of operations that could be undertaken, the tactics that might be used and even the number of casualties that might be incurred. The results, of course, were stultifying, not alone to successful battlefield tactics but to the casualty list.

7. T. E. Lawrence, "Science of Guerrilla War," *Encyclopaedia Britannica,* 14th edition, pp. 950–953.

8. Jordan, *op. cit.,* from chapter, "Employing America's Military Strength in the 1970's," p. 55.

9. Brian Crozier, *The Strategic Uses of Revolutionary War.* London: Institute for Strategic Studies, Adelphi Papers, No. 55, March, 1969, "Problems of Modern Strategy, Part Two."

10. Robert Shaplen, *The Lost Revolution.* New York: Harper & Row, 1965, p. 151.

11. Mark S. Watson, *Chief of Staff: Pre-War Plans and Preparations (U.S. Army in World War II).* Historical Division, Washington: U.S. Government Printing Office, 1950, p. 12.

## 3» The World of Tomorrow

1. Thomas B. Macaulay in a letter to Henry S. Randall, May 23, 1857.

2. George Santayana, *Character and Opinion in the United States.* New York: Charles Scribner's Sons, 1921. Harold Nicolson noted these trends in the United States in 1943. In a diary entry of August 13, 1943 (*Diaries and Letters of Harold Nicolson,* Vol. II, *The War Years,* ed., Nigel Nicolson. New York: Atheneum, 1967, p. 310), Nicolson records a conversation with Norman Angell, author, journalist and political scientist, who had just returned to England from an extended visit in the United States: "He agrees with me that America (having run out of the frontier and limitless opportunity) will be faced with the rise of an internal proletariat, composed partly of their Negro population and partly of the non Anglo-Saxon immigrants. Already, he says, in left wing circles, it is a disability to possess an Anglo-Saxon name."

3. Sir Halford Mackinder, *Democratic Ideals and Reality.* New York: 1919. Nicholas John Spykman, *America's Strategy in World Politics.* New York: Harcourt Brace, 1942.

4. John Findley Green Lecture by C. P. Snow at Westminster College, Fulton, Missouri, November 12, 1968. The *New York Times,* November 13, 1968. George W. Ball has estimated that 3 billion additional human beings will be added to the world's population in the next forty years, requiring double the present food output. "Calcutta, now a cesspool of three to five millions, threatens us by the year 2000 with a prospective population of from thirty to sixty million." (Quoted by George Ball, *The Discipline of Power.* Boston: Atlantic–Little, Brown, 1968, p. 231, from an article "Counterrevolutionary America" by Robert Heilbroner.)

5. "In Latin America, the seizure of political power by the military is virtually commonplace. Though extreme, Bolivia's record is not atypical; its military coup in 1964 was the 180th revolution in 138 years of nationhood . . . by any standard, Latin America is in revolutionary ferment." Lieutenant Colonel Paul F. Gorman, "Internal Defense and the Less De-

veloped Countries," in Jordan, *op. cit.*, p. 131. Since this book was written, another coup in Bolivia has taken place.

6. Leonard A. Lecht, *Goals, Priorities and Dollars: The Next Decade.* New York: Free Press, 1966, p. 267.

7. Samuel P. Huntington, "Military Intervention, Political Involvement and the Unlessons of Vietnam," paper delivered at the conference on Vietnam, Adlai Stevenson Institute, Chicago, 1968.

8. *Ibid.* Mr. Huntington quoted approvingly a study by Frank L. Klingberg, "The Historical Alteration of Moods in American Foreign Policy," *World Politics,* IV, January, 1952, pp. 239–273. Mr. Klingberg's studies pointed out that the history of the United States recorded eight alternating periods of introversion and extroversion in American attitudes toward foreign affairs, with the periods of introversion averaging 21 years, of extroversion 27 years. The cycles, as recorded by him, were:

| Introversion | Extroversion |
|---|---|
| 1776-1793 | 1798-1824 |
| 1824-1844 | 1844-1871 |
| 1871-1891 | 1891-1919 |
| 1919-1940 | 1940- |

9. Ithiel de Sola Pool, paper delivered at the conference on Vietnam, Adlai Stevenson Institute, Chicago, 1968.

10. Perhaps even more important will be the potential capability of the Russians to "saturate" and shadow U.S. missile submarines. Moscow is embarked upon what is, by far, the largest peacetime submarine construction program in history. A large number of her new submarines are nuclear-powered attack types which can be used to shadow and neutralize missile submarines. The Soviet submarine expansion program is a major part of her bid for dominance at sea. The U.S. Navy, in late 1969, stated "that Soviet nuclear submarine construction capacity is estimated to be some 20 units per year. With a crash program, having no restraints on manpower or materials, they could produce a considerably higher number. Intelligence estimates are that the Soviets will construct between 100 and 150 new submarines by 1978, and 80 to 100 per cent of that construction will be nuclear. In the past the Soviets have built some five nuclear submarines per year. Today we believe they are building double that number. . . . The future, unfortunately, does not look quite so bright."

*Jane's Fighting Ships,* in the foreword to its latest (72nd) edition, quotes a report of the U.S. House Armed Services Subcommittee on Seapower as stating that "the Soviet Union has outpaced the United States in new construction—the Soviet Navy boasting 1,575 vessels against the United States' 894.

"It was pointed out," the *Jane's* foreword continues, "that the average age of the U.S. ships was 17½ years and that 58 per cent of them were more than 20 years old, while only one in a hundred Soviet ships was that old."

Some of the newest U.S. ships are, as *Jane's* says, "the finest instruments of sea power ever devised." Our technology at its best is superb, and, in over-all skills and capabilities, the United States Navy is still—despite deficiencies in surface-to-surface missiles; small, fast, missile-carrying craft like the Russian *Komar* and *Osa* types; and long-range, stand-off, air-to-surface missiles—the best in the world. But the *trend* is highly unfavorable; the challenge at sea is major, and we are not meeting it.

P. Eleson, writing in *Ordnance Magazine* (November-December, 1969, p. 258) states—too flatly—that "as a matter of premeditated policy, the U.S. may be about to abdicate its primacy in the ocean to the Soviet Union." He stresses the Soviet nuclear submarine construction program and cites the 1969 announcement by Secretary of Defense Melvin R. Laird that the U.S. is not "going to try to match the U.S.S.R." in numbers of submarines. Eleson concludes: "We have decided to cede dominance in the oceans to the Soviet Union. Before that is an irreversible fact, we would do well to think more on the consequences of such a decision."

For a calm and thorough study, see *Soviet Sea Power*, Special Report Series No. 10, June, 1969, of the Center for Strategic and International Studies, Georgetown University, Washington, D.C.

11. Zbigniew Brzezinski, "Peace and Power—Looking Towards the 1970's," *Encounter*, October, 1968.

12. William R. Kintner and Harriet Fast Scott, eds., *The Nuclear Revolution in Soviet Military Affairs*. Norman, Okla.: University of Oklahoma Press, 1968, p. 390.

13. Admiral Arleigh Burke, speech to International Sea Power Symposium, Naval War College, Newport, R.I., November 19, 1969.

14. Robert F. Byrnes, *International Negotiation*. A memorandum prepared at the request of the Subcommittee on National Security and International Operations of the Committee on Government Operations, U.S. Senate, October 17, 1969. Washington: U.S. Government Printing Office, p. 19.

## 4» Colossus Under Strain

1. For a study of the Soviet economy and its influence upon the U.S. military budget, see "Part 3. The Economic Basis of the Russian Military Challenge to the United States, June 23 and June 24, 1969," *Hearings Before the Subcommittee on Economy in Government of the Joint Economic Committee of the Congress of the United States (The Military Budget and National Economic Priorities),* 91st Congress, 1st Session. Washington: U.S. Government Printing Office, 1969.

2. Hal Borland, *Countryman: A Summary of Belief.* Philadelphia: Lippincott, 1965, pp. 121–122.

3. Lecht, *op. cit.,* pp. 50–51.

4. There are, of course, loopholes and escape hatches in all these agreements, as General Harold K. Johnson, then Chief of Staff of the U.S. Army, pointed out in testimony to the Preparedness Investigating Subcommittee of the Senate Armed Services Committee, on February 23, 1967 (Washington: U.S. Government Printing Office, 1967, Part 2, p. 187):

". . . all of them [the treaties] provide that we are to consult and to provide forces in conformity with our respective constitutional processes —so that we do not have specific force commitments stated in these treaties."

5. Stephen Maxwell, *Rationality in Deterrence.* London: Institute for Strategic Studies, Adelphi Papers, No. 50, August, 1968.

6. James C. Thompson, Jr., "The Effect of Our Involvement in Vietnam on Future U.S. Patterns of Intervention," paper delivered at the conference on Vietnam, Adlai Stevenson Institute, Chicago, 1968.

7. See the interesting paper by William R. Kintner, "U.S. Overseas Defense Commitments Now and in the 1970's," Foreign Policy Research Institute, University of Pennsylvania, June, 1968.

## 5» This We Must Defend

1. Statement by Secretary of Defense Robert S. McNamara on the Fiscal Year 1969-70 Defense Program and the 1969 Defense Budget before the Senate Armed Services Committee, p. 64.

2. Statement of General Earle G. Wheeler, Chairman of the Joint Chiefs of Staff, "Status of U.S. Strategic Power," *Hearings Before the Preparedness Investigating Subcommittee of the Committee on Armed Services, United States Senate,* 90th Congress, 2nd Session, Part I, April 23, 24 and 26,

353

1968. Washington: U.S. Government Printing Office, 1968, p. 2.

3. Dr. Harold Brown, Secretary of the Air Force, told a Preparedness Investigating Subcommittee of the Senate Armed Services Committee:

> To insure deterrence, we must be able to inflict an unacceptable level of damage on the Soviets after we have absorbed a Soviet first-strike. Exactly what that level is will depend on the judgments of enemy leaders about the outcome of actual war. Mr. McNamara, in his recent posture testimony, stated that the question could not be answered precisely, but judged that a capability to destroy 20 to 25 per cent of the Soviet population and 50 per cent of her industry should serve as an effective deterrent.
>
> Of course, even 25 per cent Soviet casualties might not be enough for deterrence if U.S. casualties were disproportionately higher—if the Soviets thought they would be able to recover in some period of time while the United States would take three or four times as long, or would never recover, then the Soviets might not be deterred. "Status of U.S. Strategic Power," *Hearings,* 90th Congress, 2nd Session, Part II, 1968, p. 177.

4. Albert Wohlstetter, "The Role of the ABM in the 1970's." Statement before the Senate Armed Services Committee, April 23, 1969. Reprinted in William R. Kintner, ed., *Safeguard: Why the ABM Makes Sense.* New York: Hawthorn Books, 1969, pp. 336–337.

5. McNamara, *op. cit.,* p. 64.

6. The limitations as well as the capabilities of satellite intelligence systems should, however, be remembered. No satellite, for instance, will be able to tell Washington how many MIRV's (Multiple Independently Targetable Re-entry Vehicles) are carried by each Soviet rocket, and satellites are by no means infallible at penetrating camouflage or discovering carefully concealed or underground sites. Moreover, mobile missiles, on land or sea, are extremely hard to keep under surveillance constantly; the problem is to achieve a "real time readout," or continuous and instant surveillance of moving objects without a time lag which would make this knowledge useless for targeting purposes.

7. Albert Wohlstetter, Statement to Subcommittee on National Security and International Operations of the Committee on Government Operations, U.S. Senate, "Planning-Programming-Budgeting; Defense Analysis: Two Examples." Washington: U.S. Government Printing Office, 1969, p. 5.

8. This extensive discussion of Cuba has been republished in modified form from an article by the author, "A Military Perspective," a chapter in the book *Cuba and the United States*, edited by John Plank, and published by the Brookings Institution. Copyright © 1967 by The Brookings Institution. I am indebted to the Brookings Institution for permission to reprint this material.

9. For a case history of how *not* to conduct U.S.–Latin-American relations, see Mario Lanzo's *Dagger in the Heart: American Policy Failures in Cuba*. New York: Funk & Wagnalls, 1968.

10. John Mander, *The Unrevolutionary Society*. New York: Knopf, 1969.

11. Captain Raymond J. Toner, USN (Ret.), "The Latin American Military," *U.S. Naval Institute Proceedings*, November, 1968.

12. Samuel P. Huntington commented ("Military Intervention, Political Involvement and the Unlessons of Vietnam," *op. cit.*) that:

> The American commitment to social reform . . . presupposes the existence in the recipient country of a political system sufficiently well-developed and authoritative as to be capable of inaugurating such reforms. As the first five years of the Alliance for Progress amply demonstrate, this assumption is of questionable validity in much of Latin America. . . . If the United States is to make social reform a condition for economic assistance, it may also have some responsibility to develop the political institutions required to make such reforms a reality.

## 6» The Defense of Europe

1. Horace Walpole, letter to Horace Mann, November 24, 1774.

2. U.S. capital invested in Western Europe was estimated in 1967 at $14 billion in plants and equipment. See Jean Jacques Servan-Schreiber's study, *The American Challenge*. New York, Atheneum, 1968.

3. General Lyman L. Lemnitzer, "Report on Europe," Annual Meeting of the Association of the U.S. Army, Washington, D.C., October 28, 1968.

4. George W. Ball, *The Discipline of Power*. Boston: Atlantic–Little, Brown, 1968, pp. 166–167. Trade between West Germany and the Soviet bloc has expanded considerably in recent years.

5. It is questionable what influence the advent in 1969 of a Socialist government in Bonn will have upon the "Look-to-the-East" school in Germany. Western commentators frequently comfort themselves with the

shibboleth that socialist governments are the strongest enemies of Communism. In the crunch when the chips are finally down, this may well be true —though it is necessary to distinguish among socialist governments—but such governments also have a tendency to attempt to reconcile the irreconcilable, to seek accommodations and relations with other left-wing groups, and sometimes to make compromises which impair future freedom of maneuver. Specifically, in the case of West Germany it seems likely that Willy Brandt will try to bridge the gaps between East and West Germany and to improve materially relations with Russia and her Eastern European satellites to a greater degree than his predecessors. This is a commendable objective, provided it does not imply dangerous concessions. It seems unlikely that such concessions will be made; Brandt's background as the stalwart Mayor of West Berlin, beleaguered and isolated in a Communist sea, would appear to militate against such a course. It is clear, however, that there are considerable political risks for the West—as well as the East— in such bridge-building efforts.

6. The defense of northern Norway has been built, in NATO planning, around airborne and amphibious forces, backed by powerful naval task forces, including two to four aircraft carriers, at least half of them supplied by the United States. This would appear to be a desirable but marginal requirement, which might be reduced, or eliminated, with relatively small risk, in the decade ahead.

7. Lemnitzer, *op. cit.* For a discussion of the Soviet threat and NATO, see Stefan T. Possony, "NATO's Defense Posture," *Ordnance Magazine*, July –August, 1969. Mr. Possony strongly stresses the need to adopt a nuclear-defense concept for Europe.

8. Dwight D. Eisenhower, "Let's Be Honest with Ourselves," *The Saturday Evening Post*, March, 1963.

9. Zbigniew Brzezinski, "Meeting Moscow's 'Limited Coexistence,' " *The New Leader*, December 16, 1968.

# 7» The Mediterranean and Middle East

1. The quotation cited continues:

> Some 1,200 of the 1,500 ships at sea would belong to members of the [NATO] alliance. The goods and materials carried in these ships are essential for the economic life of the allied countries concerned, particularly for Italy, Greece and Turkey, who depend very heavily on sea transport to satisfy their needs. This is illustrated by the fact

that only about 90,000 tons of goods are carried in and out of these three countries by air, whereas by sea the total comes to about 160,000,000 tons. For these three countries, in particular, the protection of the sea lanes in the Mediterranean is vital.

From Committee on Defense Questions and Armaments, Assembly, Western European Union, "Defense of the Mediterranean and the NATO Southern Flank," Preliminary Draft Report, submitted by Mr. Goedhart, Rapporteur, Paris, 30 October, 1967, p. 3.

The Assembly of the Western European Union is an unofficial but active body composed of representatives, chiefly legislators, of NATO members.

2. *Ibid.*, p. 2.

3. Michael Howard and Robert Hunter, *Israel and the Arab World—The Crisis of 1967*, London: Institute for Strategic Studies, Adelphi Papers, No. 41, October, 1967, pp. 43–44.

4. Georgetown University: American Institute on Problems of European Unity, October 17-19, 1969.

# 8» East of Suez

1. The Middle East produces about 28 percent of the world's oil and has about 58 percent of the world's *known* resources. Average crude oil production costs (1967 figures) were about 15 cents a barrel for the Middle East generally (6.26 cents in Kuwait, the lowest known costs), as compared with $1.31 a barrel in the United Staes and perhaps 80 cents in Russia. Before the oil reaches the consumer overseas, there must be added, of course, refinery costs and the cost of transportation, via pipeline and tanker. With the development of supertankers, transportation costs have decreased, and Middle East oil is lower-priced, in its principal markets, than its competitors'. The conclusion of most experts is that Middle East oil is now, and probably long will be, the non-Communist world's principal supply. The Aramco handbook, *Oil and the Middle East*, published by the Arabian American Oil Company at Dhahran, Saudi Arabia (revised edition, July 1, 1968), is a rich store of information about Middle East oil. See also *The Gulf—Implications of British Withdrawal*, Georgetown University, Center for Strategic and International Studies, February, 1969; also *The Soviet Dilemma in the Middle East*, Parts I and II, by Robert E. Hunter, London: Institute for Strategic Studies, Adelphi Papers, Nos. 59 and 60, September-October, 1969.

2. Moscow has spent millions on propaganda in India; large sums go to

help support left-wing papers and Communist causes. The Russian efforts are aided by the peculiarly parochial view of the world depicted in the Indian press, and by the egocentric Indian character.

3. The Indian Army consists of about 1,000,000 men, plus another 100,-000 undergoing 50 weeks of training. The basic soldier signs up for a long term—a minimum of 8 years, normally about 15—and there are about seven applications for every vacancy. The Army is organized in 24 divisions—13 infantry, 10 mountain and 1 armored division—and 2 parachute brigades, plus other independent brigades and units, which swell the total to the equivalent of 29 to 30 divisions. The Army is backed for internal security duties by the Central Reserve Police (a federal force) and the State Armed Police (paramilitary units with light infantry equipment), amounting in all to about 250,000 men, and by smaller border security forces. The greatest weakness of the Army, in addition to logistics, reserves (perhaps 4 additional divisions, only lightly equipped, could be raised and trained in six months), ammunition and equipment, is potentially its officer corps. The British influence is fading, and the new breed of native officers—unlike the British-selected officers, drawn not only from the martial races (Sikhs and Gurkas) but also from all classes in India, including the former "untouchables"—are an unknown equation.

4. Calcutta, in some ways the cesspool of the world, a vast city designed for 1 million people with 5 million in its environs (half a million of them living, literally, on the sidewalks), is perhaps the worst case history of the meaning of population explosion. But, though worse than other examples, it is not untypical of the overcrowding, starvation, economic and social discrepancies, poverty, filth and ignorance that beset the so-called Indian democracy. India, despite its Gandhian tradition of meekness, has a history of violence. Its street mobs, volatile and easily excited, spill over into bloodshed easily; its crimes committed in the name of religion have probably caused more deaths than any civil war in history; dacoits (bandits, extortionists, a traditional criminal class) roam many sections of the countryside, and the dead hand of Hinduism, with its multiple gods and goddesses and its enshrinement of the cow and the monkey virtually alongside man, mean that life is cheap in India and its millions violently and unpredictably emotional.

Agronomists believe that India's tremendous, though spotty, progress since 1967, in agricultural mechanization, utilization of fertilizers, new high-yield crops, the development of tube wells and irrigation, has demonstrated India's capability of feeding her own population. Hunger and periodic famines could, theoretically, be completely eliminated, the experts

NOTES

believe, even if the Indian population increased to one billion people by the year 2000. However, these projections, though based on the progress of recent years, are still hopes. For fulfillment, they will depend upon a variety of factors: relaxation of the dead hand of the Hindu religion, slowdown in population growth, extension to much of India of the mechanization-irrigation projects which have been successful in the Punjab and some political and economic stability. The odds are still in favor of famine.

5. Ernest Lefever, "Africa, a Background Paper," Research Resources Conference, October 24–25, 1969, Center for Strategic and International Studies, Georgetown University, Washington, D.C.

6. *Ibid.*, pp. 8 and 9.

7. *Ibid.*, p. 10.

8. Anthony Harrigan, "Naval Defense of the Southern Oceans," American Security Council, Washington Report WR 69-32, August 18, 1969.

9. *Ibid.* See also D. C. Watt, "The Continuing Strategic Importance of Simonstown" *U.S. Naval Institute Proceedings*, October, 1969.

10. Ball, *op. cit.*, p. 258.

11. In 1966 about 274,250,000 net tons of shipping passed through the Suez Canal. Of this total, tanker tonnage represented more than 206,-000,000 tons. Today, with the canal reopened, the proportion of tanker to total tonnage would greatly decrease. The development of giant supertankers, of pipelines and of North African oil sources has permanently altered the flow of oil traffic. But U.S.S.R. tanker tonnage southbound, fully loaded, from the Black Sea fields, would be routed, until the depletion of the Black Sea–Caspian reserves, via Suez. For an interesting study, see *The Indian and Pacific Oceans: Some Strategic Considerations*, by T. B. Millar, London: Institute for Strategic Studies, Adelphi Papers, No. 57, May, 1969. Also Committee on Defense Questions and Armaments, Western European Union, *op. cit.* p. 4. Also a dated but extremely interesting overview, *India and the Indian Ocean* by K. M. Panikkar, New York, Macmillan, 1945, a study from the Indian point of view, stressing India's dependence on maritime power.

12. Lefever, *op. cit.*, pp. 16, 17. See also pages 13 and 15 of this excellent summary.

# 9» Asia and the Broad Pacific

1. Coral Bell, *The Asian Balance of Power—A Comparison with European Precedents.* London: Institute for Strategic Studies, Adelphi Papers, No. 48, February, 1968.

2. About 90 percent of the world's supply of natural rubber comes from Indonesia, Malasia, Ceylon, Thailand and (until the disruption of the war) Vietnam.

3. More than 98 percent of U.S. imports of zircon, the basic ore from which zirconium is produced, came from Australia in 1965.

4. Kei Wakaizumi, "Japan Beyond 1970," *Foreign Affairs,* April, 1969.

5. There were, in late 1968, 149 U.S. military installations of all sorts in Japan, ranging from the Yokosuka naval ship repair base and airfields to offices, warehouses and antenna sites. This number compares with more than 3,800 U.S. installations in the main Japanese islands during the Korean War, and is still being steadily reduced. U.S. forces in Japan numbered about 38,000 in 1968, and also were on the decline.

6. Joungwon A. Kim, "North Korea's New Offensive," *Foreign Affairs,* October, 1969.

7. SEATO members are Australia, Britain, France, New Zealand, Pakistan, the Philippines, Thailand and the United States. The organization, which covers the Southwest Pacific and Southeast Asia below 21-30 north latitude, is to a large extent a "paper" one, though it has served a useful consultative purpose and has helped, if but to a minor degree, in its avowed purpose of increasing the collective and military strength of the area. The treaty members were supposedly committed to discuss joint action in case of an attack, direct or indirect, against any member—or against the so-called "protocol states" of South Vietnam, Laos and Cambodia. Unlike NATO, SEATO has no organized international command or military structure. And events have eroded its strength and, to some extent, its common purpose. Cambodia and Laos have forsworn SEATO'S protection; Pakistan is completely inactive; France—since Dienbienphu and her subsequent withdrawal from Indochina—has no real presence in Asia; and the planned British withdrawal from Singapore and the Far East will leave the United States the only major power as a participant in Seato.

8. Saigon is only about 31 airline miles—slightly more by road—from the nearest point on the Cambodian frontier. The so-called "parrot's beak" of Cambodia juts out threateningly toward South Vietnam's capital city.

9. Tillman Durdin, veteran Asian correspondent and the most knowledgeable *New York Times* expert on Chinese affairs, noted in a dispatch to the *Times*, October 2, 1969, that

Maoist China faces its third decade with massive problems and handicaps. With the gross national product probably no higher today than it was 10 years ago, an annual population growth of 15 million to 20 million has negated attempts to raise the standards of living.

The dangerous dispute with the Soviet Union over borders and ideological influence and the continued hostility toward not only the United States but most other countries add to the strains and uncertainties. Given stability, practical domestic guidelines and policies of peaceful adjustment in foreign relations, the Chinese Communist state would stand a good chance of pulling out of its present slump and making new progress. But these factors appear difficult to assure under a leadership headed by . . . Mao or any other leader now on the horizon.

10. One of the great miscalculations by most of our Communist experts was the prediction, before the event, that U.S. intervention in Vietnam would reduce Sino-Soviet friction and act as a unifying force in the Communist world. The opposite appeared to be true, but whether Vietnam really had any major effect upon the course of Communist dissension is uncertain. Both powers continued their unilateral aid to North Vietnam and increased it; the conflict between Russia and China grew more and more serious as the war continued. But about the only effect that was of indirect importance to the United States was the withdrawal, since 1968, of sizable Chinese ground forces from Yünnan province, near the North Vietnamese border, apparently to reinforce the Chinese-Russian frontier.

11. William E. Griffith, "The American Stake in the Russia-China Confrontation," *Reader's Digest*, September, 1969.

## 10» Strategy for Tomorrow

1. Sir Robert Thompson, *No Exit from Vietnam*. New York: David McKay, 1969.

2. The *New York Times*, Section 3, page 1, September 7, 1969. Article by Gerd Wilcke.

3. Brooks Emeney, *The Strategy of Raw Materials*. New York: Macmillan, 1934.

361

4. Rear Admiral J. C. Wylie, USN, contends in his interesting little book, *Military Strategy* (New Brunswick: Rutgers University Press, 1967), that there are four principal strategic concepts, or schools of thought: continental, maritime, aerospace, and the Mao theory of guerrilla warfare. To this writer the Mao concept appears to be rather a derivative of the continental concept, or a tactic used in gaining continental control, rather than an entirely new strategic concept. Nevertheless Wylie is of course correct when he points out that there is interdependence and overlap among these concepts and that none alone fits all conditions. He is also correct in stressing that the objective of war is to exert control of some kind and degree over an enemy, and that it is impossible to predict with certainty the nature or pattern of a future war. This, of course, means that we must hedge many bets and that our military forces must have at least an initial capability to fight nearly any kind of war anywhere, holding the fort, so to speak, until the pattern of the war, and its peculiar and special needs, can be determined and met. This tremendously complicates the problem of force mix and of training.

5. The John Foster Dulles strategy of "massive retaliation" was an attempt to reduce the great costs of maintaining large armed forces for both conventional and nuclear war. It was not so much an answer to the enemy as a formula keyed to domestic economics—a "bigger bang for a buck." Admiral Arthur W. Radford, USN (Ret.), then Chairman of the Joint Chiefs of Staff, frankly stated in an interview with me in 1953 that the principal reason why he had changed the opinions he held before taking office and now tended to place his major reliance on nuclear weapons was costs; "We can't afford both," he said. But even during the heyday of this temporary policy, which was quickly outdated by Russia's growing nuclear strength and the lack of credibility of the threat of "massive retaliation" (world opinion refused to believe nuclear weapons would be used to repel aggression except in the defense of really vital U.S. interests), the United States maintained large ground forces in Europe and in Asia.

6. The psychological and political as well as the military importance of tactical nuclear weapons in the defense of island positions was well illustrated in the case of Quemoy, the Chinese Nationalist island about one mile from the Communist-held mainland. This island is geographically perhaps the most vulnerable of all insular positions—seemingly susceptible to an overwhelming amphibious assault. It was under blockade by bombardment and naval interdiction in the offshore island crisis of 1958. President Eisenhower ordered U.S. Marines to emplace 8-inch howitzers,

362

capable of firing nuclear shells, in Quemoy. The gesture, which was well publicized, had an immediate effect. The nuclear artillery shells were never made available to the Nationalists, but the Communists knew that one transport aircraft could break the blockade and could bring in enough shells to doom any attempted amphibious assault. The assault never took place; the bombardment and blockade petered out.

7. The principal disadvantage of the submarine-launched missile is the relative vulnerability of its land-based command and control system to destruction by sudden enemy surprise attack. Submerged missile submarines constantly monitor high-powered, VLF (very low frequency) radio stations, which represent the instruments of Washington's command and control apparatus. VLF radio waves penetrate water, at least to shallow depths, and the submerged submarines can, if necessary, trail a wire antenna buoyed by a small float, or can project fixed atennas just above the surface. But the powerful low-frequency stations required to communicate with submerged submarines are relatively few in number, and their locations are known and are necessarily immobile on land bases. Hence, theorists argue, at the start of any nuclear war an enemy could "zero in" against these stations and cripple the command and control system for our missile submarines. The argument, when examined, is largely fallacious; there are alternative methods of communication, and, in any case, the interruption of regular communications would alert all submarine commanders to emergency procedures. When surfaced or running at shallow depths with antennas above water, other radio stations or satellite communications systems could substitute for the low-frequency stations. Project Sanguine, the Navy's proposal to use the earth itself as a kind of giant antenna, is an R and D project to insure constant communications.

8. Force levels in any security structure, no matter what the strategic concept, will be tied to "commitments" and to the budget. The concept enunciated in this chapter would probably require (after Vietnam) an army in the continental United States, including Alaska, of seven or eight divisions—all of them ready and full-strength—plus one or two divisions in Europe, one (for the time being) in Korea and several brigades in Panama or at forward island bases.

9. Dr. Cora Bell, *op. cit.*

10. These self-imposed limitations, already approved by President Nixon, upon chemical, biological and radiological warfare should never limit our development of *protective* measures against possible enemy use. And—a fact the average citizen rarely understands—there is no possible way of

developing adequate *defenses* without, at the same time, developing, *experimentally, offensive techniques, means and methods.* The stockpiling of chemical agents is also an essential precautionary measure. The psychological and political revulsion against the use of lethal and disabling chemical-warfare agents is so great that the political and psychological price of using them is not worth the military gain in most circumstances. But the fact remains that the revulsion is not entirely justified on the basis of the relative degree of "humaneness" of any weapon. Gas, in World War I, caused 4.6 percent of all combat injuries, but only 1.32 percent of the fatalities, and gas casualties were neither maimed nor horribly wounded as were the victims of high explosive. Modern gas warfare, with its disabling and incapacitating agents, can probably—under favorable conditions of terrain, climate, weather and geography—save lives. The various forms of tear and nausea gas, used by police forces around the world, defoliants—derivatives of commercial chemicals—and perhaps some of the disabling chemical agents should never be included in any self-imposed or internationally agreed ban. The price would be, in another war, U.S. blood. See *Chemicals in War* by Lieutenant Colonel Augustin M. Prentiss, U.S. Army. New York: McGraw-Hill, 1937.

11. Letter to the author, February 21, 1969.

12. These figures increase to between $15,000 and $20,000 per year to maintain one U.S. soldier in *combat* overseas.

13. There used to be much talk, pre-McNamara, of service rivalries (they still exist, though they are muted). Some of these rivalries were carried to absurd lengths. Nevertheless, some of them represented healthy competition. More important, the old system—preunification—of independent executive departments, the War Department and the Navy Department, and the independent service committees of Congress provided built-in checks and balances in both the executive and the legislative departments of government. Rivalries within the services and inter- as well as intraservice competition for funds—between the various bureaus of the Navy Department (now abolished) and between the chiefs of the combat arms and services in the Army (also abolished)—acted as effective *military* restraints upon too much concentration of power in too few hands. Similarly, the dual federal-state National Guard system and the organized reserves provided additional political checks upon an overconcentration of power. The various reorganizations of the Pentagon since unification, and the centralized management philosophy of Secretary McNamara, resulted in the elimination of most of these traditional military checks and balances, and

the unprecedented concentration of power in the hands of a civilian Defense Secretary and a political-intelligentsia secretariat.

14. Secretary McNamara was a detail man, who had an amazing propensity for absorbing—and sometimes misinterpreting—facts, tremendous energy and—the quality that endeared him to two administrations—loyalty up. But he violated the rule of the good administrator; few decisions were left to his subordinates. Once during the Pentagon's attempts to help the government diminish the outflow of gold he told this writer that he personally examined every Defense Department overseas contract in excess of $100,000. He acted as his own project officer on the F-111, and actually had engineering progress meetings with Convair, Grumann and United Aircraft executives, as well as with several of his chief assistants, every two weeks. He told Admiral George Anderson how the Navy should run the Cuban blockade during the missile crisis, and he repeatedly intervened in details of armaments, weapons, spare parts, etc., which should have been, and could have been, settled with greater effectiveness and speed by subordinates.

15. A thorough study of the *Pueblo* incident, revealing the confusion, the uncertainties and the indecision of the command structure, was made by a subcommittee of the House Armed Services Committee. See *Inquiry into the U.S.S.* Pueblo *and EC-121 Plane Incidents*, Report of the Special Subcommittee on the U.S.S. *Pueblo* of the Committee on Armed Services, House of Representatives, 91st Congress, 1st Session, July 28, 1969. Washington: U.S. Government Printing Office, 1969.

# Acknowledgments

THIS BOOK was written under an annual Distinguished Writer's Award granted by the Center for Strategic and International Studies, Georgetown University, Washington, D.C. The Center is a private, nonprofit, nongovernmental organization that seeks to advance the understanding of international policy issues through interdisciplinary study of emerging world problems. The Center does not take a position on any policy issue, and the views expressed in works it sponsors are those of the individual author.

I am indebted to Admiral Arleigh Burke, USN (Ret.) the Chairman of the Center, to Dr. David M. Abshire, who was Executive Director during the writing of this book, and to the staff of the Center for their encouragement, suggestions, criticisms and advice and for access to the treasury of fact and opinion the Center provides.

Mr. Hobart Lewis, Editor-in-Chief of the *Reader's Digest*, helped to provide funds for an extensive fact-finding trip to many of the areas discussed in this book. Parts of Chapters 2 and 6, in very abbreviated and modified form, have appeared in the *Digest*, and the extensive discussion of the Middle East–Persian Gulf situation in Chapters 7 and 8 was based, in part, upon an article prepared for the *Digest* and upon articles published in the *New York Times*.

Part of Chapter 1 appeared in *Army* magazine. The extensive discussion of the Cuban situation in Chapter 5 appeared originally in modified form in a chapter by the author, "A Military Perspective," in the book, *Cuba and the United States*, edited by John Plank and published by The Brookings Institution in 1967.

I have also drawn, at various places in the book, particularly in Chapter 10, upon some of the thoughts and some of the phraseology incorporated in a series of lectures I delivered at Claremont College, California, in 1950, published by the college in book form, under the title of *Power and Politics: The Price of Security in the Atomic Age.*

I have also utilized parts of a magazine article published in the *New York Times Sunday Magazine* of June 9, 1968, and portions of other articles I prepared during my thirty-eight years with the *New York Times*. I have, of course, also drawn heavily upon the experience and background of a lifetime as a military and political analyst and reporter.

I am indebted to two of the luminaries of the *New York Times* Washington Bureau—William Beecher and Edwin L. Dale, Jr.—for their aid in checking facts and statistics. I am also indebted to all the publications and institutions cited for the use of material and for their helpfulness during the preparation of this book. My thanks are also due to the uniform helpfulness of military information officers in the Pentagon and to countless officers and officials in this country and overseas.

My wife has lived through this book's birth throes with the patience and affection that have always characterized her, and her judgments have helped materially.

Though *Strategy for Tomorrow* was suggested, sponsored and made possible by the Georgetown Center for Strategic and International Studies, it should be again emphasized that the Center bears no responsibility for the omissions and commissions of the end result. My opinions, which might, in many instances, differ sharply from those of the Center, are mine alone, and errors of fact or interpretation are also mine. But whatever credit the book may merit must rightfully be shared with "31-Knot" Burke, and with "Dave" Abshire and their cohorts.

HANSON W. BALDWIN

*Roxbury, Connecticut*
*January, 1970*

368

# Index

369

# About the Author

Hanson Baldwin was born in Baltimore, Maryland, and is a graduate of the United States Naval Academy at Annapolis. Commissioned an ensign in 1924, he served aboard battleships and destroyers on the East Coast, the Caribbean and in the European Squadron. In 1927 Mr. Baldwin resigned from the Navy to travel and write. A reporter on the Baltimore *Sun* for a year, Mr. Baldwin joined the *New York Times* in 1929. Since 1942 and until his recent retirement he was the military editor and analyst for the *Times*. His career as a military journalist has taken him to three wars and to military bases here and abroad.

In 1942 Mr. Baldwin was awarded a Pulitzer Prize for a series of articles on the South Pacific situation. A contributor to many national magazines, Mr. Baldwin is also the author of many books including *The Price of Power, The Great Arms Race, Great Mistakes of the War, World War I* and *Battles Lost and Won*. He is now a roving editor for The Reader's Digest, and is President of the U. S. Naval Academy Alumni Association.

70 71 72 73 10 9 8 7 6 5 4 3 2

# THE WORLD IN 1970

Communist bloc countries